PRENTICE HALL

WORLD STUDIES

Don't miss these powerful teacher timesavers!

Teacher's Edition Step-by-step guide for teachers ensures that objectives are met, provides reading strategies, makes point-of-use suggestions for using resources, and offers differentiated instruction.

Teaching Resources

All-in-One Teaching Resources Everything you need to teach in one location—including lesson plans, worksheets, tests, and transparency planner—making it easy to find materials, prep for class, and teach exciting lessons.

PRENTICE HALL

TeacherEXPRESS™

Plan • Teach • Assess

TeacherExpress CD-ROM Powerful lesson planning, resource management, testing, and an interactive Teacher's Edition, all in one place, make class preparation quick and easy!

Teacher's Edition

PRENTICE HALL

WORLD STUDIES

FOUNDATIONS of GEOGRAPHY

PEARSON

Prentice
Hall

Needham, Massachusetts
Upper Saddle River, New Jersey

Program Consultants

Heidi Hayes Jacobs

Heidi Hayes Jacobs has served as an education consultant to more than 1,000 schools across the nation and abroad. Dr. Jacobs serves as an adjunct professor in the Department of Curriculum on Teaching at Teachers College, Columbia University. She has written two best-selling books and numerous articles on curriculum reform. She received an M.A. from the University of Massachusetts, Amherst, and completed her doctoral work at Columbia University's Teachers College in 1981. The core of Dr. Jacobs' experience comes from her years teaching high school, middle school, and elementary school students. As an educational consultant, she works with K–12 schools and districts on curriculum reform and strategic planning.

Michal L. LeVasseur

Michal LeVasseur is the Executive Director of the National Council for Geography Education. She is an instructor in the College of Education at Jacksonville State University and works with the Alabama Geographic Alliance. Her undergraduate and graduate work were in the fields of anthropology (B.A.), geography (M.A.), and science education (Ph.D.). Dr. LeVasseur's specialization has moved increasingly into the area of geography education. Since 1996 she has served as the Director of the National Geographic Society's Summer Geography Workshops. As an educational consultant, she has worked with the National Geographic Society as well as with schools and organizations to develop programs and curricula for geography.

Senior Reading Consultants

Kate Kinsella

Kate Kinsella, Ed.D., is a faculty member in the Department of Secondary Education at San Francisco State University. A specialist in second-language acquisition and adolescent literacy, she teaches coursework addressing language and literacy development across the secondary curricula. Dr. Kinsella earned her M.A. in TESOL from San Francisco State University and her Ed.D. in Second Language Acquisition from the University of San Francisco.

Kevin Feldman

Kevin Feldman, Ed.D., is the Director of Reading and Early Intervention with the Sonoma County Office of Education (SCOE) and an independent educational consultant. At the SCOE, he develops, organizes, and monitors programs related to K–12 literacy. Dr. Feldman has an M.A. from the University of California, Riverside, in Special Education, Learning Disabilities and Instructional Design. He earned his Ed.D. in Curriculum and Instruction from the University of San Francisco.

Acknowledgments appear on page 187, which constitutes an extension of this copyright page.

ISBN 0-13-128033-3
345678910   08 07 06 05 04

Cartography Consultant

DK Andrew Heritage

Andrew Heritage has been publishing atlases and maps for some 25 years. In 1991, he joined the leading illustrated nonfiction publisher Dorling Kindersley (DK) with the task of building an international atlas list from scratch. The DK atlas list now includes some 10 titles, which are constantly updated and appear in new editions either annually or every other year.

Academic Reviewers

Africa
Barbara B. Brown, Ph.D.
African Studies Center
Boston University
Boston, Massachusetts

Ancient World
Evelyn DeLong Mangie, Ph.D.
Department of History
University of South Florida
Tampa, Florida

Central Asia and the Middle East
Pamela G. Sayre
History Department,
    Social Sciences Division
Henry Ford Community College
Dearborn, Michigan

East Asia
Huping Ling, Ph.D.
History Department
Truman State University
Kirksville, Missouri

Eastern Europe
Robert M. Jenkins
Center for Slavic, Eurasian and
    East European Studies
University of North Carolina
Chapel Hill, North Carolina

Latin America
Dan La Botz
Professor, History Department
Miami University
Oxford, Ohio

Medieval Times
James M. Murray
History Department
University of Cincinnati
Cincinnati, Ohio

North Africa
Barbara E. Petzen
Center for Middle Eastern Studies
Harvard University
Cambridge, Massachusetts

Religion
Charles H. Lippy, Ph.D.
Department of Philosophy
    and Religion
University of Tennessee
    at Chattanooga
Chattanooga, Tennessee

Russia
Janet Vaillant
Davis Center for Russian
    and Eurasian Studies
Harvard University
Cambridge, Massachusetts

South Asia
Robert J. Young
Professor Emeritus
History Department
West Chester University
West Chester, Pennsylvania

United States and Canada
Victoria Randlett
Geography Department
University of Nevada, Reno
Reno, Nevada

Western Europe
Ruth Mitchell-Pitts
Center for European Studies
University of North Carolina
    at Chapel Hill
Chapel Hill, North Carolina

Reviewers

Sean Brennan
Brecksville-Broadview Heights
    City School District
Broadview Heights, Ohio

Stephen Bullick
Mt. Lebanon School District
Pittsburgh, Pennsylvania

William R. Cranshaw, Ed.D.
Waycross Middle School
Waycross, Georgia

Dr. Louis P. De Angelo
Archdiocese of Philadelphia
Philadelphia, Pennsylvania

Paul Francis Durietz
Social Studies
    Curriculum Coordinator
Woodland District #50
Gurnee, Illinois

Gail Dwyer
Dickerson Middle School,
    Cobb County
Marietta, Georgia

Michal Howden
Social Studies Consultant
Zionsville, Indiana

Rosemary Kalloch
Springfield Public Schools
Springfield, Massachusetts

Deborah J. Miller
Office of Social Studies,
    Detroit Public Schools
Detroit, Michigan

Steven P. Missal
Newark Public Schools
Newark, New Jersey

Catherine Fish Petersen (Retired)
East Islip School District
Islip Terrace, New York

Joe Wieczorek
Social Studies Consultant
Baltimore, Maryland

FOUNDATIONS of GEOGRAPHY

Develop Skills

Use these pages to develop students' reading, writing, and geography skills.

Focus on Geography

Introduce students to the basic tools and concepts of geography.

MAP MASTER™

 Video/DVD

- Practice your skills with every map in this book.
- Interact with every map online and on CD-ROM.

Maps and illustrations created by DK help build your understanding of the world. The DK World Desk Reference Online keeps you up to date.

The World Studies Video Program takes you on field trips to study countries around the world.

The *World Studies* Interactive Textbook online and on CD-ROM uses inter-active maps and other activities to help you learn.

COUNTRY DATABANK

Read about the countries that make up the regions of the world.

Literature

A selection by a noted author brings geography to life.

DIAGRAPHICS

Investigate geographic concepts using diagrams, maps, and photographs.

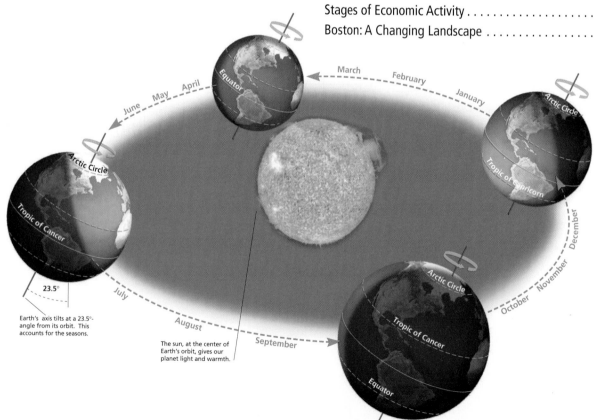

Earth's axis tilts at a 23.5°-angle from its orbit. This accounts for the seasons.

The sun, at the center of Earth's orbit, gives our planet light and warmth.

Links

See the fascinating links between social studies and other disciplines.

Skills for Life

Teach skills that students will use all of their lives.

Target Reading Skills

Chapter-by-chapter reading skills help students read and understand social studies concepts.

DK Eyewitness Technology

Detailed drawings show how technology shapes places and societies.

Discovery Channel School Video/DVD

Explore the geography, history, and cultures of the countries of the world.

Maps and Charts

MAP MASTER™

MAP MASTER™ Interactive

Go online to find an interactive version of every MapMaster Skills Activity map in this book. Use the Web Code provided to gain direct access to these maps.

How to Use Web Codes:

1. Go to **www.PHSchool.com**.
2. Enter the Web Code.
3. Click Go!

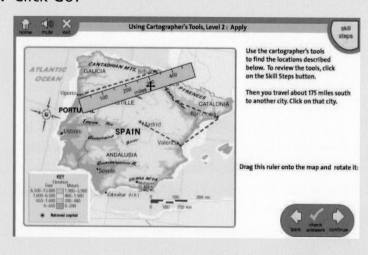

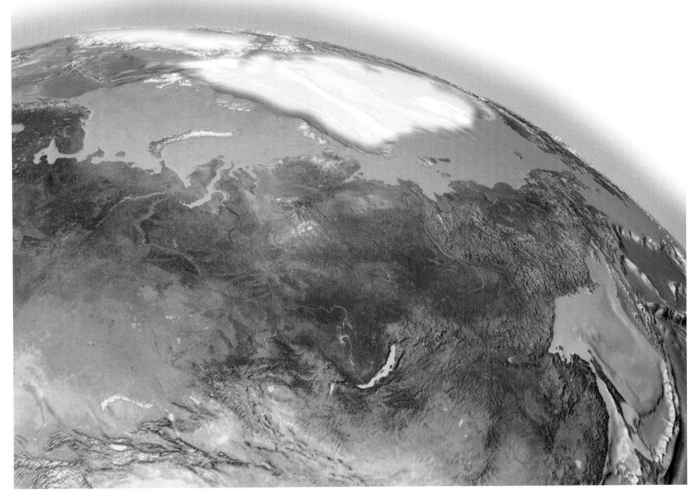

NCLB Implications for Social Studies

The No Child Left Behind (NCLB) legislation was a landmark in educational reform designed to improve student achievement and create a fundamental shift in American education. In the essay that follows, we will explore the implications of NCLB on social studies curriculum, instruction, assessment, and instructional programs.

Facts about NCLB

The No Child Left Behind Act of 2001 (NCLB) calls for sweeping educational reform, requiring all students to perform proficiently on standardized tests in reading, mathematics, and (soon to be added) science by the year 2014. Under NCLB, schools will be held accountable for students' academic progress. In exchange for this accountability, the law offers more flexibility to individual states and school districts to decide how best to use federal education funds. NCLB places an emphasis on implementing scientifically proven methods in teaching reading and mathematics, and promotes teacher quality. It also offers parental choice for students in failing schools.

Effects on Curriculum, Instruction, and Assessment

Since the primary focus of NCLB is on raising the achievement of students in reading and mathematics, some educators have wondered how it relates to social studies. Some teachers have expressed concerns that since NCLB does not require yearly testing of social studies, state and school districts may decide to shift resources and class time away from teaching social studies. However, NCLB considers the social studies areas of history, geography, economics, and government and civics to be core academic subjects. Many states are requiring middle grades social studies teachers to be highly qualified in history and geography in order to comply with the principle of improving teacher quality in NCLB.

NCLB sets the goal of having every child meet state-defined education standards. Since social studies educators have been leaders in the development of standards-based education and accountability through student testing over the past decade, many state and local districts have their own standards and assessments for social studies already in place. Assessment, including screening, diagnostic, progress-monitoring—including end-of-year, end-of-schooling, grade level, district, and state testing—and large-scale assessments, will continue to play a significant role in shaping social studies curriculum and instruction in the near future.

Integrating Reading into Social Studies Instruction

Due to the increased emphasis on reading and mathematics required by NCLB, social studies teachers may be called on to help improve their students' reading and math skills. For example, a teacher might use a graph about exports and imports to reinforce math skills, or a primary source about a historical event to improve reading skills. The connection between reading and social studies is especially important. Since many state and local assessments of reading require students to read and interpret informational texts, social studies passages are often used in the exams. Therefore, social studies teachers may assist in raising reading scores by integrating reading instruction into their teaching of social studies content.

Implications for Instructional Programs

The environment created by the NCLB legislation has implications for instructional programs. In keeping with the spirit of NCLB, social studies programs should clearly tie their content to state and local standards. Programs should also provide support so that all students can master these standards, ensuring that no child is left behind. An ideal instructional program is rooted in research, embeds reading instruction into the instructional design, and provides assessment tools that inform instruction—helping teachers focus on improving student performance.

Prentice Hall Response

We realize that raising the achievement level of all students is the number one challenge facing teachers today. To assist you in meeting this challenge, Prentice Hall enlisted a team of respected consultants who specialize in middle grades issues, reading in the content areas, and geographic education. This team created a middle grades world studies program that breaks new ground and meets the changing needs of you and your students.

With Prentice Hall, you can be confident that your students will not only be motivated, inspired, and excited to learn world studies, but they will also achieve the success needed in today's environment of the No Child Left Behind (NCLB) legislation and testing reform.

In the following pages, you will find the key elements woven throughout this World Studies program that truly set it apart and assure success for you and your students.

Teacher's Edition Contents in Brief

Research on Effective Reading Instruction

Why do many students have difficulty reading textbooks? How can we help students read to learn social studies? In the pages that follow, we examine the research on the challenge of reading textbooks; explain the direct, systematic, and explicit instruction needed to help students; and then show how Prentice Hall has responded to this research.

What is skilled reading?

Recent research (Snow et al., 2002) suggests that skillful and strategic reading is a long-term developmental process in which "readers learn how to simultaneously extract and construct meaning through interaction with written language." In other words, successful readers know how to decode all kinds of words, read with fluency and expression, have well-developed vocabularies, and possess various comprehension strategies such as note-taking and summarizing to employ as the academic reading task demands.

Many students lack reading skills

Sadly, many secondary students do not have solid reading skills. In the early years, students read mainly engaging and accessible narratives, such as stories, poems, and junior biographies. But in the upper elementary years, they shift toward conceptually dense and challenging nonfiction, or expository texts. It is no accident that the infamous "Fourth-Grade Slump" (Chall and Jacobs, 2003; Hirsch 2003)—a well-documented national trend of declining literacy after grade four—occurs during this time. The recent National Assessment of Educational Progress (NAEP, 2002) found that only 33 percent of eighth-grade students scored at or above the proficient level in reading.

Even students quite skilled in reading novels, short stories, and adolescent magazines typically come to middle school ill-equipped for the rigors of informational texts or reading to learn. They tend to dive right into a social studies chapter as if reading a recreational story. They don't first preview the material to create a mental outline and establish a reading purpose. They have not yet learned other basic strategies, including reading a section more than once, taking notes as they read, and reading to answer specific questions.

Dr. Kate Kinsella
Reading Consultant for *World Studies*
Department of Secondary Education
San Francisco State University, CA

Dr. Kevin Feldman
Reading Consultant for *World Studies*
Director of Reading and Early Intervention
Sonoma County, CA

"Even students quite skilled in reading novels, short stories, and adolescent magazines typically come to middle school ill-equipped for the rigors of informational texts or reading to learn."

The unique demands of textbooks

The differences between textbooks and the narratives students are used to reading are dramatic. The most distinctive challenges include dense conceptual content, heavy vocabulary load, unfamiliar paragraph and organizational patterns, and complex sentence structures. Academic texts present such a significant challenge to most students that linguists and language researchers liken them to learning a foreign language (Schleppegrell, 2002). In other words, most secondary students are second language learners: they are learning the academic language of informational texts!

Effective reading instruction

Research illustrates that virtually all students benefit from direct, systematic, and explicit instruction in reading informational texts (Baker & Gersten, 2000). There are three stages to the instructional process for content-area reading:

(1) **before reading:** instructional frontloading;

(2) **during reading:** guided instruction;

(3) **after reading:** reflection and study.

Before reading

Placing a major emphasis on preteaching, or "front-loading" your instruction—building vocabulary, setting a purpose for reading, and explicitly teaching students strategies for actively engaging with the text—helps you structure learning to ensure student success (see Strategies 1 and 2 on pages T32-T33). Frontloading strategies are especially critical in mixed-ability classrooms with English language learners, students with special needs, and other students performing below grade level in terms of literacy.

During reading

In guided instruction, the teacher models approaches for actively engaging with text to gain meaning. The teacher guides students through the first reading of the text using passage reading strategies (see Strategies 3-7 on pages T33-35), and then guides discussion about the content using participation strategies (see Strategies 8-11 on pages T35-T37). Finally, students record key information in a graphic organizer.

After reading

During the reflection and study phase, the teacher formally checks for student understanding, offers remediation if necessary, and provides activities that challenge students to apply content in a new way. To review the chapter, students recall content, analyze the reading as a whole, and study key vocabulary and information likely to be tested.

References

Baker, Scott and Russell Gersten. "What We Know About Effective Instructional Practices for English Language Learners." *Exceptional Children*, 66 (2000):454–470.

Chall, Jeanne S. and Vicki A. Jacobs. "Poor Children's Fourth-Grade Slump." *American Educator* (Spring 2003):14.

Donahue, P.L., et al. *The 1998 NAEP Reading Report Card for the Nation and the States* (NCES 1999-500). Washington, D.C.: U.S. Department of Education, Office of Education Research and Improvement, National Center for Education Statistics, 1999.

Grigg, W.S. et al. *The Nation's Report Card: Reading 2002* (NCES 2003-521). Washington D.C.: U.S. Department of Education, Institute of Education Sciences, National Center for Education Statistics, 2003.

Hirsch, E.D., Jr. "Reading Comprehension Requires Knowledge—of Words and the World." *American Educator* (Spring 2003):10-29.

Kinsella, Kate, et al. *Teaching Guidebook for Universal Access.* Upper Saddle River, NJ: Prentice Hall, 2002.

Schleppegrell, M. "Linguistic Features of the Language of Schooling." *Linguistics and Education*, 12, no. 4 (2002): 431–459.

Snow, C., et al. *Reading for Understanding: Toward an R&D Program in Reading Comprehension.* Santa Monica, California: The Rand Corporation, 2002.

Reading Support

Putting Research Into Practice

Prentice Hall enlisted the assistance of Dr. Kate Kinsella and Dr. Kevin Feldman to ensure that the new middle grades world studies program would provide the direct, systematic, and explicit instruction needed to foster student success in reading informational texts. To help students rise to the challenge of reading an informational text, *World Studies* embedded reading support right into the student text.

Embedded Reading Support in the Student Text

Before students read

- **Objectives** set the purpose for what students will read.
- **Target Reading Skill** for the section is explained.
- **Key Terms** are defined up front with pronunciation and part of speech.

During the section

- **Target Reading Skill** is applied to help students read and understand the narrative.
- **Key Terms** are defined in context, with terms and definitions called out in blue type.
- **Reading Checks** reinforce students' understanding by slowing them down to review after every concept is discussed.
- **Caption Questions** draw students into the art and photos, helping them to connect the content to the images.

After students read

- **Section Assessment** revisits the **Key Terms**, provides an opportunity to master the **Target Reading Skill**, allows student to rehearse their understanding of the text through the **Writing Activity**.

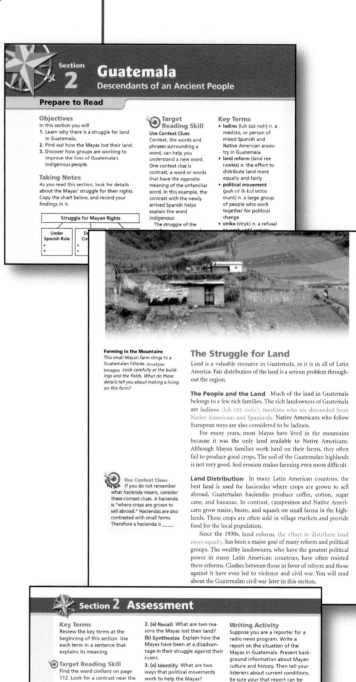

T16

Putting Research Into Practice

World Studies offers teachers guidance in direct, systematic, and explicit reading instruction. The instructional sequence in the Teacher's Edition explicitly guides you in the use of effective strategies at each stage of the instructional process.

Reading Instruction in *World Studies* Teacher's Edition

Before Reading

Every lesson plan begins with suggestions that help you integrate frontloading strategies into your teaching. Build Background Knowledge activates and builds prior knowledge. Set a Purpose for Reading prompts students to predict and anticipate content and motivates students to engage with the text. Preview Key Terms helps students learn Key Terms to understand the text. Target Reading Skill models a reading strategy to help students gain meaning from the text. Vocabulary Builder gives teachers definitions and sample sentences to help teach high-use words.

During Reading

In the "Instruct" part of the lesson plan, you can use suggestions for getting students actively engaged in the text. Guided Instruction clarifies high-use words, applies a passage-reading strategy to promote text comprehension, and guides discussion to construct meaning. Independent Practice prompts students to reread and take notes in the graphic organizer provided to rehearse understanding.

After Reading

The lesson plan closes with specific strategies for the reflection and study phase after reading is completed. Monitor Progress checks students' note taking, and verifies students' prereading predictions. Assess and Reteach measures students' recall of content and provides additional instruction if needed. Review Chapter Content promotes retention of key concepts and vocabulary.

Integrated Reading Resources

The *World Studies* program provides instructional materials to support the reading instruction in the Teacher's Edition.

The **All-in-One Teaching Resources** provides reading instruction support worksheets, such as a Reading Readiness Guide, Word Knowledge, and Vocabulary Development.

Students can use the **Reading and Vocabulary Study Guide** (English and Spanish) to reinforce reading instruction and vocabulary development, and to review section summaries of every section of the student text.

Research on Differentiated Instruction

It's basic, but it's true—not all our students learn in the same manner and not all our students have the same academic background or abilities. As educators, we need to respond to this challenge through the development and utilization of instructional strategies that address the needs of diverse learners, or the number of children who "fall through the cracks" will continue to rise (Kame'enui & Carnine, 1998).

Providing universal access

Universal access happens when curriculum and instruction are provided in ways that allow all learners to participate and to achieve (Kinsella, et al., 2002). Teachers who teach in heterogeneous, inclusive classrooms can provide universal access by modifying their teaching to respond to the needs of typical learners, gifted learners, less proficient readers, English language learners, and special needs students. Many of these learner populations benefit from extensive reading support (see pages T14-T17).

It is also critical to properly match the difficulty level of tasks with the ability level of students. Giving students tasks that they perceive as too hard lowers their expectations of success. However, giving students assignments that they think are too easy, undermines their feelings of competence (Stipek, 1996). Therefore, it is important for a program to give teachers leveled activities that allow them to match tasks with the abilities of their individual students.

When students connect to and are engaged with the content, comprehension and understanding increase. Technology, such as online activities, can provide an ideal opportunity for such engagement. It also can be used to provide additional opportunities to access content. For example, a less proficient reader may reinforce understanding of a key concept through watching a video. A complete social studies program makes content available in a variety of formats, including text, audio, visuals, and interactivities.

> "Universal access happens when curriculum and instruction are provided in ways that allow all learners to participate and to achieve (Kinsella, et al., 2002)."

Kame'enui, Edward and Douglas Carnine. *Effective Teaching Strategies that Accommodate Diverse Learners*. Upper Saddle River, NJ: Prentice Hall, 1998.

Kinsella, Kate, et al. *Teaching Guidebook for Universal Access*. Upper Saddle River, NJ: Prentice Hall, 2002.

Stipek, D.J. "Motivation and Instruction," in R.C. Clafee and D.C. Berlinger (Eds.), *Handbook of Educational Psychology*. New York: Macmillan, 1996.

Differentiated Instruction

Putting Research Into Practice

Prentice Hall recognizes that today's classrooms include students with diverse backgrounds and ability levels. Accordingly, the *World Studies* program was designed to provide access to the content for all students. The program provides both the instructional materials to meet the learning needs of all students and the guidance you need to accommodate these needs.

Differentiated Instruction in the Teacher's Edition

The Teacher's Edition was designed to make it easy for teachers to modify instruction for diverse learners. Teaching strategies, provided by Dr. Kate Kinsella and Dr. Kevin Feldman, to help you modify your teaching are incorporated into every lesson plan. Specific activities help you differentiate instruction for individual students in five categories—less proficient readers, advanced readers, special needs students, gifted and talented, and English language learners. Resources are identified as being appropriate for use by each of these categories. All resources are also assigned a level—basic, average, and above average—so you know exactly how to assign tasks of appropriate difficulty level.

All-in-One Teaching Resources

Everything you need to provide differentiated instruction for each lesson, including reading support, activities and projects, enrichment, and assessment—in one convenient location.

World Studies Video Program

Students will benefit from our custom-built video program—the result of an exclusive partnership with Discovery Channel School—making content accessible through dynamic footage and high-impact stories.

Student Edition on Audio CD

The complete narrative is read aloud, section by section, providing extra support for auditory learners, English language learners, and reluctant readers. Also available is the Guided Reading Audio CD (English/Spanish), containing section summaries read aloud.

Interactive Textbook—The Student Edition Online and on CD-ROM

The Interactive Textbook allows students to interact with the content, including reading aids, visual and interactive learning tools, and instant feedback assessments.

Differentiated Instruction

For Less Proficient Readers L1
Have students read the section in the Reading and Vocabulary Study Guide. This version provides basic-level instruction in an interactive format with questions and write-on lines.

Chapter 4, Section 1, **Latin America Reading and Vocabulary Study Guide,** pp. 42–44

For Special Needs Students L1
Have students read the section as they listen to the recorded version on the Student Edition on Audio CD. Check for comprehension by pausing the CD and asking students to share their answers to the Reading Checks.

Chapter 4, Section 1, **Student Edition on Audio CD**

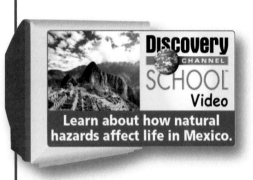

Discovery CHANNEL SCHOOL Video
Learn about how natural hazards affect life in Mexico.

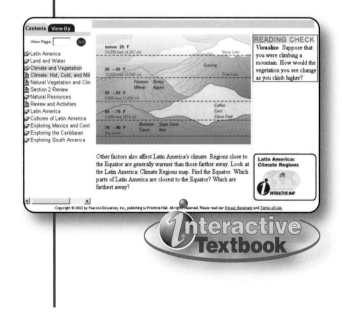

Interactive Textbook

Research on Geographic Literacy

As the *Geography for Life: National Geography Standards* (1994) state, "There is now a widespread acceptance among the people of the United States that being literate in geography is essential if students are to leave school equipped to earn a decent living, enjoy the richness of life, and participate responsibly in local, national, and international affairs." A middle grades social studies program needs to help teachers produce students who are literate in geography.

Geographic literacy defined

Results for the 2001 National Assessment of Educational Progress (NAEP) Geography assessment show that the average scores of fourth- and eighth-grade students have improved since 1994. The average score of twelfth-grade students, however, has not changed significantly. In order to make the critical leap from basic geography skills to the kind of geographic literacy needed by the twelfth grade and beyond, a program must teach both geography content and geography skills, and then help students think critically. Geography content is made up of the essential knowledge that students need to know about the world. Geography skills are the ability to ask geographic questions, acquire and analyze geographic information, and answer these questions. To be truly literate in geography, students must be able to apply their knowledge and skills to understand the world.

Elements for success in middle grades

Students in the elementary grades don't always get enough training in geography. In order to help all students gain a base upon which to build middle grades geographic literacy, a program should introduce basic geography skills at the beginning of the school year.

The quality of maps is also vital to the success of a middle grades world studies program. Maps must be developmentally appropriate for middle grades students. They should be clean, clear, and accurate. Maps should be attractive and present subject matter in appealing ways, so that students *want* to use them to learn.

Another element that can lead to success is the incorporation of technology into the teaching and learning of geography, specifically the Internet. Research has shown that 8th grade students with high Internet usage scored higher in geography (NAEP, 2001).

U.S. Department of Education, Office of Educational Research and Improvement, National Center for Education Statistics, National Assessment of Educational Progress (NAEP), 2001 Geography Assessment.

Andrew Heritage
Head of Cartography
Dorling Kindersley (DK)

"Maps should be attractive and present subject matter in appealing ways, so that students *want* to use them to learn."

Putting Research Into Practice

Prentice Hall partnered with DK—internationally known for their dynamic atlases—to develop the *World Studies* program. DK's Andrew Heritage and his world-renowned cartography team designed all maps, resulting in stunning, high quality maps that are middle grades appropriate.

The MapMaster™ System

Chapter 1 introduces students to the basic tools and concepts of geography, with a special focus on essential map skills.

Introduce Basic Map Skills

Chapter 1 introduces students to the basic tools and concepts of geography, with a special focus on essential map skills.

Build Geographic Literacy with Every Map

Scaffolded questions start with questions that require basic geography content and skills, and then ask students to demonstrate geographic literacy by thinking critically about the map.

Activate Learning Online

MapMaster™ Interactive—online and on CD-ROM—allows students to put their knowledge of geography skills and content into practice through interactivities.

Extend Learning with DK

- **DK World Desk Reference Online** is filled with up-to-date data, maps, and visuals that connect students to a wealth of information about the world's countries.

- **DK Compact Atlas of the World** with Map Master™ Teacher's Companion provides activities to introduce, develop, and master geography and map skills.

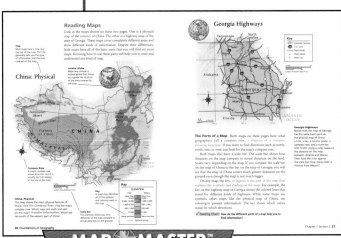

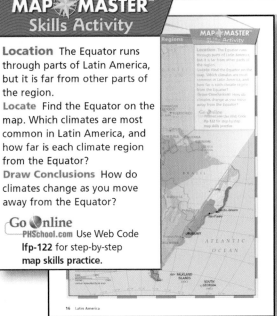

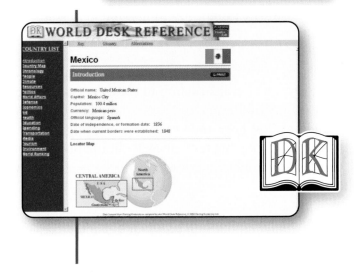

Research on Assessment

Meeting the NCLB challenge will necessitate an integrated approach to assessment with a variety of assessment tools. With the spotlight now on *improving* student performance, it is essential to use assessment results to inform instruction.

Assessments Tools for Informing Instruction

The key to success is using a variety of assessment tools coupled with data analysis and decision making. Teachers work with information coming from four kinds of assessment.

Screening assessments are brief procedures used to identify at-risk students who are not ready to work at grade level.

Diagnostic assessments provide a more in-depth analysis of strengths and weaknesses that can help teachers make instructional decisions and plan intervention strategies.

Progress-monitoring assessments (sometimes referred to as benchmark tests) provide an ongoing, longitudinal record of student achievement detailing individual student progress toward meeting end-of-year and end-of-schooling, grade level, district, or state standards.

Large-scale assessments, such as state tests and standardized tests, are used to determine whether individual students have met the expected standards and whether a school system has made adequate progress in improving its performance.

Ongoing Assessment

Daily assessment should be embedded in the program before, during, and after instruction in the core lessons. Legitimate test preparation experiences also should be embedded in the program. Test preparation involves teaching students strategies for taking tests, such as eliminating answers, reading comprehension, and writing extended response answers.

Eileen Depka
Supervisor of Standards and Assessment
Waukesha, WI

"Meeting the NCLB challenge will necessitate an integrated approach to assessment with a variety of assessment tools."

Putting Research Into Practice

Prentice Hall developed the *World Studies* program with a variety of assessment tools, including ongoing assessment in the student text.

Assessments for Informing Instruction

World Studies was designed to provide you with all four kinds of assessment.

- **Screening test** identifies students who are reading 2-3 years below grade level.

- **Diagnostic tests** focus on skills needed for success in social studies, including subtests in geographic literacy, visual analysis, critical thinking and reading, and communications skills, as well as vocabulary and writing.

- **Benchmark tests**, to be given six times throughout the year, monitor student progress in the course.

- **Outcome test**, to be administered at the end of the year, evaluates student mastery of social studies content standards.

Ongoing Assessment

- **Student Edition** offers section and chapter assessments with questions building from basic comprehension to critical thinking and writing.

- **Test Prep Workbook** and **Test-taking Strategies with Transparencies** develop students' test-taking skills and improve their scores on standardized tests.

- *ExamView® Test Bank CD-ROM* allows you to quickly and easily develop customized tests from a bank of thousands of questions.

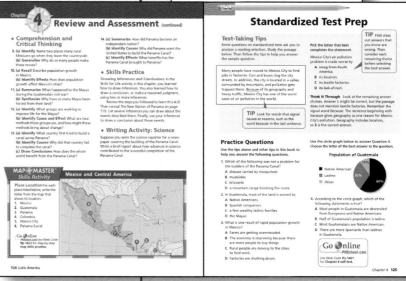

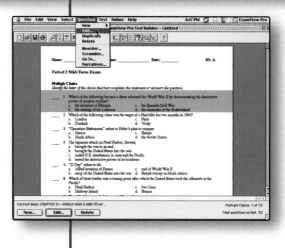

Foundations of Geography Skills Scope and Sequence

Prentice Hall *World Studies* contains a comprehensive program of core skills. Each skill is taught in every book of the series. A Target Reading Skill is located at the beginning of each chapter and expanded upon in each section within the chapter. Core skills are also taught either in the "Skills for Life Activity" in the Student Edition, or in a "Skills Mini Lesson" in the Teacher's Edition. In addition, worksheets for the students' use in completing each skill are located in the All-in-One Teaching Resources. The chart below lists the skills covered in *Prentice Hall World Studies: Foundations of Geography* and the page where each skill is taught.

Foundations of Geography Analysis Skills	SE	TE
Analyzing Graphic Data	pp. 48–49	pp. 48–49, 65
Analyzing Images		p. 35
Analyzing Primary Sources		p. 122
Clarifying Meaning	pp. 8, 10, 12, 13, 16, 17, 22	pp. 8b, 10, 16,
Comparing and Contrasting	pp. 58, 60, 62, 66, 67, 68, 71, 74, 76, 79, 80, 81, 84	pp. 44, 58b, 60, 67, 74, 80
Decision Making		p. 83
Distinguishing Fact and Opinion		p. 107
Drawing Inferences and Conclusions		p. 12
Identifying Cause and Effect/Making Predictions	pp. 126–127	pp. 30, 126–127
Identifying Frame of Reference and Point of View		p. 69
Identifying Main Ideas/Summarizing	pp. 112, 114, 115, 119, 120, 122, 125, 128, 131, 132	pp. 76, 112b, 114, 120, 128,
Making Valid Generalizations	pp. 102–103	pp. 102–103
Problem Solving		p. 118
Recognizing Bias and Propaganda		p. 94
Sequencing	pp. 90, 92, 95, 96, 97, 101, 104, 106, 108	pp. 18, 90b, 92, 96, 104
Supporting a Position		p. 131
Synthesizing Information		p. 100
Transferring Information From One Medium to Another		p. 53
Using the Cartographer's Tool		p. 43
Using Context	pp. 26, 28, 30, 32, 33, 35, 39, 40, 43, 47, 50, 52, 54	pp. 26b, 28, 33, 40, 50
Using Reliable Information	pp. 14–15	pp. 14–15
Using Special-Purpose Maps	pp. 72–73	pp. 72–73

Pacing Options

World Studies offers many aids to help you plan your instruction time, whether regular class periods or block scheduling. Section-by-section lesson plans for each chapter include suggested times, based on the 9-week course configuration below. Teacher Express CD-ROM will help you manage your time electronically.

Foundations of Geography Pacing Options			9-week unit	12-week unit
Chapter 1	Section 1 Section 2	The Five Themes of Geography The Geographer's Tools	4.5 4	6 5
Chapter 2	Section 1 Section 2 Section 3 Section 4	Our Planet, Earth Forces Shaping Earth Climate and Weather How Climate Affects Vegetation	2 1.5 3 3	2 2.5 4 4.5
Chapter 3	Section 1 Section 2 Section 3 Section 4	Population Migration Economic Systems Political Systems	1.5 3 1.5 4.5	2 4 2 6.5
Chapter 4	Section 1 Section 2 Section 3	Understanding Culture Culture and Society Cultural Change	1.5 3.5 3.5	2 4.5 4.5
Chapter 5	Section 1 Section 2 Section 3	Natural Resources Land Use People's Effect on the Environment	1.5 3 3.5	2 4 4.5
		Total Number of Days	**45**	**60**

Correlation to *Geography for Life*, the National Geography Standards

On the following pages, *Prentice Hall World Studies Foundations of Geography* is correlated with *Geography for Life*, the National Geography Standards. These standards were prepared in response to the Goals 2000, Educate America Act, by the Geography Education Standards Project. Participating in the project were the American Geographical Society, the Association of American Geographers, the National Council for Geographic Education, and the National Geographic Society. Concepts and skills contained in the Geography Standards are incorporated throughout the program. This correlation displays places where the standards are directly addressed.

Standard	Foundations of Geography
The World in Spatial Terms	
Standard 1 Use maps and other geographic representations, tools, and technologies to acquire, process, and report information from a spatial perspective.	World Overview, 1:1–2, 2:1–4, 3:1, 3:2, 4:2, 5:1–3, Review and Assessment: Chs. 1–5
Standard 2 Use mental maps to organize information about people, places, and environments in a spatial context.	2:4, 3:1, Skills for Life: Ch. 3, Review and Assessment: Ch. 1
Standard 3 Analyze the spatial organization of people, places, and environments on Earth's surface.	World Overview, 1:1–2, 2:2, 2:3, 2:4, 3:1, 3:2, 3:3, 4:2, 5:2, Skills for Life: Ch. 3, Review and Assessment: Chs. 1, 2, 4
Places and Regions	
Standard 4 Understand the physical and human characteristics of places.	World Overview, 1:1, 2:1–4, 3:1–4, 4:1, 4:2, 5:2, 5:3, Skills for Life: Ch. 2, Review and Assessment: Chs. 2, 3, 4, 5
Standard 5 Understand that people create regions to interpret Earth's complexity.	World Overview, 1:1–2, 2:1, 2:4, 3:1, 3:3, 3:4, Review and Assessment: Chs. 1, 3
Standard 6 Understand how culture and experience influence people's perception of places and regions.	World Overview, 2:1, 3:1–4, 4:1–3, 5:2, 5:3, Review and Assessment: Chs. 3, 4, 5
Physical Systems	
Standard 7 Understand the physical processes that shape the patterns of Earth's surface.	World Overview, 2:1–4, 3:1, Review and Assessment: Ch. 2
Standard 8 Understand the characteristics and spatial distribution of ecosystems on Earth's surface.	2:2, 2:3, 2:4, 3:1, 5:1–3, Review and Assessment: Chs. 2, 5

Correlation to *Geography for Life*, the National Geography Standards *(continued)*

Standard	Foundations of Geography
Human Systems	
Standard 9 Understand the characteristics, distribution, and migration of human populations on Earth's surface.	World Overview, 3:1–4, 4:1–3, 5:1–3, Review and Assessment: Chs. 3, 4
Standard 10 Understand the characteristics, distribution, and complexity of Earth's cultural mosaics.	3:1, 3:2, 3:3, 4:1–3, 5:2, Review and Assessment: Chs. 3, 4, 5
Standard 11 Understand the patterns and networks of economic interdependence on Earth's surface.	3:1, 3:2, 3:3, 4:3, 5:1–3, Review and Assessment: Chs. 3, 5
Standard 12 Understand the processes, patterns, and functions of human settlement.	3:1, 3:2, 4:1, 4:2, 5:2, Review and Assessment: Chs. 3, 4, 5
Standard 13 Understand how the forces of cooperation and conflict among people influence division and control of Earth's surface.	3:1, 3:2, 3:3, 4:1–3, 5:1–3, Review and Assessment: Chs. 3, 4, 5
Environment and Society	
Standard 14 Understand how human actions modify the physical environment.	3:1, 3:2, 3:3, 4:1, 5:1–3, Review and Assessment: Chs. 3, 5
Standard 15 Understand how physical systems affect human systems.	World Overview, 2:2, 2:3, 2:4, 3:1, 4:1, 5:1–3, Review and Assessment: Chs. 2, 3, 4, 5
Standard 16 Understand the changes that occur in the meaning, use, distribution, and importance of resources.	2:2, 3:1, 3:2, 3:3, 4:1, 4:3, 5:1–3, Review and Assessment: Chs. 3, 4, 5
The Uses of Geography	
Standard 17 Understand how to apply geography to interpret the past.	World Overview, 1:1, 2:2, 3:1, 3:2, 3:3, 4:1–3, 5:1–3, Review and Assessment: Chs. 3, 4, 5
Standard 18 Understand how to apply geography to interpret the present and plan for the future.	3:1, 3:2, 3:3, 4:2, 4:3, 5:1–3, Review and Assessment: Chs. 3, 4, 5

Correlation to the NCSS Curriculum Standards

On the following pages *Prentice Hall World Studies Foundations of Geography* is correlated with *Expectations of Excellence*, the Curriculum Standards for Social Studies. These standards were developed by the National Council for the Social Studies to address overall curriculum design and comprehensive student performance expectations.

Standard	Foundations of Geography
Performance Expectations 1: Culture	
• compare similarities and differences in the ways groups, societies, and cultures meet human needs and concerns • explain how information and experiences may be interpreted by people from diverse cultural perspectives and frames of reference • explain and give examples of how language, literature, the arts, architecture, other artifacts, traditions, beliefs, values, and behaviors contribute to the development and transmission of culture • explain why individuals and groups respond differently to their physical and social environments and/or changes to them on the basis of shared assumptions, values, and beliefs • articulate the implications of cultural diversity, as well as cohesion, within and across groups	4:1–3, 5:2, Review and Assessment: Chs. 4, 5
Performance Expectations 2: Time, Continuity, and Change	
• demonstrate an understanding that different scholars may describe the same event or situation in different ways but must provide reasons or evidence for their view • identify and use key concepts such as chronology, causality, change, conflict, and complexity to explain, analyze, and show connections among patterns of historical change and continuity • identify and describe selected historical periods and patterns of change within and across cultures • identify and use processes important to reconstructing and reinterpreting the past • develop critical sensitivities regarding attitudes, values, and behaviors of people in different historical contexts • use knowledge of facts and concepts drawn from history, along with methods of historical inquiry, to inform decision-making about and action-taking on public issues	2:2, 3:1, 3:2, 3:3, 4:1, 4:3, 5:2, Review and Assessment: Chs. 3, 4
Performance Expectations 3: People, Places, and Environment	
• elaborate mental maps of locales, regions, and the world that demonstrate understanding of relative location, direction, size, and shape • create, interpret, use, and distinguish various representations of the earth • use appropriate resources, data sources, and geographic tools to generate, manipulate, and interpret information • estimate distance, calculate scale, and distinguish geographic relationships • locate and describe varying landforms and geographic features and explain their relationship with the ecosystem • describe physical system changes and identify geographic patterns associated with them • describe how people create places that reflect cultural values and ideals • examine, interpret, and analyze physical and cultural patterns and their interactions • describe ways that historical events have been influenced by, and have influenced, physical and human geographic factors in local, regional, national, and global settings • observe and speculate about social and economic effects of environmental changes and crises resulting from natural phenomena • propose, compare, and evaluate alternative uses of land and resources in communities, regions, nations, and the world	World Overview, 1:1–2, 2:1–4, 3:1, 3:2, 3:3, 4:1–3, 5:1–3, Skills for Life: Chs. 2, 3, Review and Assessment: Chs. 1–5

Correlation to the NCSS Curriculum Standards *(continued)*

Standard	Foundations of Geography
Performance Expectations 4: Individual Development and Identity	
• relate personal changes to social, cultural, and historical contexts • describe personal connections to place—as associated with community, nation, and world • describe the ways family, gender, ethnicity, nationality, and institutional affiliations contribute to personal identity • relate such factors as physical endowment and capabilities, learning, motivation, personality, perception, and behavior to individual development • identify and describe ways regional, ethnic, and national cultures influence individuals' daily lives • identify and describe the influence of perception, attitudes, values, and beliefs on personal identity • identify and interpret examples of stereotyping, conformity, and altruism • work independently and cooperatively to accomplish goals	3:1, 3:2, 3:3, 4:1–3, 5:2, 5:3, Review and Assessment: Chs. 3, 4, 5
Performance Expectations 5: Individuals, Groups, & Institutions	
• demonstrate an understanding of concepts such as role, status, and social class in describing interactions of individuals and social groups • analyze group and institutional influences on people, events, and elements of culture • describe the various forms institutions take and the interactions of people with institutions • identify and analyze examples of tensions between expressions of individuality and group or institutional efforts to promote social conformity • identify and describe examples of tensions between belief systems and government policies and laws • describe the role of institutions in furthering both continuity and change • apply knowledge of how groups and institutions work to meet individual needs and promote the common good	3:3, 3:4, 4:1, 4:2, Review and Assessment: Chs. 3, 4
Performance Expectations 6: Power, Authority, and Governance	
• examine persistent issues involving the rights, roles, and status of the individual in relation to general welfare • describe the purpose of government and how its powers are acquired, used, and justified • analyze and explain ideas and governmental mechanisms to meet needs and wants of citizens, regulate territory, manage conflict, and establish order and security • describe the ways nations and organizations respond to forces of unity and diversity affecting order and security • identify and describe the basic features of the political system in the United States, and identify representative leaders from various levels and branches of government • explain conditions, actions, and motivations that contribute to conflict and cooperation within and among nations • describe and analyze the role of technology as it contributes to or helps resolve conflicts • explain how power, role, status, and justice influence the examination of persistent issues and social problems • give examples and explain how governments attempt to achieve their stated ideals at home and abroad	3:3, 3:4, 4:1, Review and Assessment: Ch. 3

Correlation to the NCSS Curriculum Standards *(continued)*

Standard	Foundations of Geography
Performance Expectations 7: Production, Distribution, and Consumption	
• give examples of ways that economic systems structure choices about how goods and services are to be produced and distributed • describe the role that supply and demand, prices, incentives, and profits play in determining what is produced and distributed in a competitive market system • explain differences between private and public goods and services • describe a range of examples of the various institutions that make up economic systems • describe the role of specialization and exchange in the economic process • explain and illustrate how values and beliefs influence different economic decisions • differentiate among various forms of exchange and money • compare basic economic systems according to who determines what is produced, distributed, and consumed • use economic concepts to help explain historical and current events in local, national, or global concepts • use economic reasoning to compare different proposals for dealing with contemporary social issues	3:3, 4:3, 5:1–3, Review and Assessment: Chs. 3, 5
Performance Expectations 8: Science, Technology, and Society	
• examine and describe the influence of culture on scientific and technological choices and advancement • show through specific examples how science and technology have changed peoples' perceptions of their social and natural world • describe examples in which values, beliefs, and attitudes have been influenced by new scientific and technological knowledge • explain the need for laws and policies to govern scientific and technological applications • seek reasonable and ethical solutions to problems that arise when scientific advancements and social norms or values come into conflict	1:2, 2:1–4, 3:1, 3:3, 4:1, 4:3, 5:1–3, Review and Assessment: Chs. 2, 3, 4, 5
Performance Expectations 9: Global Connections	
• describe instances in which language, art, music, and belief systems, and other cultural elements can facilitate global understanding or cause misunderstanding • analyze examples of conflict, cooperation, and interdependence among groups, societies, and nations • describe and analyze the effects of changing technologies on the global community • explore the causes, consequences, and possible solutions to persistent contemporary and emerging global interests • describe and explain the relationships and tensions between national sovereignty and global interests • demonstrate understanding of concerns, standards, issues, and conflicts related to universal human rights • identify and describe the roles of international and multinational organizations	3:1, 3:2, 3:3, 4:1–3, 5:1–3, Review and Assessment: Chs. 3, 4, 5

Correlation to the NCSS Curriculum Standards *(continued)*

Standard	Foundations of Geography
Performance Expectations 10: Civic Ideals and Practices	
• examine the origins and continuing influence of key ideals of the democratic republican form of government, such as individual human dignity, liberty, justice, equality, and rule of law • identify and interpret sources and examples of the rights and responsibilities of citizens • locate, access, analyze, organize, and apply information about selected public issues—recognizing and explaining multiple points of view • practice forms of civic discussion and participation consistent with the ideals of citizens in a democratic republic • explain and analyze various forms of citizen action that influence public policy decisions • identify and explain the roles of formal and informal political actors in influencing and shaping public policy and decision-making • analyze the influence of diverse forms of public opinion on the development of public policy and decision-making • analyze the effectiveness of selected public policies and citizen behaviors in realizing the stated ideals of a democratic republican form of government • explain the relationship between policy statements and action plans used to address issues of public concern • examine strategies designed to strengthen the "common good," which consider a range of options for citizen action	4:1–3, 5:1, 5:3, Review and Assessment: Ch. 4

Instructional Strategies for Improving Student Comprehension

In response to today's environment of the NCLB legislation and testing reform, Prentice Hall asked Dr. Kate Kinsella and Dr. Kevin Feldman to provide specific instructional strategies you can use to improve student comprehension. Their guidance informed the development of the *World Studies* Teacher's Edition. The lesson plans in this Teacher's Edition incorporate the following instructional strategies to enhance students' comprehension.

There is no single magical strategy that will solve all of the difficulties students encounter in reading challenging content area texts. Secondary students in mixed-ability classrooms depend on teachers to use a consistent set of research-informed and classroom-tested strategies in a patient and recursive manner—not the occasional or random use of different strategies. Students will not become skillful readers of content area texts in a week or two of instruction. However, when teachers engage students in the consistent use of a well-chosen set of content reading strategies appropriately matched to the demands of the text and the students' level of knowledge, their ability to comprehend difficult grade level texts will be dramatically enhanced.

Strategy 1: Set a Purpose for Reading

This program has two types of activities designed to help students set a purpose for reading: an Anticipation Guide and a KWL chart. The two types rotate by section.

A. Anticipation Guide

Purpose: To focus students' attention on key concepts, and guide them to interact with ideas in the text

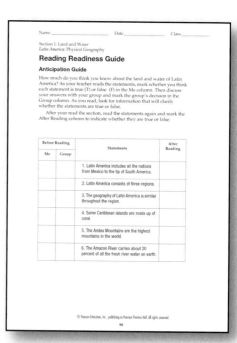

1. Distribute the *Reading Readiness Guide*. Read each statement aloud, and then ask students to react to the statements individually and in groups, marking their responses in the Before Reading column.

2. Use the worksheet as a springboard for discussing the section's key concepts as a unified class. Refrain from revealing the correct responses at this time, to avoid taking away the need for them to read the text.

3. Have students read the section with the purpose of finding evidence that confirms, disproves, or elaborates each statement in the *Reading Readiness Guide*.

4. After students finish reading, have them return to the statements and mark the After Reading column on their worksheets. Have them locate information from the text that supports or disproves each statement.

5. Discuss what the class has learned and probe for any lingering confusion about key concepts.

B. KWL

Purpose: To engage students before, during, and after reading

The KWL worksheet guides students to recall what they **K**now, determine what they **W**ant to learn, and identify what they **L**earn as they read.

1. Distribute the *Reading Readiness Guide.* Brainstorm with the group about what they already know about the topic. List students' ideas on the board. Encourage students to generate questions at points of ambiguity.

2. Students then list pieces of information they already know and questions they want to answer in the first two columns of their worksheets.

3. As students read the section, ask them to note information that answers their questions or adds to what they know.

4. After reading, facilitate a class discussion about what the students have learned. Clarify any lingering confusion about key concepts.

Strategy 2: Teach High-Use Academic Words

Purpose: To teach students words used often in academic texts, beyond the content-specific Key Terms

How to Do It

1. Have students rate how well they know each word on their *Word Knowledge* worksheets. Tell them there is no penalty for a low rating.

2. Survey students' ratings to decide which words need the most instruction.

3. Provide a brief definition or sample sentence for each word. (See Vocabulary Builder at the beginning of each section for definitions and sample sentences.) Rephrase your explanation, leaving out the word and asking students to substitute it aloud.

4. Work with students as they fill in the "Definition or Example" column of their *Word Knowledge* worksheets.

5. Point out each word in context as you read the chapters. Consider allowing students to earn extra credit if they use a word correctly in class discussion or assignments.

Strategy 3: Oral Cloze

Purpose: To help students read actively while the teacher reads aloud

How to Do It

1. Choose a passage and direct students to "read aloud silently using their inner voices." Be sure students understand reading is an active process, not simply a listening activity, and their job is to follow along—eyes riveted to each word, saying the words to themselves as you read aloud.

2. Tell students to be on their "reading toes," for you will be leaving out an occasional word and their task is to chorally supply the word.

3. The first few times you use the Oral Cloze, demonstrate by telling the students in advance what word you will be leaving out, directing them to read the word at the right time. Practice this a few times until they have the feel for the procedure. Leave out fewer words as students become more familiar with the Oral Cloze and require less direction to remain focused during teacher read alouds.

Strategies for Improving Student Comprehension *(continued)*

Strategy 4: Choral Reading

Purpose: To have students attend to the text in a non-threatening atmosphere

How to Do It

1. Choose a relatively short passage.

2. Tell students that you will all read the text aloud at once. Direct students to "keep your voice with mine" as they read.

3. Read the passage slowly and clearly.

4. Have students read the text again silently.

Strategy 5: Structured Silent Reading

Purpose: To give students a task as they read silently to increase their attentiveness and accountability

How to Do It

1. Assign a section to read silently. Pose a question for the whole class to answer from their silent reading, such as the Reading Check question at the end of each subsection. Model how one thinks while reading to find answers to a question.

2. When students get used to reading to answer the Reading Check question, pose more in-depth questions, progressing from factual recall to questions that stimulate interpretive or applied thinking.

3. Teach students to ask and answer their own questions as they read. Model this process by reading a section aloud and asking and answering your own questions as you read.

4. After the students have finished reading, engage the class in a brief discussion to clarify questions, vocabulary, and key concepts.

Strategy 6: Paragraph Shrinking

Purpose: To increase comprehension during reading

How to Do It

1. Partner struggling students with more proficient students and assign a manageable portion of the text.

2. Ask one member of each pair to identify the "who or what" the paragraph is about and tell the other.

3. Have the other member of the pair identify important details about the "who or what" and tell the other.

4. Ask the first member to summarize the paragraph in fifteen to twenty words or less using the most important details. The second member of the pair monitors the number of words and says "Shrink it!" if the summary goes over twenty words.

5. Have the partners reverse roles and continue reading.

6. Discuss the reading as a class to make sure students' paragraphs have correctly hit upon the main ideas of the passage.

Strategy 7: ReQuest (Reciprocal Questioning)

Purpose: To ask and answer questions during reading to establish a purpose for reading and monitor one's own comprehension

How to Do It

1. Prepare students to read by doing the section's Build Background Knowledge, Set a Purpose for Reading, and Preview Key Terms activities.

2. Begin reading a brief portion of the text aloud. Ask and answer your own questions about the text, progressing from recall to critical thinking questions.

3. After modeling this question and response pattern with a brief passage, ask students to read the next section of the text. Tell students that they will be taking turns asking you questions about what they read, and you will answer their questions, just like you modeled for them.

4. Ask students to read the next section. Inform them that you will be asking them questions about the section and they will be answering your questions.

5. Continue to alternate between student-generated questions and teacher-generated questions until the entire designated passage has been read. As students become used to the strategy, they gradually assume more responsibility in the process.

6. When the students have read enough information to make predictions about the remainder of the assignment, stop the exchange of comprehension questions. Instead, ask prediction questions, such as, "What do you think will be discussed in the next section? Why do you think so?"

7. Assign the remaining portion for students to read silently. Then lead a wrap-up discussion of the material.

Strategy 8: Idea Wave

Purpose: To engage students in active class discussions

How to Do It

1. Pose a question or task.

2. Give students quiet time to consider what they know about the topic and record a number of responses.

3. Whip around the class in a fast-paced and structured manner (e.g. down rows, around tables), allowing as many students as possible to share an idea in 15 seconds or less.

4. After several contributions, if there tends to be repetition, ask students to point out similarities in responses rather than simply stating that their idea has already been mentioned.

Strategies for Improving Student Comprehension *(continued)*

Strategy 9: Numbered Heads

Purpose: To engage students in active class discussions

How to Do It

1. Seat students in groups of four and number off one through four (if possible, combine established partners to form groups of four).

2. After giving the discussion prompt, allow students to discuss possible responses for an established amount of time.

3. Remind students to pay close attention to the comments of each group member because you will be randomly selecting one student to represent the best thinking of the entire group.

4. Call a number (one through four), and ask all students with that number to raise their hands, ready to respond to the topic at hand in a teacher-directed, whole-class discussion.

5. Add comments, extend key ideas, ask follow-up questions, and make connections between individual student's comments to create a lively whole-class discussion.

6. Provide any summary comments required to ensure that all students understand critical points.

Strategy 10: Think-Write-Pair–Share

Purpose: To engage students in responding to instruction

How to Do It

1. **Think**—Students listen while the teacher poses a question or a task related to the reading or classroom discussion. The level of questions should vary from lower level literal to higher order inferential or analytical.

2. **Write**—Provide quiet thinking or writing time for students to deal with the question, and go back to the text or review notes. Have students record their ideas in their notebooks.

3. **Pair/Share**—Cue students to find a partner and discuss their responses, noting similarities and differences. Teach students to encourage one another to clarify and justify responses.

4. Randomly call on students to share during a unified class discussion after they have all rehearsed answers with their partners.

5. Invite any volunteers to contribute additional ideas and points of view to the discussion after calling on a reasonable number of students randomly.

6. Direct students to go back to notes and add any important information garnered during the partner and class discussions.

Strategy 11: Give One, Get One

Purpose: To foster independent reflection and peer interaction prior to a unified class discussion

How to Do It

1. Pose a thought-provoking question or a concrete task to the class.

2. Allow three to five minutes of quiet time for students to consider what they may already know about the topic and jot down a number of potential responses.

3. Ask students to place a check mark next to the two or three ideas that they perceive as their strongest and then draw a line after their final idea to separate their ideas from those that they will gather from classmates.

4. Give students a set amount of time (about eight to ten minutes) to get up from their seats and share ideas with classmates. After finding a partner, the two students exchange papers and first quietly read each other's ideas. They discuss the ideas briefly, then select one idea from their partner's list and add it to their own, making sure to accurately copy the idea alongside the partner's name.

5. When one exchange is completed, students move on to interact with a new partner.

6. At the end of the exchange period, facilitate a unified class discussion. Call on a volunteer to share one new idea acquired from a conversation partner. The student whose idea has just been reported then shares the next idea, gleaned from a different conversation partner.

Professional Development

For more information about these strategies, see the end of each chapter's Interleaf.

Reading and Writing Handbook

Step-by-Step Instruction

Objectives

- Learn how to read nonfiction critically by analyzing an author's purpose, distinguishing between facts and opinions, identifying evidence, and evaluating credibility.

Prepare to Read

Build Background Knowledge `L2`

Write the phrase "Don't believe everything you read" on the board. Ask students to brainstorm examples that illustrate the saying. Provide a few simple examples to get them started (*tall tales, advertisements.*)

Instruct

Reading Informational Texts `L2`

Guided Instruction

- Tell students that they must actively evaluate the information in most of the nonfiction they read.

- Read the sample editorial on this page aloud. Tell students that an editorial usually expresses a person's opinion. Ask students to consider why the author wrote this editorial. *(The author expresses the opinion that the proposal to build the new shopping center should have been approved.)* Ask **How might this purpose affect what the editorial says?** *(The author may present information in the best possible light to prove his or her belief.)*

- Another important step in evaluating nonfiction is distinguishing between facts and opinions. Ask each student to write one fact and one opinion, on any subject, in their notebooks. Use the Idea Wave strategy (TE, p. T35) to get students to share their facts and opinion. If students have incorrectly categorized examples, help them to see why.

Reading Informational Texts

Reading a magazine, an Internet page, or a textbook is not the same as reading a novel. The purpose of reading nonfiction texts is to acquire new information. On page RW6 you'll read about some ⟲ **Target Reading Skills** that you'll have a chance to practice as you read this textbook. Here we'll focus on a few skills that will help you read nonfiction with a more critical eye.

Analyze the Author's Purpose

Different types of materials are written with different purposes in mind. For example, a textbook is written to teach students information about a subject. The purpose of a technical manual is to teach someone how to use something, such as a computer. A newspaper editorial might be written to persuade the reader to accept a particular point of view. A writer's purpose influences how the material is presented. Sometimes an author states his or her purpose directly. More often, the purpose is only suggested, and you must use clues to identify the author's purpose.

Distinguish Between Facts and Opinions

It's important when reading informational texts to read actively and to distinguish between fact and opinion. A fact can be proven or disproven. An opinion cannot—it is someone's personal viewpoint or evaluation.

For example, the editorial pages in a newspaper offer opinions on topics that are currently in the news. You need to read newspaper editorials with an eye for bias and faulty logic. For example, the newspaper editorial at the right shows factual statements in blue and opinion statements in red. The underlined words are examples of highly charged words. They reveal bias on the part of the writer.

> More than 5,000 people voted last week in favor of building a new shopping center, but the opposition won out. The margin of victory is irrelevant. Those <u>radical</u> voters who opposed the center are obviously <u>self-serving elitists</u> who do not care about anyone but themselves.
>
> This month's unemployment figure for our area is 10 percent, which represents an increase of about 5 percent over the figure for this time last year. These figures mean unemployment is getting worse. But the people who voted against the mall probably do not care about creating new jobs.

Reading and Writing Handbook

- Tell students that identifying evidence is another way to read nonfiction critically. Ask students to look again at the facts highlighted in the sample editorial. **Does the evidence presented in these facts convince you that building a new shopping center is a good idea?** *(The evidence is incomplete—the author has not shown that the new shopping center would solve the unemployment problem.)*

- Tell students that analyzing an author's purpose, distinguishing between fact and opinions, and identifying evidence are all ways to evaluate the credibility of the author. Tell students to look at the checklist for evaluating Web sites. Ask students to think about Web sites they have visited. Do those Web sites pass the checklist's test? Why or why not?

Identify Evidence

Before you accept an author's conclusion, you need to make sure that the author has based the conclusion on enough evidence and on the right kind of evidence. An author may present a series of facts to support a claim, but the facts may not tell the whole story. For example, what evidence does the author of the newspaper editorial on the previous page provide to support his claim that the new shopping center would create more jobs? Is it possible that the shopping center might have put many small local businesses out of business, thus increasing unemployment rather than decreasing it?

Evaluate Credibility

Whenever you read informational texts, you need to assess the credibility of the author. This is especially true of sites you may visit on the Internet. All Internet sources are not equally reliable. Here are some questions to ask yourself when evaluating the credibility of a Web site.

- ❑ Is the Web site created by a respected organization, a discussion group, or an individual?
- ❑ Does the Web site creator include his or her name as well as credentials and the sources he or she used to write the material?
- ❑ Is the information on the site balanced or biased?
- ❑ Can you verify the information using two other sources?
- ❑ Is there a date telling when the Web site was created or last updated?

Reading and Writing Handbook **RW1**

Independent Practice

Ask students to bring in an editorial from the local newspaper, or distribute copies of an appropriate editorial. Ask students to critically assess their editorial by analyzing the author's purpose; underlining facts and circling opinions in the text of the editorial; summarizing the evidence presented in the editorial; and finally drawing a conclusion about the credibility of the editorial.

Monitor Progress

Pair students and have them share their editorial assessments. Ask them to explain the reasoning behind the conclusions they drew about the editorial's credibility. Circulate and offer assistance as needed.

Assess and Reteach

Assess Progress   L2
Collect students' papers and review their assessments.

Reteach   L1
If students are struggling, tell them to approach the task by asking themselves the following questions as they read a piece of nonfiction: **Why** did the author write this? **How** has the author made his or her points, using facts or opinions? **What** evidence has the author used to support the main idea? **Who** is the author, and what sources has he or she used?

Extend   L3
To extend this lesson, tell students to turn to the Table of Contents in the Student Edition and pick a chapter name that intrigues. Then, ask them to search the internet and find two Web sites about the chapter's topic. Finally, ask them to use the checklist on this page to evaluate each Web site and compare the two in terms of credibility.

Differentiated Instruction

For Advanced Readers   L3
Draw students' attention to the checklist under the heading "Evaluate Credibility." Ask students to create a similar checklist for analyzing an author's purpose, distinguishing between fact and opinion, and identifying evidence.

For Special Needs Students   L1
If special needs students are having trouble making the distinction between facts and opinions, partner them with more proficient students to do the *Distinguishing Fact and Opinion* lesson on the Social Studies Skill Tutor CD-ROM.

◉ *Distinguishing Fact and Opinion,* **Social Studies Skill Tutor CD-ROM**

Objectives

- Use a systematic approach to write narrative, persuasive, expository, and research essays.

Prepare to Read

Build Background Knowledge [L2]

As a group, brainstorm all the ways that people use writing to communicate. Start them with these examples: labeling a folder, writing an email. Conduct an Idea Wave (TE, p. T35) and write students' responses on the board. Tell them that people often write to express ideas or information. Give them *Four Purposes for Writing* and tell them to keep it in their notebooks for future reference.

All in One Foundations of Geography Teaching Resources, *Four Purposes for Writing,* p. 5

Instruct

Narrative Essays [L2]

Guided Instruction

- Tell students that narrative essays tell a story about their own experiences. Discuss the steps listed in the Student Edition.

- Choose an event in your own life (or invent one) such as visiting friends in another city. Write your topic on the board and model how to list details *(what the trip was like, what you did while you were there, what your friends are like.)* Cross out the least interesting details.

- Think aloud as your form your topic into a sentence that conveys the main idea of your essay.

- Tell students that you will go on to flesh out the details into a colorful story.

Independent Practice

- Tell students to write a narrative essay about a recent positive experience. Have student pairs brainstorm topics.

Writing for Social Studies

Writing is one of the most powerful communication tools you will ever use. You will use it to share your thoughts and ideas with others. Research shows that writing about what you read actually helps you learn new information and ideas. A systematic approach to writing—including prewriting, drafting, revising, and proofing—can help you write better, whether you're writing an essay or a research report.

Narrative Essays

Writing that tells a story about a personal experience

① Select and Narrow Your Topic

A narrative is a story. In social studies, it might be a narrative essay about how an event affected you or your family.

② Gather Details

Brainstorm a list of details you'd like to include in your narrative.

③ Write a First Draft

Start by writing a simple opening sentence that conveys the main idea of your essay. Continue by writing a colorful story that has interesting details. Write a conclusion that sums up the significance of the event or situation described in your essay.

④ Revise and Proofread

Check to make sure you have not begun too many sentences with the word *I*. Replace general words with more colorful ones.

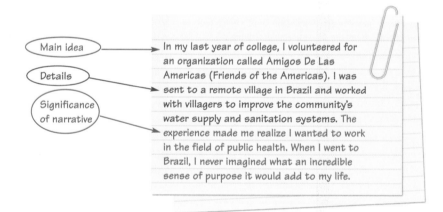

Main idea → In my last year of college, I volunteered for an organization called Amigos De Las Americas (Friends of the Americas). I was

Details → sent to a remote village in Brazil and worked with villagers to improve the community's water supply and sanitation systems. The

Significance of narrative → experience made me realize I wanted to work in the field of public health. When I went to Brazil, I never imagined what an incredible sense of purpose it would add to my life.

- Give students *Writing to Describe* to help them write their essays. After they have written the body of their essay, give them *Writing the Conclusion* to help them complete it.

All in One Foundations of Geography Teaching Resources, *Writing to Describe,* p. 6; *Writing the Conclusion,* p. 7

Monitor Progress

Have students share their drafts with their partners. Give them *Using the Revision Checklist* and ask them to review their partners' papers. Urge them to provide constructive criticism and suggestions for improvement.

All in One Foundations of Geography Teaching Resources, *Using the Revision Checklist,* p. 8

Persuasive Essays

Writing that supports an opinion or position

① Select and Narrow Your Topic

Choose a topic that provokes an argument and has at least two sides. Choose a side. Decide which argument will appeal most to your audience and persuade them to understand your point of view.

② Gather Evidence

Create a chart that states your position at the top and then lists the pros and cons for your position below, in two columns. Predict and address the strongest arguments against your stand.

③ Write a First Draft

Write a strong thesis statement that clearly states your position. Continue by presenting the strongest arguments in favor of your position and acknowledging and refuting opposing arguments.

④ Revise and Proofread

Check to make sure you have made a logical argument and that you have not oversimplified the argument.

Main Idea

Supporting (pro) argument

Opposing (con) argument

Transition words

> It is vital to vote in elections. When people vote, they tell public officials how to run the government. Not every proposal is carried out; however, politicians do their best to listen to what the majority of people want. Therefore, every vote is important.

Guided Instruction

■ Tell students that the purpose of writing a persuasive essay is to convince other people to believe your point of view. However, you must use solid, reliable evidence and arguments to make your points.

■ Model the thought process by pointing out how the writer presents his or her argument in the paragraph on this page.

Independent Practice

■ Tell students to write a persuasive essay about a topic that is important to them. Have students form pairs. One student in each pair should state his or her position. The other student then shares opposing arguments, which the first student should refute in his or her essay. Then the pairs switch roles.

■ Give students *Writing to Persuade* to help them write their essays.

  All in One **Foundations of Geography Teaching Resources,** *Writing to Persuade,* p. 9

Monitor Progress

If students are having trouble structuring their paragraphs, give them *Structuring Paragraphs* and *Creating Paragraph Outlines* to provide a framework.

  All in One **Foundations of Geography Teaching Resources,** *Structuring Paragraphs,* p. 10; *Creating Paragraph Outlines,* p. 11

Differentiated Instruction

For Less Proficient Readers L1

Tell students to use looping to help them focus on a topic. Have them follow these steps: Write freely on your topic for about five minutes. Read what you have written and circle the most important idea. Write for five minutes on the circled idea. Repeat the process until you isolate a topic narrow enough to cover well in a short essay.

Expository Essays L2

Guided Instruction

- Read the steps for writing expository essays with students.

- Tell students that the graphic organizer example given on the Student Edition page is for a cause and effect expository essay. They might use a Venn diagram for a compare and contrast essay and a flow-chart for a problem and solution essay.

- Model how to create a topic sentence from the information in the cause and effect graphic organizer. *(Sample topic sentence: In Mexico, several factors are causing rural families to move from the countryside to the city.)*

- Create a brief outline showing how you will organize the paragraphs in your essay.

Independent Practice

Tell students to write an expository essay based on a recent current event. Have them brainstorm ideas with a partner, then choose which type of essay best suits their topic (cause and effect, compare and contrast, or problem and solution.) Give them *Writing to Inform and Explain* and *Gathering Details* to help them start drafting their essays.

All in One **Foundations of Geography Teaching Resources,** *Writing to Inform and Explain,* p. 12; *Gathering Details,* p. 13

Monitor Progress

If students are struggling with their essays, give them *Writing a Cause-and-Effect Essay* or *Writing a Problem-and-Solution Essay.*

All in One **Foundations of Geography Teaching Resources,** *Writing a Cause-and-Effect Essay,* p. 14; *Writing a Problem-and-Solution Essay,* p. 15

Research Papers L2

Guided Instruction

Go over the steps for writing a research paper carefully. Ask students to share questions about the process, using the Idea Wave strategy (p. T35). Answer any questions they might have.

Reading and Writing Handbook

Expository Essays

Writing that explains a process, compares and contrasts, explains causes and effects, or explores solutions to a problem

1 Identify and Narrow Your Topic

Expository writing is writing that explains something in detail. It might explain the similarities and differences between two or more subjects (compare and contrast). It might explain how one event causes another (cause and effect). Or it might explain a problem and describe a solution.

2 Gather Evidence

Create a graphic organizer that identifies details to include in your essay.

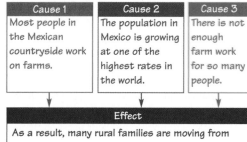

Cause 1	Cause 2	Cause 3
Most people in the Mexican countryside work on farms.	The population in Mexico is growing at one of the highest rates in the world.	There is not enough farm work for so many people.

Effect
As a result, many rural families are moving from the countryside to live in Mexico City.

3 Write Your First Draft

Write a topic sentence and then organize the essay around your similarities and differences, causes and effects, or problem and solutions. Be sure to include convincing details, facts, and examples.

4 Revise and Proofread

Research Papers

Writing that presents research about a topic

1 Narrow Your Topic

Choose a topic you're interested in and make sure that it is not too broad. For example, instead of writing a report on Panama, write about the construction of the Panama Canal.

2 Acquire Information

Locate several sources of information about the topic from the library or the Internet. For each resource, create a source index card like the one at the right. Then take notes using an index card for each detail or subtopic. On the card, note which source the information was taken from. Use quotation marks when you copy the exact words from a source.

Source #1
McCullough, David. *The Path Between the Seas: The Creation of the Panama Canal, 1870-1914.* N.Y., Simon and Schuster, 1977.

3 Make an Outline

Use an outline to decide how to organize your report. Sort your index cards into the same order.

Outline
I. Introduction
II. Why the canal was built
III. How the canal was built
    A. Physical challenges
    B. Medical challenges
IV. Conclusion

RW4 Reading and Writing Handbook

Differentiated Instruction

For Gifted and Talented L3

Tell students that a verb is in active voice when the subject performs the action named by the verb. A verb is in passive voice when the subject undergoes the action named by the verb.

Give these examples:

Passive voice: The house is being painted by my sister and me.

Active voice: My sister and I are painting the house.

Tell students that using the active voice whenever possible will make their writing more dynamic and concise.

Introduction

Building the Panama Canal

Ever since Christopher Columbus first explored the Isthmus of Panama, the Spanish had been looking for a water route through it. They wanted to be able to sail west from Spain to Asia without sailing around South America. However, it was not until 1914 that the dream became a reality.

Conclusion

It took eight years and more than 70,000 workers to build the Panama Canal. It remains one of the greatest engineering feats of modern times.

4 Write a First Draft

Write an introduction, a body, and a conclusion. Leave plenty of space between lines so you can go back and add details that you may have left out.

5 Revise and Proofread

Be sure to include transition words between sentences and paragraphs. Here are some examples:

To show a contrast—*however, although, despite.*

To point out a reason—*since, because, if.*

To signal a conclusion—*therefore, consequently, so, then.*

Evaluating Your Writing

Use this table to help you evaluate your writing.

	Excellent	Good	Acceptable	Unacceptable
Purpose	Achieves purpose—to inform, persuade, or provide historical interpretation—very well	Informs, persuades, or provides historical interpretation reasonably well	Reader cannot easily tell if the purpose is to inform, persuade, or provide historical interpretation	Purpose is not clear
Organization	Develops ideas in a very clear and logical way	Presents ideas in a reasonably well-organized way	Reader has difficulty following the organization	Lacks organization
Elaboration	Explains all ideas with facts and details	Explains most ideas with facts and details	Includes some supporting facts and details	Lacks supporting details
Use of Language	Uses excellent vocabulary and sentence structure with no errors in spelling, grammar, or punctuation	Uses good vocabulary and sentence structure with very few errors in spelling, grammar, or punctuation	Includes some errors in grammar, punctuation, and spelling	Includes many errors in grammar, punctuation, and spelling

Reading and Writing Handbook **RW5**

Differentiated Instruction

For English Language Learners L2

To help students understand the tasks you have given them, provide them with an example of a well-executed essay from a different class or a previous year. The example essay should be well written and organized but not above grade level. You could look for and save good examples each year you teach.

Independent Practice

- Have students consider topics for a research paper. Give them *Choosing a Topic* to help them learn how to evaluate potential topics.

  All in One **Foundations of Geography Teaching Resources,** *Choosing a Topic,* p. 16

- Once students have selected a topic, tell them they will need facts to support their ideas. Give them *Using the Library, Summarizing and Taking Notes,* and *Preparing Note Cards* to help them start their research.

  All in One **Foundations of Geography Teaching Resources,** *Using the Library,* p. 17; *Summarizing and Taking Notes,* p. 18; *Preparing Note Cards,* p. 19

Monitor Progress

Give students *Writing an Introduction* and *Writing the Body of an Essay* to help them write their essays.

All in One **Foundations of Geography Teaching Resources,** *Writing an Introduction,* p. 20; *Writing the Body of an Essay,* p. 21

Assess and Reteach

Assess Progress L2

Ask student to pick the best essay they have written so far and evaluate it using the rubric on this page.

Reteach L1

Collect students' essays and self-evaluations. Meet with students to go over good points and areas for improvement. Revisit each type of essay as needed with the whole class.

Extend L3

To extend this lesson, tell students there are many other different types of writing. Have them complete *Writing for Assessment* and *Writing a Letter* to learn about two more types of writing.

All in One **Foundations of Geography Teaching Resources,** *Writing for Assessment,* p. 22; *Writing a Letter,* p. 23

Teaching the Target Reading Skills

The Prentice Hall *World Studies* program has interwoven essential reading skills instruction throughout the Student Edition, Teacher's Edition, and ancillary resources. In Foundations of Geography, students will learn five reading skills.

Student Edition The *World Studies* Student Edition provides students with reading skills instruction, practice, and application opportunities in each chapter within the program.

Teacher's Edition The *World Studies* Teacher Edition supports your teaching of each skill by providing full modeling in each chapter's interleaf and modeling of the specific sub-skills in each section lesson.

All in One Teaching Resources The *World Studies* All-in-One Teaching Resources provides a worksheet explaining and supporting the elements of each Target Reading Skill. Use these to help struggling students master skills, or as more practice for every student.

How to Read Social Studies

Target Reading Skills

The Target Reading Skills introduced on this page will help you understand the words and ideas in this book and in other social studies reading you do. Each chapter focuses on one of these reading skills. Good readers develop a bank of reading strategies, or skills. Then they draw on the particular strategies that will help them understand the text they are reading.

Chapter 1 Target Reading Skill
Clarifying Meaning If you do not understand something you are reading right away, you can use several skills to help clarify the meaning of the word or idea. In this chapter you will practice these strategies for clarifying meaning: rereading, reading ahead, and paraphrasing.

Chapter 2 Target Reading Skill
Using Context Using the context of an unfamiliar word can help you understand its meaning. Context includes the words, phrases, and sentences surrounding a word. In this chapter you will practice using these context clues: descriptions, definitions, comparisons, and examples.

Chapter 3 Target Reading Skill
Comparing and Contrasting You can use comparison and contrast to sort out and analyze information you are reading. Comparing means examining the similarities between things. Contrasting is looking at differences. In this chapter you will practice these skills: comparing and contrasting, identifying contrasts, making comparisons, and recognizing contrast signal words.

Chapter 4 Target Reading Skill
Using Sequence Noting the order in which significant events take place can help you understand and remember them. In this chapter you will practice these sequence skills: sequencing, or finding the order of events, sequencing important changes, and recognizing sequence signal words.

Chapter 5 Target Reading Skill
Identifying the Main Idea Since you cannot remember every detail of what you read, it is important that you identify the main ideas. The main idea of a section or paragraph is the most important point and the one you want to remember. In this chapter you will practice these skills: identifying stated and implied main ideas and identifying supporting details.

RW6 Foundations of Geography

Assessment Resources

Use the diagnosing readiness tests from **AYP Monitoring Assessments** to help you identify problems before students begin to study geography.

Determine students' reading level and identify challenges:

📄 *Screening Tests*, pp. 1–10

Evaluate students' verbal skills:

📄 *Critical Thinking and Reading Tests*, pp. 25–34

📄 *Vocabulary Tests*, pp. 45–52

📄 *Writing Tests*, pp. 53–60

FOUNDATIONS of GEOGRAPHY

Are you curious about our world? Do you want to know why winters are cold and summers are hot? Have you wondered why some people live and work in cities and others work on farms in the countryside? If you answered yes to any of these questions, you want to know more about geography.

Guiding Questions

The text, photographs, maps, and charts in this book will help you discover answers to these Guiding Questions.

1 **Geography** What are Earth's major physical features?

2 **History** How have people's ways of life changed over time?

3 **Culture** What is a culture?

4 **Government** What types of government exist in the world today?

5 **Economics** How do people use the world's natural resources?

Project Preview

You can also discover answers to the Guiding Questions by working on projects. Project possibilities are listed on page 136 of this book.

Assess students' social studies skills:

- *Geographic Literacy Tests,* pp. 13–20
- *Visual Analysis Tests,* pp. 21–24
- *Communications Tests,* pp. 35–44

The World Studies program provides instruction and practice for all of these skills. Use students' test results to pinpoint the skills your students have mastered and the skills they need to practice. Then use *Correlation to Program Resources* to prescribe skills practice and reinforcement.

> *Correlation to Program Resources,* pp. 64–77

FOUNDATIONS of GEOGRAPHY

Guiding Questions

- This book was developed around five Guiding Questions about the foundations of geography. They appear on the reduced Student Edition page to the left. The Guiding Questions are intended as an organizational focus for the book. The Guiding Questions act as a kind of umbrella under which all of the material falls.

- You may wish to add your own Guiding Questions to the list in order to tailor them to your particular course.

- Draw students' attention to the Guiding Questions. Ask them to write the questions in their notebooks for future reference.

- In the Teacher's Edition, each section's themes are linked to a specific Guiding Question at the beginning of each chapter. Then, an activity at the end of the chapter returns to the Guiding Questions to review key concepts.

Project Preview

- The projects for this book are designed to provide students with hands-on involvement in the content area. Students are introduced to some projects on page 136.

- *Book Projects* give students directions on how to complete these projects, and more.

  All in One **Foundations of Geography Teaching Resources,** *Book Project: Focus on Part of the Whole,* pp. 27–29; *Book Project: The Geography Game,* pp. 30–32; *Book Project: Desktop Countries,* pp. 33–35; *Book Project: World News Today,* pp. 36–38

- Assign projects as small group activities, whole-class projects, or individual projects. Consider assigning a project at the beginning of the course.

Objectives

- Examine country borders that are shaped by geography, politics, and culture.

- Locate and name the seven continents.

- Analyze a physical map of the world to learn about elevation.

- Examine landforms and bodies of water that act as barriers to movement across countries and continents.

- Analyze the population density of the world and investigate the world's urban and rural populations.

Prepare to Read

Build Background Knowledge **L2**

Have students brainstorm similarities and differences among the world's continents. Encourage them to think about physical and cultural similarities and differences. Tell students that they will either confirm or revise these comparisons during their study of Earth's geography.

Instruct

Investigate the Political World **L2**

Guided Instruction

- Read the introductory and Location paragraphs as a class. Direct students' attention to the border between the country of Canada and state of Alaska. Ask **Do you think the border is shaped by politics or geography? Explain.** *(politics, because the border is straight)*

- Hand out the *World Overview* worksheet. Direct students to fill in the answers to the questions as they read.

All in One Foundations of Geography Teaching Resources, *World Overview,* pp. 43–45

Answers

LOCATION Rivers and lakes may form the crooked portion of the border in the east. The straight portion of the border was probably shaped by politics.

Investigate the Political World

There are more than 190 independent countries in the world. Some of those countries have dependencies, or areas outside of those countries that belong to them. Every land area where people live belongs to some country. The blue areas on maps in this book show the world's oceans, seas, and lakes. The other colors on this map show the areas of the world's countries and dependencies.

Go Online PHSchool.com Use Web Code **lep-3020** for the **interactive maps** on these pages.

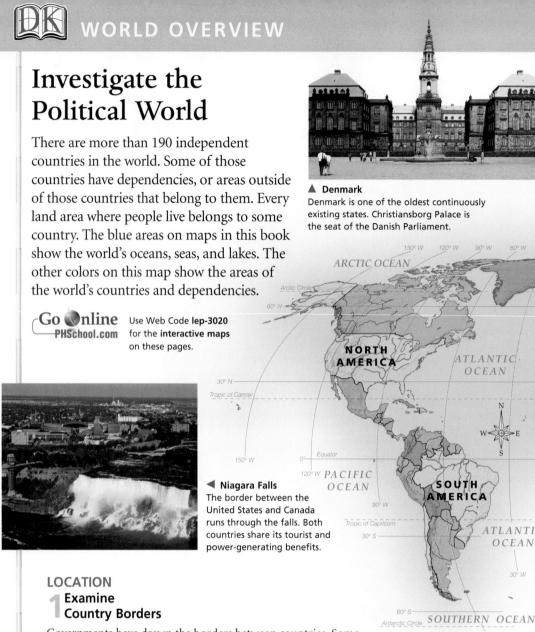

▲ **Denmark**
Denmark is one of the oldest continuously existing states. Christiansborg Palace is the seat of the Danish Parliament.

◄ **Niagara Falls**
The border between the United States and Canada runs through the falls. Both countries share its tourist and power-generating benefits.

LOCATION

1 Examine Country Borders

Governments have drawn the borders between countries. Some borders follow mountains or rivers. Others are straight lines. On the map, look at the United States and Canada. These are the large yellow and pink countries in North America. Parts of their borders are straight, but others are crooked. Why might this be? What might explain the location of other borders on this map?

The World: Political Key

— National border
- - - Disputed border

Mental Mapping

The Shape of the World Have students close their textbooks. Take down or cover any maps of the world that may be hanging in your classroom. Then give each student a blank piece of paper. Ask them to draw a map of the seven continents.

Encourage them to draw the shapes of the continents as accurately as possible. Have them draw in any continent borders that appear on land. Remind them to label the continents.

PLACE

2 Analyze the Continents

Notice the six black labels on the world map. These labels name continents. Which continent's name is also the name of a country? You can see that some continents have more countries than others. Which continent is made up mostly of small countries?

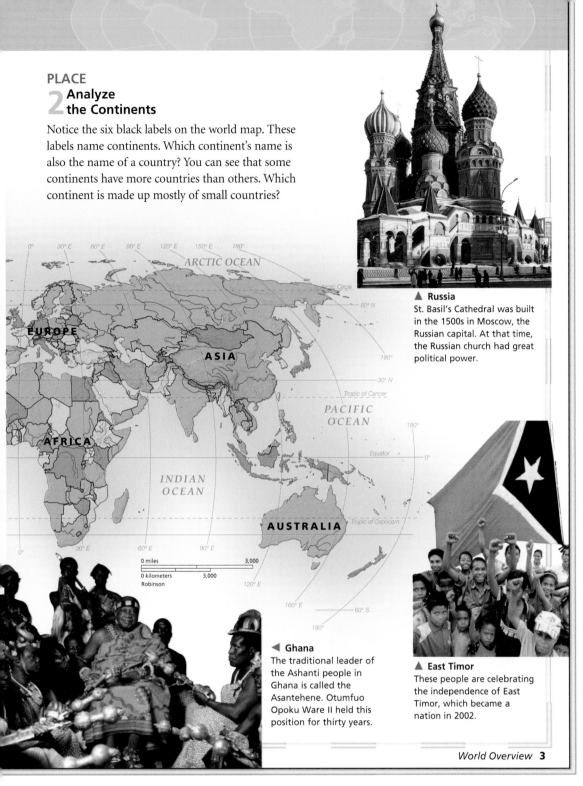

ARCTIC OCEAN

Arctic Circle

60° N

EUROPE

ASIA

180°

30° N

Tropic of Cancer

PACIFIC OCEAN

180°

AFRICA

Equator   0°

INDIAN OCEAN

AUSTRALIA   Tropic of Capricorn

0 miles   3,000
0 kilometers   3,000
Robinson

160° E   60° S

180°

▲ **Russia**
St. Basil's Cathedral was built in the 1500s in Moscow, the Russian capital. At that time, the Russian church had great political power.

◄ **Ghana**
The traditional leader of the Ashanti people in Ghana is called the Asantehene. Otumfuo Opoku Ware II held this position for thirty years.

▲ **East Timor**
These people are celebrating the independence of East Timor, which became a nation in 2002.

World Overview **3**

Background: Links Across Time

Historical Borders Geographic features such as rivers and mountains have played an important role in history. By 1803, the United States stretched from the Atlantic Ocean to the Mississipi River. France controlled the territory—called Louisiana—that extended from the Mississippi River west to the Rocky Mountains. In 1803, the United States purchased Louisiana, extending the United States to the Rocky Mountains. Today, the Mississippi River still serves as a border—but between neighboring states rather than neighboring country territories.

Guided Instruction (continued)

■ Read the Place paragraph and the photo captions. Ask students if they know where Russia, Ghana, and East Timor are located. If students cannot locate the countries, display *Transparency FG 22: The World: Political* and have student volunteers point to the locations of these countries. Have volunteers name the continent on which each is located.

📖 **Foundations of Geography Transparencies,** *Color Transparency FG 22: The World: Political*

■ Using the transparency, have a student trace his or her finger along the border between Asia and Europe. Ask students **Which countries are located in both Europe and Asia?** *(Turkey and Russia)*

■ Ask **Which continents are east of North and South America across the Atlantic Ocean?** *(Europe and Africa)* **Which continents are west of North America and South across the Pacific Ocean?** *(Asia and Australia)*

Independent Practice

Distribute *Transparency FG 27: Latin America: Physical-Political.* Ask students to find borders or partial borders that are made by rivers. Have them write down the names of the countries that share these borders.

📖 **Foundations of Geography Transparencies,** *Color Transparency FG 27: Latin America: Physical-Political*

Monitor Progress

Circulate to make sure students are able to identify river borders and are recording the proper country names. If students are having difficulty reading the map, assign *Reading a Political Map* to give them more practice.

All in One **Foundations of Geography Teaching Resources,** *Reading a Political Map,* p. 46

Answers

PLACE
Australia; Europe

Investigate the Physical World

Guided Instruction

- Read the introduction and the Place paragraphs. Have students study the physical map of the world. Ask them to use the map key to determine the highest range of elevations in Asia and Australia. *(Asia—more than 13,000 feet [3,960 meters]; Australia—1,600–6,500 feet [480–1,980 meters])*

- Ask students to identify the elevation range of Scandinavia's northern and western coasts. *(0–650 feet [0–200 meters])*

- Read the Human-Environment Interaction paragraph. Direct students' attention to Europe and Asia. Have them again locate the border between these two continents. Ask **What physical feature serves as a physical barrier between these two continents?** *(Ural Mountains)*

- After students have read the caption about Mount Fuji, ask them to trace their finger over the islands along the rim of the Pacific Ocean. Be sure they locate the islands on both pages of the map. Point out that some of these islands are considered to be part of Asia and others are part of a region that is sometimes called Oceania. The islands off the east coast of Asia from Japan south to Sumatra and Java and east to New Guinea are part of Asia while the islands of Micronesia, Melanesia, and Polynesia are part of Oceania.

- Have students continue to complete the *World Overview* worksheet.

  All in One Foundations of Geography Teaching Resources, *World Overview,* pp. 43–45

Answer

PLACE The elevation of the Amazon Basin is 0 to 650 feet or 0 to 200 meters above sea level. The landscape around the Tigre River appears very flat. You would expect to see tall peaks in the Andes.

Investigate the Physical World

People's lives are constantly shaped by their physical environment. The physical features of a place often determine where and how people live. Yet the physical world is always changing, too. Some changes come very slowly. For example, it took millions of years for Earth's crust to lift and form mountains. Other changes are fast and dramatic, such as when a volcano erupts or an earthquake hits.

▲ **Alaska**
Glaciers like this one at Portage, Alaska, have shaped the land for thousands of years.

PLACE

3 Infer From a Map

Notice the bumpy texture and brownish colors on the map. These indicate a mountainous landscape. Now find the continent of South America. Look for the Amazon Basin. What does the key tell you about its elevation? Notice the photograph of the Tigre River as it weaves through the basin. Describe that landscape. Now find the Andes on the map, and describe what you would expect to see there.

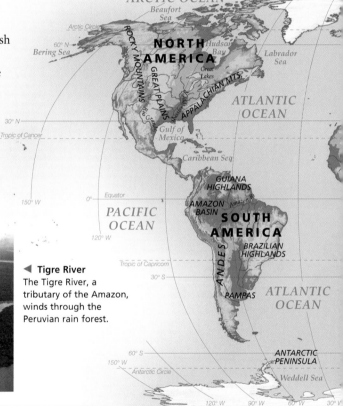

◄ **Tigre River**
The Tigre River, a tributary of the Amazon, winds through the Peruvian rain forest.

Differentiated Instruction

For Less Proficient Readers   **L1**

For students having trouble reading the physical map of the world, distribute *Reading a Physical Map* and *Elevation on a Map*. Have students complete the activities in pairs.

All in One Foundations of Geography Teaching Resources, *Reading a Physical Map,* p. 47; *Elevation on a Map,* p. 48

For Advanced Readers   **L3**

Tell students that another way mapmakers can show elevation on a map is by using isolines. Assign *Understanding Isolines* and *Reading a Contour Map* to help students explore this concept.

All in One Foundations of Geography Teaching Resources, *Understanding Isolines,* p. 49; *Reading a Contour Map,* p. 50

HUMAN-ENVIRONMENT INTERACTION

4 Examine Landforms as Barriers

Physical barriers can make movement between areas difficult. For example, take a look at the continents in the map below. Some of them are separated from one another by vast areas of water. Examine the elevation key. Look closely at the map's labels. What other physical landforms might have acted as barriers to movement?

▲ **Mount Fuji, Japan**
Volcanoes such as this one have created islands along the rim of the Pacific Ocean.

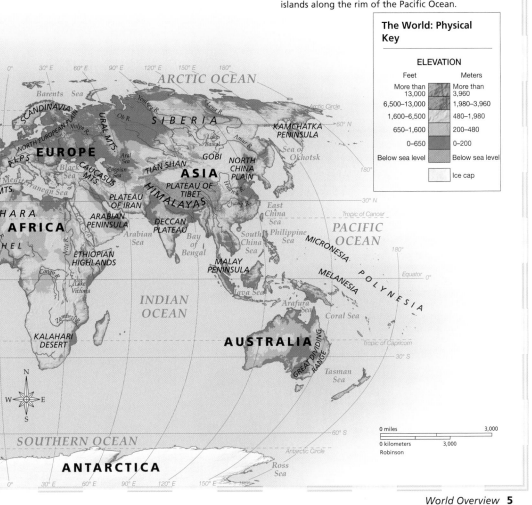

The World: Physical Key

ELEVATION

Feet	Meters
More than 13,000	More than 3,960
6,500–13,000	1,980–3,960
1,600–6,500	480–1,980
650–1,600	200–480
0–650	0–200
Below sea level	Below sea level
	Ice cap

World Overview **5**

Independent Practice

■ Have students explore the location of the world's highest peaks by placing them on an outline map.

■ Give them the following statistics:

Continent	Highest Point	Elevation
Africa	Kilimanjaro	19,340 feet
Antarctica	Vinson Massif	16,864 feet
Asia	Mount Everest	29,035 feet
Australia	Mount Kosciusko	7,310 feet
North America	Mount McKinley	20,320 feet
South America	Mount Aconcagua	22,834 feet

■ Have them research the location of the highest point on each continent. Then distribute *Outline Map 1: The World: Physical.* Ask students to create a symbol to represent the highest point and show it in a map key. Then have them label the points on each continent. Ask them to write in the height of each point near each label.

All in One **Foundations of Geography Teaching Resources,** *Outline Map 1: The World: Physical,* p. 51

Monitor Progress

Make sure students are creating maps correctly. Check student maps for map keys and appropriate labels.

Answer

HUMAN-ENVIRONMENT INTERACTION
Possible answer: Mountain ranges and deserts also might have acted as barriers to movement.

Investigate Population

Guided Instruction

- Use the Choral Reading technique (TE, p. 34) to read the text.

- Ask students **Which color on the map represents the most densely populated areas?** *(purple)* **Which color represents the most sparsely populated areas?** *(yellow)*

- Direct students' attention to Africa on the map. Tell them to use what they know about Africa's physical geography to explain why much of North Africa is sparsely populated. *(Much of North Africa is covered by the Sahara.)*

- Have students study the circle graphs at the bottom of p. 6. Ask **In which of these countries does the greatest percentage of people live in urban areas?** *(the United Kingdom)*

Independent Practice

Display *Color Transparency FG 5: The World: Continents and Oceans* and *Color Transparency FG 6: Some Major Cities of the World.* Have students compare them with the population density map on pp. 6–7 in the Student Edition. Ask students to list one densely populated city on each continent. Then have them compare the transparencies with the physical map on pp. 4–5 of the Student Edition. Have them locate the cities they listed on the physical map and their nearby landforms. Finally, ask them to synthesize the information by writing a sentence about each city.

📖 **Foundations of Geography Transparencies,** *Color Transparency FG 5: The World: Continents and Oceans; Color Transparency FG 6: Some Major Cities of the World*

Monitor Progress

Circulate to make sure students are able to locate the most populated cities on the maps. Check students' sentences for appropriate details.

Answer

REGIONS Much of Europe, eastern North America, and southeastern and southern Asia have many people, while Northern North America, Australia, and northern Asia have few people. Possible answer: People choose where to live based on climate and geography.

Investigate Population

For thousands of years, the world's population grew slowly. In the past 200 years, however, health care, living conditions, and food production have greatly improved. This has led to a huge population burst. In 1800, the world's population numbered less than 1 billion people. Today, it is more than 6 billion, and growing quickly.

▲ **China**
A crowd of people walk through a park in the capital city of Beijing. China has the largest population of any country in the world.

REGIONS

5 Analyze Population Density

A population density map shows you where the world's people live. Study the world population map. Which places have many people? Which have few? Why do you think people live where they do? As you study the map, refer to the world physical map on the previous page. It may give you some clues to help you answer these questions.

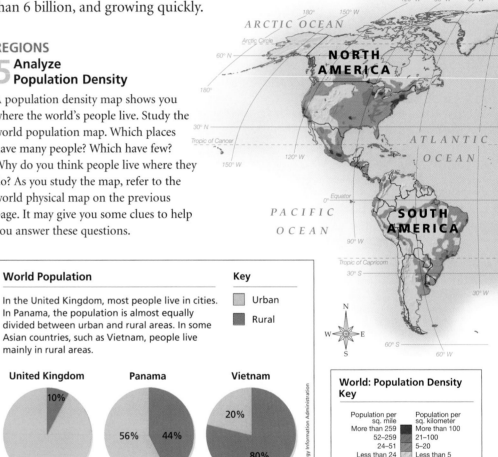

World Population

In the United Kingdom, most people live in cities. In Panama, the population is almost equally divided between urban and rural areas. In some Asian countries, such as Vietnam, people live mainly in rural areas.

Key
- Urban
- Rural

United Kingdom
10%

Panama
56% 44%

Vietnam
20%
80%

Source: Energy Information Administration

World: Population Density Key

Population per sq. mile	Population per sq. kilometer
More than 259	More than 100
52–259	21–100
24–51	5–20
Less than 24	Less than 5

—— National border
- - - Disputed border

Differentiated Instruction

For English Language Learners 〔L1〕
Spend extra time reviewing the meaning of important terms that may be difficult for English language learners such as *population density, urban,* and *rural.* Point out the map key and review what a square mile is. Have students find at least one area on the map that corresponds to each density range and have them say aloud the number of people it represents as they point to the area on the map.

MOVEMENT

6 Compare Continents

When high population densities cover large areas, those areas have large populations. Look at the continents on the map. Which continent do you think has the largest population, based on the size of its areas of high population density? Which continent do you think has the lowest population? Compare North America and South America on the map. Which continent do you think has the larger population?

▲ **New Zealand**
The Whanganui River flows through a New Zealand national park. New Zealand has a low population density.

0 miles 3,000
0 kilometers 3,000
Robinson

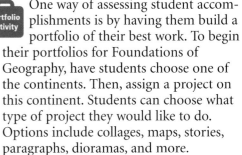

PRACTICE YOUR GEOGRAPHY SKILLS

1. In Asia there is a ring of dense population next to an area with low population. Look at the physical map of the world on pages 4 and 5. What landform may explain this difference?

2. Look at northern Africa. Find the area of heavy population that forms a curving line on the map. How does the physical map on pages 4 and 5 explain this?

Monaco is the most densely populated European nation. ▶

Differentiated Instruction

For Advanced Readers L3
Have students complete the *Urban Population, Past and Projected* activity individually so they can learn more about the world's urban population.

Go Online
PHSchool.com **For:** Environmental and Global Issues: *Urban Population, Past and Projected*
Visit: PHSchool.com
Web Code: led-3307

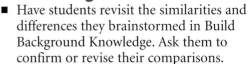

Assess and Reteach

Assess Progress L2
- Have students revisit the similarities and differences they brainstormed in Build Background Knowledge. Ask them to confirm or revise their comparisons.
- Ask students to complete Practice Your Geography Skills on page 7.

Reteach L1
Have students review key concepts in the World Overview by completing *DK Compact Atlas of the World Activity: Reading a Political Map, DK Compact Atlas of the World Activity: Reading a Physical Map,* and *Reading a Population Density Map* in partners or small groups.

All in One Foundations of Geography Teaching Resources, *DK Compact Atlas of the World Activity: Reading a Political Map,* p. 52; *DK Compact Atlas of the World Activity: Reading a Physical Map,* p. 53; *Reading a Population Density Map,* p. 54

Extend L3

 One way of assessing student accomplishments is by having them build a portfolio of their best work. To begin their portfolios for Foundations of Geography, have students choose one of the continents. Then, assign a project on this continent. Students can choose what type of project they would like to do. Options include collages, maps, stories, paragraphs, dioramas, and more.

- Give students *Writing an Outline for Research* to help them get started.

All in One Foundations of Geography Teaching Resources, *Writing an Outline for Research,* p. 55

Answers

MOVEMENT Possible answer: Asia, because it seems to have the largest areas of high population density. Australia, because most of it has low population density and there is very little area with a high population density. North America, because it has larger areas of high population density.

PRACTICE YOUR GEOGRAPHY SKILLS

1. Possible answer: the Plateau of Tibet, the Gobi desert
2. The Nile River is located along the curving line of dense population.

1 The World of Geography

Chapter Overview

DISCOVERY
CHANNEL
SCHOOL
Video

Overview

Section 1 — The Five Themes of Geography
1. Learn about the study of Earth.
2. Discover five ways to look at Earth.

What Is Geography?
Length: 3 minutes, 25 seconds
Use with Section 1
Explores the many facets of geography.

Section 2 — The Geographer's Tools
1. Find out how maps and globes show information about Earth's surface.
2. See how mapmakers show Earth's round surface on flat maps.
3. Learn how to read maps.

Geography Tools and Map Skills
Length: 4 minutes, 5 seconds
Use with Section 2
Introduces geography as a profession with a focus on maps.

Technology Resources

Go Online PHSchool.com

Students use embedded Web codes to access Internet activities, chapter self-tests, and additional map practice. They may also access Dorling Kindersley's Online Desk Reference to learn more about each country they study.

Interactive Textbook

Use the Interactive Textbook to make content and concepts come alive through animations, videos, and activities that accompany the complete basal text—online and on CD-ROM.

PRENTICE HALL
TeacherEXPRESS
Plan · Teach · Assess

Use this complete suite of powerful teaching tools to make planning lessons and administering tests quicker and easier.

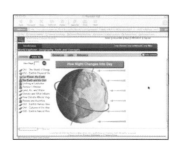

Reading and Assessment

Reading and Vocabulary Instruction

🎯 Model the Target Reading Skill

Clarifying Meaning Explain to students that they can use several strategies to clarify the meaning of unfamiliar words and concepts in the text. They can reread a difficult passage and try to make connections between familiar and unfamiliar words or ideas. They can read ahead to see if the author provides definitions or examples later in the passage. After reading, students can solidify their knowledge of a passage by paraphrasing, or putting what they have read into their own words.

Model clarifying meaning by thinking aloud as you read the paragraph below, from page 17, to the class.

A geographic information system, or GIS, is a computer-based system that links information to locations. Think aloud: What does *link information to locations* mean? I'll keep reading, maybe the author will give me a definition or example. *A GIS is useful not only to geographers but also to governments and businesses. A GIS connects information with places. For example, if a business needs to decide where to open an office, it can use a GIS to choose a location where it will reach the most customers.* Think aloud: This is an example of linking information (number of possible customers) to locations (possible site of new office). To paraphrase, a GIS is used by geographers, governments, and businesses to determine information about specific locations.

Use the following worksheets from All-in-One Foundations of Geography Teaching Resources (pp. 68–69) to support this chapter's Target Reading Skill.

Vocabulary Builder
High-Use Academic Words

Use these steps to teach this chapter's high-use words:

1. Have students rate how well they know each word on their Word Knowledge worksheets (All-in-One Foundations of Geography Teaching Resources, p. 70).

2. Pronounce each word and ask students to repeat it.

3. Provide a brief definition and sample sentence (provided on TE pp. 11 and 17).

4. Work with students as they fill in the "Definition or Example" column of their Word Knowledge worksheets.

Assessment

Formal Assessment

Test students' understanding of core knowledge and skills.

Chapter Tests A and B, All-in-One Foundations of Geography Teaching Resources, pp. 96–101

Customize the Chapter Tests to suit your needs.

ExamView® Test Bank CD-ROM

Skills Assessment

Assess geographic literacy.

MapMaster Skills, Student Edition, pp. 22, 24

Assess reading and comprehension.

Target Reading Skills, Student Edition, pp. 12, 17, and in Section Assessments

Chapter 1 Assessment, Reading and Vocabulary Study Guide, p. 12

Performance Assessment

Assess students' performance on this chapter's Writing Activities using the rubric from All-in-One Foundations of Geography Teaching Resources.

Rubric for Assessing a Writing Assignment, p. 95

Assess students' work through performance tasks.

Small Group Activity: Plotting a Route Around the World, All-in-One Foundations of Geography Teaching Resources pp. 73–76

Online Assessment

Have students check their own understanding.

Chapter Self-Test

Test Preparation

Assess students' skills and diagnose problems as students begin their study of this region.

Screening Tests and Diagnosing Readiness Tests, AYP Monitoring Assessments, pp. 1–11, 13–63

Section 1 The Five Themes of Geography

3.5 periods, 1.75 blocks (includes Skills for Life)

Social Studies Objectives
1. Learn about the study of Earth.
2. Discover five ways to look at Earth.

Reading/Language Arts Objective
Reread or read ahead to clarify the meaning of unfamiliar words and ideas.

Prepare to Read	Instructional Resources	Differentiated Instruction
Build Background Knowledge Show students a video, and then ask them to think about the five themes of geography. **Set a Purpose for Reading** Have students evaluate statements on the *Reading Readiness Guide*. **Preview Key Terms** Teach the section's Key Terms using a "See It—Remember It" chart. **Target Reading Skill** Introduce the section's Target Reading Skill of **rereading or reading ahead**.	**All in One Foundations of Geography Teaching Resources** L2 Reading Readiness Guide, p. 61 L2 Reread or Read Ahead, p. 68 **World Studies Video Program** L2 What is Geography?	**Spanish Reading and Vocabulary Study Guide** L1 Chapter 1, Section 1, pp. 5–6 ELL

Instruct	Instructional Resources	Differentiated Instruction
The Study of Earth **Five Ways to Look at Earth** Discuss the ways people study Earth and its people. **Target Reading Skill** Review **reading ahead**.	**All in One Foundations of Geography Teaching Resources** L2 Guided Reading and Review, p. 62 L2 Reading Readiness Guide, p. 61 **Foundations of Geography Transparencies** L2 Section Reading Support Transparency FG 43	**All in One Foundations of Geography Teaching Resources** L2 Skills for Life, p. 72 AR, GT, LPR, SN **Spanish Support** L2 Guided Reading and Review (Spanish), p. 4 ELL

Assess and Reteach	Instructional Resources	Differentiated Instruction
Assess Progress Evaluate student comprehension with the section assessment and section quiz. **Reteach** Assign the Reading and Vocabulary Study Guide to help struggling students. **Extend** Extend the lesson by having students do a map activity.	**All in One Foundations of Geography Teaching Resources** L2 Section Quiz, p. 63 L3 Understanding Hemispheres, p. 79 L3 Understanding Grids, p. 80 L3 Using a Grid, p. 81 L3 Understanding Latitude and Longitude, p. 82 L3 Using Latitude and Longitude, p. 83 Rubric for Assessing a Writing Assignment, p. 95 **Reading and Vocabulary Study Guide** L1 Chapter 1, Section 1, pp. 6–8	**Spanish Support** L2 Section Quiz (Spanish), p. 5 ELL **Teacher's Edition** L1 For Less Proficient Readers, TE p. 15 L1 For Special Needs Students, TE p. 15 **Social Studies Skills Tutor CD-ROM** L1 Using Reliable Information ELL, LPR, SN

Key

L1 Basic to Average   L3 Average to Advanced   LPR Less Proficient Readers   GT Gifted and Talented

L2 For All Students   AR Advanced Readers   ELL English Language Learners

                                               SN Special Needs Students

Section 2 The Geographer's Tools

 4 periods, 2 blocks (includes Chapter Review and Assessment)

Social Studies Objectives
1. Find out how maps and globes show information about Earth's surface.
2. See how mapmakers show Earth's round surface on flat maps.
3. Learn how to read maps.

Reading/Language Arts Objective
Paraphrase to clarify the meaning of unfamiliar words and ideas.

Prepare to Read	**Instructional Resources**	**Differentiated Instruction**
Build Background Knowledge Ask students to preview the section and predict what they will learn about maps and globes. **Set a Purpose for Reading** Have students begin to fill out the *Reading Readiness Guide.* **Preview Key Terms** Teach the section's Key Terms. **Target Reading Skill** Introduce the section's Target Reading Skill of **paraphrasing**.	**All in One Foundations of Geography Teaching Resources** L2 Reading Readiness Guide, p. 65 L2 Paraphrase, p. 69	**Spanish Reading and Vocabulary Study Guide** L1 Chapter 1, Section 2, pp. 7–8 ELL

Instruct	**Instructional Resources**	**Differentiated Instruction**
Target Reading Skill Review **paraphrasing**. **Globes and Maps** Ask about the creation and uses of maps and globes. **Getting It All on the Map** Ask about the different kinds of map projections. **Reading Maps** Discuss the parts of a map.	**All in One Foundations of Geography Teaching Resources** L2 Guided Reading and Review, p. 66 L2 Reading Readiness Guide, p. 65 **Foundations of Geography Transparencies** L2 Section Reading Support Transparency FG 44 **World Studies Video Program** L2 Geography Tools and Map Skills	**All in One Foundations of Geography Teaching Resources** L3 Understanding Projection, Maps with Accurate Shapes, Maps with Accurate Areas, Maps with Accurate Directions, pp. 84–87 AR GT L3 Enrichment, p. 71 ELL, LPR, SN L1 Outline Map 1, p. 91 ELL, LPR, SN L3 Captain Scott's Letter to the British Public, pp. 92–93 AR, GT L2 Using the Map Key, Using the Compass Rose, Using the Map Scale, pp. 88–90 ELL L3 Small Group Activity, pp. 73–76 AR, GT **Teacher's Edition** L3 For Gifted and Talented, TE pp. 19, 21 L1 For Special Needs Students, TE p. 20 L3 For Advanced Readers, TE p. 20 L2 For English Language Learners, TE p. 21

Assess and Reteach	**Instructional Resources**	**Differentiated Instruction**
Assess Progress Evaluate student comprehension with the section assessment and section quiz. **Reteach** Assign the Reading and Vocabulary Study Guide to help struggling students. **Extend** Extend the lesson by having students create their own maps.	**All in One Foundations of Geography Teaching Resources** L2 Section Quiz, p. 67 Rubric for Assessing a Writing Assignment, p. 95 L2 Vocabulary Development, p. 94 L2 Word Knowledge, p. 70 L2 Chapter Tests A and B, pp. 96–101	**Spanish Support** L2 Section Quiz (Spanish), p. 7 ELL L2 Chapter Summary (Spanish), p. 8 ELL L2 Vocabulary Development (Spanish), p. 9 ELL **Reading and Vocabulary Study Guide** L1 Chapter 1, Section 2, pp. 9–11

Key

L1 Basic to Average   L3 Average to Advanced   LPR Less Proficient Readers   GT Gifted and Talented
L2 For All Students   AR Advanced Readers   ELL English Language Learners
SN Special Needs Students

Professional Development

Reading Background

Previewing and Prereading

Students who do a brief, preliminary reading of complex material are in a strategic position to take control of their learning and comprehension. Previewing also helps students identify the text structure and develop a mental framework for ideas to be encountered in the text. Follow the steps below to teach students how to preview and preread, using Section 1 of this chapter as an example:

1. Tell students that previewing will help them identify the text structure and develop a mental outline of ideas they will encounter in the text.

2. Skim the section, getting clues from such features as titles, bold-faced headings, captions, and discussion questions. Take notes as you go along. (*Notes could include: the study of Earth; five ways to look at Earth; location; latitude and longitude; regions; place; movement; human-environment interaction.*)

3. Use these notes to make predictions about what you will learn from the selection. (*Think aloud: "This section will probably be about how people study Earth. They use five different methods to study it. Some of these might include location, regions, place, movement, and human-environment interaction."*)

4. Reflect on what you've previewed. Write down any questions you may have. (*Questions may include: I am not sure what latitude and longitude are. What kind of movement are they referring to? How do humans interact with their environments and how does this relate to geography?*)

5. Return to the notes and questions after reading part of the selection. Revise your predictions as needed, and answer your questions.

Pre-Teaching Vocabulary

Research literature on academic vocabulary instruction indicates that effective strategies require students to go beyond simply looking up dictionary definitions or examining the context. Vocabulary learning must be based on the learner's dynamic engagement in constructing understanding.

If students are not retaining the meaning of the Key Terms or high-use words, use this extended vocabulary sequence to engage them in learning new words.

World Studies Background

The Longitude Problem

Due to the absence of landmarks at sea, sailors must determine their location by measuring latitude and longitude. In the late 1600s, sailors could measure latitude but had no tool for measuring longitude. After several disasters caused by navigation errors, the British government announced it would give an award to the person who could discover a way to measure longitude at sea.

British carpenter John Harrison solved the problem. He developed a timekeeper that looked like a large pocket watch. This watch kept the time of Greenwich, England. Everywhere the sailors went, they could find the local time by the position of the sun, and compare it to the time in Greenwich, determining longitude.

Fields of Geography

The study of geography is divided into the three professional subcategories of study: physical, human, and regional geography. Although distinct fields, they are interrelated in many ways. Physical geography is the study of the surface of Earth, including the examination of human impact on the environment. Human geography is the analysis of the attributes and populations of different societies. Regional geography is a narrower study of a particular region. It combines elements of physical and human geography because regional geographers look at the physical boundaries, climates, and cultural features of regions.

Infoplease® provides a wealth of useful information for the classroom. You can use this resource to strengthen your background on the subjects covered in this chapter. Have students visit this advertising-free site as a starting point for projects requiring research.

Use Web code **led-3100** for **Infoplease.**

1. Present the word in writing and point out the part of speech.
2. Pronounce the word and have students pronounce the word.
3. Provide a range of familiar synonyms (or "it's like" words) before offering definitions.
4. Provide an accessible definition and concrete examples, or "showing sentences."
5. Rephrase the simple definition or example sentence, asking students to complete the statement by substituting the word aloud.
6. Check for understanding by providing an application task/question requiring critical thinking.

Sample instructional sequence:

1. Our first word is *geography*. It is a noun, a word that names a person, place, or thing.
2. Say the word *geography* after me. (Students repeat.)
3. *Geography* is similar to *geology* because both involve studying something on Earth.
4. The word *geography* means *the study of Earth*. By taking *geography*, we learned a lot more about our world.
5. We learned more about our world by taking _____ . (Students substitute missing word.)
6. Would studying the stars in the sky be part of *geography*? Yes-No-Why? (Students answer the question.)

Scaffolding Tips

Scaffolding is a technique used to help students transition from seeing and hearing the teacher demonstrate and model a particular skill to performing the skill independently. A teacher may begin with a recall question about a topic and lead students toward forming their own interpretive question. Scaffolding is especially effective for less proficient readers, English language learners, and some special needs students. When the teacher uses scaffolding, students should eventually be able to perform the skill completely on their own. To test the effectiveness of scaffolding, ask yourself each time students do an activity how much you had to help them. The answer should decrease with every attempt.

The Trimetrogon Method

Before World War II, many countries lacked detailed maps of their national areas. In fact, by 1940 only about 10 percent of the world was mapped out in any detail. Because airplane pilots needed more comprehensive maps during the war, the United States Air Force developed the trimetrogon method of mapping to create the World Aeronautical Charts.

The trimetrogon mapping technique is a system in which land is photographed, and then plotted for data such as elevation. Remote areas of Earth are now charted in a large enough scale to be significant, using the trimetrogon method. Today, about 62 percent of the world is mapped adequately.

Maps of the Moon

The only celestial body that has been mapped in any detail besides Earth is the moon. Two German astronomers, Wilhelm Beer and Johann Heinrich von Mädler, published the first comprehensive map of the moon in 1836. The map included a detailed study of the moon's surface. A year later, the pair supplemented the map with a book that gave the measurements of 148 of the moon's craters and 830 of its mountains.

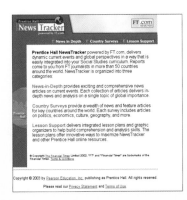

Get in-depth information on topics of global importance with **Prentice Hall Newstracker**, powered by FT.com

Use Web code **led-3101** for **Prentice Hall Newstracker**.

The World of Geography

Guiding Questions

Remind students about the Guiding Questions introduced at the beginning of the book.

Section 1 relates to **Guiding Question** ❶ **What are Earth's major physical features?** *(The five central themes of geography are location, regions, place, movement, and human-environment interaction.)*

Section 2 relates to **Guiding Question** ❶ **What are Earth's major physical features?** *(Tools such as globes and maps communicate important information about Earth's physical features.)*

➲ Target Reading Skill

In this chapter, students will learn and apply the reading skill of clarifying meaning. Use the following worksheets to help students practice this skill:

All in One Foundations of Geography Teaching Resources, *Reread or Read Ahead,* p. 68; *Paraphrase,* p. 69

Chapter Preview

This chapter will introduce you to the study of Earth, the planet where we live.

Section 1
The Five Themes of Geography

Section 2
The Geographer's Tools

⊙ Target Reading Skill

Clarifying Meaning In this chapter you will focus on clarifying meaning by learning how to read ahead and how to paraphrase.

▶ A satellite launched from the space shuttle *Discovery* orbits Earth.

8 Foundations of Geography

Bibliography

For the Teacher
Dorling Kindersley. *Geography of the World.* DK Publishing, 2003.
Rhatigan, Joe and Smith, Heather. *Geography Crafts for Kids: 50 Cool Projects and Activities for Exploring the World.* Lark Books, NC, 2002.
Five Themes of Geography. 100 Percent Education, 2002. Videocassette.

For the Student
L1 American Education. *The Complete Book of Maps & Geography.* American Education Publishing, 1998.
L1 Johnson, Sylvia. *Mapping the World.* Atheneum, 1999.
L2 National Geographic Society. *National Geographic Student Atlas of the World.* National Geographic Society, 2001.
L3 Young, Karen Romano. *Maps and Map Making.* Scholastic Paperbacks, 2002.

Reach Into Your Background Draw students' attention to the picture and caption on pages 8–9. Remind them that satellites travel hundreds of miles above Earth's surface.

Discuss the idea that mapmakers can use satellite pictures of Earth to make maps of our planet. There are even detailed satellite maps of cities. Have students discuss ways people might take pictures to make a map of their neighborhood. Have students share their ideas. *(Possible answer: take pictures from a helicopter or airplane)*

Chapter Resources

Teaching Resources
Letter Home, p. 59
L2 Vocabulary Development, p. 94
L2 Skills for Life, p. 72
L2 Chapter Tests A and B, pp. 96–101

Spanish Support
Spanish Letter Home, p. 3
Spanish Vocabulary Development, p. 9
Spanish Chapter Summary, p. 8

Media and Technology
L1 Student Edition on Audio CD
L1 Guided Reading Audiotapes, English and Spanish
L2 Social Studies Skills Tutor CD-ROM
ExamView® Test Bank CD-ROM

Discovery World Studies
CHANNEL Video Program
SCHOOL

interactive Textbook

PRENTICE HALL

Teacher**EXPRESS**
Plan · Teach · Assess

Section 1

Step-by-Step Instruction

Objectives

Social Studies

1. Learn about the study of Earth.
2. Discover five ways to look at Earth.

Reading/Language Arts

Reread or read ahead to clarify the meaning of unfamiliar words and ideas.

Prepare to Read

Build Background Knowledge [L2]

Tell students that they will begin their study of geography by learning five important ideas of geography. Show the video *What is Geography?*, then ask students to list the five themes of geography. Ask students what topics they think they will learn about within each theme, and have them use the Think-Write-Pair-Share strategy (TE, p. T36) to share their ideas.

📼 *What Is Geography?*, **World Studies Video Program**

Set a Purpose for Reading [L2]

■ Preview the Objectives.

■ Read each statement in the *Reading Readiness Guide* aloud. Ask students to mark the statements true or false.

All in One Foundations of Geography Teaching Resources, *Reading Readiness Guide*, p. 61

■ Have students discuss the statements in pairs or groups of four, then mark their worksheets again. Use the Numbered Heads participation strategy (TE, p. T36) to call on students to share their group's perspectives.

Vocabulary Builder

Preview Key Terms [L2]

Create a three column "See It—Remember It" chart of the Key Terms on the board. Write a term in the first column, a short definition in the second column, and a sketch in the third column. Guide students as they copy and complete the chart.

Answer

✓**Reading Check** Where are things located? Why are they there?

Prepare to Read

Objectives

In this section you will
1. Learn about the study of Earth.
2. Discover five ways to look at Earth.

Taking Notes

As you read the section, look for details about each of the five themes of geography. Copy the web diagram below and write down details related to each theme. Add ovals as needed for additional themes or details.

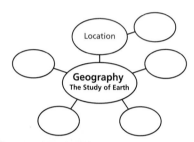

🎯 Target Reading Skill

Reread or Read Ahead If you do not understand a passage, reread it to look for connections among the words and sentences. Reading ahead can also help. Words and ideas may be clarified further on.

Key Terms

- **geography** (jee AHG ru fee) *n.* the study of Earth
- **cardinal directions** (KAHR duh nul duh REK shunz) *n.* the directions north, east, south, and west
- **latitude** (LAT uh tood) *n.* the distance north or south of Earth's Equator, in degrees
- **longitude** (LAHN juh tood) *n.* the distance east or west of the Prime Meridian, in degrees
- **hemisphere** (HEM ih sfeer) *n.* a half of Earth
- **parallel** (PA ruh lel) *n.* a line of latitude
- **meridian** (muh RID ee un) *n.* a line of longitude

Geographers use maps and other tools to understand Earth.

10 Foundations of Geography

The Study of Earth

Geography is the study of Earth, our home planet. Geographers try to answer two basic questions: Where are things located? and, Why are they there? To find answers to these questions, geographers consider Earth from many points of view.

✓**Reading Check** What questions do geographers try to answer?

Five Ways to Look at Earth

Five themes can help you organize information about Earth and its people. These themes are location, regions, place, movement, and human-environment interaction. They can help you understand where things are located, and why they are there.

🎯 Target Reading Skill [L2]

Reread or Read Ahead Point out the Target Reading Skill. Tell students that rereading a difficult passage or reading ahead in the text can help them clarify meaning.

Model rereading using the first paragraph on this page to find the meaning of the word *geographer*. By rereading, students will see that geographers are people who study Earth. Model reading ahead using this sentence from p. 11: "Longitude is the distance east or west of the Prime Meridian, measured in degrees." Students can read ahead to find an explanation of the Prime Meridian.

Give students *Reread or Read Ahead*. Have them complete the activity in groups.

All in One Foundations of Geography Teaching Resources, *Reread or Read Ahead*, p. 68

Location Geographers begin to study a place by finding where it is, or its location. Geographers use both cardinal and intermediate directions to describe location. The **cardinal directions** are north, east, south, and west. Intermediate directions lie between the cardinal directions. For example, northwest is halfway between north and west.

Geographers also use two special measurements of Earth to describe location. **Latitude** is the distance north or south of the Equator, measured in units called degrees. Degrees are units that measure angles. **Longitude** is the distance east or west of the Prime Meridian, measured in degrees.

Lines of latitude are east-west circles around the globe. All points on the circle have the same latitude. The line of latitude around the middle of the globe, at 0 degrees (0°) of latitude, is the Equator. Lines of longitude run north and south. The Prime Meridian is the line of longitude that marks 0° of longitude.

Learn more about the themes of geography.

The Hemispheres

The Equator and the Prime Meridian both divide Earth in two. Each half of Earth is called a **hemisphere.** The Equator divides Earth into Northern and Southern hemispheres. The Prime Meridian divides Earth into Eastern and Western hemispheres.

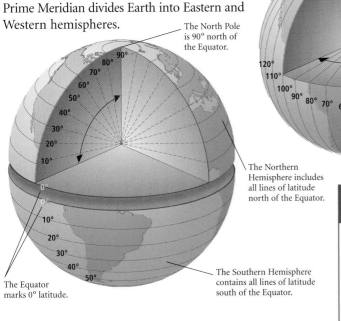

The Western Hemisphere includes the area from the Prime Meridian west to 180° of longitude.

The Eastern Hemisphere includes the area from the Prime Meridian east to 180° of longitude.

The North Pole is 90° north of the Equator.

The Northern Hemisphere includes all lines of latitude north of the Equator.

The Prime Meridian marks 0° longitude.

The Equator marks 0° latitude.

The Southern Hemisphere contains all lines of latitude south of the Equator.

GEOGRAPHY SKILLS PRACTICE

Location Geographers can pinpoint the location of any place on Earth using lines of latitude and longitude. **Use Latitude and Longitude** What place on Earth is located at 0° longitude and 90° north latitude?

Vocabulary Builder

Use the information below to teach students this section's high-use words.

High-Use Word	Definition and Sample Sentence
theme, p. 10	*n.* the main subject or idea of something The students identified the **theme** of the paragraph.
traditional, p. 13	*adj.* something handed down from generation to generation Her mother taught her to make a **traditional** Italian meal.

Show students *What is Geography?* Ask **Why is geography an important part of everyday life?** *(How people live is often determined by where they live.)*

Instruct

The Study of Earth [L2]

Five Ways to Look at Earth [L2]

Guided Instruction

- **Vocabulary Builder** Clarify the high-use words **theme** and **traditional** before reading.

- Read The Study of Earth and Five Ways to Look at Earth, using the Paragraph Shrinking strategy (TE, p. T34). Have students study the diagrams on this page and page 12.

- Have students name the five themes that geographers use to organize information about Earth and its people, then brainstorm examples of each. *(The five themes and an example of each are: location—the United States is in the Western Hemisphere; regions—a physical region of the United States is the Mojave Desert; place—the climate of the Mojave Desert is hot and dry; movement—radios have helped spread music from the United States to many parts of the world; human-environment interaction— people have cut trails into a mountainside. Other examples will vary, but should illustrate an understanding of each theme.)*

- Ask students **How are latitude and longitude similar? How are they different?** *(Similar: both are measurements of Earth to describe location; both are measured in degrees. Different: latitude is distance north or south of the Equator; longitude is distance east or west of the Prime Meridian.)*

Answer

Geography Skills Practice **Use Latitude and Longtitude** the North Pole

Guided Instruction (continued)

■ Ask students to link their area to the theme of regions. Have them name a region that their location could fall into. Next, ask them to think of an example of the themes of movement and human-environment interaction in their area. *(Responses will vary.)*

Independent Practice

Ask students to create the Taking Notes graphic organizer on a blank piece of paper. Then have them complete the organizer with the information they have just learned. Briefly model how to identify which details to record.

Monitor Progress

■ Show *Section Reading Support Transparency FG 43* and ask students to check their graphic organizers individually. Go over key concepts and clarify key vocabulary as needed.

📖 Foundations of Geography Transparencies, *Section Reading Support Transparency FG 43*

■ Tell students to fill in the last column of the *Reading Readiness Guide.* Probe for what they learned that confirms or invalidates each statement.

All in One Foundations of Geography Teaching Resources, *Reading Readiness Guide, p. 61*

🎯 Target Reading Skill   L2

Read Ahead As a follow up, ask students to answer the Target Reading Skill question in the Student Edition. *(Areas that share physical features, such as landforms or a particular climate, are often defined as regions, such as the Rocky Mountains or the Mojave Desert.)*

Answers

Geography Skills Practice **Compare and Contrast** the Equator; the Prime Meridian

12 *Foundations of Geography*

The Global Grid

Lines of longitude and latitude form a global grid. Geographers can identify the absolute location of any point on Earth by finding the latitude and longitude lines that intersect at that point. Lines of latitude are also called **parallels,** because they run east and west and are parallel to one another. This means that they never cross. Lines of longitude are also called **meridians.** Meridians run north and south, from the North Pole to the South Pole.

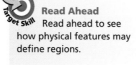

The North Pole has the greatest latitude north of the Equator.

The Equator, at 0° latitude, circles Earth midway between the North and South poles.

The Equator is the parallel around the middle of the globe.

A line of longitude

The Prime Meridian, at 0° longitude, runs through Greenwich, England.

The South Pole has the greatest latitude south of the Equator.

GEOGRAPHY SKILLS PRACTICE

Location Latitude and longitude are measured in degrees from imaginary lines on Earth's surface. **Compare and Contrast** From which line is latitude measured? Where do degrees of longitude start?

Read Ahead
Read ahead to see how physical features may define regions.

Lines of longitude and latitude form a global grid. This grid allows geographers to state the absolute location, or exact address, of any place on Earth. For example, Savannah, Georgia, is located at 32° north latitude and 81° west longitude.

Geographers also discuss relative location, or the location of a place relative to another place. A geographer might give the relative location of Tallahassee, Florida, by saying, "Tallahassee is about 400 miles northwest of Miami."

Regions Geographers use the theme of regions to group places that have something in common. A region has a unifying human or physical feature such as population, history, climate, or landforms. For example, a country is a region with a common national government, and a city is a region with a common local government. A school district is a region defined by a common school system. Land areas can also be divided into regions that share physical features, such as mountains or a dry climate. Physical regions of the western United States include the Rocky Mountains and the Mojave (mo HAH vee) Desert.

12 Foundations of Geography

🔴 Skills for Life **Skills Mini Lesson**

Drawing Inferences and Conclusions   L2

1. Explain that inferences are based on facts and that conclusions are based on inferences.

2. Students can practice the skill using the photograph on p. 10. Have them identify what the photograph shows *(Fact: The geographer is using a map.),* connect it to the themes of geography *(Inference: She is locating a place on the map.),* and then draw a conclusion about which theme the geographer is focusing on *(She is focusing on location.)*

3. Have students compare the photographs on pp. 10 and 13, to draw conclusions about where the weather is warmer. *(The farmers' weather is warmer.)*

Place Geographers also study place. Place includes the human and physical features at a specific location. To describe physical features, you might say the climate is hot or cold. Or you might say that the land is hilly. To discuss human features, you might talk about how many people live in a place and the kinds of work they do. You might also describe their religions or the languages they speak.

Movement The theme of movement helps explain how people, goods, and ideas get from one place to another. For example, when people from other countries came to the United States, they brought traditional foods that enriched the American way of life. The theme of movement helps you understand such cultural changes. Movement helps you understand many other facts about the world. For example, radios and computers have helped music from the United States to spread and become popular around the world.

Human-Environment Interaction This theme explores how people affect their environment, or their natural surroundings, and how their environment affects them. Perhaps they have cut trails into the mountainside. Or they may have learned how to survive with little water.

Farmers in India
These women are using the wind to separate grain for flour from chaff, or husks. Farming is an example of human-environment interaction. **Infer** *Do you think that these farmers use much modern machinery?*

✓ **Reading Check** What is the purpose of the five themes of geography?

Section 1 Assessment

Key Terms
Review the key terms at the beginning of this section. Use each term in a sentence that explains its meaning.

Target Reading Skill
What did you learn about physical features and regions by reading ahead?

Comprehension and Critical Thinking
1. (a) **Recall** What do geographers study?

(b) **Explain** What basic questions guide geographers?
2. (a) **Explain** How can the five themes help geographers?
(b) **Predict** How might a geographer use the theme of movement to describe the area where you live?
3. (a) **Define** What does the theme of location cover?
(b) **Contrast** How would a description of your home town as a place be different from a description of your home town's location?

Writing Activity
Read the passage above on human-environment interaction. Then write a paragraph describing ways that people in your area interact with their natural environment.

For: An activity on the five themes of geography
Visit: PHSchool.com
Web Code: led-3101

Chapter 1 Section 1 **13**

Writing Activity
Use the *Rubric for Assessing a Writing Assignment* to evaluate students' paragraphs.

All in One Foundations of Geography Teaching Resources, *Rubric for Assessing a Writing Assignment,* p. 95

Go Online PHSchool.com Typing in the Web code when prompted will bring students directly to detailed instructions for this activity.

Assess Progress   L2
Have students complete the Section Assessment. Administer the *Section Quiz.*

All in One Foundations of Geography Teaching Resources, *Section Quiz,* p. 63

Reteach   L1
If students need more instruction, have them read this section in the Reading and Vocabulary Study Guide.

📖 Chapter 1, Section 1, **Foundations of Geography Reading and Vocabulary Study Guide**, pp. 6–8

Extend   L3
Organize students into five groups. Ask each group to complete one of the worksheets listed below to help them fully understand latitude and longitude. Have each group give a brief presentation of its work.

All in One Foundations of Geography Teaching Resources, *Understanding Hemispheres, Understanding Grids, Using a Grid, Understanding Latitude and Longitude, Using Latitude and Longitude,* pp. 79–83

Answers

Infer Probably not, because they are separating grain from straw by hand.

✓ **Reading Check** They are ways to organize information about Earth and its people

Section 1 Assessment

Key Terms
Students' sentences should reflect knowledge of each Key Term.

Target Reading Skill
Physical features refer to climate and landforms, and can be used to form regions.

Comprehension and Critical Thinking
1. (a) Earth (b) Where are things located? Why are they there?

2. (a) They help geographers organize information about Earth and its people. (b) The geographer could explain how people, goods, and ideas came to the area.

3. (a) finding a particular place (b) For place, you might use human and physical features to describe the town; for location, you might use longitude and latitude to describe where the town is.

Objective

Learn to determine the reliability of information.

Prepare to Read

Build Background Knowledge   **L2**

Ask students to suppose that they are going to a movie. Have them list the information that they will need. *(start time, location of theater, cost of ticket)* Discuss possible sources of information *(newspaper, friend, Web site)* and what may happen if they use unreliable sources. *(may arrive late, may not be able to find the theater, may not have enough money to cover the cost of a ticket)*

Instruct

Using Reliable Information   **L2**

Guided Instruction

- Read the steps for judging the reliability of information as a class and write them on the board.

- Practice the skill by following the steps on p. 14 as a class. Model each step of the activity by selecting a topic, such as the location of the capital of a country or state, and researching it. Students should identify the source of the information they have found *(examples: an atlas, an encyclopedia, or other source)*, determine whether the information is current *(by checking the publication date)*, consult multiple sources to be sure that they agree *(by comparing information in two or more sources)*, and investigate the author to check for his or her qualifications and possible biases.

Independent Practice

Assign *Skills for Life* and have students complete it individually.

All in One **Foundations of Geography Teaching Resources**, *Skills for Life*, p. 72

Using Reliable Information

Would you seek medical advice from a plumber? Would you go to an encyclopedia to keep track of this season's basketball scores? Of course you wouldn't. Information is only as good as its source. To get reliable information, you have to go to an appropriate, trustworthy, and knowledgeable source.

Learn the Skill

Follow these steps to determine whether information is reliable.

1 **Find out the source of the information.** If it comes from a printed source, find out the name of the source, the author, and the date of publication. If it appeared on television, find out the name, date, and type of program (news, drama, or documentary). Do not accept information from Internet sites that do not give a date and an author.

2 **Find out if the information is recent enough for your purpose.** If you need current information, search for recent newspaper articles and up-to-date Web sites. Even if your topic is historic, researchers may have discovered new information about it. Seek the most current information.

3 **Find out if the information is accurate.** On certain topics, nearly all sources agree. For other topics, try to find information on which several respected sources agree. To be clear, you might say, "Several sources agree that" or "According to." If reliable sources disagree, you might note that disagreement in your writing.

4 **Look up the author's qualifications and methods.** When you check out an author's qualifications, always ask yourself whether he or she has a bias, or a one-sided view.

Is it Reliable?

To see if a source is reliable, ask
- What is the source?
- Is it recent enough?
- Is it accurate?
- Is the author qualified or biased?

Monitor Progress

Monitor students doing the *Skills for Life* worksheet, checking to make sure they understand the skill steps.

Practice the Skill

Now use steps 1–4 to answer some questions about reliable information.

1 Where might you go to find information on the location of the capital of Japan? On the population of North Carolina? On the major industries of Cuba? On presidential election results in Russia?

2 Would a 20-year-old encyclopedia be a reliable source of information on active volcanoes in Hawaii? On the type of money used in Europe? On the longest river in the world? Explain your answers.

3 If you heard in a television documentary that most of the world's diamonds are mined in southern Africa, how could you check the accuracy of that statement?

4 Suppose you do an Internet search for information on the amount of beef produced in the United States last year. The search leads you to articles by three authors. Who would be the best source of information: an economist for the U.S. Department of Agriculture, the largest cattle rancher in Texas, or a leading university expert on beef production? Explain your answer.

Apply the Skill

If you had to research a report on the health of children in India, what kinds of sources would you search for reliable information? Name at least two sources, and explain why they would be reliable.

These boys are playing ball in front of the famed Taj Mahal, in India.

Assess and Reteach

Assess Progress ▪️L2

Ask students to do the Apply the Skill activity.

Reteach ▪️L1

If students are having trouble applying the skill steps, have them review the skill using Level 1 of the interactive Social Studies Skills Tutor CD-ROM.

⊙ *Using Reliable Information,* **Social Studies Skills Tutor CD-ROM**

Extend ▪️L3

Have students create a bibliography for Chapter 1, Section 1 that contains at least three sources. Students should explain why they consider each source to be reliable.

Differentiated Instruction

For Less Proficient Readers ▪️L1

Partner these students with more proficient readers to do Level 1 of the *Using Reliable Information* lesson on the interactive Social Studies Skills Tutor CD-ROM. When they have successfully completed Level 1, they can move on to Level 2 alone.

⊙ *Using Reliable Information,* **Social Studies Skills Tutor CD-ROM**

For Special Needs Students ▪️L1

Have students make a two-column chart with the headings *10-Year-Old Encyclopedia* and *This Year's Almanac.* Students should list five questions in each column that could be answered reliably by each source. Then, have students write a sentence explaining how they determined the reliability of each source for their questions.

Answers
Apply the Skill

Possible answers: A Web site containing government data or a recent book by a well-regarded expert would be good sources because the information would be recent, and the authors would be reliable. Student answers will vary, but should reflect that students understand the skill steps for determining if a source is reliable.

Section 2
Step-by-Step Instruction

Objectives

Social Studies

1. Find out how maps and globes show information about Earth's surface.
2. See how mapmakers show Earth's round surface on flat maps.
3. Learn how to read maps.

Reading/Language Arts

Paraphrase to clarify the meaning of unfamiliar words and ideas.

Prepare to Read

Build Background Knowledge L2

Tell students that in this section they will learn about maps and globes. Have them glance through the section, paying attention to the visuals and headings. Then write the headings Maps and Globes on the board. Under each heading, make a list of what students already know and what they think they will learn. Use the Idea Wave participation strategy (TE, p. T35) to help generate a list of suggestions. Students can refer to these lists when they are filling in the first two columns of their *Reading Readiness Guides*.

Set a Purpose for Reading L2

- Preview the Objectives.

- Organize students into pairs or groups of four. Distribute the *Reading Readiness Guide*. Ask the students to fill in the first two columns of the chart. Use the Numbered Heads participation strategy (TE, p. T36) to call on students to share one piece of information they already know and one piece of information they want to know.

  All in One **Foundations of Geography Teaching Resources,** *Reading Readiness Guide,* p. 65

Vocabulary Builder
Preview Key Terms L2

Pronounce each Key Term, then ask students to say the word with you. Provide a simple explanation such as, "A compass rose is a diagram showing north, south, east, and west on a map."

Prepare to Read

Objectives

In this section you will

1. Find out how maps and globes show information about Earth's surface.
2. See how mapmakers show Earth's round surface on flat maps.
3. Learn how to read maps.

Taking Notes

As you read this section, look for details about each of the following map topics: comparing maps with globes, map projections, and parts of a map. Copy the outline below and write each detail under the correct topic.

> I. Maps and globes
>   A. Globes
>   B.
>   1.
>   2.
> II. Projections
>   A.

A map can help you find directions.

16 Foundations of Geography

Target Reading Skill

Paraphrase When you paraphrase, you restate what you have read in your own words. For example, you could paraphrase the first paragraph after the heading Globes and Their Weaknesses this way:

"Mapmakers found that globes are the best way to show the shapes of continents, but at a different size."

As you read this section, paraphrase or restate the information after each red or blue heading.

Key Terms

- **scale** (skayl) *n.* relative size
- **distortion** (dih STAWR shun) *n.* loss of accuracy
- **geographic information systems** (jee uh GRAF ik in fur MAY shun SIS tumz) *n.* computer-based systems that provide information about locations
- **projection** (proh JEK shun) *n.* a way to map Earth on a flat surface
- **compass rose** (KUM pus rohz) *n.* a diagram of a compass showing direction
- **key** (kee) *n.* the section of a map that explains the symbols and colors on the map

Globes and Maps

As people explored Earth, they collected information about the shapes and sizes of islands, continents, and bodies of water. Map makers wanted to present this information accurately.

Globes and Their Weaknesses The best way was to put the information on a globe, or a model with the same round shape as Earth itself. By using an accurate shape for Earth, mapmakers could show the continents and oceans of Earth much as they really are. The only difference would be the **scale,** or relative size.

But there is a problem with globes. Try making a globe large enough to show the streets in your town. The globe might have to be larger than your school building. Imagine putting a globe that big in your pocket every morning! A globe just cannot be complete enough to be useful for finding directions and at the same time small enough to be convenient for everyday use.

Target Reading Skill L2

Paraphrase Point out the Target Reading Skill. Tell students that saying or writing a difficult passage in their own words can help them clarify meaning.

Model paraphrasing using the paragraph under the heading Aerial Photographs and Satellite Images on p. 17. (*Aerial photographs and satellite images provide information about Earth's surface in great detail. However, they cannot show objects that are hidden from the air, and they show a distorted view of Earth's surface.*)

Give students *Paraphrase.* Have them complete the activity in their groups.

All in One **Foundations of Geography Teaching Resources,** *Paraphrase,* p. 69

Maps and Mapping People, therefore, use flat maps. Flat maps, however, present another problem. Earth is round. A map is flat. Can you flatten an orange peel without stretching or tearing it? There will be sections that are stretched or bent out of shape. The same thing happens when mapmakers create flat maps. It is impossible to show Earth on a flat surface without some **distortion,** or loss of accuracy. Something will look too large, too small, or out of place. Mapmakers have found ways to limit distortion of shape, size, distance, and direction.

Mapmakers rely on ground surveys, or measurements made on the ground, to make maps. They also use aerial photographs and satellite images.

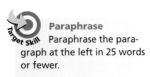

Paraphrase
Paraphrase the paragraph at the left in 25 words or fewer.

Aerial Photographs and Satellite Images
Aerial photographs are photographs of Earth's surface taken from the air. Satellite images are pictures of Earth's surface taken from a satellite in orbit. Both types of image are valuable sources of information for mapmakers because they provide current information about Earth's surface in great detail. But they are not useful for finding objects that are hidden, such as underground transit lines, or features such as streams that may be covered by vegetation. Also, like any map, flat aerial photographs and satellite images give a distorted view of Earth's surface.

Geographic Information Systems A geographic information system, or GIS, is a computer-based system that links information to locations. A GIS is useful not only to geographers but also to governments and businesses. A GIS connects information with places. For example, if a business needs to decide where to open an office, it can use a GIS to choose a location where it will reach the most customers. Military planners may use a GIS to improve their knowledge of the places where troops will operate. A GIS also may be used to produce maps.

✓ **Reading Check** What are the advantages and disadvantages of each way of showing Earth's surface?

Satellite Image of North and South America
This satellite view shows parts of North and South America. A storm system covers part of the southeastern United States. **Analyze Images** *How might this image pose problems as a source for making maps?*

Paraphrase As a follow up, ask students to complete the Target Reading Skill activity on this page of the Student Edition. *(Answers will vary, but should include an explanation of why flat maps have distortion.)*

Instruct

Globes and Maps 📖

Guided Instruction
■ **Vocabulary Builder** Clarify the high-use words **transit** and **vegetation** before reading.

■ Read Globes and Maps using the Oral Cloze reading strategy (TE, p. T33).

■ Have students discuss one use for a globe and one use for a map. *(globe: to see an accurate view of Earth; map: to show roads in your state or streets in your town)*

■ Ask students **How does technology help geographers understand Earth better?** *(Aerial photographs and satellite images provide current information about Earth's surface, while a GIS links geographical information to places.)*

Independent Practice
Ask students to create the Taking Notes graphic organizer on a blank piece of paper. Have them fill in details about maps and globes.

Monitor Progress
As students fill in the graphic organizer, circulate and make sure individuals are choosing the correct details.

Answers

✓**Reading Check** globes—show accurate shape, distance, and direction; not convenient for everyday use; maps—easy to use; some distortion of shape, distance, and/or direction; aerial photographs and satellite images—provide current information, but do not show features that are hidden; GIS—links information to location, but is probably not useful for navigating

Analyze Images Clouds and vegetation block the view of parts of Earth's surface.

⌐ **Vocabulary Builder** ──────

Use the information below to teach this section's high-use words.

High-Use Word	Definition and Sample Sentence
transit, p. 17	*adj.* movement from one place to another Many large cities have public **transit** systems.
vegetation, p. 17	*n.* plant life Rainforests have a wide variety of **vegetation**.
available, p. 19	*adj.* that can be gotten, used, or reached She sat in the last **available** seat on the crowded bus.
symbol, p. 21	*n.* a mark or sign that represents another object or an idea A key lists the **symbols** that a map uses.

Show students *Geography Tools and Map Skills*. Ask students to explain why maps are a geographer's most important tool. *(Since geographers study Earth from many points of view, the variety of maps, such as climate maps and relief maps, are essential to a geographer's work.)*

Getting It All on the Map

L2

Guided Instruction

- **Vocabulary Builder** Clarify the high-use word **available.**

- Read Getting It All on the Map with students. As students read, circulate and make sure individuals can answer the Reading Check question.

- Have students describe a Mercator projection. *(Mercator maps expand the area between the longitudes near the poles.)*

- Ask students who these maps were useful to, and why. *(to sailors, because they showed directions accurately)*

- Have students study Making a Mercator Map diagram and discuss the problem with Mercator projections. *(Distances and size become distorted the farther the area is from the Equator.)*

Getting It All on the Map

In 1569, a mapmaker named Gerardus Mercator (juh RAHR dus mur KAY tur) created a flat map to help sailors navigate, or plan journeys, around the globe. To make his map flat and to keep his grid rectangular, Mercator expanded the area between lines of longitude near the poles. Mercator's map was very useful to sailors because it showed directions accurately, even though sizes and distances were distorted. More than 400 years later, nearly all seagoing navigators still use the Mercator **projection,** or method of mapping Earth on a flat surface.

The Mercator Projection Mercator maps make areas near the poles look bigger than they are. This is because on a globe, the lines of longitude meet at the poles. To keep lines of longitude straight up and down, Mercator had to stretch the spaces between them north and south of the Equator. Land near the Equator was about the right size, but land areas near the poles became much larger. For example, on Mercator's map, Greenland looks bigger than South America. Greenland is actually only about one eighth as big as South America. Geographers call a Mercator projection a conformal map. It shows correct shapes but not true distances or sizes. What other areas, besides Greenland, do you think might look larger than they should?

Making a Mercator Map

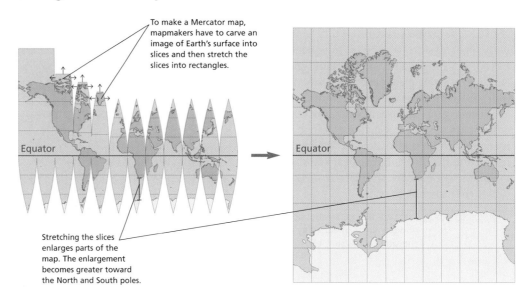

To make a Mercator map, mapmakers have to carve an image of Earth's surface into slices and then stretch the slices into rectangles.

Equator

Stretching the slices enlarges parts of the map. The enlargement becomes greater toward the North and South poles.

Equator

Skills Mini Lesson

Sequencing   L2

1. Teach the skill by explaining that sequencing means putting pieces of information in a logical order, using a diagram if necessary.

2. Help students practice the skill by looking at the visuals on p. 18. As a class, first identify the topic, then the steps in the process, and then the order. Then draw a flowchart of the process on the board. *(flowchart will have three boxes: get image of Earth's surface, cut image into gores, stretch gores to form rectangle)*

3. Have students apply the skill by creating a similar flowchart about equal-area maps. *(flowchart will have three boxes : get image of Earth's surface, cut image into gores, squeeze gores into oval)*

Equal-Area Projections An equal-area map shows the correct size of landmasses, but their shapes are altered. Lines that would be straight on Earth may be forced into curves to fit on the map's flat surface.

The Robinson Projection This projection is named for its designer, Arthur Robinson. Today, many geographers believe that the Robinson projection is the best world map available. It is used for most of the world maps in this book. This projection shows most distances, sizes, and shapes quite accurately. However, even a Robinson projection has distortions, especially in areas around the edges of the map.

Other Projections There are many other types of projections besides the ones shown here. Some are useful for showing small areas but not for showing the whole world. Others are good for specific purposes, such as planning a plane's flight route.

✓ **Reading Check** What are the strengths and weaknesses of the Mercator, equal-area, and Robinson projections?

Making an Equal-Area Map

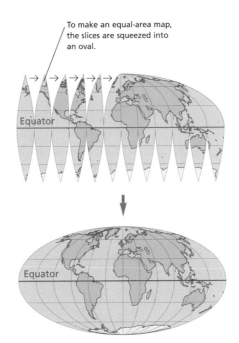

To make an equal-area map, the slices are squeezed into an oval.

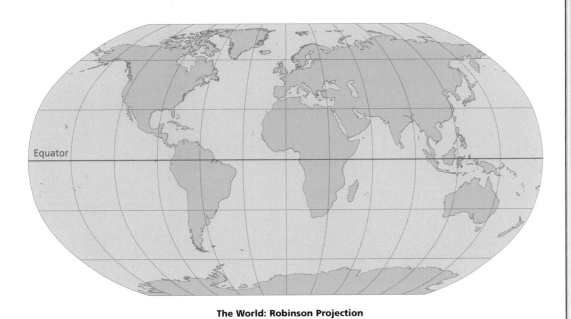

The World: Robinson Projection

- Have students describe an equal-area projection. *(shows the correct size of landmasses, but alters their shapes)*

- Ask students **Why do geographers believe that the Robinson projection is the best world map available?** *(It shows most distances, sizes, and shapes accurately.)*

- Ask students **If you were planning to travel by ship from Los Angeles to Hong Kong, which map projection would you use? Why?** *(Mercator—its accurate directions are useful for navigation at sea.)*

Independent Practice

Have students continue filling in the graphic organizer with details from the information they have just learned.

Monitor Progress

As students fill in the graphic organizer, circulate and make sure individuals are choosing appropriate details. Provide assistance as needed.

Differentiated Instruction

For Gifted and Talented [L3]

Challenge students to learn more about map projections. Assign *Understanding Projection, Maps with Accurate Shapes: Conformal Maps, Maps with Accurate Areas: Equal-Area Maps,* and *Maps with Accurate Directions: Azimuthal Maps.*

Then, have students identify one instance in which each type of map would be used.

All in One Foundations of Geography Teaching Resources, *Understanding Projection, Maps with Accurate Shapes: Conformal Maps, Maps with Accurate Areas: Equal-Area Maps,* and *Maps with Accurate Directions: Azimuthal Maps,* pp. 84–87

Answer

✓ **Reading Check** Mercator—shows shapes and directions accurately, but distances and sizes are distorted; equal-area—shows correct size of landmasses, but shapes are distorted; Robinson—most distances, sizes, and shapes are accurate, but some distortions around edges of map

Reading Maps

Guided Instruction

- **Vocabulary Builder** Clarify the high-use word **symbol** before reading.

- Ask students to read Reading Maps and to review the maps on pp. 20–22.

- Have students list the parts of the map shown on the China: Physical and Georgia Highways maps. Then ask students **How does each part help you read a map?** *(title tells you what type of information the map contains and what area it is focusing on; locator globe shows the area's location on a globe; compass rose shows direction; scale bar shows how distances on the map compare to distances on land; a key identifies symbols and coloring)*

- Have students discuss what the colors show on the physical map of China. *(The colors show ranges of elevation.)*

- Ask students **What is the distance between Atlanta and Augusta? Which highway connects the two cities?** *(about 130 miles or 200 kilometers; Interstate 20)*

Reading Maps

Look at the maps shown on these two pages. One is a physical map of the country of China. The other is a highway map of the state of Georgia. These maps cover completely different areas and show different kinds of information. Despite their differences, both maps have all of the basic parts that you will find on most maps. Knowing how to use these parts will help you to read and understand any kind of map.

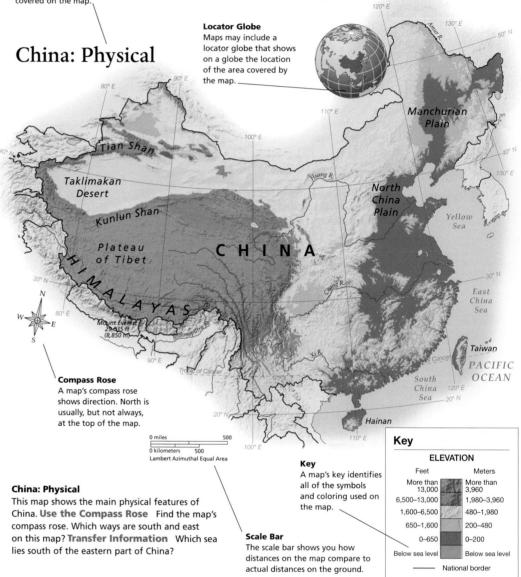

Title
Most maps have a title near the top of the map. The title generally tells you the type of information and the area covered on the map.

Locator Globe
Maps may include a locator globe that shows on a globe the location of the area covered by the map.

Compass Rose
A map's compass rose shows direction. North is usually, but not always, at the top of the map.

China: Physical
This map shows the main physical features of China. **Use the Compass Rose** Find the map's compass rose. Which ways are south and east on this map? **Transfer Information** Which sea lies south of the eastern part of China?

Scale Bar
The scale bar shows you how distances on the map compare to actual distances on the ground.

Key
A map's key identifies all of the symbols and coloring used on the map.

Key

ELEVATION

Feet	Meters
More than 13,000	More than 3,960
6,500–13,000	1,980–3,960
1,600–6,500	480–1,980
650–1,600	200–480
0–650	0–200
Below sea level	Below sea level
—— National border	

20 Foundations of Geography

Differentiated Instruction

For Special Needs Students   L1
Have students work with more advanced students to complete *Enrichment*. Then hand out *Outline Map 1* and have them color and label the continents and oceans.

All in One Foundations of Geography Teaching Resources, *Enrichment,* p. 71; *Outline Map 1: The World: Physical,* p. 91

For Advanced Readers   L3
Have students read *Captain Scott's Letter to the British Public* to learn about his expedition to the South Pole. Have students research and chart the journey on a map.

All in One Foundations of Geography Teaching Resources, *Captain Scott's Letter to the British Public,* pp. 92–93

Answers

Use the Compass Rose south is down and east is to the right **Transfer Information** South China Sea

Georgia Highways

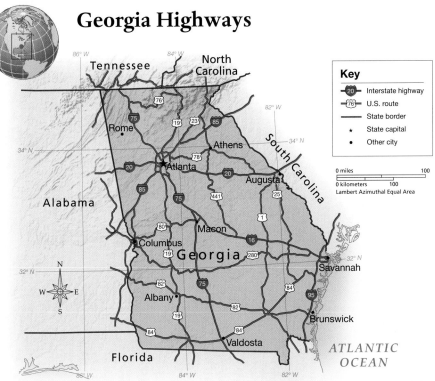

Key
- 20   Interstate highway
- 76   U.S. route
- ———   State border
- ★   State capital
- •   Other city

0 miles   100
0 kilometers   100
Lambert Azimuthal Equal Area

The Parts of a Map Both maps on these pages have what geographers call a **compass rose,** a diagram of a compass showing direction. If you want to find directions such as north, south, east, or west, just look for the map's compass rose.

Both maps also have a scale bar. The scale bar shows how distances on the map compare to actual distances on the land. Scales vary, depending on the map. If you compare the scale bar on the map of China to the bar on the map of Georgia, you will see that the map of China covers much greater distances on the ground even though the map is not much bigger.

On any map, the **key,** or legend, is the part of the map that explains the symbols and shading on the map. For example, the key on the highway map of Georgia shows the colored lines that stand for different kinds of highways. While some maps use symbols, other maps, like the physical map of China, use coloring to present information. The key shows which colors stand for which elevations.

✓ **Reading Check** How do the different parts of a map help you to find information?

Georgia Highways
Notice that this map of Georgia has the same basic parts as the physical map of China: a title, a key, a locator globe, a compass rose, and a scale bar.
Use Scale *Using a ruler, measure the distance on the map between Atlanta and Macon. Then hold the ruler against the scale bar. How many miles is Atlanta from Macon?*

- Ask students **What are the scales used in the two maps of London on page 22?** (*Greater London: 0 to 10 miles or 0 to 15 km; Central London: 0 to 1 mile or 0 to 1 km*) **Which map provides the most detail?** (*Central London*) **Why would the smaller scale not be used for the map of Greater London?** (*If the map of Greater London showed the same area using a smaller scale, it would make the map quite large and too detailed for its use.*)

Independent Practice
Have students complete their graphic organizers by adding a head labeled "Parts of a Map" and filling in the details they have just learned.

Monitor Progress
- Show *Section Reading Support Transparency FG 44* and ask students to check their graphic organizers individually. Go over key concepts and clarify key vocabulary as needed.

  📖 **Foundations of Geography Transparencies,** *Section Reading Support Transparency FG 44*

- Tell students to fill in the last column of the *Reading Readiness Guide.* Ask them to evaluate if what they learned was what they had expected to learn.

  All in One **Foundations of Geography Teaching Resources,** *Reading Readiness Guide,* p. 65

Differentiated Instruction

For English Language Learners   L2
To sharpen students' map skills, have them complete *Using the Map Key, Using the Compass Rose,* and *Comparing Maps of Different Scale.*

All in One **Foundations of Geography Teaching Resources,** *Using the Map Key, Using the Compass Rose, Using the Map Scale,* pp. 88–90

For Gifted and Talented   L3
Form students into groups. Have each group plot a trip around the world by completing *Small Group Activity: Plotting a Route Around the World.*

All in One **Foundations of Geography Teaching Resources,** *Small Group Activity: Plotting a Route Around the World,* pp. 73–76

Answers
Use Scale about 80 miles

✓ **Reading Check** compass rose—shows directions; scale bar—shows how map distances compare to actual distances; key—explains map's symbols and shading; title—tells subject of map; grid—helps find locations

Assess and Reteach

Assess Progress L2

Have students complete the Section Assessment. Administer the *Section Quiz*.

All in One **Foundations of Geography Teaching Resources,** *Section Quiz*, p. 67

Reteach L1

If students need more instruction, have them read this section in the Reading and Vocabulary Study Guide.

📖 Chapter 1, Section 2, **Foundations of Geography Reading and Vocabulary Study Guide,** pp. 9–11

Extend L3

Have students invent their own country and create a map including a title, a key, a scale bar, a grid, and a compass rose. Students should include their country's major cities, physical features, and major sites such as airports or tourist attractions.

Answers

MAP MASTER Skills Activity **Analyze** the map titled Greater London; the map titled Central London

Go Online PHSchool.com Students may practice their map skills using the interactive online version of this map.

Section 2 Assessment

Key Terms

Students' sentences should reflect knowledge of each Key Term.

Target Reading Skill

Answers will vary, but should include the strengths and weaknesses of the Mercator projection.

Comprehension and Critical Thinking

1. (a) ground surveys, aerial photographs, and satellite images **(b)** ground surveys—record details at ground level, but can be out of date; aerial photographs and satellite images—provide current, detailed information, but some features can be hidden from the air and flat photographs and images can distort Earth's curved surface **(c)** ground survey

2. (a) Mercator projection—shows directions and shapes accurately, but distances and sizes are distorted; equal-area projection—shows correct size of landmasses, but shapes are distorted **(b)** Mercator

22 *Foundations of Geography*

Maps of Different Scale

On the scale bar for the map of Greater London, a mile covers a small space. This map has a small scale. It gives a general picture of a large area. Maps with a larger scale, such as the map of Central London, show more detail and are useful for finding landmarks.

Greater London

Central London

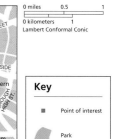

MAP MASTER Skills Activity

Two Maps of London
The map of Central London zooms in on the area inside the red box on the map of Greater London. **Analyze** Which map shows the city's size? Which shows tourist attractions?

Go Online PHSchool.com Use Web Code **lep-3112** for step-by-step **map skills practice.**

Section 2 Assessment

Key Terms
Review the key terms at the beginning of this section. Use each term in a sentence that explains its meaning.

Target Reading Skill
Go back and find the paragraph under the heading The Mercator Projection. Paraphrase this paragraph, or rewrite it in your own words.

Comprehension and Critical Thinking
1. (a) Identify What information sources do mapmakers use?
(b) Evaluate What are the advantages and disadvantages of each information source?

(c) Predict To make a map of small streams in an area of thick vegetation, what source would a mapmaker most likely use?
2. (a) Recall What are the advantages and disadvantages of a Mercator projection and of an equal-area projection?
(b) Apply Information Which projection would you use to plan a voyage by ship in a straight line across an ocean?
3. (a) Define On a map, what are the key, title, compass rose, and scale bar?
(b) Synthesize Information If you made a map of places to shop in your area, what might you put in the map's key?

Writing Activity
Look at the physical map of China. Plan a route for a trip from its east coast to its western border. Using information from the map, describe the landscape that you will see along the way.

Go Online PHSchool.com

For: An activity on maps
Visit: PHSchool.com
Web Code: led-3102

22 Foundations of Geography

---

3. (a) key—explains map's symbols and shading; title—tells subject of map; compass rose—shows directions; scale bar—shows how map distances compare to actual distances **(b)** Answers will vary, but should show an understanding of a key's purpose.

Writing Activity

Use the *Rubric for Assessing a Writing Assignment* to evaluate students' descriptions.

All in One **Foundations of Geography Teaching Resources,** *Rubric for Assessing a Writing Assignment*, p. 95

Go Online PHSchool.com Typing in the Web code when prompted will bring students directly to detailed instructions for this activity.

Review and Assessment

Review Chapter Content

- Tell students that each statement in the Chapter Summary is an answer to one of the chapter's Guiding Questions. Have students determine the number of the Guiding Question that relates to each statement and then pair students to discuss their classifications. Refer to p. 1 of the Student Edition for text of Guiding Questions.

- Assign *Vocabulary Development* for students to review Key Terms.

    All in One **Foundations of Geography Teaching Resources,** *Vocabulary Development,* p. 94

◆ Chapter Summary

Section 1: The Five Themes of Geography

- Geography is the study of Earth.
- Geographers can pinpoint any location on the surface of Earth using lines of latitude and longitude, which form an imaginary grid.
- There are five themes of geography—location, regions, place, movement, and human-environment interaction. They offer five ways to gather and understand information about places on Earth.

Section 2: The Geographer's Tools

- Maps can show more details of Earth's surface than globes, but showing Earth's round surface on flat maps causes distortion.
- Projections are different ways of showing Earth's round surface on a flat map.
- Parts of the map such as the key, compass rose, and scale bar can help you to find and understand information on any map.

Earth viewed from space

◆ Key Terms

Each of the statements below contains a key term from the chapter. If the statement is true, write *true*. If it is false, rewrite the statement to make it true.

1. The cardinal directions are north, east, south, and west.

2. Latitude is a measure of the distance north or south of Earth's Equator.

3. Longitude is a measure of the distance north or south of the Equator.

4. A hemisphere is a half of Earth.

5. A meridian is a line of latitude.

6. The scale is the part of the map that shows cardinal directions.

7. A projection is a way of mapping the flat surface of Earth onto a round globe.

8. The compass rose is the part of a map that shows symbols and their meanings.

9. The key is the part of the map that shows relative distances.

── Vocabulary Builder ──

Revisit this chapter's high-use academic words:

available	transit	vegetation
symbol	theme	traditional

Ask students to review the definitions they recorded on their *Word Knowledge* worksheets.

All in One **Foundations of Geography Teaching Resources,** *Word Knowledge,* p. 70

Consider allowing students to earn extra credit if they use the words in their answers to the questions in the Chapter Review and Assessment. The words must be used correctly and in a natural context to earn the extra points.

Answers

Key Terms

1. True

2. True

3. False. Longitude is a measure of the distance east or west of the Prime Meridian.

4. True

5. False. A meridian is a line of longitude.

6. False. The scale is the part of the map that shows how distances on the map compare to actual distances on the land.

7. False. A projection is a way of mapping the round surface of Earth onto a flat surface.

8. False. A compass rose shows direction on a map.

9. False. The key is the part of the map that explains the map's symbols and shading.

Review and Assessment

Comprehension and Critical Thinking

10. (a) location, regions, place, movement, human-environment interaction
(b) human-environment interaction

11. (a) by giving its longitude and latitude
(b) Knowing the exact location of a place could enable you to measure its distance from your current location, or find out how to travel there.

12. (a) human or physical features **(b)** Yes; a single place might fit into one political region, but another region based on the physical features of the area.

13. (a) A globe with enough detail for daily use would be enormous. Maps have some degree of distortion of size, distance, shape, and/or direction. **(b)** globe

14. (a) shows directions and shapes accurately, but distances and sizes are distorted **(b)** Navigators are most interested in plotting routes in the correct direction. **(c)** when you were most interested in accurate distances or sizes

15. (a) compass rose, scale bar, key, title, grid **(b)** compass rose—shows directions; scale bar—shows how distances on a map compare to actual distances; key—explains map's symbols and shading; title—tells subject of map; grid—helps find locations

Skills Practice

Students' answers will vary. Some may say that the first three sentences are reliable because the writer makes firsthand observations, while the last sentence is not reliable because the writer is making an assumption.

Writing Activity: Geography

Students' answers will vary, but should show an understanding of each of the five themes of geography.

Use *Rubric for Assessing a Writing Assignment* to evaluate students' descriptions.

All in One Foundations of Geography Teaching Resources, *Rubric for Assessing a Writing Assignment,* p. 95

Review and Assessment (continued)

◆ Comprehension and Critical Thinking

10. (a) List What five themes can help you organize infomation about Earth?
(b) Categorize Under which theme would you discuss building a dam on a river in a desert?

11. (a) Recall How do geographers pinpoint the exact location of any place on Earth?
(b) Infer Why might it be useful to know the exact location of a place?

12. (a) Identify What unifying characteristics might be used to describe a region?
(b) Draw Conclusions Might a single place be part of more than one region? Explain.

13. (a) Recall What are the disadvantages of globes? What are the disadvantages of maps?
(b) Apply Information Which would be more helpful for studying the exact shapes of continents, a globe or a map?

14. (a) Describe What are the main features of the Mercator projection?
(b) Infer Why is the Mercator projection still used by navigators today?
(c) Generalize When might you want to use a projection other than the Mercator projection?

15. (a) List What are the basic parts that most maps have?
(b) Synthesize Information How can you use the parts of a new map to understand it?

◆ Skills Practice

Using Reliable Information In the Skills for Life activity in this chapter, you learned how to use reliable information. Review the steps for this skill. Then apply them to the text below. Suppose you found this text in a teen magazine. Decide whether you think the information is reliable. Write a sentence that explains why or why not.

"Japan is a very clean country. I spent a whole week in Japan. The buses and trains were very clean. I didn't go inside a Japanese home, but I bet they are very clean, too."

◆ Writing Activity: Geography

Write down the name of the place where you live. Below that name, list the five themes of geography. Next to each theme, describe how it applies to your city, town, or state.

MAP MASTER™ Skills Activity

The Globe

Place Location For each place listed below, write the letter from the map that shows its location.
1. Prime Meridian
2. Equator
3. North Pole
4. South Pole
5. Europe
6. Africa
7. South America
8. North America

Go Online
PHSchool.com Use Web Code lep-3113 for an interactive map.

MAP MASTER™ Skills Activity

1. A	**2.** F
3. B	**4.** H
5. C	**6.** E
7. G	**8.** D

Go Online
PHSchool.com Students may practice their map skills using the interactive online version of this map.

Standardized Test Prep

Test-Taking Tips

Some questions on standardized tests ask you to make mental maps. Do the exercise in the box below. Then follow the tips to answer the sample question.

Draw a simple map of the world based on maps you have seen. Draw a rough shape for each landmass. Draw the Prime Meridian and the Equator across the map.

TIP Find the continents on your map. How is the world divided into hemispheres?

Pick the letter that best answers the question.

Which continent lies completely in both the Northern Hemisphere and the Western Hemisphere?

A Europe
B Greenland
C North America
D Australia

TIP Beware of careless errors. Read the question twice and think carefully about each answer choice.

Think It Through Australia is located completely in both the Southern Hemisphere and the Eastern Hemisphere. Europe is in the Northern Hemisphere but also mostly in the Eastern Hemisphere. Greenland is completely in both the Northern Hemisphere and the Western Hemisphere—as the question asks. But be careful! Greenland is not a continent. The answer is C.

Practice Questions

Use the tips above and other tips in this book to help you answer the following questions.

1. Which of the following is NOT a tool a geographer would use to study absolute location?
   A cardinal directions
   B climate
   C lines of latitude
   D degrees

2. What disadvantage do all flat maps share?
   A They have some sort of distortion.
   B They are hard to carry.
   C There are few sources to create them.
   D They can only show areas at a small scale.

3. A map with cities and colored lines marked with numbers is probably a type of
   A climate map.
   B road map.
   C physical map.
   D vegetation map.

Read the passage below and answer the question that follows.

This area is located in the United States, west of the Mississippi River. It is mainly hot and dry, with little rainfall, so people have built many dams there. Its landforms include rivers, canyons, and deserts.

4. Which of the five themes are used to describe this area?
   A location, movement, regions
   B movement, place, regions, human-environment interaction
   C regions, location, movement
   D location, place, human-environment interaction

Go Online
PHSchool.com

Use Web Code lea-3103
for a **Chapter 1 self-test.**

Earth's Physical Geography

Overview

Our Planet, Earth

Section 1

1. Learn about Earth's movement in relation to the sun.
2. Explore seasons and latitude.

Forces Shaping Earth

Section 2

1. Learn about the planet Earth.
2. Explore the forces inside Earth.
3. Explore the forces on Earth's surface.

Climate and Weather

Section 3

1. Learn about weather and climate.
2. Explore latitude, landforms, and precipitation.
3. Discover how oceans affect climate.

How Climate Affects Vegetation

Section 4

1. Investigate the relationship between climate and vegetation.
2. Explore Earth's vegetation regions.
3. Study vertical climate zones.

Video

The Ever-Changing Earth
Length: 3 minutes, 33 seconds
Use with Section 2

This segment explores how Earth may have looked over 200 million years ago, when all the continents formed a huge single landmass. The segment also examines the theory of plate tectonics. It explains how Earth's surface has changed. Students will learn about the consequences of tectonic plate movements, such as earthquakes and volcanoes.

Technology Resources

Go Online
PHSchool.com

Students use embedded Web codes to access Internet activities, chapter self-tests, and additional map practice. They may also access Dorling Kindersley's Online Desk Reference to learn more about each country they study.

Interactive Textbook

Use the Interactive Textbook to make content and concepts come alive through animations, videos, and activities that accompany the complete basal text—online and on CD-ROM.

PRENTICE HALL

TeacherEXPRESS™
Plan • Teach • Assess

Use this complete suite of powerful teaching tools to make planning lessons and administering tests quicker and easier.

Reading and Assessment

Reading and Vocabulary Instruction

🔄 Model the Target Reading Skill

Using Context Clues Using context clues involves reading the words and sentences that surround an unfamiliar word or idea to clarify its meaning. The context can describe, define, or restate the term, or provide a comparison that allows you to figure out the term's meaning. Model using context clues by writing the following sentences on the board:

1. An archipelago is a series of island chains.
2. A tsunami is like a wall of water 15 to 30 feet above the usual level of the sea.
3. The river carved out an enormous gorge, or deep, narrow valley with steep, rocky walls.

Ask students to circle the unfamiliar word in each sentence, and then underline the context clues that help to define it. Explain that in the first sentence, the context clue is a definition—*is a series of island chains* defines *archipelago*. In the second sentence, *like a wall of water 15 to 30 feet above the usual level of the sea* provides a comparison. In the third sentence, *or deep narrow valley with steep, rocky walls* restates the word *gorge*. Challenge students to find unfamiliar words in the chapter and write down how they used context clues to gain an understanding of these words.

Use the following worksheets from All-in-One Foundations of Geography Teaching Resources (pp. 121–124) to support this chapter's Target Reading Skill.

Vocabulary Builder
High-Use Academic Words

Use these steps to teach this chapter's high-use words:

1. Have students rate how well they know each word on their Word Knowledge worksheets (All-in-One Foundations of Geography Teaching Resources, p. 125).
2. Pronounce each word and ask students to repeat it.
3. Give students a brief definition and sample sentence (provided on TE pp. 29, 34, 41, and 51).
4. Work with students as they fill in the "Definition or Example" column of their Word Knowledge worksheets.

Assessment

Formal Assessment

Test students' understanding of core knowledge and skills.

Chapter Tests A and B, All-in-One Foundations of Geography Teaching Resources, pp. 151–156

Customize the Chapter Tests to suit your needs.
ExamView Test Bank CD-ROM

Skills Assessment

Assess geographic literacy.

MapMaster Skills, Student Edition, pp. 29, 43, 44, 45, 53, 56

Assess reading and comprehension.

Target Reading Skills, Student Edition, pp. 30, 35, 43, 52, and in Section Assessments

Chapter 2 Assessment, Foundations of Geography Reading and Vocabulary Study Guide, p. 25

Performance Assessment

Assess students' performance using the following rubrics from All-in-One Foundations of Geography Teaching Resources.

Rubric for Assessing a Student Poem, p. 146

Rubric for Assessing a Role-Playing Activity, p. 147

Rubric for Assessing a Bar Graph, p. 148

Rubric for Assessing a Line Graph, p. 149

Rubric for Assessing a Poster, p. 150

Assess students' work through performance tasks.

Small Group Activity, All-in-One Foundations of Geography Teaching Resources, pp. 128–131

Online Assessment

Have students check their own understanding.

Chapter Self-Test

Test Preparation

Foundations of Geography Benchmark Test 1, AYP Monitoring Assessments, pp. 81–84

Section 1 Our Planet, Earth

 *2 periods, 1 block*

Social Studies Objectives

1. Learn about Earth's movement in relation to the sun.
2. Explore seasons and latitude.

Reading/Language Arts Objective

Use context clues from surrounding phrases to determine the meaning of unfamiliar words.

Prepare to Read

Build Background Knowledge
Ask students to predict the effect of Earth's movements.

Set a Purpose for Reading
Have students begin to fill out the *Reading Readiness Guide*.

Preview Key Terms
Teach the section's Key Terms.

Target Reading Skill
Introduce the section's Target Reading Skill of **using context clues**.

Instructional Resources

All in One Foundations of Geography Teaching Resources
- L2 Reading Readiness Guide, p. 106
- L2 Use Context Clues: General Knowledge, p. 121

Differentiated Instruction

Spanish Reading and Vocabulary Study Guide
- L1 Chapter 2, Section 1, pp. 10–11 ELL

Instruct

Earth and the Sun
Discuss how the Earth's rotation affects the way we keep track of time.

Seasons and Latitude
Ask questions about the Earth's tilt and how it relates to the seasons.

Target Reading Skill
Review **using context clues**.

Instructional Resources

All in One Foundations of Geography Teaching Resources
- L2 Guided Reading and Review, p. 107
- L2 Reading Readiness Guide, p. 106

Foundations of Geography Transparencies
- L2 Section Reading Support Transparency FG 45

Differentiated Instruction

All in One Foundations of Geography Teaching Resources
- L3 Enrichment, p. 126 AR, GT
- L1 Understanding Movements of the Earth, p. 134 ELL, LPR, SN

Teacher's Edition
- L3 For Gifted and Talented, TE p. 31
- L1 For Less Proficient Readers, TE p. 31

Spanish Support
- L2 Guided Reading and Review (Spanish), p. 10 ELL

Assess and Reteach

Assess Progress
Evaluate student comprehension with the section assessment and section quiz.

Reteach
Assign the Reading and Vocabulary Study Guide to help struggling students.

Extend
Extend the lesson by assigning an Activity Shop Lab.

Instructional Resources

All in One Foundations of Geography Teaching Resources
- L2 Section Quiz, p. 108
- L3 Activity Shop Lab: The Earth's Seasons, pp. 132–133
  Rubric for Assessing a Writing Assignment, p. 145

Reading and Vocabulary Study Guide
- L1 Chapter 2, Section 1, pp. 13–15

Differentiated Instruction

Spanish Support
- L2 Section Quiz (Spanish), p. 11 ELL

Key

L1 Basic to Average   L3 Average to Advanced
L2 For All Students

LPR Less Proficient Readers
AR Advanced Readers
SN Special Needs Students

GT Gifted and Talented
ELL English Language Learners

Section 2 Forces Shaping Earth

 1.5 periods, .75 block

Social Studies Objectives

1. Learn about the planet Earth.
2. Explore the forces inside Earth.
3. Explore the forces on Earth's surface.

Reading/Language Arts Objective

Use context clues, such as restatement, to determine the meaning of an unfamiliar word or phrase.

Prepare to Read	Instructional Resources	Differentiated Instruction
Build Background Knowledge Show a video to start a discussion about how forces shape Earth. **Set a Purpose for Reading** Have students begin to fill out the *Reading Readiness Guide.* **Preview Key Terms** Teach the section's Key Terms. **Target Reading Skill** Introduce the section's Target Reading Skill of **using context clues.**	**All in One Foundations of Geography Teaching Resources** L2 Reading Readiness Guide, p. 110 L2 Use Context Clues: Definition/Description, p. 122 **World Studies Video Program** L2 The Ever-Changing Earth	**Spanish Reading and Vocabulary Study Guide** L1 Chapter 2, Section 2, pp. 12–13 ELL

Instruct	Instructional Resources	Differentiated Instruction
Understanding Earth Discuss the properties of Earth, from its core to its atmosphere. **Target Reading Skill** Review **using context clues.** **Forces Inside Earth** Discuss the different forces beneath Earth's surface. **Forces on Earth's Surface** Discuss how the surface of Earth is changing.	**All in One Foundations of Geography Teaching Resources** L2 Guided Reading and Review, p. 111 L2 Reading Readiness Guide, p. 110 **Foundations of Geography Transparencies** L2 Section Reading Support Transparency FG 46	**All in One Foundations of Geography Teaching Resources** L3 A Huge Black Umbrella, pp. 138–140 AR, GT **Teacher's Edition** L1 For English Language Learners, TE p. 36 L3 For Gifted and Talented, TE p. 36 **Spanish Support** L2 Guided Reading and Review (Spanish), p. 12 ELL

Assess and Reteach	Instructional Resources	Differentiated Instruction
Assess Progress Evaluate student comprehension with the section assessment and section quiz. **Reteach** Assign the Reading and Vocabulary Study Guide to help struggling students. **Extend** Extend the lesson by assigning a Small Group Activity.	**All in One Foundations of Geography Teaching Resources** L2 Section Quiz, p. 112 L3 Small Group Activity: Simulation: Making a Poster for the Whitney Classic, pp. 128–131 Rubric for Assessing a Writing Assignment, p. 145 **Reading and Vocabulary Study Guide** L1 Chapter 2, Section 2, pp. 16–18	**Spanish Support** L2 Section Quiz (Spanish), p. 13 ELL

Key

L1 Basic to Average   L3 Average to Advanced
L2 For All Students

LPR Less Proficient Readers
AR Advanced Readers
SN Special Needs Students

GT Gifted and Talented
ELL English Language Learners

Section 3 Climate and Weather

 3 periods, 1.5 blocks (includes Skills for Life)

Social Studies Objectives

1. Learn about weather and climate.
2. Explore latitude, landforms, and precipitation.
3. Discover how oceans affect climate.

Reading/Language Arts Objective

Use context clues that give a comparison to determine the meaning of a word or phrase.

Prepare to Read

Build Background Knowledge
Have students share ideas about weather and climate.

Set a Purpose for Reading
Have students begin to fill out the *Reading Readiness Guide.*

Preview Key Terms
Teach the section's Key Terms.

Target Reading Skill
Introduce the section's Target Reading Skill of **using context clues.**

Instructional Resources

All in One Foundations of Geography Teaching Resources
- **L2** Reading Readiness Guide, p. 114
- **L2** Use Context Clues: Compare and Contrast, p. 123

Differentiated Instruction

Spanish Reading and Vocabulary Study Guide
- **L1** Chapter 2, Section 3, pp. 14–15 ELL

Instruct

Weather or Climate?
Why Climates Vary
Discuss climate and weather.

Oceans and Climates
Discuss how the ocean affects climate.

Target Reading Skill
Review **using context clues.**

Eyewitness Technology
Have students read about weather forecasting, and then create an outline of the information they learned.

Raging Storms
Ask a question about the characteristics that different storms have in common.

Instructional Resources

All in One Foundations of Geography Teaching Resources
- **L2** Guided Reading and Review, p. 115
- **L2** Reading Readiness Guide, p. 114

Foundations of Geography Transparencies
- **L2** Section Reading Support Transparency FG 47
- **L3** Color Transparency FG 41: Climate Graphs

Differentiated Instruction

All in One Foundations of Geography Teaching Resources
- **L1** Reading a Climate Map, p. 135 ELL, LPR, SN
  Rubric for Assessing a Student Poem, p. 146 AR, GT
- **L3** Writing a Letter, p. 143 AR, GT
- **L2** Skills for Life, p. 127 AR, GT, LPR, SN
- **L1** Reading a Climate Graph, p. 136 ELL, LPR, SN

Teacher's Edition
- **L1** For Special Needs Students, TE p. 42
- **L1** For Less Proficient Readers, TE p. 45
- **L3** For Gifted and Talented, TE p. 45
- **L1** For English Language Learners, TE p. 46
- **L3** For Advanced Readers, TE p. 46

Student Edition on Audio CD
- **L1** Chapter 2, Section 3 ELL, LPR, SN

Assess and Reteach

Assess Progress
Evaluate student comprehension with the section assessment and section quiz.

Reteach
Assign the Reading and Vocabulary Study Guide to help struggling students.

Extend
Extend the lesson by assigning a role-playing activity.

Instructional Resources

All in One Foundations of Geography Teaching Resources
- **L2** Section Quiz, p. 116
  Rubric for Assessing a Role-Playing Activity, p. 147
  Rubric for Assessing a Writing Assignment, p. 145
  Rubric for Assessing a Bar Graph, p. 148
  Rubric for Assessing a Line Graph, p. 149

Reading and Vocabulary Study Guide
- **L1** Chapter 2, Section 3, pp. 19–21

Differentiated Instruction

Spanish Support
- **L2** Section Quiz (Spanish), p. 15 ELL

Teacher's Edition
- **L1** For Special Needs Students, TE p. 49

Social Studies Skills Tutor CD-ROM
- **L1** Analyzing Graphic Data ELL, LPR, SN

Key

- **L1** Basic to Average
- **L3** Average to Advanced
- **L2** For All Students

LPR Less Proficient Readers
AR Advanced Readers
SN Special Needs Students

GT Gifted and Talented
ELL English Language Learners

Section 4 How Climate Affects Vegetation

 3 periods, 1.5 blocks (includes Chapter Review and Assessment)

Social Studies Objectives
1. Investigate the relationship between climate and vegetation.
2. Explore Earth's vegetation regions.
3. Study vertical climate zones.

Reading/Language Arts Objective
Use context to determine the meaning of a word or phrase when examples are provided.

Prepare to Read

Build Background Knowledge
Have students brainstorm how climate zones affect daily life.

Set a Purpose for Reading
Have students evaluate statements on the *Reading Readiness Guide*.

Preview Key Terms
Teach the section's Key Terms.

Target Reading Skill
Introduce the section's Target Reading Skill of **using context clues**.

Instructional Resources

All in One Foundations of Geography Teaching Resources
- L2 Reading Readiness Guide, p. 118
- L2 Use Context Clues: Examples, p. 124

Differentiated Instruction

Spanish Reading and Vocabulary Study Guide
- L1 Chapter 2, Section 4, pp. 16–17 ELL

Instruct

Climate and Vegetation
Discuss the five broad types of climate.

Earth's Vegetation Regions
Ask a question about the locations of various vegetation regions.

Target Reading Skill
Review **using context clues**.

Vertical Climate Zones
Discuss climates in higher elevations.

Instructional Resources

All in One Foundations of Geography Teaching Resources
- L2 Guided Reading and Review, p. 119
- L2 Reading Readiness Guide, p. 118

Foundations of Geography Transparencies
- L2 Section Reading Support Transparency FG 48
- L2 Color Transparency FG 10: The World: Annual Precipitation (Base)
- L2 Color Transparency FG 12: The World: Desert and Desert Scrub Vegetation Regions (Overlay)

Differentiated Instruction

All in One Foundations of Geography Teaching Resources
- L3 The Endless Steppe, pp. 141–142 AR, GT
- L1 Reading a Natural Vegetation Map, p. 137 ELL, LPR, SN

Teacher's Edition
- L3 For Advanced Readers, TE p. 52
- L1 For Less Proficient Readers, TE p. 52

Spanish Support
- L2 Guided Reading and Review (Spanish), p. 16 ELL

Assess and Reteach

Assess Progress
Evaluate student comprehension with the section assessment and section quiz.

Reteach
Assign the Reading and Vocabulary Study Guide to help struggling students.

Extend
Extend the lesson by having students create posters.

Instructional Resources

All in One Foundations of Geography Teaching Resources
- L2 Section Quiz, p. 120
    Rubric for Assessing a Poster, p. 150
    Rubric for Assessing a Writing Assignment, p. 145
- L2 Vocabulary Development, p. 144
- L2 Word Knowledge, p. 125
- L2 Chapter Tests A and B, pp. 151–156

Reading and Vocabulary Study Guide
- L1 Chapter 2, Section 4, pp. 22–24

Differentiated Instruction

Spanish Support
- L2 Section Quiz (Spanish), p. 17 ELL
- L2 Chapter Summary (Spanish), p. 18 ELL
- L2 Vocabulary Development (Spanish), p. 19 ELL

Key
- L1 Basic to Average
- L3 Average to Advanced
- L2 For All Students
- LPR Less Proficient Readers
- AR Advanced Readers
- SN Special Needs Students
- GT Gifted and Talented
- ELL English Language Learners

Section Lesson Planner

Reading Background

Paragraph Puzzles

In this activity, students are asked to put a paragraph's sentences in the correct order. Explain to students that this activity will help them understand paragraph structure. The activity teaches students to distinguish a topic sentence that contains the main idea from the supporting details. Doing a paragraph puzzle activity also helps students practice sequencing steps and ideas.

Begin by writing a paragraph on a piece of paper with each sentence on its own line. Cut the sentences into narrow strips, and place the strips in an envelope. Divide students into pairs and distribute one envelope to each pair. Ask students to arrange the sentences into a logical paragraph.

Extend this strategy by challenging students to recall the plot of a short story, the sequence of events necessary to solve a math problem, or the steps involved in a scientific experiment. Ask students to write down the sentences, cut them into individual sentences, and place them in an envelope. Have students exchange envelopes with a partner and put the sentences in the correct order. Students should then explain their rationale.

Power Notes

This strategy can help students clarify the difference between main ideas and details. The Power Notes strategy is similar to creating an outline, but simpler because main ideas and details are assigned different numbers. Main ideas are power 1 ideas. Details are either power 2s or 3s. Students can use this technique to organize information for reading, writing, and studying.

Write the following on the board:

> **Power 1:** Main Idea
>> **Power 2:** Detail or support for power 1
>>> **Power 3:** Detail or support for power 2

Model this approach by using information from the chapter:

> **Power 1:** The effect of Earth's tilt on its axis
>> **Power 2:** Toward the sun creates Summer
>>> **Power 3:** Longer daylight and more direct sunlight
>> **Power 2:** Away from the sun creates Winter
>>> **Power 3:** Shorter daylight and sunlight is less direct

Another way to practice this skill is to write power 1s from the chapter on the board and have students take turns filling in the supporting details.

World Studies Background

Our Solar System

The nine planets of our solar system orbit around the sun in a counterclockwise direction. The innermost planets—Mercury, Venus, Earth, and Mars—are relatively small and have solid surfaces. They have few or no moons and no ring systems. The outermost planets—Jupiter, Saturn, Uranus, and Neptune—are larger and are made up of gases. They have many moons, ranging in number from eight for Neptune to at least 18 for Saturn. Each of the outer planets has a ring system. Pluto is in a category by itself because it resembles the icy moons of the outer planets. It has only one moon and does not have any rings.

Volcanoes

More than 80 percent of Earth's surface—above and below sea level—is of volcanic origin. Most volcanoes are located on the edges of continents, along island chains, or beneath the sea in long mountain ranges. About 500 volcanoes have erupted above sea level throughout history. More than half of them encircle the Pacific Ocean to form the Ring of Fire. After Indonesia and Japan, the United States has the highest number of historically active volcanoes.

Infoplease® provides a wealth of useful information for the classroom. You can use this resource to strengthen your background on the subjects covered in this chapter. Have students visit this advertising-free site as a starting point for projects requiring research.

Use Web code **led-3200** for **Infoplease.**

Using the Choral Reading Technique Effectively

The Choral Reading strategy encourages participation by all students because it provides a non-threatening reading environment. To maximize success with this strategy, choose shorter passages (fewer than 500 words) and encourage students to stay with your voice, so that everyone reads at the same rate. When students have finished reading in unison, allow time for students to reread the passage silently, focusing on new or unfamiliar words.

Read-Cover-Recite-Check

Read-Cover-Recite-Check is a useful strategy for helping students to retain the information they read. It can be especially effective when students are studying for a test. Model the steps for using Read-Cover-Recite-Check to read the first paragraph on page 28 of the Student Edition.

1. Read the paragraph quickly to grasp the main ideas. (*Think aloud about the main idea: this paragraph is about a galaxy.*)
2. Reread the paragraph, looking for details and key information. (*Think aloud, noting the details: the Milky Way is a galaxy. It is made up of Earth, the sun, other planets, and stars. Our sun is a star in the Milky Way.*)
3. Cover the paragraph with your hand or a piece of paper. Recall and repeat the information from the paragraph, including the topic and important details. (*Think aloud: repeat the main idea and details from steps 1 and 2, using different phrasing.*)
4. Rephrase the paragraph in your own words. (*The Milky Way is a galaxy that includes planets and stars. It looks like a white streak across the sky. The sun is not the center of the Milky Way, but it is the center of Earth's orbit.*)
5. Check to make sure you remembered correctly.

Weather Conditions

Weather takes place in the lowest region of the atmosphere known as the troposphere. Geographic features such as mountains and large bodies of water significantly impact the weather. The temperature of the ocean can be responsible for a drought in one area and heavy rains in another. Because weather has such a great effect on human settlement patterns, food production, and personal comfort, people are often reliant on forecasts. The National Meteorological Center (NMC) collects data from devices such as weather satellites, barometers, and radar. This information is used to create weather maps for geographic regions throughout the world.

The Amazon Rainforest

The Amazon Rainforest in northern South America exists because of the high rainfall, high humidity, and high temperatures of the region. About half of the Amazon's rainfall is evaporated moisture from the Atlantic. The rest is moisture evaporated from the rainforest itself. Blanketing an area of 2,300,000 square miles (6,000,000 sq km), this rainforest is the world's richest and most biologically diverse, with millions of species of animals and plants.

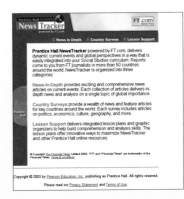

Get in-depth information on topics of global importance with **Prentice Hall Newstracker,** powered by FT.com.

Use Web code **led-3203** for **Prentice Hall Newstracker.**

Chapter 2

Guiding Questions

Remind students about the Guiding Questions introduced at the beginning of the book.

Section 1 relates to **Guiding Question** ❶
What are Earth's major physical features?
(Earth's movement in relation to the sun causes day and night. The tilt of Earth combined with Earth's rotation around the sun causes seasons.)

Section 2 relates to **Guiding Question** ❶
What are Earth's major physical features?
(More than 70 percent of Earth's surface is made up of water. Landforms such as mountains, plains, hills, volcanoes, and plateaus cover the other 30 percent of Earth's surface.)

Section 3 relates to **Guiding Question** ❶
What are Earth's major physical features?
(Earth's oceans and landforms can affect climates. Places located on coasts have more moderate temperatures due to the slow cooling and heating of the ocean. Mountains can also affect climates.)

Section 4 relates to **Guiding Question** ❶
What are Earth's major physical features?
(Vegetation varies widely across Earth according to climate and type of soil.)

⊙ Target Reading Skill

In this chapter, students will learn and apply the reading skill of using context clues. Use the following worksheets to help students practice this skill:

All in One Foundations of Geography Teaching Resources, *Use Context Clues: General Knowledge,* p. 121; *Use Context Clues: Definition/Description,* p. 122; *Use Context Clues: Compare and Contrast,* p. 123; *Use Context Clues: Examples,* p. 124

Differentiated Instruction

The following Teacher's Edition strategies are suitable for students of varying abilities.

Advanced Readers, pp. 46, 52
English Language Learners, pp. 36, 46
Gifted and Talented, pp. 31, 36, 45
Less Proficient Readers, pp. 31, 45, 52
Special Needs Students, pp. 42, 49

Chapter 2 — Earth's Physical Geography

Chapter Preview

This chapter will introduce you to the physical geography of Earth, including the planet's structure, climate, and vegetation.

Section 1
Our Planet, Earth

Section 2
Forces Shaping Earth

Section 3
Climate and Weather

Section 4
How Climate Affects Vegetation

 Target Reading Skill

Context In this chapter you will focus on using context to help you understand unfamiliar words. Context includes the words, phrases, and sentences surrounding a word.

▶ Delicate Arch in Arches National Park, Utah

Bibliography

For the Teacher
Erickson, Jon and Ernest H. Muller. *Plate Tectonics: Unraveling the Mysteries of the Earth.* Checkmark Books, 2001.
Zeilinga De Boer, Jelle and Donald Theodore Sanders. *Volcanoes in Human History: The Far-Reaching Effects of Major Eruptions.* Princeton University Press, 2001.

For the Student
L1 Arthus-Bertrand, Yann. *Earth from Above for Young Readers.* Abrams, 2002.
L2 Berger, Melvin. *Why Do Volcanoes Blow Their Tops?* Scholastic Reference, 2000.
L3 Oldershaw, Cally, *Atlas of Geology and Landforms.* Scholastic Library, 2001.

Chapter 2 **27**

Reach Into Your Background Draw students' attention to the caption accompanying the picture on page 26.

Discuss the visual with your students. What strikes them about the image in this photo? Encourage students to share their ideas about how these rock formations may have formed. Ask students to share any experiences they have had traveling to state and national parks to see unusual landforms.

Chapter Resources

Teaching Resources

[L2] Vocabulary Development, p. 144
[L2] Skills for Life, p. 127
[L2] Chapter Tests A and B, pp. 151–156

Spanish Support

[L2] Spanish Chapter Summary, p. 18
[L2] Spanish Vocabulary Development, p. 19

Media and Technology

[L1] Student Edition on Audio CD
[L1] Guided Reading Audiotapes, English and Spanish
[L2] Social Studies Skills Tutor CD-ROM
ExamView Test Bank CD-ROM

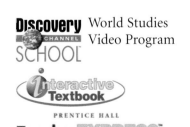

Discovery World Studies
CHANNEL Video Program
SCHOOL

interactive Textbook
PRENTICE HALL

TeacherEXPRESS™
Plan • Teach • Assess

Section 1
Step-by-Step Instruction

Objectives
Social Studies
1. Learn about Earth's movement in relation to the sun.
2. Explore seasons and latitude.

Reading/Language Arts
Use context clues from surrounding phrases to determine the meaning of unfamiliar words.

Prepare to Read

Build Background Knowledge `L2`
Tell students that they will learn about Earth's movements and how they affect the seasons and latitude in this section. Ask students to look through the section and predict the effects of Earth's movements. Provide a few simple examples to get students started. Conduct an Idea Wave (TE, p. T35) to generate a list.

Set a Purpose for Reading `L2`
- Preview the Objectives.
- Form students into pairs or groups of four. Distribute the *Reading Readiness Guide*. Ask students to fill in the first two columns of the chart. Use the Numbered Heads participation strategy (TE, p. T36) to call on students to share one piece of information they already know and one piece of information they want to know.

  All in One Foundations of Geography Teaching Resources, *Reading Readiness Guide*, p. 106

Vocabulary Builder
Preview Key Terms `L2`
Create a three-column "See It—Remember It" chart of the Key Terms on the board. Write a term in the first column, a short definition in the second column, and a sketch in the third column. Guide students as they copy and complete the chart.

Section 1
Our Planet, Earth

Prepare to Read

Objectives
In this section you will
1. Learn about Earth's movement in relation to the sun.
2. Explore seasons and latitude.

Taking Notes
Copy the table below. As you read this section, fill in the table with information about the movements of Earth relative to the sun, days and nights, seasons, and latitude. Add more lines as you need them.

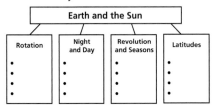

```
              Earth and the Sun
    ┌──────────┬──────────┬───────────┬──────────┐
  Rotation   Night      Revolution   Latitudes
             and Day     and Seasons
    •          •            •           •
    •          •            •           •
    •          •            •           •
```

🎯 Target Reading Skill
Use Context Clues You can sometimes find the meaning of a word by using context—the words and sentences around that word. In some cases the context will describe the word. In this example, the phrase in italics describes a planet:

> A planet is a *large object that circles a star.*

As you read, look at the context for the word *galaxy* in the paragraph below. What do you think *galaxy* means?

Key Terms
- **orbit** (AWR bit) *n.* the path one body makes as it circles around another
- **revolution** (rev uh LOO shun) *n.* circular motion
- **axis** (AK sis) *n.* an imaginary line through Earth between the North and South poles, around which Earth turns
- **rotation** (roh TAY shun) *n.* a complete turn

Earth and the Sun

Earth, the sun, the planets, and the stars in the sky are all part of a galaxy, or family of stars. Our galaxy is just one of the billions of galaxies in the universe. We call our galaxy the Milky Way because, in a dark night sky, away from city lights, its billions of stars look like a trail of spilled milk. Our sun is one of those stars. The sun is just a tiny speck compared to the rest of the Milky Way, but it is the center of everything for Earth and the other planets in the solar system. The solar system includes Earth, the other planets, and other objects that orbit the sun.

Even though the sun is about 93 million miles (150 million kilometers) away, it provides Earth with heat and light. Earth travels around the sun in a nearly circular **orbit,** which is the path one body makes as it circles around another. Earth takes $365\frac{1}{4}$ days, or one year, to complete one **revolution,** or circular motion, in its orbit around the sun.

The Milky Way Galaxy

🎯 Target Reading Skill `L2`

Use Context Clues Point out the Target Reading Skill. Tell students that information surrounding an unknown word can provide clues to the word's meaning.

Model context clues to find the meaning of *polar zones* in this sentence from page 32: "The areas above the Arctic Circle and below the Antarctic Circle are the high latitudes, or the polar zones." (*The* polar zones *are defined in context as the areas of high latitude above the Arctic Circle and below the Antarctic Circle.*)

Give students *Use Context Clues: General Knowledge.* Have them complete the activity in groups.

All in One Foundations of Geography Teaching Resources, *Use Context Clues: General Knowledge*, p. 121

Understanding Days and Nights   As Earth circles the sun, it also spins in space. Earth turns around its **axis**—an imaginary line running through Earth between the North and South poles. Each complete turn, or **rotation,** takes about 24 hours. As Earth rotates, it is night on the side away from the sun. As Earth turns toward the sun, the sun appears to rise. When a side of Earth faces the sun, it is daytime. Then, as that side of Earth turns away from the sun, the sun appears to set.

Time Zones   Earth rotates toward the east, so the day starts earlier in the east. The time difference is just a few seconds per mile. If every town had its own local time, it would be very confusing. So, governments have divided the world into standard time zones. Times in neighboring zones are one hour apart. There are also a few nonstandard time zones with times less than a full hour away from their neighbors.

✔ **Reading Check**   What is the connection between Earth's rotation and the change from day to night?

Links to
Math
Time Zones and Longitude
Earth's surface is divided into 360 degrees of longitude: 180 degrees east and west of the Prime Meridian. Since Earth rotates at a steady rate in about 24 hours, its 24 standard time zones are centered the same number of degrees of longitude apart. Can you find this number? (*Hint:* The number is 360° ÷ 24.)

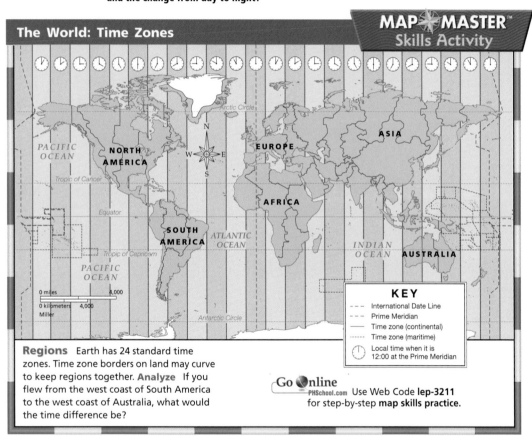

The World: Time Zones

MAP★MASTER™
Skills Activity

KEY
- - - International Date Line
- - - Prime Meridian
—— Time zone (continental)
······ Time zone (maritime)
🕐 Local time when it is 12:00 at the Prime Meridian

Regions Earth has 24 standard time zones. Time zone borders on land may curve to keep regions together. **Analyze** If you flew from the west coast of South America to the west coast of Australia, what would the time difference be?

Go Online PHSchool.com Use Web Code **lep-3211** for step-by-step **map skills practice.**

Chapter 2 Section 1 **29**

Vocabulary Builder

Use the information below to teach students this section's high-use words.

High-Use Word	Definition and Sample Sentence
standard, p. 29	*n.* something set up as a rule or model with which others are compared Juan's excellent presentation set the **standard** for the rest of the class.
relative, p. 30	*adj.* as compared with someone or something else My teacher is very short **relative** to the principal.

Instruct

Earth and the Sun   L2

Guided Instruction
- **Vocabulary Builder** Clarify the high-use word **standard** before reading.

- Read Earth and the Sun using the Paragraph Shrinking strategy (TE, p. T34). Ask students to study The World: Time Zones map and the caption on this page.

- Ask students **What is the relationship between Earth's rotation and time zones?** (*It takes 24 hours for Earth to rotate through each of its 24 time zones.*)

- Ask students to predict how the cycle of day and night would be affected if Earth's rotation were slower. (*If Earth's rotation were slower, the day would be longer than 24 hours.*)

- Tell students that every four years is a leap year of 366 days. Have them draw a conclusion as to why. (*If there are 365 1/4 days every year, then every four years there is one extra day, so leap year has 366 days.*)

Independent Practice
Ask students to create the Taking Notes graphic organizer on a blank piece of paper. Then have them fill in the "Rotation" and "Night and Day" boxes with information they have just learned. Briefly model how to identify which details to record.

Monitor Progress
As students fill in the graphic organizer, circulate and make sure individuals are selecting the correct details. Provide assistance as needed.

Links

Read the **Links to Math** box on this page with students. Guide them as they calculate that 360 divided by 24 is 15.

Answers

✔**Reading Check** As Earth rotates, it is night on the side facing away from the sun. When the side away from the sun faces the sun, it is daytime.

MAP★MASTER Skills Activity **Analyze** 11 hours

Seasons and Latitude L2

Guided Instruction

■ **Vocabulary Builder** Clarify the high-use word **relative** before reading.

■ Read how Earth's movement and latitude affect the seasons in Seasons and Latitude. Ask students to study the diagram titled The Revolution of Earth. As a class, answer the Geography Skills Practice question.

■ Ask students **What happens in the Northern Hemisphere during the summer solstice?** *(The Northern Hemisphere is tilted farthest toward the sun.)* **How does this tilt affect the region?** *(The days are longer and the temperature is higher.)*

■ Ask students **What is the season in Australia when it is winter in the United States?** *(summer)*

⊙ Target Reading Skill L2

Using Context Clues As a follow up, ask students to perform the Target Reading Skill activity in the Student Edition. Then ask **What words in the text describe the summer solstice?** *(the Northern Hemisphere is tilted farthest toward the sun)*

Use Context Clues If you do not know what the summer solstice is, look at the words that follow this term in the text. They describe the summer solstice.

Seasons and Latitude

The axis of Earth is tilted relative to its orbit. At different points in Earth's orbit, the Northern Hemisphere may tilt toward or away from the sun. At other points in the orbit, neither hemisphere tilts toward or away from the sun. The revolution of the tilted planet Earth causes seasons.

At the summer solstice, the Northern Hemisphere is tilted farthest toward the sun. Places in this hemisphere have longer daylight and more direct sunlight at the solstice than at other times of the year. This direct sunlight causes the heat of summer.

The Revolution of Earth

As Earth travels around the sun, the tilt of its axis causes our seasons. Each hemisphere shifts from the long days and direct sun of summer to the short days and indirect sun of winter, and then back again. This diagram shows seasons in the Northern Hemisphere.

Spring ▶
At the spring equinox, about March 21, days and nights are nearly equal in length. Earth's axis tilts "sideways." The sun is directly over the Equator.

Summer ▶
At the summer solstice, about June 21, the sun is directly over the Tropic of Cancer. North of the Arctic Circle, the sun never sets, and there is continuous daylight.

23.5°
Earth's axis tilts at a 23.5° angle from its orbit. This accounts for the seasons.

◀ **A Beach in Maine**
During the long, warm days of summer, green plants grow and people head for beaches.

The sun, at the center of Earth's orbit, gives our planet light and warmth.

Diagram not to scale

30 Foundations of Geography

✓ Skills Mini Lesson

Identifying Cause and Effect

1. Teach identifying cause and effect by pointing out that students can choose a specific event as a starting point and look at earlier events to determine possible causes. They can look at later events to help them identify effects.

2. Help students practice the skill by looking at the diagram on pp. 30–31. Have students determine an effect of Earth's movement.

3. Have students apply the skill by determining the effect of the following cause: the sun is directly over the Tropic of Cancer north of the Arctic Circle at summer solstice.

As Earth moves through its orbit, the Northern Hemisphere is tilted farther from the sun. Sunlight is less direct, and we have the chill of fall. When the Northern Hemisphere is tilted farthest from the sun at the winter solstice, days are short, the sun's rays reach us at a steep angle, and we have cold weather. Finally, Earth's revolution moves the Northern Hemisphere back toward the sun, and we have the warming trend of spring.

When the Northern Hemisphere is tilted toward the sun, the Southern Hemisphere is tilted away, and vice versa, so the seasons are reversed in the Southern Hemisphere.

▼ **Winter**
About December 21, at winter solstice, the sun is directly over the Tropic of Capricorn, and the area north of the Arctic Circle is in constant darkness.

▲ **Winter in the Arctic**
Iqaluit, Canada, is near the Arctic Circle. In winter, there is very little sun, and temperatures are bitterly cold.

◄ **Fall**
By about September 23, the sun is again directly over the Equator. Less direct sunlight in the Northern Hemisphere brings cooler temperatures.

GEOGRAPHY SKILLS PRACTICE

Regions Earth's tilt means that the seasons are different in the Northern and Southern hemispheres. **Compare and Contrast** When it is spring in the Northern Hemisphere, what is the season in the Southern Hemisphere?

Chapter 2 Section 1 **31**

Guided Instruction (continued)
■ Ask students **Where are the high latitudes located?** (*above the Arctic and below the Antarctic circles*) **If this area receives very long hours of sunlight, why do you think it is so cold?** (*The sun is not directly overhead and therefore doesn't cause the temperature to rise.*)

Independent Practice
Have students complete the graphic organizer by filling in the "Revolution and Seasons" and "Latitudes" boxes.

Monitor Progress
■ Show *Section Reading Support Transparency FG 45* and ask students to check their graphic organizers individually. Go over key concepts and clarify key vocabulary as needed.
📖 **Foundations of Geography Transparencies,** *Section Reading Support Transparency FG 45*

■ Tell students to fill in the last column of their *Reading Readiness Guides.* Ask them to evaluate if what they learned was what they had expected to learn.
All in One Foundations of Geography Teaching Resources, *Reading Readiness Guide,* p. 110

Answer
Geography Skills Practice Compare and Contrast Fall

Assess and Reteach

Assess Progress

Have students complete the Section Assessment. Administer the *Section Quiz.*

Reteach

If students need more instruction, have them read this section in the Reading and Vocabulary Study Guide.

 Chapter 2, Section 1, **Foundations of Geography Reading and Vocabulary Study Guide,** pp. 13–15

Extend

To extend the lesson, pair students and distribute the *Activity Shop Lab: The Earth's Seasons.* Have students make a model of Earth's path around the sun. Then, have them describe their observations as they follow the activity's steps as well as answer the questions provided.

Answer

✓ Reading Check The higher the latitude the longer the winter, and the lower the latitude the longer the summer. For the middle latitude, the four seasons are more distinct.

Section 1 Assessment

Key Terms
Students' sentences should reflect knowledge of each Key Term.

 Target Reading Skill
The winter solstice occurs when the Northern Hemisphere is tilted farthest from the sun. The clue is given in the phrase before the term in the sentence.

Comprehension and Critical Thinking
1. (a) A rotation is one complete turn of Earth around its axis, which takes 24 hours.
(b) As Earth rotates, it is night on the side facing away from the sun. As that side of Earth turns toward the sun, it becomes day.

2. (a) Answers will vary, but students should be able to identify the correct time zone.
(b) Answers will vary, but students should correctly calculate the time difference between the Prime Meridian and where they live.

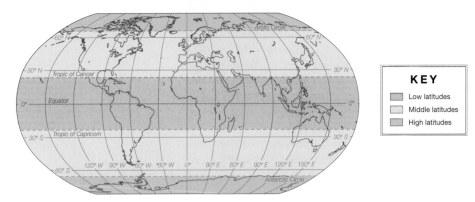

KEY

- Low latitudes
- Middle latitudes
- High latitudes

Zones of Latitude
The low latitudes, or tropics, are the single orange band around the Equator. The middle latitudes are the two yellow bands just to the north and south. The two green zones in the far north and south are the high latitudes, or polar zones.

Latitudes The areas between the Tropic of Cancer and the Tropic of Capricorn are called the low latitudes, or the tropics. The tropics have fairly direct sunlight and hot weather all year.

The areas above the Arctic Circle and below the Antarctic Circle are the high latitudes, or the polar zones. Though the polar zones may receive long hours of sunlight during the summer, the sun is never directly overhead. They are cool or very cold all year.

The areas between the high and low latitudes are the middle latitudes, or the temperate zones. In summer, these areas receive fairly direct sunlight. In winter, they get very indirect sunlight. So, the middle latitudes have marked seasons: a hot summer, a cold winter, and a moderate spring and fall.

✓ Reading Check What is the relation between seasons and latitude?

Section 1 Assessment

Key Terms
Review the key terms at the beginning of this section. Use each term in a sentence that explains its meaning.

Target Reading Skill
Find the phrase *winter solstice* on page 31. Use context to figure out its meaning. What do you think it means? What clues helped you find a meaning?

Comprehension and Critical Thinking
1. (a) Define What is the rotation of Earth?

(b) Synthesize Information How is Earth's rotation connected to the change from day to night?
2. (a) Identify On the time zone map on page 29, find the time zone where you live.
(b) Evaluate What is the time difference between your home and Greenwich, England?
(c) Analyze How is this time difference related to Earth's rotation?
3. (a) Recall What is Earth's tilt?
(b) Describe How does Earth's orbit affect its tilted hemispheres?

(c) Identify Cause and Effect How do Earth's tilt and orbit cause the seasons?

Writing Activity
Write a short passage for a younger child, explaining the movements of Earth.

For: An activity on our planet, Earth
Visit: PHSchool.com
Web Code: led-3201

(c) Earth is divided into 24 standard time zones because Earth takes about 24 hours to rotate. The time at a location differs depending on how far from the Prime Meridian its time zone is located.

3. (a) Earth's tilt is the degree to which Earth leans toward or away from the sun. **(b)** At different points in Earth's orbit, the hemispheres tilt at varying degrees toward or away from the sun. **(c)** The shift in Earth's tilt causes the seasons by changing the distance and angle of different parts of the Earth from the sun.

Writing Activity
Use the *Rubric for Assessing a Writing Assignment* to evaluate students' passages.

Go Online PHSchool.com Typing in the Web code when prompted will bring students directly to detailed instructions for this activity.

Forces Shaping Earth

Prepare to Read

Objectives
In this section you will
1. Learn about the planet Earth.
2. Explore the forces inside Earth.
3. Explore the forces on Earth's surface.

Taking Notes
As you read this section, look for details about Earth's structure, Earth's landforms, forces inside Earth, how continents move, and forces on Earth's surface. Copy the web diagram below, add more branches and ovals as needed, and write each detail in the correct oval.

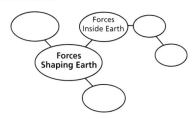

⊙ Target Reading Skill
Use Context Clues You can sometimes find the meaning of a word or phrase by using context. Sometimes the context will define or restate the word. In this example, the phrase in italics defines *continent*:

  A continent, or *one of Earth's large land areas* . . .

As you read, look at the context for the phrase *Ring of Fire* in the paragraph below. What do you think the phrase *Ring of Fire* means?

Key Terms
- **core** (kawr) *n.* the sphere of very hot metal at the center of Earth
- **mantle** (MAN tul) *n.* the thick layer around Earth's core
- **crust** (krust) *n.* the thin, rocky layer on Earth's surface
- **magma** (MAG muh) *n.* soft, nearly molten rock
- **plate** (playt) *n.* a huge block of Earth's crust
- **weathering** (WETH ur ing) *n.* a process that breaks rocks down into small pieces
- **erosion** (ee ROH zhun) *n.* the removal of small pieces of rock by water, ice, or wind

Understanding Earth

Around the rim of the Pacific Ocean is a string of volcanoes and earthquake belts called the "Ring of Fire." About 80 percent of the world's earthquakes and many of the world's active volcanoes occur in that ring. Earthquakes and volcanoes are two forces that shape and reshape Earth. They are one reason why Earth's surface constantly changes. They also provide clues about Earth's structure.

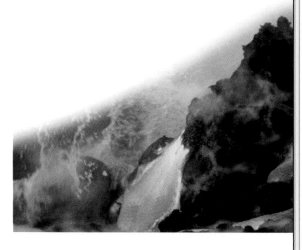

Hot rock from inside Earth flows into the Pacific Ocean to form new land in Hawaii.

Objectives

Social Studies
1. Learn about the planet Earth.
2. Explore the forces inside Earth.
3. Explore the forces on Earth's surface.

Reading/Language Arts
Use context clues, such as restatement, to determine the meaning of an unfamiliar word or phrase.

Prepare to Read

Build Background Knowledge L2
Tell students that in this section they will learn about the forces that shape Earth, both inside and out. Show students the *The Ever-Changing Earth*. Then ask students how moving plates cause volcanic eruptions. Use the Give One, Get One participation strategy (TE, p. T37) to generate answers.

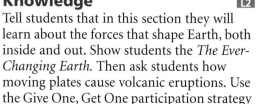
The Ever-Changing Earth, **World Studies Video Program**

Set a Purpose for Reading L2
- Preview the Objectives.
- Read each statement in the *Reading Readiness Guide* aloud. Ask students to mark the statements true or false.
- Have students discuss the statements in pairs or groups of four, then mark their worksheets again. Use the Numbered Heads participation strategy (TE, p. T36) to call on students to share their group's perspectives.

All in One Foundations of Geography Teaching Resources, *Reading Readiness Guide,* p. 110

Vocabulary Builder
Preview Key Terms
Pronounce each Key Term, then ask the students to say the word with you. Provide a simple explanation such as, "The shifting of Earth's plates can sometimes be felt as an earthquake."

⊙ Target Reading Skill L2
Use Context Clues Point out the Target Reading Skill. Tell students that using context clues, such as definition and restatement, is one way to find the meaning of an unfamiliar word or phrase.

Model using context clues to find the meaning of fresh water in this sentence from page 35: "Very little of Earth's water is fresh water, or water without salt." (*The phrase* fresh water *means* water without salt.)

Give students *Use Context Clues: Definition/Description.* Have them complete the activity in groups.

All in One Foundations of Geography Teaching Resources, *Use Context Clues: Definition/Description,* p. 122

Instruct

Understanding Earth L2

Guided Instruction

■ **Vocabulary Builder** Clarify the high-use word **force** before reading.

■ Read Understanding Earth using the Oral Cloze strategy (TE, p. T33). Ask students to review the diagram of Earth's Layers on this page. As a class, answer the Analyze Images question. Allow students to discuss their answers with a partner before sharing them with the class.

■ Ask students to name the sources of heat that help shape Earth's crust. *(the core: a ball of very hot metal at the center of the earth; the mantle: the hot, rocky layer around the core)*

What Is Earth Made Of? To understand the forces that shape Earth, you must study Earth's structure. A sphere of very hot metal at the center of Earth is called the **core**. The **mantle** is a thick, hot, rocky layer around the core. The thin layer of rocks and minerals that surrounds the mantle is called the **crust**. In effect, the crust floats on top of the mantle. The heat of the core and mantle helps shape Earth's crust. The surface of the crust includes Earth's land areas as well as the ocean floors.

Earth's Layers

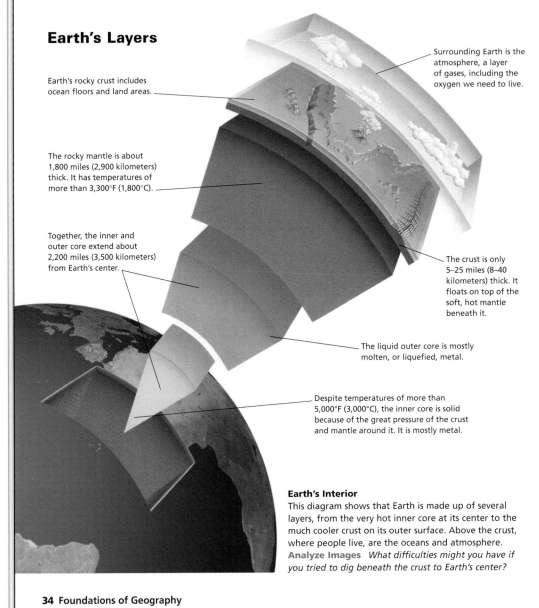

Surrounding Earth is the atmosphere, a layer of gases, including the oxygen we need to live.

Earth's rocky crust includes ocean floors and land areas.

The rocky mantle is about 1,800 miles (2,900 kilometers) thick. It has temperatures of more than 3,300°F (1,800°C).

Together, the inner and outer core extend about 2,200 miles (3,500 kilometers) from Earth's center.

The crust is only 5–25 miles (8–40 kilometers) thick. It floats on top of the soft, hot mantle beneath it.

The liquid outer core is mostly molten, or liquefied, metal.

Despite temperatures of more than 5,000°F (3,000°C), the inner core is solid because of the great pressure of the crust and mantle around it. It is mostly metal.

Earth's Interior
This diagram shows that Earth is made up of several layers, from the very hot inner core at its center to the much cooler crust on its outer surface. Above the crust, where people live, are the oceans and atmosphere.
Analyze Images *What difficulties might you have if you tried to dig beneath the crust to Earth's center?*

Answers

Analyze Images Possible answers: A person could not withstand the extremely high temperatures; the disturbance might cause a volcano to erupt or an earthquake; the escaping gases might affect the atmosphere that surrounds Earth.

Vocabulary Builder

Use the information below to teach students this section's high-use words.

High-Use Word	Definition and Sample Sentence
force, p. 33	*n.* strength, power, energy The pitcher threw the baseball with great **force**.
collide, p. 37	*v.* to crash against each other The icy road conditions caused the two cars to **collide**.
surge, p. 37	*v.* to swell and move with force She felt her energy **surge** after her third cup of coffee.
splinter, p. 37	*v.* to split into fragments or parts If the wind blows hard enough, the dead tree may **splinter** and fall.

Water and Air Less than 30 percent of Earth's surface is land. Water covers more than 70 percent of Earth's surface in lakes, rivers, seas, and oceans. The oceans hold about 97 percent of Earth's water. This water is salty. Very little of Earth's water is fresh water, or water without salt. Most fresh water is frozen in ice sheets near the North and South poles. People can use only a small part of Earth's fresh water. This fresh water comes from lakes, rivers, and ground water, which are fed by rain.

Above Earth's surface is the atmosphere, a layer of gases a few miles thick. It provides life-giving oxygen to people and animals, and carbon dioxide to plants.

Landforms Many different landforms, or shapes and types of land, cover Earth's land surfaces. Mountains are landforms that rise more than 2,000 feet (610 meters) above sea level or the surrounding flatlands. They are wide at the bottom and rise steeply to a narrow peak or ridge. A volcano is a kind of mountain. Hills are landforms with rounded tops, which rise above the surrounding land but are lower and less steep than mountains. A plateau is a large, mostly flat area that rises above the surrounding land. At least one side of a plateau has a steep slope. Plains are large areas of flat or gently rolling land.

✓ **Reading Check** Which layer of Earth contains all of its landforms?

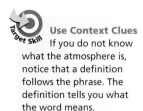

Use Context Clues If you do not know what the atmosphere is, notice that a definition follows the phrase. The definition tells you what the word means.

Land and Water
Ice floes float near Alexander Island, off the coast of Antarctica. Salt water covers most of Earth's surface. Most fresh water is ice, frozen in polar regions such as Antarctica. **Analyze Images** *What landforms can you see in this photograph?*

■ Ask students **What is the atmosphere and why is it important to our survival on Earth?** *(The atmosphere is a thick layer of gases, including the air we breathe.)*

■ Ask students to draw a conclusion about how much of the world's water is fresh water if 97 percent of the world's water is in oceans. *(about 3 percent)*

■ Ask students to name four types of land-forms that cover Earth's surface. *(mountains, hills, plateaus, and plains)* Then have students list landforms in your county or state that are one of these four types. *(Answers will vary, but should show an understanding of these landforms.)*

Independent Practice
Ask students to create the Taking Notes graphic organizer on a blank piece of paper. Then have them add more branches and circles in order to fill in the information about Earth's structure and landforms.

Monitor Progress
As students fill in the graphic organizer, circulate and make sure individuals are selecting the correct details. Provide assistance as needed.

Target Reading Skill   L2
Using Context Clues As a follow up, ask students to review the Target Reading Skill in the Student Edition. *(a thick layer of gases)*

Skills for Life Skills Mini Lesson

Analyzing Images

1. Teach the skill by pointing out to students that to analyze an image, they can ask these questions: Who or what is the image is showing? When or where does the scene take place? What general feeling do you get from the image? Who created the image and why?

2. Help students practice the skill by looking at the image of the volcano on page 37. Ask students What evidence besides the caption indicates that the molten rock is very hot? *(The color of the liquid pouring out from the top of the volcano shows it is hot.)*

3. Have students apply the skill by answering this question: What might have been the photographer's reason for taking the photo on page 37? *(to show how erupting volcanoes change the surface of Earth)*

Answers
✓ **Reading Check** Earth's crust
Analyze Images mountains

Forces Inside Earth L2

Guided Instruction

- **Vocabulary Builder** Clarify the high-use words **collide, surge,** and **splinter** before reading.

- Read how the movement underneath Earth's surface affects our planet in Forces Inside Earth. As a class, study the diagram and captions under How Continents Move and partner students to answer the Geography Skills Practice question on page 37.

- Ask students **What forces inside Earth cause mountains to form?** (*The pressure exerted where two plates push against each other causes Earth's crust to bend and buckle, forming mountains.*)

- Ask students **Which different forces inside Earth cause volcanoes in Hawaii and earthquakes in California?** (*Volcanoes form when ocean crust plunges beneath continental crust and streams of magma to rise to the surface. Earthquakes occur when blocks of crust rub against each other along faults, releasing huge amounts of energy.*)

Forces Inside Earth

Heat deep inside Earth is constantly reshaping the planet's surface. The intense heat causes rock to rise toward the surface. Where streams of this soft, nearly molten rock called **magma** reach Earth's crust, they push up the crust to form volcanoes. Volcanoes spew molten rock, or lava, from inside Earth. Streams of magma may also push the crust apart along seams. Huge blocks of Earth's crust called **plates** are separated by these seams. Plates may include continents or parts of continents. Each plate also includes part of the ocean floor. Along seams, mainly beneath oceans, streams of magma rise from inside Earth. As the magma cools, it forms new crust and pushes the old crust away from the seams.

How Continents Move

Rising magma forms new crust along seams between Earth's plates. Beneath the surface, some scientists believe, magma moves like a conveyor belt. The belt drags the growing plates and the continents that they carry.

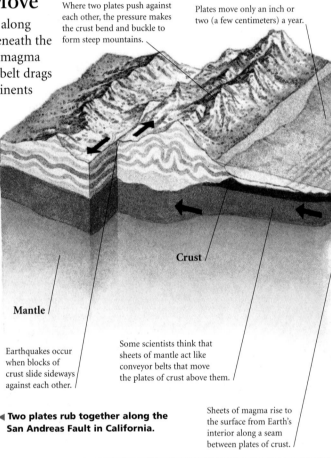

Where two plates push against each other, the pressure makes the crust bend and buckle to form steep mountains.

Plates move only an inch or two (a few centimeters) a year.

Crust

Mantle

Some scientists think that sheets of mantle act like conveyor belts that move the plates of crust above them.

Earthquakes occur when blocks of crust slide sideways against each other.

Sheets of magma rise to the surface from Earth's interior along a seam between plates of crust.

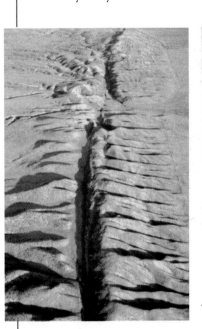

◀ **Two plates rub together along the San Andreas Fault in California.**

Differentiated Instruction

For English Language Learners L1
Students may have difficulty pronouncing some of the longer words in this section, such as *reshaping, continental, boundaries, earthquakes,* and *geographers.* Encourage students to break down these words into smaller parts to help them sound out the pronunciations.

For Gifted and Talented L3
The forces of nature can affect people both directly and indirectly. Ask students to read the selection *A Huge Black Umbrella* to experience how an event altered the lives of several individuals.

All in One Foundations of Geography Teaching Resources, *A Huge Black Umbrella,* pp. 138–140

Volcanoes and Earthquakes Where a plate of ocean crust collides with a plate of continental crust, the ocean crust plunges underneath the continental plate and melts. Molten rock surges upward, exploding onto the surface through a volcano. The Ring of Fire surrounds the plates that make up the Pacific Ocean. Streams of magma also form volcanoes at places other than plate boundaries. Such volcanoes have shaped the Hawaiian Islands, which are far from a plate boundary.

When two plates push together, the crust cracks and splinters from the pressure. The cracks in Earth's crust are called faults. When blocks of crust rub against each other along faults, they release huge amounts of energy in the form of earthquakes.

▲ **Molten rock pours from a volcano in Hawaii.**

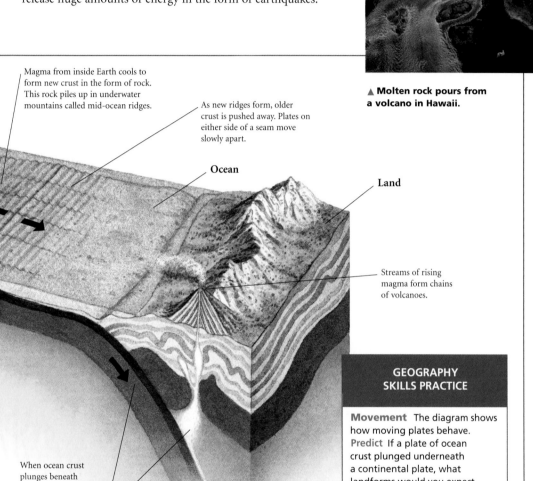

Magma from inside Earth cools to form new crust in the form of rock. This rock piles up in underwater mountains called mid-ocean ridges.

As new ridges form, older crust is pushed away. Plates on either side of a seam move slowly apart.

Ocean

Land

Streams of rising magma form chains of volcanoes.

When ocean crust plunges beneath land, it melts into streams of magma that rise to the surface.

GEOGRAPHY SKILLS PRACTICE

Movement The diagram shows how moving plates behave. **Predict** If a plate of ocean crust plunged underneath a continental plate, what landforms would you expect to develop?

Chapter 2 Section 2 **37**

Guided Instruction (continued)

- Have students review the maps on page 38 and ask **How do some scientists believe that continents move?** (*Magma beneath Earth's crust may act like a slow-moving conveyor belt, dragging the plates that carry the continents a few centimeters a year.*) Then, using The World: Physical map in the Atlas on pp. 140–141, have students discuss ways of how the continents could have once been one land mass.

- Ask students **How can magma cause the plates that carry the continents to move apart?** (*Sheets of magma rise to the surface along a seam between the plates to form ridges in the crust. As new ridges form, older crust is pushed away, forcing the plates on either side of a seam to move slowly apart.*)

Independent Practice
Have students continue to fill in the graphic organizer web by including details from the information they have just learned. Remind them to add more branches and circles if necessary.

Monitor Progress
Survey the class and determine if individuals are absorbing the content. Provide assistance as needed.

Background: Links Across Time

A New Island For thousands of years, magma from underwater volcanoes built up until it rose above sea level to create the Hawaiian Islands. Today, a new island, named Loihi (low EE hee), is forming just southeast of the big island of Hawaii. Already more than two miles (about 3.7 kilometers) high, it has 3,180 feet (969 meters) to go before it breaks the ocean's surface. Loihi erupts often, causing earthquakes and tidal waves.

Answer
Geography Skills Practice **Predict**
volcanoes and islands

Show students *The Ever-Changing Earth*. Ask **According to the video, what is the cause of volcanic eruptions and earthquakes?** *(the movement of plates of the Earth's crust)*

Forces on Earth's Surface

Guided Instruction   L2

- Read Forces on Earth's Surface. Circulate to make sure individuals can answer the Reading Check question.

- Ask students **What is weathering?** *(a process that breaks down rocks into tiny pieces)* **How does it differ from erosion?** *(Weathering is the breaking down of rocks into tiny pieces while erosion is the removal of these pieces.)*

- Ask students to predict what the area where they live might look like 10,000 years from now. *(Answers will vary but students should note that forces such as weathering and erosion will change a region over time.)*

Independent Practice
Have students complete their graphic organizers.

Monitor Progress

- Show *Section Reading Support Transparency FG 46* and ask students to check their graphic organizers individually. Go over key concepts and clarify key vocabulary as needed.

    📖 **Foundations of Geography Transparencies,** *Section Reading Support Transparency FG 46*

- Tell students to fill in the last column of their *Reading Readiness Guides*. Probe for what they learned that confirms or invalidates each statement.

    All in One **Foundations of Geography Teaching Resources,** *Reading Readiness Guide,* p. 110

Answers

✓ Reading Check Parts of Earth's crust called plates shift in response to movements of magma beneath the crust.
Analyze According to the first map, all of the present-day continents were once joined together. **Identify** the Cocos Plate

---

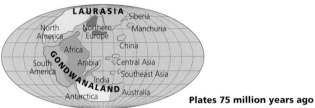

Explore the movement of continental plates.

A World of Moving Plates For hundreds of years, geographers wondered how Earth's landmasses took their present shapes and positions. When they looked at the globe, they thought they saw matching shapes in continents that are very far apart. Now that they know how forces inside Earth move continents, they know that those continents were once close together.

✓ Reading Check How do continents move apart?

Plate Movements

Plates 250 million years ago

Plates Shifting Through Time
Most geographers believe that long ago Earth had only one huge continent. They call it Pangaea (pan JEE uh). About 200 million years ago, they conclude, plate movement began to split Pangaea apart. They think that these pieces came to form the continents that we know today. **Analyze** *According to these maps, which present-day continents were once joined together?*

Plates 150 million years ago

Present-Day Plates
The map below shows Earth's modern plates and plate edges. It also shows how the plates are moving. Earthquakes and volcanoes cluster along plate edges. **Identify** *Which plate is colliding with the North American Plate?*

Plates 75 million years ago

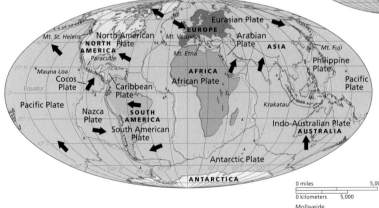

KEY	
—	Plate boundary
➡	Plate movement
▨	Earthquake zone
▲	Volcano

0 miles 5,000
0 kilometers 5,000
Mollweide

38 Foundations of Geography

— Background: Biography —

One Big Landmass Alfred Lothar Wegener (1880–1930) studied astronomy and taught meteorology. Even though his education focused on the sky, Wegener was interested in the shapes of continental landmasses. In 1912, Wegener proposed that a single large landmass broke apart to form the continents we see today. As evidence, he pointed to closely related fossil organisms and similar rock strata that occur on the continents. Geologists rejected his ideas. More than forty years later, precise dating of rocks on the opposite sides of the Atlantic Ocean indicated that Wegener's ideas were not only plausible, but likely.

Forces on Earth's Surface

Forces inside Earth move plates apart, produce volcanoes, and slowly build up Earth's crust. Other forces slowly wear it down and reshape it. The forces that wear Earth down are not as dramatic as volcanoes, but over time they are just as effective.

Weathering is a process that breaks rocks down into tiny pieces. Water, ice, and living things like lichens on rocks all cause weathering. Weathering helps create soil, too. Tiny pieces of rock combine with decayed animal and plant material to form soil.

Once this breaking down has taken place, landforms are reshaped by **erosion,** or the removal of small pieces of rock by water, ice, or wind. Hundreds of millions of years ago, the Appalachian Mountains in the eastern United States were as high as the Rocky Mountains of the western United States now are. Rain, snow, and wind slowly wore them down into much lower peaks.

When water, ice, and wind remove material, they deposit it downstream or downwind to create new landforms. Plains are often made of material carried from upstream by rivers.

✓ **Reading Check** What landforms are products of weathering and erosion?

Weathering and erosion formed this natural sandstone bridge in Jordan.

Section 2 Assessment

Key Terms
Review the key terms at the beginning of this section. Use each term in a sentence that explains its meaning.

Target Reading Skill
Find the word *landforms* in the last paragraph of page 35. Use the context to find its meaning. What does it mean? What clues did you use to find its meaning?

Comprehension and Critical Thinking
1. (a) List What are Earth's three main layers?

(b) **Synthesize Information** How do those layers interact?
2. (a) **Recall** What forces inside Earth shape Earth's surface?
(b) **Explain** How do these forces explain the movement of the continents?
(c) **Predict** How might a continent split in two?
3. (a) **Identify** What forces cause weathering and erosion?
(b) **Compare and Contrast** How is erosion different from weathering?

Writing Activity
Think about the region where you live. Does it have steep mountains or volcanoes, rounded hills, or plains? Write a paragraph describing some of the natural forces that are slowly reshaping your region.

For: An activity on Pangaea
Visit: PHSchool.com
Web Code: led-3202

Assess and Reteach

Assess Progress   L2
Have Students complete the Section Assessment. Administer the *Section Quiz.*

All in One **Foundations of Geography Teaching Resources,** *Section Quiz*, p. 112

Reteach   L1
If students need more instruction, have them read this section in the Reading and Vocabulary Study Guide.

📖 Chapter 2, Section 2, **Foundations of Geography Reading and Vocabulary Study Guide,** pp. 16–18

Extend   L3
Have students learn more about varying landforms and elevations from Death Valley to Mt. Whitney by completing the *Small Group Activity: Simulation: Making a Poster for the Whitney Classic.*

All in One **Foundations of Geography Teaching Resources,** *Small Group Activity: Simulation: Making a Poster for the Whitney Classic,* p. 128–131

Answer

✓ Reading Check   hills, some mountains, deserts, and plains

Writing Activity
Use the *Rubric for Assessing a Writing Assignment* to evaluate students' paragraphs.

All in One **Foundations of Geography Teaching Resources,** *Rubric for Assessing a Writing Assignment,* p. 145

Go Online PHSchool.com Typing in the Web code when prompted will bring students directly to detailed instructions for this activity.

Section 2 Assessment

Key Terms
Students' sentences should reflect knowledge of each Key Term.

Target Reading Skill
Landforms are shapes and types of land. Clue: The meaning of landforms was restated after the word.

Comprehension and Critical Thinking
1. (a) the crust, the mantle, and the core
(b) The crust floats on top of the mantle and the heat of the mantle and the core help shape Earth's crust.

2. (a) magma and moving plates (b) Some scientists think that sheets of mantle form conveyor belts that move the plates of crust above them, causing the continents to move. (c) A continent that sits on two or more of Earth's plates can split apart when those plates move in opposite directions.

3. (a) water, ice, living things, and wind
(b) Weathering is a process that breaks down rocks into small pieces. Erosion is the removal of small pieces of rock by water, ice, or wind.

Section 3
Climate and Weather

Objectives

Social Studies

1. Learn about weather and climate.
2. Explore latitude, landforms, and precipitation.
3. Discover how oceans affect climate.

Reading/Language Arts

Use context clues that give a comparison to determine the meaning of a word or phrase.

Prepare to Read

Build Background Knowledge `L2`

Tell students that in this section they will explore climate and weather. Ask students to think about what they know about weather, and then look at the two photographs and related captions on pp. 40 and 41. Then ask what they think the difference between weather and climate is. Conduct an Idea Wave (TE, p. T35) to share ideas as a class.

Set a Purpose for Reading `L2`

■ Preview the Objectives.

■ Form students into pairs or groups of four. Distribute the *Reading Readiness Guide.* Ask students to fill in the first two columns of the chart. Use the Numbered Heads participation strategy (TE, p. T36) to call on students to share one piece of information they already know and one piece of information they want to know.

All in One Foundations of Geography Teaching Resources, *Reading Readiness Guide,* p. 114

Vocabulary Builder
Preview Key Terms

Pronounce each Key Term, then ask the students to say the word with you. Provide a simple explanation such as, "The tropical cyclone arrived on shore with such force that roads were flooded, trees and power lines were torn down, and many homes were damaged."

Answer

✓ **Reading Check** Weather is the condition of the air and sky from day to day. Climate is the average weather of a place over many years.

40 *Foundations of Geography*

Prepare to Read

Objectives

In this section you will

1. Learn about weather and climate.
2. Explore latitude, landforms, and precipitation.
3. Discover how oceans affect climate.

Taking Notes

As you read this section, look for topics related to climate and weather, such as landforms, precipitation, oceans, and storms. Copy the outline below and add headings as needed to show the relationships among these topics.

```
I.  Weather
II. Climate
    A. Latitudes
    B.
       1.
       2.
III. Storms
```

🎯 Target Reading Skill

Use Context Clues You can sometimes learn the meaning of a word or phrase when the context gives a comparison. In this example, the word *cyclone* is compared to the phrase in italics.

A cyclone is like *a huge spiral escalator moving air upward.*

Key Terms

- **weather** (WETH ur) *n.* the condition of the air and sky from day to day
- **precipitation** (pree sip uh TAY shun) *n.* water that falls to the ground as rain, sleet, hail, or snow
- **temperature** (TEM pur uh chur) *n.* how hot or cold the air is
- **climate** (KLY mut) *n.* the average weather over many years
- **tropical cyclone** (TRAHP ih kul SY klohn) *n.* an intense wind and rain storm that forms over oceans in the tropics.

This Inuit woman and child are dressed for their cold climate.

40 Foundations of Geography

Weather or Climate?

Every morning, most people check the weather before they get dressed. But in some parts of India, people have very serious reasons for watching the **weather,** or the condition of the air and sky from day to day. In parts of India, it rains only during one time of year. No one living there wants the rainy days to end too soon. That rain must fill the wells with enough fresh water to last for the entire year.

In India, people are concerned about **precipitation,** or water that falls to the ground as rain, sleet, hail, or snow. When you get dressed in the morning, you may want to know the **temperature,** or how hot or cold the air is. Weather is mainly measured by temperature and precipitation.

The **climate** of a place is the average weather over many years. Climate is not the same as weather. Weather is what people see from day to day. Climate is what usually happens from year to year.

✓ **Reading Check** What is the difference between weather and climate?

🎯 Target Reading Skill `L2`

Use Context Clues Point out the Target Reading Skill. Tell students that one way to find the meaning of a word or phrase is to look for comparisons between the unfamiliar word and a familiar word or phrase within the context.

Model using comparison context clues by finding the meaning of *tsunami.* Write the following sentence on the board: "The tsunami approached the southern coast of Japan like an enormous tower of water and crashed upon the shore flooding everything it its path." (enormous tower of water *and* crashed upon the shore *implies a large wave*) Point out to students that words such as *like* and *as* signal that a comparison is being made.

Give students *Use Context Clues: Compare and Contrast.* Have them complete the activity in groups.

All in One Foundations of Geography Teaching Resources, *Use Context Clues: Compare and Contrast,* p. 123

Why Climates Vary

Earth has many climates. Some climates are so hot that people rarely need to wear a sweater. In some cold climates, snow stays on the ground most of the year. And there are places on Earth where more than 30 feet (9 meters) of rain falls in a single year.

Climate depends on location. Places in the low latitudes, or tropics, have hot climates, because they get direct sunlight. Places in the high latitudes, or polar regions, have cold climates, because their sunlight is indirect.

Air and water spread heat around the globe as they move. Without wind and water, places in the tropics would overheat. Oceans gain and lose heat slowly, so they keep temperatures mild near coasts. Mountains can also affect climates.

✓ **Reading Check** How does latitude affect temperature?

Cherrapunji, India, averages 37 feet (11 meters) of rain a year.

The Water Cycle

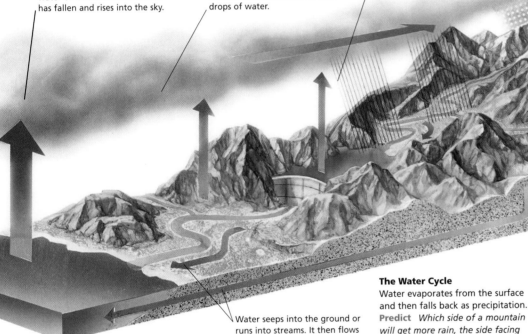

Water evaporates from bodies of water or land areas where rain has fallen and rises into the sky.

The heated water vapor condenses to form clouds made up of little drops of water.

As moist air rises, it cools and drops its moisture. This can happen when air is forced up a mountain slope or when air rises in a storm system.

Water seeps into the ground or runs into streams. It then flows to the sea or evaporates again.

The Water Cycle
Water evaporates from the surface and then falls back as precipitation. **Predict** *Which side of a mountain will get more rain, the side facing the wind, or the side facing away?*

Vocabulary Builder

Use the information below to teach students this section's high-use words.

High-Use Word	Definition and Sample Sentence
indirect, p. 41	*adj.* not direct or straight; by a longer way He took an **indirect** route home in order to pass by his friend's house and see if she was home.
distribute, p. 43	*v.* to give or spread out Many people **distribute** candy on Halloween.

Instruct

Weather or Climate? 🄻2

Why Climates Vary 🄻2

Guided Instruction

- **Vocabulary Builder** Clarify the high-use word **indirect** before reading.

- Read Weather or Climate? and Why Climates Vary using the Choral Reading strategy (TE, p. T34). Ask students to study the diagram and captions for The Water Cycle. As a class, answer the caption question. Allow students to briefly discuss their responses with a partner before sharing with the class.

- Ask students **What is climate?** (*It is the average weather over many years.*) **Why do climates vary?** (*location, including elevation; wind patterns; mountains*)

- Ask students **How is weather measured?** (*It is mainly measured by temperature and precipitation.*) **What is precipitation and what forms can it take?** (*Precipitation is water that falls to the ground as rain, sleet, hail, or snow.*)

- Ask students **Once rain has fallen, how does water return to the ocean?** (*through rivers, streams, and groundwater runoff*)

Independent Practice

Ask students to create the Taking Notes graphic organizer outline on a blank piece of paper. Have students fill in information related to climate and weather.

Monitor Progress

As students fill in the graphic organizer, circulate and make sure individuals are selecting the correct details. Provide assistance as needed.

Answers

✓ **Reading Check** Low latitudes receive direct sunlight; therefore, the temperature is hot. High latitudes receive indirect sunlight; therefore, the temperature is cold.
Predict the side facing the wind

Oceans and Climates L2

Guided Instruction

- **Vocabulary Builder** Clarify the high-use word **distribute** before reading.

- Review the diagram and map on pages 42 and 43 with students. Read how global wind patterns and bodies of water affect the regions of the world in Oceans and Climates.

- Ask students **What do wind and air currents move?** (*heat and moisture between different parts of Earth*) **How are they affected by latitude?** (*The currents flow in regular circular patterns depending on the latitude through which they are moving.*)

- Ask students **What happens when air rises?** (*The moisture it contains condenses and falls as rain or snow.*) **What happens when air sinks?** (*The air becomes drier creating dry climates such as those at the poles or in the desert.*)

Air Circulation and Wind

Winds and air currents move heat and moisture between different parts of Earth. These currents follow regular patterns related to latitude. The diagram below shows these circular patterns of air movement, which form a series of belts, or cells, that circle Earth.

A strong onshore wind blows in Miami Beach, Florida.

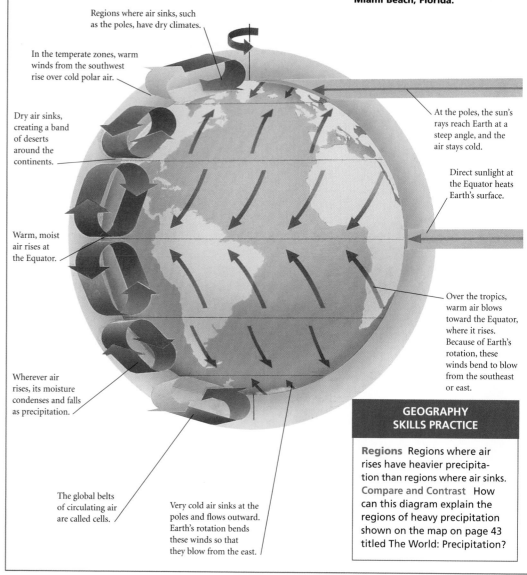

Regions where air sinks, such as the poles, have dry climates.

In the temperate zones, warm winds from the southwest rise over cold polar air.

Dry air sinks, creating a band of deserts around the continents.

Warm, moist air rises at the Equator.

Wherever air rises, its moisture condenses and falls as precipitation.

At the poles, the sun's rays reach Earth at a steep angle, and the air stays cold.

Direct sunlight at the Equator heats Earth's surface.

Over the tropics, warm air blows toward the Equator, where it rises. Because of Earth's rotation, these winds bend to blow from the southeast or east.

The global belts of circulating air are called cells.

Very cold air sinks at the poles and flows outward. Earth's rotation bends these winds so that they blow from the east.

GEOGRAPHY SKILLS PRACTICE

Regions Regions where air rises have heavier precipitation than regions where air sinks. **Compare and Contrast** How can this diagram explain the regions of heavy precipitation shown on the map on page 43 titled The World: Precipitation?

42 Foundations of Geography

Differentiated Instruction

For Special Needs Students L1

Have students read the section as they listen to the recorded version on the Student Edition on Audio CD. Check for comprehension by pausing the CD and asking students to share their answers to the Reading Check.

⊙ *Chapter 2, Section 3,* **Student Edition on Audio CD**

Answer

Geography Skills Practice **Compare and Contrast** The regions of heavy precipitation on the map have belts of warm, moist air that rises, causing heavy precipitation.

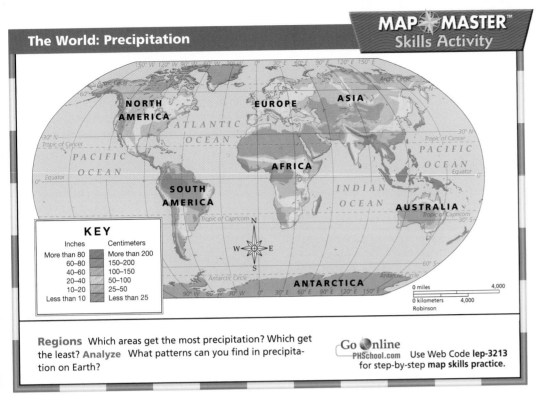

MAP MASTER™
Skills Activity

KEY

Inches	Centimeters
More than 80	More than 200
60–80	150–200
40–60	100–150
20–40	50–100
10–20	25–50
Less than 10	Less than 25

0 miles   4,000
0 kilometers   4,000
Robinson

Regions Which areas get the most precipitation? Which get the least? **Analyze** What patterns can you find in precipitation on Earth?

Go Online
PHSchool.com Use Web Code **lep-3213**
for step-by-step **map skills practice.**

Oceans and Climates

The oceans help distribute Earth's heat and shape climates. Global wind patterns help create ocean currents, which are like vast rivers in the oceans. Ocean currents move across great distances. Generally, warm water flows away from the Equator, while cold water moves toward the Equator.

Oceans and Currents In the Atlantic Ocean, the Gulf Stream, a warm current, travels northeast from the tropics. The Gulf Stream and the North Atlantic Current carry warm water all the way to western Europe. That warm water gives western Europe a milder climate than other regions at the same latitude.

The cold Peru Current moves north from Antarctica along the coast of South America. The city of Antofagasta (ahn toh fah GAHS tah) lies along that coast, in Chile. Even though Antofagasta is closer than Miami, Florida, is to the Equator, the average temperature in Antofagasta during the hottest month of summer is just 68°F (20°C).

Using Prereading Strategies
If you do not know what ocean currents are, notice that they are compared to vast rivers in the ocean. How does the comparison help you find the meaning?

Skills Mini Lesson

Using Cartographer's Tools

1. Teach the skill by pointing out that a map key explains symbols and special colors used on a map. Explain that it helps students interpret the information being shown on the map.

2. Help students practice the skill by looking at the map on this page. Read the key with students and have them identify what each color represents on the map.

3. Have students apply the skill by choosing a continent and describing its pattern of precipitation.

- Ask students **Why does western Europe have a milder climate than other regions at the same latitude?** *(The Gulf Stream and the North Atlantic Current carry warm water to western Europe.)*

- Ask students to draw a conclusion about why the temperature in Antofagasta, Chile, is not as warm as Florida, even though it is closer to the Equator. *(The cold-water current from the South Pole called the Peru Current moves north past Chile, giving Antofagasta a cooler climate than Florida.)*

Target Reading Skill   L2

Use Context Clues As a follow up, ask students to answer the Target Reading Skill question in the Student Edition. *(Possible answer: Since* river *is a familiar concept, it can help one understand a more unfamiliar concept like* ocean current.*)*

Answers

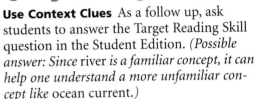 **Regions** central region of northern South America; portions of Africa's west coast; parts of Southeast Asia; island countries located in the Pacific Ocean
Analyze Generally, areas around the Equator get the most precipitation. As you move north or south of the Equator, the amount of precipitation decreases.

Go Online
PHSchool.com Students may practice their map skills using the interactive online version of this map.

Guided Instruction (continued)

- Have students discuss the cooling and warming affects of the ocean and other bodies of water.

- Have students compare and contrast the climates of San Francisco and St. Louis. *(Because San Francisco borders the Pacific Ocean, it is warmer than St. Louis in the winter and cooler than St. Louis in the summer.)* Ask students if there are any bodies of water nearby that may affect the region in which they live.

- As a class, study The World: Climate Regions on these pages. Answer the Map-Master Skills Activity questions as a class. Then, ask the class to compare the climate regions of North America and Europe. *(North America and Europe have similar types of climate regions, but the southern portion of North America has tropical regions while Europe does not.)*

The Ocean's Cooling and Warming Effects Bodies of water affect climate in other ways, too. Water takes longer to heat or cool than land. As the air and land heat up in summer, the water remains cooler. Wind blowing over the water cools the nearby land. So in summer, a region near an ocean or lake will be cooler than an inland area at the same latitude. In the winter, the water remains warmer than the land. So places near lakes or oceans are warmer in winter than inland areas.

The World: Climate Regions

You can see patterns in a map of Earth's climate regions. Notice that tropical wet climate regions hug the Equator on several continents. Farther from the Equator are arid and semiarid climate regions. Elsewhere, regions where the wind blows off the ocean have wetter climates than regions farther inland. Each climate region on this map is described more fully in the next section.

▲ **Arid** This view from the air shows the Colorado River winding through the Grand Canyon in Arizona.

Skills Mini Lesson

Comparing and Contrasting

1. Teach the skill by pointing out to students that comparison involves similarities, and contrast involves differences. It is important to first identify the topic and purpose in their comparison and contrast. Similarities and differences will then be easier to determine.

2. Help students practice the skill by looking at The World: Climate Regions map on these pages and comparing and contrasting North and South America.

3. Have students apply the skill by comparing and contrasting the climate regions of Australia and Greenland.

Consider San Francisco, California, and St. Louis, Missouri. Both cities are near 38° north latitude. However, San Francisco borders the Pacific Ocean. In winter, the ocean is warmer than the air. The ocean keeps San Francisco much warmer than St. Louis in winter. In summer, the ocean is cooler than the air, so it keeps San Francisco cool.

✓ **Reading Check** During the summer, are places near the ocean warmer or cooler than places inland?

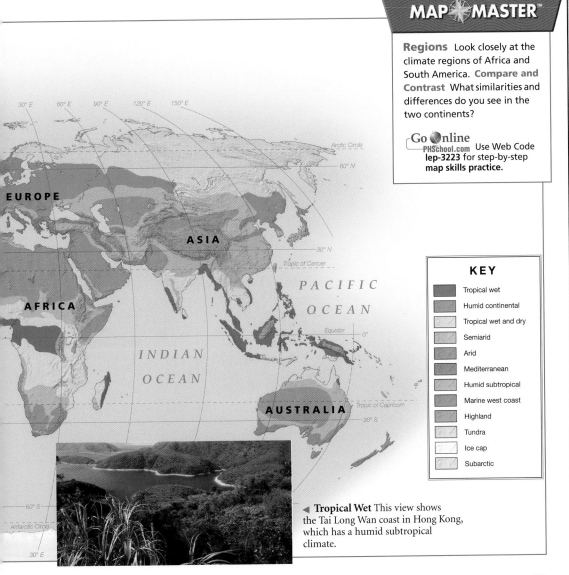

MAP✦MASTER™

Regions Look closely at the climate regions of Africa and South America. **Compare and Contrast** What similarities and differences do you see in the two continents?

Go Online
PHSchool.com Use Web Code **lep-3223** for step-by-step map skills practice.

KEY

- Tropical wet
- Humid continental
- Tropical wet and dry
- Semiarid
- Arid
- Mediterranean
- Humid subtropical
- Marine west coast
- Highland
- Tundra
- Ice cap
- Subarctic

◀ **Tropical Wet** This view shows the Tai Long Wan coast in Hong Kong, which has a humid subtropical climate.

Guided Instruction (continued)

■ Partner students to analyze the images on pages 44 and 45. Coach students to think about what each image shows and what general feeling each image inspires. Then ask them **If there were no captions, what climate regions would they assign each image based on its content?** (*The image on page 44 shows a dry, arid landscape; the image on page 45 shows a lush, tropical area with heavy vegetation.*)

Independent Practice
Have students continue to fill in their graphic organizer with details from the information they have just learned.

Monitor Progress
As students fill in the graphic organizer, circulate and make sure individuals are selecting the correct details. Provide assistance as needed.

Differentiated Instruction

For Less Proficient Readers L1
Some students may have trouble reading the climate map on pages 44 and 45. Pair these students with more able students and ask them to complete *Reading a Climate Map* together.

All in One **Foundations of Geography Teaching Resources,** *Reading a Climate Map,* p. 135

For Gifted and Talented L3
Have students choose one of the images on pages 44–45 and write a poem that describes what it must be like to live in this climate region.

All in One **Foundations of Geography Teaching Resources,** *Rubric for Assessing a Student Poem,* p. 146

Answers

✓ **Reading Check** cooler

MAP✦MASTER™ Skills Activity **Compare and Contrast**
The two continents share many of the same types of climate regions, but Africa has a much larger arid region.

Go Online
PHSchool.com Students may practice their map skills using the interactive online version of this map.

Weather Forecasting L2

Guided Instruction

Ask students to read the feature and review the images and captions. Then have students discuss why it might be important to be forewarned about weather conditions. As a class, answer the Analyzing Images question.

Independent Practice

Have students create an outline of the information on this page.

Raging Storms L2

Guided Instruction

- Read Raging Storms as a class. Make sure that individuals are able to answer the Reading Check question.

- Have students list the storms mentioned in the reading. (*tropical cyclones, hurricanes, tornadoes, blizzards, severe rainstorms, and thunderstorms*) Ask **What elements are common to these storms?** (*high winds and heavy precipitation*)

Independent Practice

Tell students to complete their graphic organizers.

Monitor Progress

- Show *Section Reading Support Transparency FG 47*. Go over key concepts and clarify key vocabulary as needed.

  📖 **Foundations of Geography Transparencies,** *Section Reading Support Transparency FG 47*

- Tell students to fill in the last column of their *Reading Readiness Guides*. Ask them to evaluate if what they learned was what they had expected to learn.

  All in One Foundations of Geography Teaching Resources, *Reading Readiness Guide,* p. 114

Answer

ANALYZING IMAGES Satellites gather information about locations all over the world. Forecasters might use the weather patterns in other parts of the world to predict what the weather might be like in their area.

Weather Forecasting

Television weather forecasters rely on scientists and equipment from all over the world. Weather stations record local conditions. Satellites orbit overhead to photograph large weather systems. Weather balloons and radar provide still more data. The results, displayed on weather maps or presented in forecasts, can warn citizens of an approaching hurricane or simply remind people to carry an umbrella.

Weather station
This ranger is measuring rainfall at a weather station on the island of Madeira in the Atlantic Ocean. Stations like this send reports to forecasters.

Solar cell panels power the spacecraft.

Weather satellites
Scientists use satellites in space to record everything from wind patterns to the height of waves.

GOES weather satellite
U.S. weather satellites are called GOES (Geostationary Operational Environmental Satellites). They circle Earth in time with Earth's rotation, so they always stay above the same spot.

A hurricane

Weather map
Forecasters track weather patterns and storm systems, and display data on weather maps.

A gathering storm

ANALYZING IMAGES
How might a satellite help forecasters predict the weather?

46 Foundations of Geography

Differentiated Instruction

For English Language Learners L1

Partner students with English speakers to reread the information on this page. Have them summarize, in their own words, the information they have read. Make sure they clarify words they find difficult to pronounce or understand.

For Advanced Readers L3

Have students write a letter to a local television weather forecaster asking three questions that would help them learn more about predicting weather. Give them *Writing a Letter* to help them get started.

All in One Foundations of Geography Teaching Resources, *Writing a Letter,* p. 143

Raging Storms

Wind and water can make climates milder, but they also can create large and dangerous storms. **Tropical cyclones** are intense wind and rain storms that form over oceans in the tropics. Tropical cyclones that form over the Atlantic Ocean are called hurricanes. The winds near the center of a hurricane can reach speeds of more than 100 miles (160 kilometers) per hour. Hurricanes produce huge swells of water called storm surges, which flood over shorelines and can destroy buildings.

Tornadoes are like funnels of wind that can reach 200 miles (320 kilometers) per hour. The winds and the low air pressure they create in their centers can wreck almost anything in their path. They can be just as dangerous as hurricanes, but they affect much smaller areas.

Other storms are less dangerous. In winter, blizzards dump huge amounts of snow on parts of North America. And severe rainstorms and thunderstorms strike the continent most often in spring and summer.

Hurricane Andrew
In 1992 Hurricane Andrew caused massive destruction and left 160,000 people homeless in south Florida. **Synthesizing Information** *Is a hurricane more likely on a tropical coast or in a polar region far from the ocean?*

✓ **Reading Check** Which storms cover larger areas, hurrricanes or tornadoes?

Section 3 Assessment

Key Terms
Review the key terms at the beginning of this section. Use each term in a sentence that explains its meaning.

🎯 **Target Reading Skill**
Find the word *tornadoes* in the second paragraph on this page. Using the context, find out its meaning. What clues did you use to find its meaning?

Comprehension and Critical Thinking
1. (a) **Identify** What is climate?
(b) **Explain** How is climate different from weather?

(c) **Analyze** Are hurricanes an example of climate or of weather?
2. (a) **Recall** What kind of climate occurs in most places near the Equator?
(b) **Contrast** Why are climates near the poles different from climates near the Equator?
3. (a) **Recall** How do bodies of water affect temperatures?
(b) **Predict** A city in the interior of a continent has very cold winters. How would you expect winter temperatures to differ in a coastal city at the same latitude as the interior city?

Writing Activity
Write a paragraph describing your region's climate, or average weather. Are winters usually warm or cold? What can you say about summers? Do oceans affect your climate? How much precipitation does your region get? Is it mostly rain, or snow, or a mix?

Writing Tip Remember that every paragraph needs a main idea. Make a general statement about your climate in a topic sentence. Then add sentences with supporting details about your climate.

Chapter 2 Section 3 **47**

Objective

Use and interpret climate graphs.

Prepare to Read

Build Background Knowledge `L2`

Invite students to brainstorm a list of all the kinds of graphs they know, such as circle, line, and bar. Then ask them what they usually want or need to know about the weather (*temperature and precipitation*). Tell students that climate graphs answer the questions most people have about weather.

Instruct

Using Climate Graphs `L2`

Guided Instruction

- Read the steps to using climate graphs as a class and write them on the board.

- Practice the skill by following the steps on page 49 as a class. Model each step in the activity by first reading the labels on the graph (*Fahrenheit degrees; inches; months of the year*); identifying what the bar and line graphs show (*bar: rainfall in inches; line: temperature in Fahrenheit degrees*); describing the shape of the line graph and look of the bar graph (*line: relatively flat indicating little temperature change; bar graph: varying heights indicating higher precipitation during the spring and summer than the fall and winter*). Remind students that seasons in the Southern Hemisphere are the reverse of seasons in the Northern Hemisphere. Then draw conclusions. (*Possible conclusions: São Paulo's temperatures remain in the same small range year round; therefore the city has a moderate climate. São Paulo has a wet and dry season. The wet season runs from October through March and the dry season runs from April through September.*)

Independent Practice

Assign *Skills for Life* and have students complete it individually.

All in One **Foundations of Geography**
Teaching Resources, *Skills for Life*, p. 127

Using Climate Graphs

People in Menghai, China, walking in the rain

" **E** verybody talks about the weather, but nobody does anything about it," goes an old joke attributed to the humorist Mark Twain. It's still true, although today we track the weather so that we can predict and prepare for it. One way geographers track weather patterns is by making a climate graph. A climate graph usually presents information about average precipitation and average temperature. Often it shows a whole year of information, so you can see how conditions change with the seasons.

Learn the Skill

To read a climate graph, follow the steps below.

1 **Identify the elements of the graph.** A climate graph is actually two graphs in one: a line graph that shows temperature and a bar graph that shows rainfall. The scale on the left side goes with the line graph, and the scale on the right side goes with the bar graph. The scale along the bottom shows a time period.

2 **Study the line graph.** Notice changes in temperature from month to month and from season to season. Draw a conclusion about the temperature of the place.

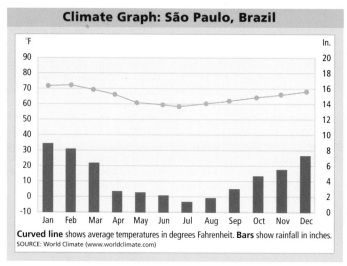

Climate Graph: São Paulo, Brazil

Curved line shows average temperatures in degrees Fahrenheit. **Bars** show rainfall in inches.
SOURCE: World Climate (www.worldclimate.com)

3 **Study the bar graph.** Again, notice changes for months and for seasons. Draw a conclusion about rainfall.

4 **Use your conclusions about both graphs to draw an overall conclusion about the climate of the location.** Does the location appear to have hot seasons and cold seasons? Or does it have a rainy season and a dry season? State your conclusion.

48 Foundations of Geography

Monitor Progress

As students are completing *Skills for Life*, circulate to make sure individuals are applying the skill steps effectively. Provide assistance as needed.

Practice the Skill

Look at the graph of São Paulo, Brazil, on page 48.

1 Read the labels on the sides and bottom of the graph. What do the numbers on the left side measure? What do the numbers on the right side measure? Look at the green bars. Which do they measure, temperature or rainfall? How do you know? Look at the line graph. What does it show? Now, look at the scale along the bottom of the graph. What period of time does it show?

2 Describe the shape of the line graph—is it generally flat, or does it go up and down? What and when is São Paulo's highest average temperature? Its lowest temperature? Do you think São Paulo has a hot season and a cold season? Write a conclusion about temperatures in the city.

3 What do the bars in the bar graph show? Are they generally the same height, or do they differ from month to month? What and when are São Paulo's highest and lowest average rainfall? Do you think São Paulo has a wet season and a dry season? Write a conclusion about rainfall in the city.

4 Using your conclusions about São Paulo's climate, write a summary that includes answers to these questions: What kind of seasons does the city have? Does the weather change much during the year?

Charleston, South Carolina

Month	Temperature (°Fahrenheit)	Precipitation (inches)
Jan	48.4	2.9
Feb	50.9	3.0
Mar	57.7	3.6
Apr	65.3	2.4
May	72.7	3.2
Jun	78.8	4.7
Jul	81.7	6.8
Aug	81.0	6.4
Sept	76.6	5.1
Oct	67.8	2.9
Nov	59.5	2.1
Dec	52.2	2.7

Apply the Skill

To make your own climate graph, draw a large square on graph paper. Divide the square into 10 horizontal rows and 12 vertical columns. Title your graph "Climate Graph of Charleston, South Carolina." Then label the left side of your graph using one colored pencil and the right side with a different colored pencil. Write the months of the year along the bottom. Using the temperature and precipitation information in the table above, plot your line graph. Draw the lines with the same colored pencils you used to make the labels for temperature and precipitation.

Assess and Reteach

Assess Progress **L2**

Ask students to do the Apply the Skill activity.

Reteach **L1**

If students are having trouble applying the skill steps, pair students and ask them to complete *Reading a Climate Graph.*

All in One Foundations of Geography, *Reading a Climate Graph,* p. 136

Extend **L3**

To extend the skill, show students *Color Transparency FG 41: Climate Graphs.* Have students follow the steps outlined in the skill feature to draw conclusions on the climates of Karachi, Pakistan, and Chennai, India. Then have students write a brief summary of their findings.

Foundations of Geography Transparencies, *Color Transparency FG 41: Climate Graphs*

Answer
Apply the Skill

Student's climate graphs should have the same format as the São Paulo climate graph but reflect the data in the table for Charleston, South Carolina.

All in One Foundations of Geography Teaching Resources, *Rubric for Assessing a Bar Graph,* p. 148; *Rubric for Assessing a Line Graph,* p. 149

Section 4
Step-by-Step Instruction

Objectives
Social Studies
1. Investigate the relationship between climate and vegetation.
2. Explore Earth's vegetation regions.
3. Study vertical climate zones.

Reading/Language Arts
Use context to determine the meaning of a word or phrase when examples are provided.

Prepare to Read

Build Background Knowledge   L2
Tell students that in this section they will learn about different climates, and the relationship between climate and vegetation. Ask students to think of ways in which their environments would be different if they lived in a different climate zone. Model the thought process by encouraging them to think about how plants and trees would be different, how buildings might be constructed differently, and how their clothing might be different. Use the Numbered Heads participation strategy (TE, p. T36) to have students generate a list.

Set a Purpose for Reading   L2
- Preview the Objectives.
- Read each statement in the *Reading Readiness Guide* aloud. Ask students to mark the statements true or false.
- Have students discuss the statements in pairs or groups of four, then mark their worksheets again. Use the Numbered Heads participation strategy (TE, p. T36) to call on students to share their group's perspectives.

  All in One Foundations of Geography Teaching Resources, *Reading Readiness Guide,* p. 118

Vocabulary Builder
Preview Key Terms
Pronounce each Key Term, then ask the students to say the word with you. Provide a simple explanation such as, "The tree canopy was so thick that very little sunlight reached the floor of the rain forest."

Section 4
How Climate Affects Vegetation

Prepare to Read

Objectives
In this section you will
1. Investigate the relationship between climate and vegetation.
2. Explore Earth's vegetation regions.
3. Study vertical climate zones.

Taking Notes
As you read, look for details about Earth's natural vegetation regions. Copy the chart below and list each type of climate in the first row of boxes. Add boxes as needed. In the box underneath each type of climate, list facts about each vegetation region that occurs in that type of climate.

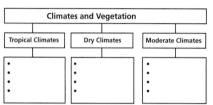

Climates and Vegetation		
Tropical Climates	Dry Climates	Moderate Climates
• • •	• • •	• • •

Target Reading Skill

Use Context Clues
You can sometimes learn the meaning of a word or phrase when the context gives examples. In the passage below, the meaning of the word *scrub* is given by the examples in italics.

> Scrub includes *bushes, small trees, and low, woody undergrowth.*

Key Terms
- **vegetation** (vej uh TAY shun) *n.* plants that grow in a region
- **tundra** (TUN druh) *n.* an area of cold climate and low-lying vegetation
- **canopy** (KAN uh pea) *n.* the layer formed by the uppermost branches of a rain forest
- **savanna** (suh VAN uh) *n.* a parklike combination of grasslands and scattered trees
- **desert scrub** (DEZ urt skrub) *n.* desert vegetation that needs little water
- **deciduous trees** (dee SIJ oo us treez) *n.* trees that lose their leaves seasonally
- **coniferous trees** (koh NIF ur us treez) *n.* trees that produce cones to carry seeds

Jackfruit, an Asian fruit, grows huge in the tropical wet climate of Hainan Island, China.

50 Foundations of Geography

Climate and Vegetation

There are five broad types of climate: tropical, dry, temperate marine, temperate continental, and polar. Each climate has its own types of natural **vegetation, or plants that grow in a region.** This is because different plants require different amounts of water and sunlight and different temperatures to survive. The map titled The World: Natural Vegetation, on page 53, shows the location of Earth's vegetation regions. If you compare this map with the map on pages 44 and 45 titled The World: Climate Regions, you will see that climate regions and vegetation regions often cover similar areas.

Tropical Climates In the tropics, there are two main climates. Both are hot. A tropical wet climate has year-round rainfall. Its typical vegetation is tropical rain forest. A tropical wet and dry climate has two seasons: a rainy season and a dry season. This climate supports grasslands and scattered trees.

Target Reading Skill   L2

Use Context Clues Point out the Target Reading Skill. Tell students that when the context of a sentence provides examples, they can help determine the meaning of an unfamiliar word or phrase.

Model the skill by finding out what vegetation makes up a tropical savanna in this sentence from page 52: "In tropical areas with winter dry seasons or more limited rainfall, there is a parklike landscape of grass-lands with scattered trees known as savanna." *(Tropical savannas are made up of grasslands and scattered trees.)*

Give students *Use Context Clues: Examples.* Have them complete the activity in their groups.

  All in One Foundations of Geography Teaching Resources, *Use Context Clues: Examples,* p. 124

Dry Climates Arid and semiarid climates have very hot summers and generally mild winters. They get very little rain. The driest arid climate regions have little or no vegetation. Others have plants that need little water. Semiarid climates get a little more rain. They support shrubs and grasses.

Temperate Marine Climates Temperate marine climates are found in the middle latitudes, usually near coastlines. There are three types: Mediterranean, marine west coast, and humid subtropical. The marine west coast and humid subtropical climates get plenty of rain. In the humid subtropical climate, the rain falls mainly in summer. Mediterranean climates get less rain, and it falls mainly in winter. All of the climates have mild winters. Mediterranean and humid subtropical climates generally have hot summers. With their heavy rainfall, marine west coast and humid subtropical climates support a variety of forests. The drier Mediterranean climates have their own vegetation, known as Mediterranean vegetation.

Temperate Continental Climates In a humid continental climate, summer temperatures are moderate to hot, but winters can be very cold. This climate supports grasslands and forests. Regions with subarctic climates are drier, with cool summers and cold winters. Most subarctic climate regions are forested.

Polar Climates The polar climates are cold all year-round. The **tundra** is an area, near the Arctic Circle, of cold climate and low-lying vegetation. The word *tundra* refers both to the vegetation and the climate, which has short, cool summers and long, very cold winters. Ice cap climates are bitterly cold all year. These areas are covered with ice. No vegetation can grow there.

✓ **Reading Check** Why are climate and vegetation related?

Earth's Vegetation Regions

Geographers divide Earth into regions that share similar vegetation. A place's vegetation depends mainly on its climate, but also on other things, such as soil quality.

Links to **Science**

Plant Fossils In ancient rocks in Wyoming, scientists have found fossils of palm trees. Millions of years ago, sediments such as sand or ash buried the plants quickly. Over thousands of years, the sediment and plants within turned to rock. Scientists study fossils to learn about ancient climate and vegetation.

Polar bears crossing the tundra in Churchill, Manitoba, Canada

Instruct

Climate and Vegetation L2

Guided Instruction

■ **Vocabulary Builder** Clarify the high-use words **marine** and **humid** before reading.

■ Read Climate and Vegetation using the Structured Silent Reading strategy (TE, p. T34). Ask students to study the photos and captions on pp. 50–51.

■ Ask students **What are the five broad types of climate?** *(tropical, dry, temperate marine, temperate continental, and polar)* **What factors are used to distinguish climates?** *(the amount or lack of rainfall and the amount or lack of heat)*

■ Ask students **What kinds of climates have forests?** *(Tropical wet climates, marine west coast, humid subtropical, and temperate continental climates all support forests.)* **Which do not and why?** *(Dry climates, tropical wet and dry climates, and Mediterranean climates do not support forests because there is not enough rainfall. Polar climates do not support forests because the temperatures are too cold.)*

Independent Practice

Ask students to create the Taking Notes graphic organizer on a blank piece of paper. Remind them to add extra boxes to include all of the broad types of climates. Then have them fill in each box with facts about vegetation for each of the five different types of climates.

Monitor Progress

As students fill in the graphic organizer, circulate and make sure individuals are selecting the correct details. Provide assistance as needed.

Links

Read the **Links to Science** box on this page. Ask students **What information do plant fossils give scientists?** *(Plant fossils help scientists learn about ancient climate and vegetation.)*

Answer

✓ **Reading Check** Different plants require different amounts of water and sunlight and different temperatures to survive.

Vocabulary Builder

Use the information below to teach students this section's high-use words.

High-Use Word	Definition and Sample Sentence
marine, p. 50	*adj.* of or relating to the sea A **marine** biologist studies ocean plants and animals.
humid, p. 51	*adj.* full of water vapor; moist The weather was hot and **humid.**
dense, p. 52	*adj.* packed in, crowded together We struggled to get through the **dense** bushes.
scatter, p. 52	*v.* to throw loosely about in no specific direction A gust of strong wind made the leaves **scatter.**

Earth's Vegetation Regions $L2$

Guided Instruction

- **Vocabulary Builder** Clarify the high-use words **dense** and **scatter** before reading.

- As a class, show students *The World: Annual Precipitation* and *The World: Desert and Desert Scrub Vegetation Regions* for a more detailed view of desert and desert scrub vegetation regions.

   Foundations of Geography Transparencies, *Color Transparency FG 10: The World: Annual Precipitation (Base); Color Transparency FG 12: The World: Desert and Desert Scrub Vegetation Regions (Overlay)*

- Write the different types of vegetation on the board. Ask students to brainstorm locations where they think the types of vegetation would be found. Have students refer to the map on page 53 to get ideas.

Independent Practice

Have students complete their graphic organizers with the information they just learned.

Monitor Progress

- Show *Section Reading Support Transparency FG 48* and ask students to check their graphic organizers individually. Go over key concepts and clarify key vocabulary as needed.

  Foundations of Geography Transparencies, *Section Reading Support Transparency FG 48*

⟳ Target Reading Skill $L2$

Use Context Clues As a follow up, ask students to answer the Target Reading Skill question in the Student Edition. *(It includes grasses, shrubs, and low trees.)*

Answer

√ Reading Check desert scrub and vegetation that has roots which can absorb water before it evaporates

---

This tropical rain forest in Brazil supports dense vegetation.

 Use Context Clues If you do not know what Mediterranean vegetation is, consider the examples and other information given by the context. What does the context tell you about this vegetation?

- **Tropical Rain Forest** Because there is so much sunlight, heat, and rain, thousands of kinds of plants grow in a rain forest. Some trees rise 130 feet (40 meters) into the air. The dense, leafy layer formed by the uppermost branches of the rainforest is called the **canopy.** Other plants grow to lower heights in the shade beneath the canopy.
- **Tropical Savanna** In tropical areas with winter dry seasons or more limited rainfall, there is a parklike landscape of grasslands with scattered trees known as **savanna.**
- **Desert** In the driest parts of deserts, there may be no vegetation at all. Elsewhere, plants grow far apart. Their roots absorb scarce water before it evaporates in the heat.
- **Desert Scrub** Semiarid areas and deserts with a little more rain support **desert scrub,** or low desert vegetation that needs little water. Some plants flower only when it rains, so that seeds have a better chance to survive.
- **Mediterranean Vegetation** Mediterranean vegetation includes grasses, shrubs, and low trees. These plants must hold water from the winter rains to survive warm, dry summers.
- **Temperate Grassland** Vast grasslands straddle regions with semiarid and humid continental climates. The wetter grasslands, in humid continental climates, have a mix of tall grasses and other plants that is sometimes called prairie.
- **Deciduous Forest** Marine west coast, humid subtropical, and humid continental climates all support forests of **deciduous trees,** or trees that lose their leaves in the fall.
- **Coniferous and Mixed Forest** These same climates also support areas of coniferous and mixed forest. **Coniferous trees** are trees that produce cones to carry seeds. They generally have needles, not leaves. These features protect trees in drier climates. Mixed forests combine both coniferous and deciduous trees.
- **Tundra** The tundra is an area of cold climate and low-lying vegetation. Tundra vegetation includes mosses, grasses, and low shrubs that bloom during the brief, cool summers.
- **Highland** In highland regions, vegetation depends on elevation, since temperatures drop as elevation rises. Tropical forests may grow at low elevations, with grasslands and coniferous forests farther up. Still higher, tundra vegetation may grow.
- **Ice Cap and Pack Ice** Around the poles, thick ice caps form on land. Masses of ice called pack ice cover the sea. No vegetation can grow there.

√ **Reading Check** What types of vegetation grow in deserts?

Differentiated Instruction

For Advanced Readers $L3$
Have students read *The Endless Steppe*. Using its location and description in the selection, have students identify its climate and vegetation regions. Then have students check their conclusions by locating Rubtsovsk in an atlas, encyclopedia, or on the Internet.

All in One **Foundations of Geography Teaching Resources,** *The Endless Steppe,* pp. 141–142

For Less Proficient Readers $L1$
To ensure students know how to read the natural vegetation map on page 53, have students complete *Reading a Natural Vegetation Map* in pairs.

All in One **Foundations of Geography Teaching Resources,** *Reading a Natural Vegetation Map,* p. 137

The World: Natural Vegetation

This map shows the natural vegetation regions of the world. The locations of these regions depend mainly on climate. Like the climates that support them, vegetation regions vary according to their distance from the Equator and the amount of precipitation they receive.

The Sahara ▶
The world's largest desert has vast sand dunes with little or no vegetation. This picture also shows an oasis, or a place in the desert where underground water allows trees or crops to grow.

MAP MASTER™
Skills Activity

Location In which parts of Earth do you find tropical rain forests? **Compare and Contrast** Find tropical wet climates on the map in the previous section titled The World: Climate Regions. How do those locations compare with the locations of tropical rain forests?

Go Online
PHSchool.com Use Web Code **lep-3214** for step-by-step **map skills practice.**

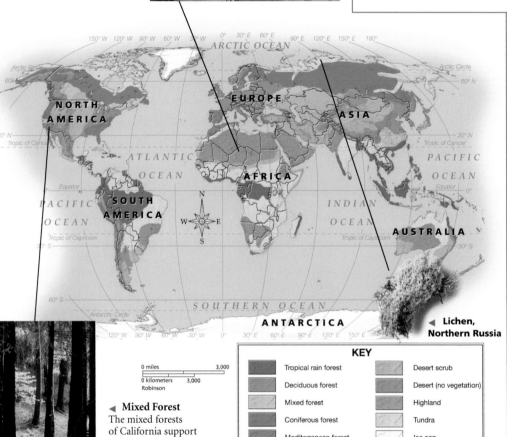

◀ **Lichen, Northern Russia**

KEY

	Tropical rain forest		Desert scrub
	Deciduous forest		Desert (no vegetation)
	Mixed forest		Highland
	Coniferous forest		Tundra
	Mediterranean forest		Ice cap
	Tropical savanna		Pack ice
	Temperate grassland		National border
			Disputed border

0 miles 3,000
0 kilometers 3,000
Robinson

◀ **Mixed Forest**
The mixed forests of California support trees such as pines, redwoods, and tan oaks.

Chapter 2 Section 4 **53**

Vertical Climate Zones 〔L2〕

Guided Instruction

- Read Vertical Climate Zones as a class. As you read, circulate to make sure students are able to answer the Reading Check question.

- Ask students **Why do mountains have a vertical climate?** *(Climate depends on elevation. Elevation changes the farther you go up a mountain causing the climate to change significantly.)*

- Ask students to predict how their clothing might change as they climb a mountain in a temperate climate. *(They might need shorts or light clothing at the base of the mountain; a jacket or coat in the coniferous forest; and polar gear as they climb toward the peak.)*

Independent Practice
Assign *Guided Reading and Review*.

All in One Foundations of Geography Teaching Resources, *Guided Reading and Review,* p. 119

Monitor Progress
Tell students to fill in the last column of their *Reading Readiness Guides*. Probe for what they learned that confirms or invalidates each statement.

All in One Foundations of Geography Teaching Resources, *Reading Readiness Guide,* p. 118

Skills for Life — Skills Mini Lesson

Transferring Information from One Medium to Another

1. Teach the skill using these skill steps: first, state the main idea you want to communicate; next, choose a visual aid such as a map, diagram, or graph that would communicate the information

clearly; finally, transfer each piece of data into the visual aid.

2. Help students practice the skill by summarizing the information in Vertical Climate Zones on page 54.

3. Have students apply the skill by transferring the main idea to a visual aid.

Answers

MAP MASTER™ Skills Activity **Location** near the Equator **Compare and Contrast** areas with tropical forests are similar to areas of tropical climates

Go Online PHSchool.com Students may practice their map skills using the interactive online version of this map.

Assess and Reteach

Assess Progress   `L2`

Have students complete the Section Assessment. Administer the *Section Quiz*.

All in One **Foundations of Geography Teaching Resources,** *Section Quiz,* p. 120

Reteach   `L1`

If students need more instruction, have them read this section in the Reading and Vocabulary Study Guide.

📖 **Foundations of Geography Reading and Vocabulary Study Guide,** pp. 22–24

Extend   `L3`

To extend the lesson, have students create a natural vegetation poster identifying at least five plants that are native to the climate region in which they live. The poster should include information about the climate region, the names of the plants and why they are suited to this particular region, and, if possible, illustrations.

All in One **Foundations of Geography Teaching Resources,** *Rubric for Assessing a Student Poster,* p. 150

Answer

✓ **Reading Check** The amount and types of vegetation decrease as the elevation increases until the cold temperature prevents any vegetation.

Section 4 Assessment

Key Terms
Students' sentences should reflect knowledge of each Key Term.

Target Reading Skill
Tundra vegetation includes mosses, grasses, and low shrubs that bloom during brief, cool summers. The examples of mosses and grasses provide clues to the meaning of the phrase.

Comprehension and Critical Thinking
1. (a) tropical, dry, temperate marine, temperate continental, and polar **(b)** Because different plants require different amounts of water, sun, and different temperatures, each climate region has its own types of vegetation. **(c)** Low-lying plants and scrub grow in climates with little precipitation and forests grow in climates with heavier precipitation.

Forested valley at the foot of Machapuchare, a mountain in Nepal

Vertical Climate Zones

The climate at the top of Mount Everest, in southern Asia, is like Antarctica's. But Mount Everest is near the Tropic of Cancer, far from the South Pole. It is so cold at the top of the mountain because the air becomes cooler as elevation increases. Mountains have vertical climate zones, where the climate and vegetation depend on elevation.

In a tropical region, vegetation that needs a tropical climate will grow only near the bottom of a mountain. Farther up is vegetation that can grow in a temperate climate. Near the top is vegetation that can grow in a polar climate.

Picture yourself on a hike up a mountain in a temperate climate. Grassland surrounds the base of the mountain, and temperatures are warm. You begin to climb and soon enter an area with more precipitation and lower temperatures than below. The grassland gives way to a coniferous forest.

As you continue to climb, you find only scattered, short trees. Finally, it is too cold even for them. There are only the low shrubs, short grasses, and mosses of a tundra. At the mountain's peak, you find permanent ice, where no vegetation grows.

✓ **Reading Check** How does vegetation change with elevation?

Section 4 Assessment

Key Terms
Review the key terms at the beginning of this section. Use each term in a sentence that explains its meaning.

🎯 Target Reading Skill
Find the phrase *tundra vegetation* on page 52. Use context to figure out its meaning. What do you think it means? What clues helped you find the meaning?

Comprehension and Critical Thinking
1. (a) List What are the five main types of climate?
(b) Evaluate How do differences in climate affect plant life?

(c) Analyze Why do low-lying plants, such as scrub or tundra, grow in some climates, while rich forests grow in others?
2. (a) Recall How do desert plants survive in dry climates?
(b) Transfer Information What features of the plants in your region allow them to grow in your region's climate?
3. (a) Define What is a vertical climate zone?
(b) Explain How do vertical climate zones affect vegetation on a mountain?
(c) Compare and Contrast Why is vegetation at the top of a tall mountain different from vegetation at the bottom?

Writing Activity
Look at the map titled The World: Natural Vegetation on page 53 in this section. Choose three places on the map that are in different natural vegetation regions. Then write a description of the types of plants you would expect to see if you visited each place you have chosen.

Writing Tip Since you are writing about three different types of natural vegetation, you may want to compare and contrast them. When you compare, you point out similarities. When you contrast, you focus on differences.

54 Foundations of Geography

---

2. (a) Desert plants have roots that absorb scarce water before it evaporates; some desert plants flower only when it rains so that as many seeds survive as possible. **(b)** Students' answers will vary by region.

3. (a) A vertical climate zone is one where the climate and vegetation depend on elevation. **(b)** The climate region at the bottom of a mountain can usually support a wide variety of vegetation because it is relatively warm. The climate region at the peak of a mountain

is usually much colder and supports less vegetation. **(c)** The climate at the top of a mountain is colder than the climate at the bottom.

Writing Activity
Use the *Rubric for Assessing a Writing Assignment* to evaluate students' essays.

All in One **Foundations of Geography Teaching Resources,** *Rubric for Assessing a Writing Assignment,* p. 145

2 Review and Assessment

◆ Chapter Summary

Section 1: Our Planet, Earth
- Earth's rotation on its axis changes day to night and night to day.
- The tilt of Earth's axis causes our seasons.

Section 2: Forces Shaping Earth
- Earth's three main layers are the crust, the mantle, and the core.
- Forces inside Earth move plates of crust to form mountains and volcanoes.
- Wind, water, and ice wear down and reshape Earth's surface.

Section 3: Climate and Weather
- Climate is the average weather in a region over a long period of time.
- Climate depends on latitude, landforms, and nearness to an ocean.
- Winds and ocean currents help spread Earth's warmth. They can also cause dangerous storms.

Section 4: How Climate Affects Vegetation
- Vegetation depends mainly on climate.
- Earth can be divided into several natural vegetation regions.
- Climate and vegetation change with elevation.

Delicate Arch, Utah

◆ Key Terms

Each of the statements below contains a key term from the chapter. If the statement is true, write *true*. If it is false, rewrite the statement to make it true.

1. Earth's movement around the sun is called rotation.

2. The mantle is a thick, rocky layer around Earth's core.

3. Earth's crust is at the center of the planet.

4. Magma is hot, flowing rock beneath Earth's surface.

5. The Appalachian Mountains have been worn down over time by erosion.

6. If you want to know how hot it will be tomorrow, you can look at a climate report.

7. Temperature measures how hot or how cold something is.

8. Vegetation is a term for the plants that grow in a region.

9. Deciduous forests grow in polar climates.

Chapter 2 **55**

┌ Vocabulary Builder ─

Revisit this chapter's high-use words:

standard	surge	marine
relative	splinter	humid
force	indirect	dense
collide	distribute	scatter

Ask students to review the definitions they recorded on their *Word Knowledge* worksheets.

All in One Foundations of Geography Teaching Resources, *Word Knowledge,* p. 125

Consider allowing students to earn extra credit if they use the words in their answers to the questions in the Chapter Review and Assessment. The words must be used correctly and in a natural context to win the extra points.

Review Chapter Content

- Review and revisit the major themes of this chapter by asking students to classify what Guiding Question each bulleted statement in the Chapter Summary answers. Have students write the Chapter Summary on a separate piece of paper. Then with a partner have them determine which Guiding Question applies to each statement and number the statements accordingly. Refer to page 1 in the Student Edition for the text of the Guiding Questions.

- Assign *Vocabulary Development* for students to review Key Terms.

  All in One Foundations of Geography Teaching Resources, *Vocabulary Development,* p. 144

Answers

Key Terms

1. False. Earth travels around the sun in an oval-shaped orbit.

2. True

3. False. Earth's core is at the center of the planet.

4. True

5. True

6. False. If you want to know how hot it will be tomorrow, you could look at a weather report.

7. True

8. True

9. False. Deciduous forests grow in marine west coast, humid subtropical, and humid continental climates.

...

Comprehension and Critical Thinking

10. (a) 24 **(b)** Earth is divided into 24 time zones because it takes 24 hours for Earth to complete one rotation.

11. (a) the summer solstice, or the longest day of the year **(b)** When a hemisphere tilts toward the sun, it receives direct sunlight, making summers hot. When a hemisphere tilts away from the sun, it receives indirect sunlight, making winters cold. **(c)** The sun is never directly overhead in Antarctica because it is in a high latitude, or polar zone, that is cold year round.

12. (a) three percent **(b)** Possible answer: Lakes, rivers, and ground water might freeze decreasing the fresh water supply.

13. (a) Wind is caused by air currents that follow regular patterns related to latitude. **(b)** Negative—tropical cyclones; hurricanes; tornadoes; Positive—wind and water can make climates milder.

14. (a) Ocean currents help distribute Earth's heat. Warm water flows away from the Equator and cold water moves away from the poles. **(b)** Water remains cooler as the air and land heats up in summer; so wind blowing over the water cools coastal land nearby.

15. (a) Different kinds of vegetation grow in each of the five broad types of climate areas because different plants require different amounts of water and sunlight and different temperatures. **(b)** Tropical climates with year-round rainfall will support a tropical rainforest, because such vegetation requires high rainfall.

Skills Practice
Paragraphs should include information about the average daily temperature changes from month to month and how the amount of precipitation stays about the same.

Writing Activity
Students' plant descriptions will vary but should include information about dry climates and desert vegetation regions.

All in One Foundations of Geography Teaching Resources, *Rubric for Assessing a Writing Assignment,* p. 145

◆ Comprehension and Critical Thinking

10. (a) Recall How many standard time zones is Earth divided into?
(b) Analyze How are time differences related to the rotation of Earth?

11. (a) Identify As Earth moves around the sun, what event happens about June 21?
(b) Explain How does Earth's movement make summers hot and winters cold?
(c) Apply Information Why is Antarctica cold even in summer?

12. (a) Recall How much of Earth's water is fresh?
(b) Predict If Earth's climate became colder, how might the fresh water supply be affected?

13. (a) Recall What causes winds?
(b) Contrast What are some negative and positive effects of wind and water in the tropics?

14. (a) Describe How do oceans shape climate?
(b) Synthesize Information Why do some coastal cities in the tropics stay cool?

15. (a) Describe How does climate affect vegetation?
(b) Evaluate A tropical climate has year-round rainfall. Can forests grow there? Explain why or why not.

◆ Skills Practice

Using Special Geography Graphs Review the steps you learned in the Skills For Life activity in this chapter. Then look at the climate graph for Helsinki, Finland, below. After you have analyzed the graph, write a paragraph that summarizes Helsinki's climate.

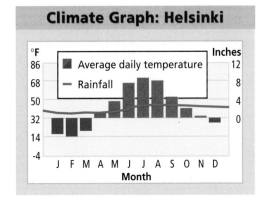

◆ Writing Activity: Science

Reread the descriptions of dry climates and of desert vegetation regions. Then design a plant that could live in these regions. Describe how it would get light, water, and nutrients.

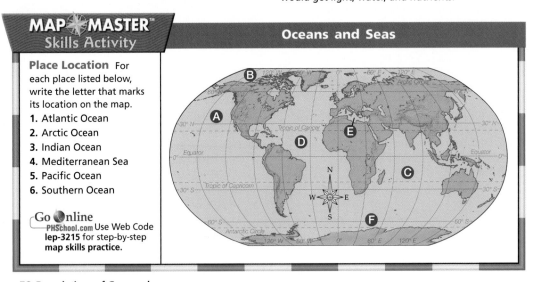

MAP MASTER Skills Activity
Oceans and Seas

Place Location For each place listed below, write the letter that marks its location on the map.
1. Atlantic Ocean
2. Arctic Ocean
3. Indian Ocean
4. Mediterranean Sea
5. Pacific Ocean
6. Southern Ocean

Go Online PHSchool.com Use Web Code **lep-3215** for step-by-step map skills practice.

MAP MASTER Skills Activity

1. D   **2.** B
3. C   **4.** G
5. E   **6.** A
7. F

Go Online PHSchool.com Students may practice their map skills using the interactive online version of this map.

Standardized Test Prep

Test-Taking Tips

Some questions on standardized tests ask you to use map keys. Read the precipitation map key below. Then follow the tips to answer the sample question.

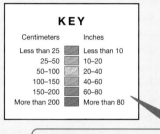

KEY

Centimeters	Inches
Less than 25	Less than 10
25–50	10–20
50–100	20–40
100–150	40–60
150–200	60–80
More than 200	More than 80

TIP On a map key, the colors line up with the data. To find information, read the numbers to the left or right of a given color.

Pick the letter that best answers the question.
On a precipitation map, the southern coastal states are colored dark green. According to the key at the left, how many inches of rain does this region get each year?

A 20–40
B 60–80
C 50–100
D 150–200

TIP To be sure you understand what the question is asking, restate it in your own words: *The color DARK GREEN on the map key stands for how many inches of rain each year?*

Think It Through The question asks about inches of rain, but the answers C and D show numbers from the centimeter column. The numbers 20–40 (answer A) are next to yellow, not dark green. The numbers 60–80 are next to dark green in the inches column. The answer is B.

Practice Questions

Use the tips above and other tips in this book to help you answer the following questions:

1. When the Northern Hemisphere has days and nights of equal length, it is
   A summer solstice.
   B spring equinox.
   C New Year's Day.
   D winter solstice.

2. Which of the following is NOT an example of a landform?
   A a mountain
   B a plateau
   C a plain
   D an atmosphere

3. In which vegetation region would you find a plant with shallow roots, meant to absorb water before it evaporates?
   A desert
   B deciduous forest
   C coniferous forest
   D tropical savanna

Study the following map key and answer the question that follows.

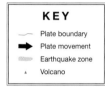

KEY

- Plate boundary
- Plate movement
- Earthquake zone
- Volcano

4. On a map with this key, you would find places where earthquakes happen by looking for
   A a brown area.
   B a red triangle.
   C a black arrow.
   D a black line.

Go Online
PHSchool.com
Use Web Code lea-3201 for a **Chapter 2 self-test**.

Standardized Test Prep

Answers

1. B
2. D
3. A
4. A

Go Online
PHSchool.com Students may use the Chapter 2 self-test on PHSchool.com to prepare for the Chapter Test.

Assessment Resources

Use *Chapter Tests A and B* to assess students' mastery of the chapter content.

Foundations of Geography Teaching Resources, Chapter Tests A and B, pp. 151–156
Tests also available on the *ExamView Test Bank CD-ROM*.

- *ExamView Test Bank CD-ROM*

Use a benchmark test to evaluate students' cumulative understanding of what they have learned in Chapters 1 and 2.

Foundations of Geography Benchmark Test 1, **AYP Monitoring Assessments**, pp. 81–84.

Earth's Human Geography

Overview

1 Section

Population
1. Learn about population distribution.
2. Explore population density.
3. Investigate population growth.

2 Section

Migration
1. Learn about migration, or people's movement from one region to another.
2. Investigate urbanization, or people's movement to cities.

3 Section

Economic Systems
1. Examine different kinds of economies.
2. Investigate levels of economic development.
3. Study global trade patterns.

4 Section

Political Systems
1. Examine different types of states.
2. Investigate types of government.
3. Learn about alliances and international organizations.

DISCOVERY CHANNEL SCHOOL Video

Migration: People on the Move
Length: 3 minutes, 57 seconds
Use with Section 2

This segment is an overview of human migration and the reasons for it. It discusses human migration in Senegal and the problems that it causes.

Technology Resources

Go Online
PHSchool.com

Students use embedded Web codes to access Internet activities, chapter self-tests, and additional map practice. They may also access Dorling Kindersley's Online Desk Reference to learn more about each country they study.

Interactive Textbook

Use the Interactive Textbook to make content and concepts come alive through animations, videos, and activities that accompany the complete basal text—online and on CD-ROM.

PRENTICE HALL
TeacherEXPRESS™
Plan · Teach · Assess

Use this complete suite of powerful teaching tools to make planning lessons and administering tests quicker and easier.

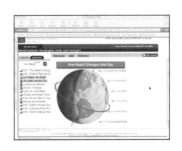

Reading and Assessment

Reading and Vocabulary Instruction

⟳ Model the Target Reading Skill

Compare and Contrast Remind students that when they compare and contrast, they analyze two objects or situations to find their similarities and differences. Model comparing and contrasting using information from page 75 of the Student Edition. Draw a Venn diagram on the board. Label the left-hand section "capitalism," the middle section "both," and the right-hand section "communism." Tell students that they make comparisons when they find similarities and contrasts when they find differences.

Ask yourself the following questions aloud, as you fill in the diagram. "What is the same about capitalism and communism? *(they are types of economic systems.)* What are the differences between capitalism and communism? *(capitalism: businesses are privately owned; communism: the government has control of the economy)* How can I summarize these comparisons and contrasts? *(Capitalism and communism are both types of economic systems, but in communism the government controls the entire economy, and capitalism has a free-market economy.)*"

Use the following worksheets from All-in-One Foundations of Geography Teaching Resources (pp. 177–179) to support this chapter's Target Reading Skill.

Vocabulary Builder
High-Use Academic Words

Use these steps to teach this chapter's high-use words:

1. Have students rate how well they know each word on their Word Knowledge worksheets (All-in-One Foundations of Geography Teaching Resources, p. 180).
2. Pronounce each word and ask students to repeat it.
3. Give students a brief definition or sample sentence (provided on TE pp. 61, 68, 75, and 81).
4. Work with students as they fill in the "Definition or Example" column of their Word Knowledge worksheets.

Assessment

Formal Assessment

Test students' understanding of core knowledge and skills.

Chapter Tests A and B, Foundations of Geography Teaching Resources, pp. 199–204

Customize the Chapter Tests to suit your needs.
ExamView Test Bank CD-ROM

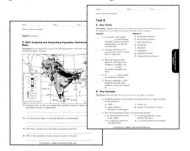

Skills Assessment

Assess geographic literacy.

MapMaster Skills, Student Edition pp. 61, 62, 63, 69, 77, 86

Assess reading skills.

Target Reading Skills, Student Edition, pp. 62, 68, 76, 81, and in Section Assessments

Chapter 3 Assessment, Foundations of Geography Reading and Vocabulary Study Guide, p. 38

Performance Assessment

Assess students' performance on this chapter's Writing Activities using rubrics from All-in-One Foundations of Geography Teaching Resources.

Rubric for Assessing a Writing Assignment, p. 197

Rubric for Assessing a Bar Graph, p. 198

Assess students' work through performance tasks.

Small Group Activity: Making an Immigration Map, All-in-One Foundations of Geography Teaching Resources, pp. 183–186

Online Assessment

Have students check their own understanding.

Chapter Self-Test

Section 1 Population

 1.5 periods, .75 block

Social Studies Objectives
1. Learn about population distribution.
2. Explore population density.
3. Investigate population growth.

Reading/Language Arts Objective
Compare and contrast to analyze information.

Prepare to Read	**Instructional Resources**	**Differentiated Instruction**
Build Background Knowledge Ask students to guess the population densities of local cities. **Set a Purpose for Reading** Have students evaluate statements on the *Reading Readiness Guide.* **Preview Key Terms** Teach the section's Key Terms. **Target Reading Skill** Introduce the section's Target Reading Skill of **comparing and contrasting**.	**All in One Foundations of Geography Teaching Resources** L2 Reading Readiness Guide, p. 162 L2 Compare and Contrast, p. 177	**Spanish Reading and Vocabulary Study Guide** L1 Chapter 3, Section 1, pp. 19–20 ELL

Instruct	**Instructional Resources**	**Differentiated Instruction**
Population Distribution Ask questions about factors that affect population size and distribution. **Target Reading Skill** Review **comparing and contrasting**. **Population Density** Compare and contrast population density and population distribution. **Population Growth** Discuss the relationship between birthrate, death rate, and population.	**All in One Foundations of Geography Teaching Resources** L2 Guided Reading and Review, p. 163 L2 Reading Readiness Guide, p. 162 **Foundations of Geography Transparencies** L2 Section Reading Support Transparency FG 49	**All in One Foundations of Geography Teaching Resources** L3 Analyzing Statistics, p. 187 AR, GT L3 Enrichment, p. 181 AR, GT **Teacher's Edition** L1 For Less Proficient Readers, TE pp. 62, 63 L1 For Special Needs Students, TE p. 62 L3 For Gifted and Talented, TE pp. 63, 64 L3 For Advanced Readers, TE p. 64 **Student Edition on Audio CD** L1 Chapter 3, Section 1 ELL, LPR, SN

Assess and Reteach	**Instructional Resources**	**Differentiated Instruction**
Assess Progress Evaluate student comprehension with the section assessment and section quiz. **Reteach** Assign the Reading and Vocabulary Study Guide to help struggling students. **Extend** Extend the lesson by assigning an Internet activity.	**All in One Foundations of Geography Teaching Resources** L2 Section Quiz, p. 164 Rubric for Assessing a Writing Assignment, p. 197 **Reading and Vocabulary Study Guide** L1 Chapter 3, Section 1, pp. 26–28 **PHSchool.com** L3 **For:** Environmental and Global Issues: Evaluating Solutions **Web Code:** led-3300	**Spanish Support** L2 Section Quiz (Spanish), p. 21 ELL

Key
L1 Basic to Average   L3 Average to Advanced
L2 For All Students

LPR Less Proficient Readers
AR Advanced Readers
SN Special Needs Students

GT Gifted and Talented
ELL English Language Learners

Section 2 **Migration**

 3 periods, 1.5 blocks (includes Skills for Life)

Social Studies Objectives
1. Learn about migration, or people's movement from one region to another.
2. Investigate urbanization, or people's movement to cities.

Reading/Language Arts Objective
Identify contrasts to understand how situations differ.

Prepare to Read

Build Background Knowledge
Have students brainstorm why people move to different places.

Set a Purpose for Reading
Have students evaluate statements on the *Reading Readiness Guide.*

Preview Key Terms
Teach the section's Key Terms.

Target Reading Skill
Introduce the section's Target Reading Skill of **identifying contrasts.**

Instructional Resources

All in One Foundations of Geography Teaching Resources
- **L2** Reading Readiness Guide, p. 166
- **L2** Identify Contrasts, p. 178

Differentiated Instruction

Spanish Reading and Vocabulary Study Guide
- **L1** Chapter 3, Section 2, pp. 21–22 ELL

Instruct

Why People Migrate
Ask questions about migration and discuss the push-pull theory.

Target Reading Skill
Review **identifying contrasts.**

Urbanization
Ask about urbanization and discuss some problems it can cause.

Instructional Resources

All in One Foundations of Geography Teaching Resources
- **L2** Guided Reading and Review, p. 167
- **L2** Reading Readiness Guide, p. 166
- **L2** Message from the Rain Forest Amerindians, p. 188

Foundations of Geography Transparencies
- **L2** Section Reading Support Transparency FG 50
- **L2** Transparency B2: Flow Chart

World Studies Video Program
- **L2** Migration: People on the Move

Differentiated Instruction

All in One Foundations of Geography Teaching Resources
- **L3** Small Group Activity: Making an Immigration Map, pp. 183–186 AR, GT
- **L2** Skills for Life, p. 182 AR, GT, LPR, SN

Teacher's Edition
- **L3** For Advanced Readers, TE p. 70
- **L1** For English Language Learners, TE p. 70

Spanish Support
- **L2** Guided Reading and Review (Spanish), p. 22 ELL

Assess and Reteach

Assess Progress
Evaluate student comprehension with the section assessment and section quiz.

Reteach
Assign the Reading and Vocabulary Study Guide to help struggling students.

Extend
Extend the lesson by having students research an American who immigrated to the United States.

Instructional Resources

All in One Foundations of Geography Teaching Resources
- **L2** Section Quiz, p. 168
  Rubric for Assessing a Writing Assignment, p. 197

Reading and Vocabulary Study Guide
- **L1** Chapter 3, Section 2, pp. 29–31

Differentiated Instruction

Spanish Support
- **L2** Section Quiz (Spanish), p. 23 ELL

Foundations of Geography Transparencies
- **L3** Color Transparency FG 5: The World: Continents and Oceans (Base) AR, GT
- **L3** Color Transparency FG 16: The World: Population Density (Overlay) AR, GT

Teacher's Edition
- **L1** For Special Needs Students, TE p. 73

Social Studies Skills Tutor CD-ROM
- **L1** Analyzing and Interpreting Special Purpose Maps ELL, LPR, SN

Key

- **L1** Basic to Average
- **L3** Average to Advanced
- **L2** For All Students

- LPR Less Proficient Readers
- AR Advanced Readers
- SN Special Needs Students

- GT Gifted and Talented
- ELL English Language Learners

Section 3 Economic Systems

 1.5 periods, .75 block

Social Studies Objectives
1. Examine different kinds of economies.
2. Investigate levels of economic development.
3. Study global trade patterns.

Reading/Language Arts Objective
Make comparisons to understand what things have in common.

Prepare to Read	**Instructional Resources**	**Differentiated Instruction**
Build Background Knowledge Ask students to brainstorm the meaning of *economy*. **Set a Purpose for Reading** Have students evaluate statements on the *Reading Readiness Guide*. **Preview Key Terms** Teach the section's Key Terms. **Target Reading Skill** Introduce the section's Target Reading Skill of **making comparisons**.	**All in One Foundations of Geography Teaching Resources** L2 Reading Readiness Guide, p. 170 L2 Make Comparisons, p. 179	**Spanish Reading and Vocabulary Study Guide** L1 Chapter 3, Section 3, pp. 23–24 ELL

Instruct	**Instructional Resources**	**Differentiated Instruction**
Different Kinds of Economies Discuss various types of economies. **Levels of Economic Development** Discuss the differences between developed and developing countries' economies. **Target Reading Skill** Review **making comparisons**. **World Trade Patterns** Ask questions about and discuss world trade.	**All in One Foundations of Geography Teaching Resources** L2 Guided Reading and Review, p. 171 L2 Reading Readiness Guide, p. 170 **Foundations of Geography Transparencies** L2 Section Reading Support Transparency FG 51	**Teacher's Edition** L1 For Less Proficient Readers, TE p. 77 L3 For Gifted and Talented, TE p. 77 **Spanish Support** L2 Guided Reading and Review (Spanish), p. 24 ELL

Assess and Reteach	**Instructional Resources**	**Differentiated Instruction**
Assess Progress Evaluate student comprehension with the section assessment and section quiz. **Reteach** Assign the Reading and Vocabulary Study Guide to help struggling students. **Extend** Extend the lesson by assigning an Internet activity.	**All in One Foundations of Geography Teaching Resources** L2 Section Quiz, p. 172 Rubric for Assessing a Writing Assignment, p. 197 **Reading and Vocabulary Study Guide** L1 Chapter 3, Section 3, pp. 32–34 **PHSchool.com** L3 **For:** Environmental and Global Issues: Trade in a Global Economy **Web Code:** led-3306	**Spanish Support** L2 Section Quiz (Spanish), p. 25 ELL

Key

L1 Basic to Average   L3 Average to Advanced

L2 For All Students

LPR Less Proficient Readers

AR Advanced Readers

SN Special Needs Students

GT Gifted and Talented

ELL English Language Learners

Section 4 Political Systems

 4.5 periods, 2.25 blocks (includes Chapter Review and Assessment, and Literature)

Social Studies Objectives
1. Examine different types of states.
2. Investigate types of government.
3. Learn about alliances and international organizations.

Reading/Language Arts Objective
Recognize contrast signal words to understand how things are different.

Prepare to Read

Build Background Knowledge
Discuss different types of leaders.

Set a Purpose for Reading
Have students evaluate statements on the *Reading Readiness Guide.*

Preview Key Terms
Teach the section's Key Terms.

Target Reading Skill
Introduce the section's Target Reading Skill of **recognizing contrast signal words.**

Instructional Resources

All in One Foundations of Geography Teaching Resources
- L2 Reading Readiness Guide, p. 174
- L2 Identify Contrasts, p. 178

Differentiated Instruction

Spanish Reading and Vocabulary Study Guide
- L1 Chapter 3 Section 4, pp. 25–26 ELL

Instruct

Target Reading Skill
Review **using contrast signal words.**

Types of States
Discuss characteristics of different kinds of states.

Types of Government
Compare and contrast different types of government.

International Organizations
Discuss the purpose of alliances and international organizations.

Instructional Resources

All in One Foundations of Geography Teaching Resources
- L2 Guided Reading and Review, p. 175
- L2 Reading Readiness Guide, p. 174

Foundations of Geography Transparencies
- L2 Section Reading Support Transparency FG 52
- L2 Transparency B3: Tree Map/Flow Chart

Differentiated Instruction

All in One Foundations of Geography Teaching Resources
- L3 Your Government Has Returned to You! pp. 189–190 AR, GT
- L2 Creating Paragraph Outlines, p. 195 AR, GT, LPR, SN

Teacher's Edition
- L3 For Advanced Readers, TE p. 82

Spanish Support
- L2 Guided Reading and Review (Spanish), p. 26 ELL

Assess and Reteach

Assess Progress
Evaluate student comprehension with the section assessment and section quiz.

Reteach
Assign the Reading and Vocabulary Study Guide to help struggling students.

Extend
Extend the lesson by having students research alliances or international organizations from the section.

Instructional Resources

All in One Foundations of Geography Teaching Resources
- L2 Section Quiz, p. 176
  Rubric for Assessing a Writing Assignment, p. 197
- L2 Vocabulary Development, p. 196
- L2 Word Knowledge, p. 180
  Rubric for Assessing a Bar Graph, p. 198
- L2 Chapter Tests A and B, pp. 199–204

Reading and Vocabulary Study Guide
- L3 Chapter 3 Section 4 pp. 35–37

Differentiated Instruction

All in One Foundations of Geography Teaching Resources
- L3 Hatchet, pp. 191–194 AR, GT

Spanish Support
- L2 Section Quiz (Spanish), p. 27 ELL
- L2 Chapter Summary (Spanish), p. 28 ELL
- L2 Vocabulary Development (Spanish), p. 29 ELL

Key
L1 Basic to Average	L3 Average to Advanced	LPR Less Proficient Readers	GT Gifted and Talented
L2 For All Students		AR Advanced Readers	ELL English Language Learners
		SN Special Needs Students	

Professional Development

Reading Background

Structured Silent Reading

In this chapter, students will use the Structured Silent Reading technique. To achieve success, always pose a question for students to answer when they finish reading. If students have trouble reading large sections, break the text into chunks of one to four paragraphs, and give students a question to answer for each one. You may ask students to preview the Reading Check question for a selection and then read to find the answer. Students may also preview the headings to develop their own questions before they read.

Model this approach using the paragraph under the heading *New Population Clusters* on page 61 of the Student Edition. Point out that headings in the text are a good place to start when thinking of a question. Think aloud: *The heading for this paragraph is "New Population Clusters." Population means people, and clusters means groups. It must be about how groups of people came to be. So I am going to read to answer this question: "How did new groups of population form?"*

Have students use this method for other selections. Suggest to students that they write down their questions before reading.

Key Terms

Tell students that the Key Terms in Chapter 3 often appear in the news. Challenge them to find at least three of these Key Terms from the chapter used in their daily lives:

population, immigrants, urbanization, capitalism, developing nations

Encourage students to look at newspapers and magazines, listen to the radio, and watch television to find uses of these words. As "evidence," have them bring in a newspaper clipping with the word or write down the sentence in which the word was used during a radio or television broadcast, and note the time and date of the broadcast.

World Studies Background

People Counting People

Demography can trace its beginnings to the work of an English scholar named John Graunt. In 1662, Graunt published his then unique analysis of over fifty years of death and baptism records. During the next century, nations began conducting basic censuses. In 1790, the United States government conducted the first nation-wide census for a political purpose; the Constitution mandates that a census of the United States be taken every ten years because population determines representation in the House of Representatives. The idea caught on, and Britain took its first census in 1801. In 1953, China became the last major area to release its census data. Today, demographers have access to vital statistics such as births, deaths, and marriages, and to census data from virtually the entire world.

Worldwide Urbanization

Urbanization is a worldwide trend, although high levels of urbanization are becoming more common in developing countries. The top ten largest urban centers in 1975 were all in developed countries, including New York, Paris, France, and Beijing, China. In 2000, four of the top ten urban centers were in the developing nations of India and Bangladesh.

Infoplease® provides a wealth of useful information for the classroom. You can use this resource to strengthen your background on the subjects covered in this chapter. Have students visit this advertising-free site as a starting point for projects requiring research.

 Use Web code **led-3304** for **Infoplease**.

Discussion Ideas

Discussing what students have read is important for them to absorb information. Empower students by having them provide topics for discussion. Explain that they must begin with a strong idea, or seed, to spark a good discussion. The following questions will motivate students to come up with strong seeds for discussion:

What don't I understand?
What have I learned that I did not know before?
What is interesting or surprising?
What words are confusing?
What reminds me of other things I know?

Write the questions on the board, and have students read *Population Growth* on pages 64–66 of the Student Edition. Ask students to answer one of the questions above on an index card. *(For example: I am surprised that large increases in population could drain Earth of its resources. I wonder what we can do to prevent that from happening?)* When students have finished, put the index cards into a bowl. Have students take turns pulling one out and reading it to the class, and discuss each one for five minutes.

Making Choices

Help students to build their understanding of Key Terms and high-use words from the chapter by asking them to make choices between correct and incorrect examples of the words.

Word: *vary*
Example 1: I eat something different for lunch every day. *(correct)*
Example 2: I always eat chicken for dinner.

Word: *immigrants*
Example 1: People move from the country to the city looking for jobs.
Example 2: Many people move from Mexico to the United States each year. *(correct)*

Word: *consumer*
Example 1: Nancy sells her food at the grocery store.
Example 2: Nancy buys her food at the grocery store. *(correct)*

Word: *dispute*
Example 1: Frank argued with his brother over who would play with the toy. *(correct)*
Example 2: Frank and his brother shared the toy.

UNICEF

One of the best-known organizations in the world is UNICEF, the United Nations Children's Fund. Originally created in 1946 to feed the starving children of postwar Europe and China, it was so successful that it was made a permanent organization in 1953. The organization has grown into a powerful and compassionate group of over 7,000 people working in 158 countries "to overcome the obstacles that poverty, violence, disease and discrimination place in a child's path." UNICEF provides food, vaccinations, and education to children around the world, but focuses its efforts on improving the lives of children in developing nations.

Thomas Malthus

In 1798, English writer Thomas Malthus published a book on population. Malthus expressed concern that the world's population was growing too quickly. He believed that future generations would not be able to raise enough food to keep up with population growth. He predicted widespread misery and starvation unless population growth slowed. Although some of Malthus' ideas have been substantiated, others have proven incorrect.

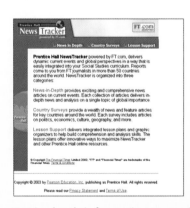

Get in-depth information on topics of global importance with **Prentice Hall Newstracker,** powered by FT.com

Use Web code **led-3305** for **Prentice Hall Newstracker.**

Chapter 3

Guiding Questions

Remind students about the Guiding Questions introduced at the beginning of the book.

Section 1 relates to **Guiding Question ⑤**

How do people use the world's natural resources? *(Many forests are disappearing as the growing world population uses trees for wood and fuel.)*

Section 2 relates to **Guiding Question ②**

How have people's ways of life changed over time? *(Since the 1800s, more people have moved from the countryside to cities.)*

Section 3 relates to **Guiding Question ⑤**

How do people use the world's natural resources? *(Some developing nations sell natural resources, such as oil, to developed nations.)*

Section 4 relates to **Guiding Question ④**

What types of government exist in the world today? *(States are controlled by different types of governments. These include absolute monarchies, dicatorships, oligarchies, constitutional monarchies, and representative democracies.)*

⤵ Target Reading Skill

In this chapter, students will learn and apply the reading skill of comparing and contrasting. Use the following worksheets to help students practice this skill:

All in One **Foundations of Geography Teaching Resources,** *Compare and Contrast,* p. 177; *Identify Contrasts,* p. 178; *Make Comparisons,* p. 179

Chapter 3 Earth's Human Geography

Chapter Preview

This chapter will introduce you to Earth's human geography, or the patterns of human activity on Earth.

Section 1
Population

Section 2
Migration

Section 3
Economic Systems

Section 4
Political Systems

↻ Target Reading Skill

Comparison and Contrast In this chapter you will focus on the text structure by learning how to compare and contrast. Comparing and contrasting can help you to sort out and analyze information.

▶ Woman harvesting rice on a terrace built by people in southern China

58 Foundations of Geography

Bibliography

For the Teacher
Gilbert, Geoffrey. *World Population: A Reference Handbook.* ABC-CLIO, 2001.
Pinder, John. *The European Union: A Very Short Introduction.* Oxford University Press, 2001.
Spellman, William M. *The Global Community: Migration and the Making of the Modern World.* Sutton Publishing, 2002.

For the Student
L1 Giesecke, Ernestine. *Governments Around the World (Kid's Guide).* Heinemean Library, 2000.
L2 Press, Petra. *European Union.* World Almanac, 2003.
L3 Tarsitano, Frank. *United Nations.* World Almanac, 2003.

Reach Into Your Background Ask students to study the photograph on pp. 58–59. Direct their attention to the caption. Tell students that in this chapter they will learn about the world's urban and rural populations, or populations in cities and the countryside. Ask them if they live in an urban or rural community. Ask students if they think the woman in the picture lives in an urban or rural area. How do they know? (*The woman probably lives in a rural area because she is working on a farm.*)

Chapter Resources

Teaching Resources

L2 Vocabulary Development, p. 196
L2 Skills for Life, p. 182
L2 Chapter Tests A and B, pp. 199–204

Spanish Support

L2 Spanish Chapter Summary, p. 28
L2 Spanish Vocabulary Development, p. 29

Media and Technology

L1 Student Edition on Audio CD
L1 Guided Reading Audiotapes, English and Spanish
L2 Social Studies Skills Tutor CD-ROM
ExamView Test Bank CD-ROM

DISCOVERY World Studies
CHANNEL Video Program
SCHOOL

Interactive Textbook

PRENTICE HALL
TeacherEXPRESS
Plan • Teach • Assess

Objectives
Social Studies
1. Learn about population distribution.
2. Explore population density.
3. Investigate population growth.

Reading/Language Arts
Compare and contrast to analyze information.

Prepare to Read

Build Background Knowledge L2

Tell students that in this section they will learn about where on Earth people live, and why they might choose to live there. To introduce the topic, write the names of two locations in your state with which students will be familiar. One should have a high population density and one should have a low population density. Ask students to predict in which location more people live and in which location less people live and why, then conduct an Idea Wave (TE, p.T35) to get students to share their ideas. After they read the section, ask them if their predictions were correct.

Set a Purpose for Reading L2

■ Preview the Objectives.

■ Read each statement in the *Reading Readiness Guide* aloud. Ask students to mark the statements true or false.

  All in One **Foundations of Geography Teaching Resources,** *Reading Readiness Guide,* p. 162

■ Have students discuss the statements in pairs or groups of four, then mark their worksheets again. Use the Numbered Heads participation strategy (TE, p. T36) to call on students to share their group's perspectives.

Vocabulary Builder
Preview Key Terms L2

Pronounce each Key Term, and then ask students to say the word with you. Provide a simple explanation such as, "Demography is the study of where people live and why."

Prepare to Read

Objectives
In this section you will
1. Learn about population distribution.
2. Explore population density.
3. Investigate population growth.

Taking Notes
Copy the concept web below. As you read this section, fill in the web with information about the causes and effects of population density and of population growth. Add more ovals as needed.

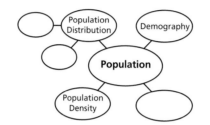

Target Reading Skill

Comparison and Contrast Comparing and contrasting can help you sort out information. When you compare, you examine the similarities between things. When you contrast, you look at the differences. As you read this section, compare and contrast population distribution and population density. Look for the similarities and differences between these two concepts.

Key Terms
- **population** (pahp yuh LAY shun) *n.* total number of people in an area
- **population distribution** (pahp yuh LAY shun dis trih BYOO shun) *n.* the way the population is spread out over an area
- **demography** (dih MAH gruh fee) *n.* the science that studies population distribution and change
- **population density** (pahp yuh LAY shun DEN suh tee) *n.* the average number of people per square mile or square kilometer
- **birthrate** (BURTH rayt) *n.* the number of live births each year per 1,000 people
- **death rate** (deth rayt) *n.* the number of deaths each year per 1,000 people

Population Distribution

The world's **population,** or total number of people, lives in uneven clusters on Earth's surface. Some places have many people. Other places are almost empty. **Population distribution** is the way the population is spread out over an area.

Demography is the science that tries to explain how populations change and why population distribution is uneven. Demographers study rates of birth, marriage, and death. And they ask why people move from one place to another.

Population and Places People usually don't move without a good reason. People may move because they can live better in a new place. Other times, people are forced to move, or they move because they cannot feed their families. However, as long as people can make a living where they are, they usually stay in that area. So, regions with large populations tend to keep them.

A crowded village on the Nile River near Aswan, Egypt

60 Foundations of Geography

Target Reading Skill L2

Compare and Contrast Point out the Target Reading Skill. Tell students that when they compare and contrast information, they identify similarities and differences.

Provide an example of comparing and contrasting by reading the paragraph on p. 63, and then identifying the similarities and differences between Japan and Canada. (*Similarities: Both countries have populations in the millions. Differences: Canada is huge in land area, yet has a population of 32 million people, and a population density of about 9 people per square mile; Japan is small in land area and has a population of 127 million people.*)

Give students *Compare and Contrast.* Have them complete the activity in groups.

  All in One **Foundations of Geography Teaching Resources,** *Compare and Contrast,* p. 177

Population and History In the past, most people lived on farms where they grew their own food. They lived where the climate provided enough water and warm weather to support crops. Regions with a long history of farming, good soil, and plenty of water became crowded. These regions still have large populations. Most places too cold or too dry for farming still have small populations.

New Population Clusters However, after about 1800, improved transportation and new ways of making a living changed things. Railroads and steamships made it easier for people to move long distances, even across oceans. New jobs in factories and offices meant that more people were living in cities, where they could make a living without farming the land. Crowded cities grew in regions that once had few people, such as the United States, Australia, and northern Europe.

Villages in France have grown through centuries of farming.

✓ **Reading Check** Why are some parts of the world more crowded than others?

Instruct

Population Distribution L2

Guided Instruction
- **Vocabulary Builder** Clarify the high-use word **cluster** before reading.

- Read Population Distribution using the Structured Silent Reading strategy (TE, p. T34).

- Discuss with students why some regions of the world have larger populations than others. Ask **What do regions with larger populations have in common?** (*Generally, they are regions with good soil and plenty of water.*)

- Ask **How did changes in technology affect the distribution of population?** (*The inventions of railroads and steamships made it easier for people to move long distances; the development of factories meant that people did not need to live on land where they could farm to make a living; cities began to develop as people moved to obtain jobs in the new industries.*)

Independent Practice
Have students create the Taking Notes concept web on a blank piece of paper. Then have them begin to fill in the ovals with the information they have just learned. Briefly model how to fill in the graphic organizer by adding one detail about population distribution or demography.

Monitor Progress
As students fill in the graphic organizer, circulate and make sure that individuals are choosing the correct details. Provide assistance as needed.

Answers

✓ **Reading Check** Some parts of the world are more crowded because they have good soil and plenty of water for farming or cities have grown up there.

MAP MASTER Skills Activity **Identify** parts of North America, South America, Europe, Asia, Africa **Analyze** Asia

Go Online PHSchool.com Students may practice their map skills using the interactive online version of this map.

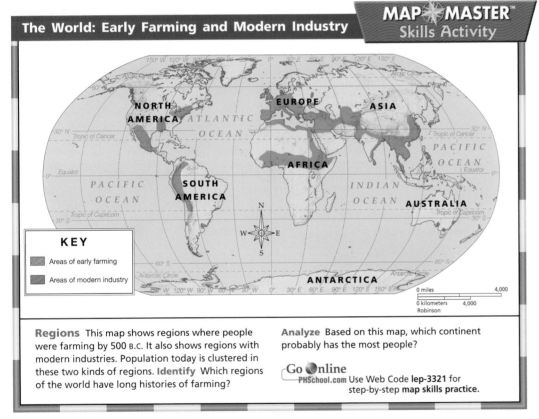

MAP MASTER Skills Activity

The World: Early Farming and Modern Industry

KEY
- Areas of early farming
- Areas of modern industry

Regions This map shows regions where people were farming by 500 B.C. It also shows regions with modern industries. Population today is clustered in these two kinds of regions. **Identify** Which regions of the world have long histories of farming?

Analyze Based on this map, which continent probably has the most people?

Go Online PHSchool.com Use Web Code lep-3321 for step-by-step **map skills practice**.

Chapter 3 Section 1 **61**

Target Reading Skill

Compare and Contrast As a follow up, ask students to answer the Target Reading Skill question in the Student Edition. *(Population density is the average number of people who live in a square mile or square kilometer. Population distribution is the number of people who actually live in an area.)*

Population Density

Guided Instruction

- **Vocabulary Builder** Clarify the high-use word **vary** before reading.

- With students, read about the differences between population density and distribution in Population Density.

- Ask **What is population density?** *(the average number of people living in one square mile or square kilometer)* **How does this differ from population distribution?** *(Population distribution gives actual numbers of people for an area.)*

- Have students find the region where their community is located on the map on pages 62 and 63. Discuss whether your area has a high or low population density. Then have students speculate why. *(Answers will vary, but student answers should give the general population density for their community and why.)*

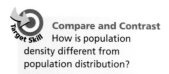

Compare and Contrast How is population density different from population distribution?

Population Density

How many people live in your neighborhood? How big is that neighborhood? If you take the population of an area and divide it by the size of that area in square miles or square kilometers, you can get a sense of how crowded or empty that area is. The average number of people per square mile or square kilometer is called **population density.**

Population distribution and population density both describe where people live. Population density differs from population distribution, however, because it gives an average number of people for an area. Population distribution gives actual numbers of people for an area.

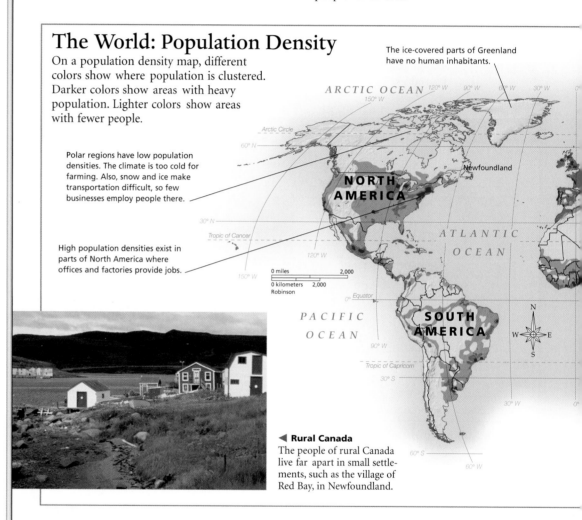

The World: Population Density

On a population density map, different colors show where population is clustered. Darker colors show areas with heavy population. Lighter colors show areas with fewer people.

The ice-covered parts of Greenland have no human inhabitants.

Polar regions have low population densities. The climate is too cold for farming. Also, snow and ice make transportation difficult, so few businesses employ people there.

High population densities exist in parts of North America where offices and factories provide jobs.

◀ **Rural Canada**
The people of rural Canada live far apart in small settlements, such as the village of Red Bay, in Newfoundland.

Differentiated Instruction

For Less Proficient Readers L1

Have students read this section in the Reading and Vocabulary Study Guide. This version provides basic-level instruction in an interactive format with questions and write-on lines.

📖 Chapter 3, Section 1, **Foundations of Geography Reading and Vocabulary Study Guide,** pp. 26–28

For Special Needs Students L1

Have students read the section as they listen to the recording on the Student Edition on Audio CD. Check for comprehension by pausing the CD and asking students to share their answers to the Reading Check questions.

⊙ Chapter 3, Section 1, **Student Edition on Audio CD**

Population density varies from one area to another. In a country with a high density, such as Japan, people are crowded together. Almost half of Japan's 127 million people live on only 17 percent of the land, or an area the size of West Virginia. In Tokyo, there is a population density of more than 25,000 people per square mile (9,664 per square kilometer). In contrast, Canada has a low overall population density. It has about 9 people per square mile (3 per square kilometer). Canada is bigger than the United States, but has only about one ninth as many people.

√ Reading Check **Which has a higher population density, a city or an area in the countryside?**

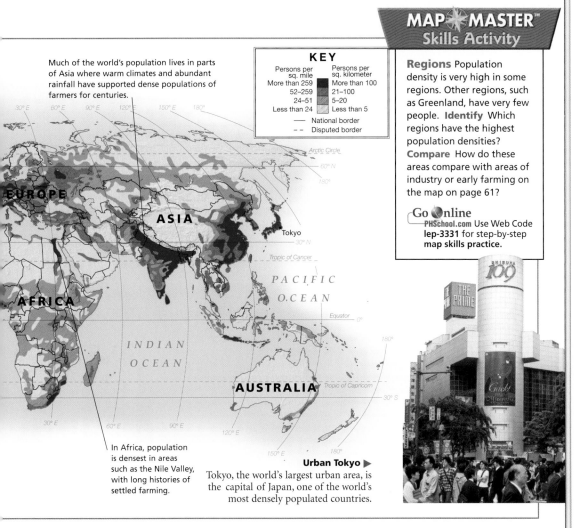

Much of the world's population lives in parts of Asia where warm climates and abundant rainfall have supported dense populations of farmers for centuries.

KEY

Persons per sq. mile	Persons per sq. kilometer
More than 259	More than 100
52–259	21–100
24–51	5–20
Less than 24	Less than 5

— National border
-- Disputed border

In Africa, population is densest in areas such as the Nile Valley, with long histories of settled farming.

Urban Tokyo ▶
Tokyo, the world's largest urban area, is the capital of Japan, one of the world's most densely populated countries.

MAP✦MASTER™ Skills Activity

Regions Population density is very high in some regions. Other regions, such as Greenland, have very few people. **Identify** Which regions have the highest population densities? **Compare** How do these areas compare with areas of industry or early farming on the map on page 61?

Go Online
PHSchool.com Use Web Code **lep-3331** for step-by-step **map skills practice.**

Differentiated Instruction

For Gifted and Talented L3
Have students do research to gather information about population densities for their community, state, and the United States. Then have them create a table showing this information.

For Less Proficient Readers L1
Remind students that it is important to read the captions that appear with pictures or photographs. Direct students' attention to the captions on pages 62 and 63. Have students reread them to find one noun to describe what is shown, and one adjective that describes the climate or vegetation.

When students are finished, ask them to describe one of the photographs without referring to its caption.

Independent Practice
Have students continue to fill in the graphic organizer by recording details about population density.

Monitor Progress
As they fill in details on their webs, make sure students understand the difference between population distribution and population density. Provide assistance as necessary.

Answers

√ Reading Check A city has a higher population density.

MAP✦MASTER Skills Activity **Identify** East and Southwest Asia, Europe, some coastal parts of Africa, northeast North America, Central Europe, and some coastal parts of South America **Compare** Many of the areas of modern industry also have high population densities. Some early farming areas, such as Asia and Europe, have high population densities, while others, such as central Africa, do not.

Go Online
PHSchool.com Students may practice their map skills using the interactive online version of this map.

Population Growth

Guided Instruction

- **Vocabulary Builder** Clarify the high-use words **method** and **aspect** before reading.

- Read how the world's human population has grown and changed over time in Population Growth.

- Ask **What does population growth depend on?** (birthrate and death rate) Then ask **What are birthrate and death rate?** (Birthrate is the number of live births each year per 1,000 people; death rate is the number of deaths each year per 1,000 people.)

- Have students study the Birth and Death Rates in Selected Countries, 2002 bar graph on page 64. Then have them predict what kinds of challenges a country like Yemen might face with such a high birthrate and a low death rate. (Answers will vary, but students should mention that it might become difficult to provide enough food, water, housing, public services, and education for so many people; the environment might also suffer.)

- Have students look at the line graph of World Population Growth A.D. 1200–2000 on page 65. Ask **About how much has the population increased in the last 100 years?** (about 4.5 billion) Ask **How has the development of modern science affected the recent population growth?** (New farming methods have increased the world's food supply; scientific advances in health and medicine have allowed people to live longer.)

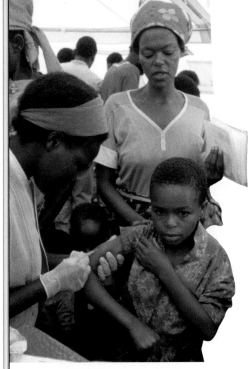

Modern Medicine
This Rwandan refugee is getting a measles vaccination in Tanzania. Modern medicine has lengthened lifespans worldwide.
Analyze Does vaccination raise birthrates or lower death rates? Explain why.

■ Graph Skills

If you subtract deaths from births, you get a country's rate of natural growth. When there are more deaths than births, the native-born population drops. **Identify** Which of the countries shown here has the highest birthrate? **Compare** Where is the population growing faster, the United States or Zimbabwe?

Population Growth

Suppose that all the years from A.D. 1 to A.D. 2000 took place in a single day. As the day began at midnight, there would be 300 million people in the world. Twelve hours later, at noon, there would be just 310 million people. By 8:24 P.M., the population would double to 600 million. It would double again by 10:05 P.M. to 1.2 billion. By 11:20, it would double again to 2.4 billion, and then double yet again by 11:48 to 4.8 billion, before reaching 6 billion as the day ended at midnight. As you can see, the world's population has grown very quickly in recent times. There are several reasons for this rapid growth.

Birthrates and Death Rates At different times in history, populations have grown at different rates. Demographers want to understand why. They know that population growth depends on the birthrate and the death rate. The **birthrate** is the number of live births each year per 1,000 people. The **death rate** is the number of deaths each year per 1,000 people.

For thousands of years, the world's population grew slowly. In those years, farmers worked without modern machinery. Food supplies often were scarce. People lived without clean water or waste removal. Many millions of people died of infectious diseases. As a result, although the birthrate was high, so was the death rate. The life expectancy, or the average number of years that people live, was short.

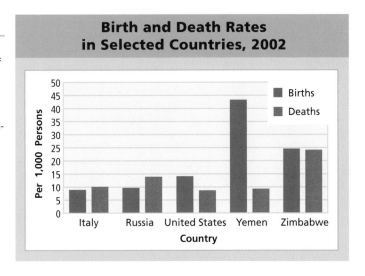

Birth and Death Rates in Selected Countries, 2002

(Bar graph showing Per 1,000 Persons on the y-axis from 0 to 50, and Country on the x-axis: Italy, Russia, United States, Yemen, Zimbabwe, with Births and Deaths shown for each.)

Differentiated Instruction

For Gifted and Talented   L3

Have students explore the concepts of demographics and statistics further by completing *Analyzing Statistics*.

All in One Foundations of Geography Teaching Resources, *Analyzing Statistics,* p. 187

For Advanced Readers   L3

To gain a better understanding of how population growth can affect the environment, assign students the *Enrichment* activity. Have students complete the activity in pairs.

All in One Foundations of Geography Teaching Resources, *Enrichment,* p. 181

Answers

Analyze Vaccinations lower death rates by improving people's immunity to disease, and therefore their life expectancy.

Graph Skills Identify Yemen
Compare the United States

Reasons for Population Growth Today This all changed after the 1700s. Death rates dropped sharply. In some countries, birthrates increased. As a result, populations have grown very fast. In some countries, the population has doubled in less than 20 years. Meanwhile, people live longer than ever. In the United States, people born in 1900 could expect to live for 47 years. Today, they can expect to live for 77 years.

Scientific progress explains much of this change. First, new farming methods have increased the world's food supply. Scientists have improved important food crops and found new ways to protect crops against insects. Scientists have also found ways to raise crops with less water. These recent scientific improvements in agriculture are called the Green Revolution.

The second set of scientific advances has come in health and medicine. Scientists have convinced local governments to provide clean drinking water and sanitary waste removal. These measures sharply reduce disease. Researchers have also developed vaccines to prevent disease and antibiotics to fight infections. As a result, people live many more years.

Due to a high birthrate and a low death rate, Yemen's population is skyrocketing.

Graph Skills

In recent centuries, population growth has soared. There are now 18 times as many people as there were 600 years ago. **Identify** Around what year did the world's population begin to rise rapidly? **Analyze a Graph** Looking at this graph, how can you tell that the world's population rose more quickly in recent years than in earlier centuries?

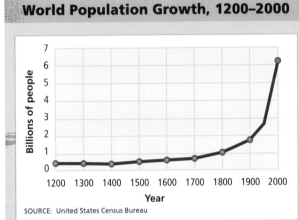

World Population Growth, 1200–2000

SOURCE: United States Census Bureau

Independent Practice

Have students complete their concept webs using the information in this section.

Monitor Progress

■ When students are finished with their concept webs, show *Section Reading Support Transparency FG 49* and ask students to check their work individually. Go over key concepts and clarify key vocabulary as needed.

📖 **Foundations of Geography Transparencies,** *Section Reading Support Transparency FG 49*

■ Tell students to fill in the last column of their *Reading Readiness Guides*. Probe for what they learned that confirms or invalidates each statement.

All in One **Foundations of Geography Teaching Resources,** *Reading Readiness Guide,* p. 162

Assess and Reteach

Assess Progress L2

Have students complete the Section Assessment. Then administer the *Section Quiz.*

All in One **Foundations of Geography Teaching Resources,** *Section Quiz,* p. 164

Reteach L1

If students need more instruction, have them read this section in the Reading and Vocabulary Study Guide.

📖 Chapter 3, Section 1, **Foundations of Geography Reading and Vocabulary Study Guide,** pp. 26–28

Skills Mini Lesson

Analyzing Graphic Data

1. Point out that information is often given in the form of charts and graphs. Tell students that charts and graphs can help them see information quickly, and can also help them draw conclusions.

2. Refer students to the bar graph on page 64. Have them practice the skill by identifying the title of the graph, the labels, and any

similarities or differences they notice in the information being presented in the graph. Then have them draw a conclusion about the populations of the countries shown on the graph.

3. Have students apply the skill by identifying the parts of the graph on this page and drawing conclusions from the information illustrated on the graph.

Answers

Graph Skills **Identify** 1800 **Analyze a Graph** because of the steep upward movement of the line between 1900 and 2000

Extend

L3

To extend the lesson, have students complete the *Evaluating Solutions* Internet activity to learn about possible solutions to the problem of overpopulation. Then have them answer the questions and partner with another student to create a chart of the options discussed.

Go Online
PHSchool.com **For:** Environmental and Global Issues: *Evaluating Solutions*
Visit: PHSchool.com
Web Code: led-3300

Answers

Infer Jobs, schools, and adequate housing may also be scarce.

✓ **Reading Check** Developments such as better farming methods and advances in health and medicine have led to a population increase.

Section 1 Assessment

Key Terms

Students' sentences should reflect an understanding of each Key Term.

Target Reading Skill

Similar: Both are used to measure and study demographics. Different: Population density is the average number of people who live in a given space; population distribution is the actual number of people who live in an area.

Comprehension and Critical Thinking

1. (a) areas with good soil and plenty of water **(b)** With advances in methods of transportation, people were able to move to other places; as industry developed, people did not need to farm to provide food and could move to work in places with factories. **(c)** Today more people live in cities than in the countryside.

2. (a) the average number of people living in a square mile or square kilometer **(b)** total population and land area.

Overcrowding in Bangladesh
These Bangladeshis are returning from a festival. Bangladesh's population has grown faster than its public services. This results in overcrowding, as seen on this train. **Infer** *What other aspects of life in Bangladesh might be affected by rapid population growth?*

The Challenges of Population Growth Today, food supplies have increased and people live longer. Even so, people in many countries still face serious problems. Some nations, such as those in Southwest Asia, do not have enough fresh water. In parts of Asia and Africa, the population is growing faster than the food supply. Often, these countries do not have enough money to buy food elsewhere.

Population growth puts pressure on all aspects of life. The populations of many countries are increasing so fast that not everyone can find jobs. There are not enough schools to educate the growing number of children. Decent housing is scarce. Public services such as transportation and sanitation are inadequate.

Rapid population growth also affects the environment. For instance, forests in many countries are disappearing. People in poorer countries cut down the trees for wood and fuel. Clearing forests causes other problems. In a forest, tree roots hold soil in place, and forest soils soak up rain. With the forest gone, heavy rainfall may wash away the soil and cause dangerous floods. Demand for wood and fuel in wealthier countries also uses up the world's scarce resources. All of Earth's people must work to meet this challenge.

✓ **Reading Check** Why have populations risen rapidly in recent times?

Section 1 Assessment

Key Terms

Review the key terms at the beginning of this section. Use each term in a sentence that explains its meaning.

Target Reading Skill

How are population density and population distribution similar? How are they different?

Comprehension and Critical Thinking

1. (a) Recall In what parts of the world did most people live before modern times?
(b) Explain How does history help explain population distribution today?

(c) Contrast How is population distribution today different from the days before modern science was developed?
2. (a) Define What is population density?
(b) Transfer Information To figure out the population density of an area, what two pieces of information do you need?
3. (a) Recall How has population growth changed in 100 years?
(b) Explain What accounts for this change?
(c) Identify Cause and Effect What are the effects of this change in population growth?

Writing Activity

Suppose that you are a demographer studying the area where you live. How does population density vary across your area? Where is population growth taking place? Write a short description of your area's demography.

Go Online
PHSchool.com
For: An activity on population
Visit: PHSchool.com
Web Code: led-3301

66 Foundations of Geography

---

3. (a) Population growth has been huge in the last 100 years. **(b)** advances in health and medicine and improved farming methods **(c)** Effects can include lack of jobs, schools, and public services and dangers to the environment.

Writing Activity

Use the *Rubric for Assessing a Writing Assignment* to evaluate students' descriptions of local demography.

All in One Foundations of Geography Teaching Resources, *Rubric for Assessing a Writing Assignment,* p. 197

Go Online
PHSchool.com Typing in the Web code when prompted will bring students directly to detailed instructions for this activity.

Prepare to Read

Objectives
In this section you will
1. Learn about migration, or people's movement from one region to another.
2. Investigate urbanization, or people's movement to cities.

Taking Notes
Copy the chart below. As you read this section, fill in the chart with information about voluntary and involuntary migration and about urbanization.

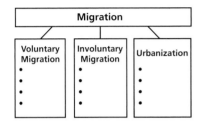

Target Reading Skill

Identify Contrasts
When you contrast two situations, you examine how they differ. Although both voluntary and involuntary migration involve the movement of people, the reasons for that movement differ. As you read, list the differences between voluntary and involuntary migration.

Key Terms
- **migration** (my GRAY shun) *n.* the movement of people from one place or region to another
- **immigrants** (IM uh grunts) *n.* people who move into one country from another
- **urbanization** (ur bun ih ZAY shun) *n.* the movement of people to cities, and the growth of cities
- **rural** (ROOR ul) *adj.* located in the countryside
- **urban** (UR bun) *adj.* located in cities and towns

Why People Migrate

For thousands of years, people have moved to new places. People's movement from one place or region to another is called **migration. Immigrants** are people who move into one country from another.

In the years from 1850 to 1930, more than 30 million Europeans moved to live in the United States. Since 1971, more than 4.5 million people have migrated here from Mexico, and more than 2.5 million have migrated from the Caribbean islands. Since 1971, Central America, the Philippines, China, and Vietnam have all lost more than 1 million immigrants to the United States. More than 800,000 immigrants have come from both South Korea and India.

During the late 1800s and early 1900s, millions of immigrants to the United States stopped at Ellis Island in New York Harbor.

Target Reading Skill [L2]

Identify Contrasts Point out the Target Reading Skill. Tell students that identifying contrasts between two situations will help them understand how they are different.

Read the first paragraph on page 71 to students. Model identifying contrasts by pointing out that in the past most Indonesians lived in rural areas, but today the population is increasingly urban; and, in 1970 about 3.9 million people lived in Jakarta, but in 2000, 11 million people lived there.

Give students *Identify Contrasts*. Have them complete the activity in groups.

All in One Foundations of Geography Teaching Resources, *Identify Contrasts,* p. 178

Objectives
Social Studies
1. Learn about migration, or people's movement from one region to another.
2. Investigate urbanization, or people's movement to cities.

Reading/Language Arts
Identify contrasts to understand how situations differ.

Prepare to Read

Build Background Knowledge [L2]
Tell students that this section is about the movement of people. Have students brainstorm a list of reasons why people might move from the countryside to the city, from one town to another, or from one country to another. Conduct an Idea Wave (TE p. T35) to elicit student responses, and then record them on the board.

Set a Purpose for Reading [L2]
- Preview the Objectives.

- Read each statement in the *Reading Readiness Guide* aloud. Ask students to mark the statements true or false.

  All in One Foundations of Geography Teaching Resources, *Reading Readiness Guide,* p. 166

- Have students discuss the statements in pairs or groups of four, then mark their worksheets again. Use the Numbered Heads participation strategy (TE, p. T36) to call on students to share their group's perspectives.

Vocabulary Builder
Preview Key Terms [L2]
Pronounce each Key Term, and then ask students to say the word with you. Provide a simple explanation such as, "New York City is urban because large numbers of people live close together there."

Instruct

Why People Migrate `L2`

Guided Instruction

- **Vocabulary Builder** Clarify the high-use word **theory** before reading.

- Read Why People Migrate using the Oral Cloze strategy (TE, p. T33).

- Discuss with students the push-pull theory. Ask **What is it and how does it work?** *(The theory helps explain why people migrate. It says that bad conditions "push" people to leave their countries, and good conditions in another country "pull" the people to migrate there.)*

- Ask **What kinds of things make people migrate voluntarily?** *(hunger or other difficulties, the search for a better quality of life, better jobs, and political freedom)* **What kinds of things force people to migrate involuntarily?** *(punishment, enslavement, war)*

⟳ Target Reading Skill `L2`

Identify Contrasts As a follow up, ask students to answer the Target Reading Skill question in the Student Edition *(Involuntary migration is when people are forced to move against their will. Voluntary migration is when people move because they want to.)*

Cubans in Little Havana
These men ordering food at a cafe are part of a large community of Cuban immigrants in Miami, Florida. **Analyze Images** *What aspects of their life in Cuba have these immigrants preserved in their new home?*

Identify Contrasts
How is involuntary migration different from voluntary migration?

Voluntary Migration in the Past Voluntary migration is the movement of people by their own choice. Today, most people move by their own choice. The push-pull theory says that people migrate because difficulties "push" them to leave. At the same time, the hope for a better life "pulls" people to a new country.

The push-pull theory helps to explain the great Irish migration in the 1840s and 1850s. In those years, 1.5 million people left Ireland for the United States. What pushed so many Irish people to come to America? In the 1840s, disease destroyed Ireland's main crop—potatoes. Hunger pushed people to migrate. Job opportunities pulled Irish families to the United States.

Voluntary Migration Today The same theory explains most migration today. The main sources of migration are countries where many people are poor and jobs are few. In some countries, such as Vietnam and Central American countries, wars have made life dangerous and difficult.

In China, Vietnam, and Cuba, governments limit people's freedom. These problems push people to leave. Meanwhile, the possibility of good jobs and political freedom pulls people to the United States and other well-off, democratic countries.

Involuntary Migration Sometimes people are forced to move. Because these people do not choose to move, their movement is known as involuntary migration. During the early 1800s, the British sent prisoners to Australia to serve their sentences. When their sentences were done, many stayed. War also forces people to migrate to escape death or serious danger.

The Transatlantic Slave Trade Perhaps the biggest involuntary migration in history was the transatlantic slave trade. From the 1500s to the 1800s, millions of Africans were enslaved and taken against their will to European colonies in North and South America. These Africans traveled under inhumane conditions across the Atlantic Ocean, chained inside ships for more than a month.

At first, their descendants in the United States lived mainly on the east coast. As cotton farming spread west, many enslaved African Americans were forced to migrate again, this time to new plantations in the Mississippi Valley and Texas.

√ Reading Check **Why do people migrate?**

Answers

Analyze Images They have preserved their Spanish language and possibly some types of food that might be sold at this cafe.

√ Reading Check Some people migrate for a better quality of life, better jobs, religious or political freedom, or safety from war or violence. Other people are forced to move through enslavement or imprisonment.

Vocabulary Builder

Use the information below to teach students this section's high-use words.

High-Use Word	Definition and Sample Sentence
theory, p. 68	*n.* an idea or belief about how something is done Laura's **theory** was that she would pass the test if she studied.
unique, p. 71	*adj.* being the only one; having no equal Many rain forest plants are **unique** because they are found nowhere else in the world.

Migration in South Asia

At the end of British colonial rule in 1947, most of South Asia was divided along religious lines into two countries. India had a Hindu majority. Pakistan was mainly Muslim. Fearing religious discrimination or violence, Muslims from India and Hindus from Pakistan fled across the new borders. Many died when violence broke out during these massive migrations.

Movement This map shows migrations by South Asians. **Identify** Which countries did South Asia's largest migrations involve? **Contrast** How do the reasons for movement out of South Asia differ from the reasons for migration within the region?

Go Online
PHSchool.com Use Web Code **lep-3312** for step-by-step **map skills practice.**

Over a million people have left South Asian countries for Europe and North America, seeking better lives.

Present-day Bangladesh was part of Pakistan in 1947. Many Hindus from the region fled to India, while Muslims from India fled to what became Bangladesh.

When India and Pakistan were separated in 1947, 5.4 million Hindus and Sikhs fled from Pakistan to India, and 6.6 million Muslims fled to Pakistan.

70° E

Indus R.

30° N

PAKISTAN

80° E

90° E

30° N

NEPAL

BHUTAN

Ganges R.

Tropic of Cancer

Arabian Sea

INDIA

BANGLADESH (formerly part of Pakistan)

20° N

70° E

20° N

90° E

Bay of Bengal

Hundreds of thousands of South Asians have left the region for Southeast Asia, Australia, and the Pacific Islands.

N
W   E
S

▲ **Chaos in India and Pakistan**
The separation of India and Pakistan uprooted millions of people and drove them to flee across the new borders.

INDIAN OCEAN

10° N

10° N

SRI LANKA

MALDIVES

80° E

KEY

➡ Involuntary migration of Hindus from Pakistan to India in 1947

➡ Involuntary migration of Muslims from India to Pakistan in 1947

➡ Voluntary migration of South Asians overseas after 1947

— National border

0 miles   500
0 kilometers   500
Lambert Azimuthal Equal Area

Chapter 3 Section 2 **69**

- Direct students' attention to the map on this page. Ask **What caused the migration of Muslims and Hindus in Southeast Asia in 1947?** *(Following the end of British colonial rule in India, most of South Asia was divided along religious lines into the countries of India and Pakistan; fearing religious discrimination or violence, Hindus and Muslims in the minority fled across the new borders.)* **Do you think this migration was voluntary or involuntary? Why?** *(Possible answer: involuntary, since people migrated to avoid possible religious persecution and violence)*

Independent Practice

Have students create the Taking Notes graphic organizer on a blank piece of paper. Model how to fill in the graphic organizer using the *Flow Chart* transparency. Students should then fill in the chart with information they have just learned.

📖 **Foundations of Geography Transparencies,** *Transparency B2: Flow Chart*

Monitor Progress

As students fill in the graphic organizer, circulate and make sure that individuals are choosing the correct details. Provide assistance as needed.

Skills Mini Lesson

Identifying Frame of Reference and Point of View

1. Explain that point of view is a person's opinion about an issue. Frame of reference is a person's background and often influences a person's point of view.

2. Have students practice the skill by reviewing the information about the division of India and Pakistan. Discuss how these people's frame of reference or point of view affected their decision to migrate.

3. Have students apply the skill by identifying Krenak's frame of reference and point of view in the following selection:

All in One Foundations of Geography Teaching Resources, *Message from the Rain Forest Amerindians,* p. 188

Answers

MAP MASTER Skills Activity **Identify** India and Pakistan **Contrast** Within the region, people migrated to avoid violence and religious persecution; they migrated outside the region to seek better lives.

Go Online
PHSchool.com Students may practice their map skills using the interactive online version of this map.

Show students *Migration: People on the Move.* Ask students to name two reasons people are migrating within Senegal. *(People are migrating to Dakar because it has a cooler climate; others are migrating to the north because the desert is encroaching on the land.)*

Urbanization `L2`

Guided Instruction

- **Vocabulary Builder** Clarify the high-use word **unique** before reading.

- Have students read Urbanization and study the bar graph and photos.

- Ask **What is the general trend in population movement since 1800?** *(More people are moving from rural to urban areas.)* **Why?** *(People are pulled to the city by the promise of better-paying jobs.)*

- Have students discuss some of the problems caused by rapid urbanization. *(Cities often cannot provide enough housing, jobs, schools, hospitals, and other services people need; traffic jams and crowds make it difficult for people to get around.)*

Independent Practice

Have students finish filling in their charts with details about urbanization.

Monitor Progress

- When students are finished with their charts, show *Section Reading Support Transparency FG 50* and ask students to check their work individually.

  📖 **Foundations of Geography Transparencies,** *Section Reading Support Transparency FG 50*

- Tell students to fill in the last column of their *Reading Readiness Guides.* Probe for what they learned that confirms or invalidates each statement.

  All in One Foundations of Geography Teaching Resources, *Reading Readiness Guide,* p. 166

Answers

Graph Skills Identify about 3–4 percent **Predict** The urban population will probably be greater than the rural population.

Learn more about migration.

Urbanization

Millions of people in many countries have migrated to cities from farms and small villages. In recent years, the population of some cities has grown tremendously. The movement of people to cities and the growth of cities is called **urbanization.**

Cities and Suburbs In Europe and North America, the growth of industry during the 1800s pulled people from the countryside to cities. They hoped for jobs in factories and offices. Since about 1950, urbanization has given way in Europe and North America to suburbanization, or the movement of people to growing suburbs. Suburbanization sometimes replaces valuable farmland with sprawling development. Because most people in suburbs rely on cars for transportation, suburban sprawl can increase pollution. However, people still move to suburbs to pursue the dream of home ownership.

Graph Skills

All over the world, city populations have soared. The photographs of Cape Town, South Africa, below, show how that city has expanded.
Identify What percent of the world's people lived in cities in 1800?
Predict Based on information from the graph, how do you think the world's rural and urban populations will compare in 2050?

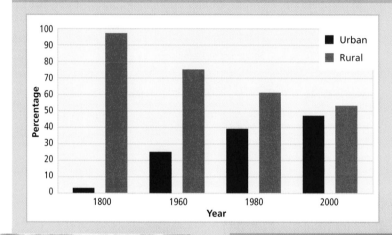

World Urban and Rural Populations, 1800-2000

Cape Town, 1938   Modern Cape Town

Differentiated Instruction

For Advanced Readers `L3`

To help students gain better understanding about immigrants and their migrations, divide them into groups to complete the *Small Group Activity: Making an Immigration Map.*

All in One Foundations of Geography Teaching Resources, *Small Group Activity: Making an Immigration Map,* pp. 183–186

For English Language Learners `L1`

Students may have difficulty pronouncing some of the longer words in this section, such as *tremendously, urbanization,* and *opportunities.* Encourage students to break down these words into smaller parts to help them sound out the pronunciations.

Urbanization on Other Continents In Asia, Africa, and Latin America, people are still streaming from the countryside to growing cities. Indonesia is an example. In the past, most Indonesians lived in **rural** areas, or areas in the countryside. Recently, more and more Indonesians have moved to **urban** areas, or areas in cities and nearby towns. For example, in 1970, about 3.9 million people lived in Greater Jakarta, Indonesia's capital. By 2000, its population was about 11 million. Jakarta is not unique. Greater São Paulo, Brazil, grew from 8 million residents in 1970 to nearly 18 million residents in 2000.

The problem in cities like Jakarta and São Paulo is that too many people are moving to the city too fast. Cities cannot keep up. They cannot provide the housing, jobs, schools, hospitals, and other services that people need. Traffic jams and crowds often make getting around a struggle.

With so many daily problems, why do people flock to São Paulo and other big cities? As hard as life is in the cities, it can be even harder in the countryside, where there are few jobs and a shortage of land to farm. Most migrants to the city are seeking a better life for their families. They are looking for jobs, modern houses, and good schools. Above all, most want better lives for their children.

✓ **Reading Check** How is the population of urban areas changing in Africa, Asia, and Latin America?

São Paulo, Brazil
São Paulo is Brazil's largest city.
Analyze Images *Do you think that this city has a high or a low population density?*

Section 2 Assessment

Key Terms
Review the key terms at the beginning of this section. Use each term in a sentence that explains its meaning.

Target Reading Skill
Contrast involuntary migration and voluntary migration. How are these two forms of migration different? List at least two differences between the two kinds of migration.

Comprehension and Critical Thinking
1. (a) Identify What are push factors and what are pull factors?
(b) Explain How do push factors and pull factors explain people's decision to migrate?
(c) Compare and Contrast Do push and pull factors account for involuntary migration? Explain why or why not.
2. (a) Recall What is urbanization?
(b) Identify Cause and Effect What are the causes and some of the effects of urbanization?

Writing Activity
Suppose that you are moving to the United States from one of the countries listed in the second paragraph on page 67. Write a paragraph describing your reasons for leaving that country and what attracts you to the United States.

For: An activity on migration
Visit: PHSchool.com
Web Code: led-3302

Assess Progress `L2`
Have students complete the Section Assessment. Then administer the *Section Quiz*.

 Foundations of Geography Teaching Resources, *Section Quiz,* p. 168

Reteach `L1`
If students need more instruction, have them read this section in the Reading and Vocabulary Study Guide.

📖 Chapter 3, Section 2, **Foundations of Geography Reading and Vocabulary Study Guide,** pp. 29–31

Extend `L3`
To extend the lesson, have students do research for a report on either a family member or famous American who immigrated to the United States. Students should identify the immigrant's country of origin and write a brief biography about the person's life and important accomplishments. Students should mention if and how immigration affected their subjects' lives.

Answers

✓ **Reading Check** The populations of urban areas in Africa, Asia, and Latin America are growing rapidly.

Analyze Images high population density

Writing Activity
Use the *Rubric for Assessing a Writing Assignment* to evaluate students' paragraphs.

All in One **Foundations of Geography Teaching Resources,** *Rubric for Assessing a Writing Assignment,* p. 197

Go Online PHSchool.com Typing in the Web code when prompted will bring students directly to detailed instructions for this activity.

Section 2 Assessment

Key Terms
Students' sentences should reflect an understanding of each Key Term.

Target Reading Skill
Involuntary migration is when people are moved against their will. Voluntary migration is when people move because they want to.

Comprehension and Critical Thinking
1. (a) push factors: reasons why people leave a place; pull factors: reasons why people are drawn to a place **(b)** Push factors explain why people leave their own country and pull factors explain why people go to another country. **(c)** Only push factors account for involuntary migration, since people are "pushed," or forced, to move to another place.

2. (a) the movement of people to cities and the growth of cities **(b)** causes: lack of jobs, shortage of land, and population growth in rural areas; effects: lack of housing and jobs, pressure on public services, crowding, traffic problems

Objective

Read and interpret population density maps.

Prepare to Read

Build Background Knowledge L2

Briefly review with students the information they learned about population density in Section 1. Ask students why it might be useful to know the population density of a particular area, and who might need to know this information. On the board, begin a concept web with *Population Density* in the center oval and two sub-ovals labeled *Why?* and *Who?* Conduct an Idea Wave (TE p. T35) to elicit student responses.

Instruct

Analyzing and Interpreting Population Density Maps L2

Guided Instruction

- Read the steps to read and interpret a population density map as a class and write them on the board.

- Practice the skill by following the steps on p. 73 with the class. Model each step by taking note of the map's topic and features *(South Asia's population density; relief and labels)*, studying the map key carefully to note what the colors show *(population density)*, using the key to identify the areas of lowest and highest population density *(lowest: parts of Afghanistan and Nepal; highest: parts of Pakistan, India, Bangladesh, and Sri Lanka)*, and writing a conclusion about South Asia's population density and possible reasons for its patterns *(Areas with lower population densities are generally mountainous and farther from coasts. This is probably because they are difficult to reach and hard to make a living in. Areas with higher population densities are near the coasts and in non-mountainous areas. This is probably because they are easier to reach and people can make a living there).*

Analyzing and Interpreting Population Density Maps

Crowds gather in Amsterdam on Queen's Day, a national holiday in the Netherlands.

How dense is the population where you live? If you drew an imaginary five-mile square around your house and counted the number of people who lived within the square, would there be many residents, or few?

Population density is the average number of persons living within a certain area. You can find out how densely populated a place is by reading a population density map.

Learn the Skill

To read and interpret a population density map, follow these steps.

1 **Read the title and look at the map to get a general idea of what it shows.** The topic of the map could be population density, physical features, or some other subject.

2 **Read the key to understand how the map uses symbols and colors.** Each color represents a different population density range, as explained in the map key.

3 **Use the key to interpret the map.** Identify areas of various densities on the map. Some places average less than one person per square mile. In other places, thousands of people might be crammed into one square mile.

4 **Draw conclusions about what the map shows.** The history, geography, and cultural traditions of a place affect its population density. Draw on this information, plus what you read on the map, to make conclusions about why particular areas have a higher or a lower population density.

Independent Practice

Assign *Skills for Life* and have students complete it individually.

All in One **Foundations of Geography Teaching Resources,** *Skills for Life,* p. 182

Monitor Progress

As students are completing *Skills for Life,* circulate to make sure individuals are applying the skill steps effectively. Provide assistance as needed.

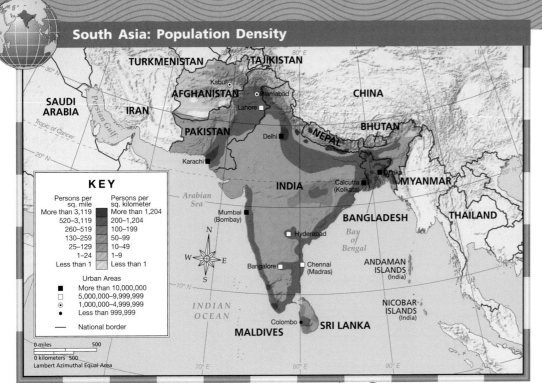

South Asia: Population Density

KEY

Persons per sq. mile	Persons per sq. kilometer
More than 3,119	More than 1,204
520–3,119	200–1,204
260–519	100–199
130–259	50–99
25–129	10–49
1–24	1–9
Less than 1	Less than 1

Urban Areas
- ■ More than 10,000,000
- ☐ 5,000,000–9,999,999
- ◉ 1,000,000–4,999,999
- • Less than 999,999
- — National border

0-miles 500
0 kilometers 500
Lambert Azimuthal Equal-Area

Practice the Skill

Use steps 1–4 to read and interpret the population density map above.

1 What is the topic of this map? Notice that the map has relief—that is, markings that indicate hills and mountains. It also has labels for cities and nations of South Asia.

2 Study the map key carefully. How many different colors are in the key? What color is used for the lowest population density? What color is used for the highest density?

3 Using the key, identify the areas of highest and lowest population densities in South Asia. Write a sentence or two that describes where the most and the fewest people are located.

4 Write a conclusion that makes a general statement about South Asia's population density and suggests possible reasons for the patterns shown on the map.

Apply the Skill

Now take a closer look at the map titled The World: Population Density on pages 62 and 63. Find the areas of greatest density. From what you already know and what you see on the map, what features do you think influence where people choose to live? Think about rivers and mountains as well as nearness to a coast or to the Equator.

Chapter 3 **73**

Assess and Reteach

Assess Progress L2

Ask students to complete the Apply the Skill activity.

Reteach L1

If students are having trouble applying the skill steps, have them review the skill using the interactive Social Studies Skills Tutor CD-ROM.

⊙ *Analyzing and Interpreting Special Purpose Maps,* **Social Studies Skills Tutor CD-ROM**

Extend L3

- To extend the lesson, ask students to apply the skill steps to the population density map on the transparency *The World: Population Density.*

📖 **Foundations of Geography Transparencies,** *Color Transparency FG 5: The World: Continents and Oceans (Base); Color Transparency FG 16: The World: Population Density (Overlay)*

- Ask students to identify what the shaded areas indicate (*population density*). Then have them identify the areas of highest population density in the world. (*parts of North America, Latin America, Asia, Europe, Africa*) Ask **Which continent has the most areas of lowest population density?** (*Antarctica*) Then discuss with students what about certain areas might cause them to have the lowest population densities. (*extremely cold areas, such as the North and South poles, and extremely hot areas, such as deserts, where harsh climates make it difficult for people to live*)

Differentiated Instruction

For Special Needs Students L1

Partner special needs students with proficient readers to do Level 1 of the *Analyzing and Interpreting Special Purpose Maps,* lesson on the Social Studies Skills Tutor CD-ROM together. When the students feel more confident, they can move onto Level 2 alone.

⊙ *Analyzing and Interpreting Special Purpose Maps,* **Social Studies Skills Tutor CD-ROM**

Answer
Apply the Skill

The areas of the highest population density probably have good farmland, adequate water, and climates that are warm enough to allow many plants to grow.

Section 3
Step-by-Step Instruction

Objectives

Social Studies
1. Examine different kinds of economies.
2. Investigate levels of economic development.
3. Study global trade patterns.

Reading/Language Arts
Make comparisons to understand what things have in common.

Prepare to Read

Build Background Knowledge [L2]
Ask students to quickly preview the headings and visuals in the section. Then, write the word *economy* on the board, and have students use the Think-Write-Pair-Share strategy (TE p. T36) to make a list of five words that they think of when they hear the word *economy (examples: money, goods, services).* Tell students to predict what *economy* might mean, and then read the section to find out if their predictions were correct.

Set a Purpose for Reading [L2]
- Preview the Objectives.
- Read each statement in the *Reading Readiness Guide* aloud. Ask students to mark the statements true or false.

  All in One Foundations of Geography Teaching Resources, *Reading Readiness Guide,* p. 170

- Have students discuss the statements in pairs or groups of four, then mark their worksheets again. Use the Numbered Heads participation strategy (TE, p. T36) to call on students to share their group's perspectives.

Vocabulary Builder
Preview Key Terms [L2]
Pronounce each Key Term, and then ask students to say the word with you. Provide a simple explanation such as, "The carpenter who builds a table is a producer. The person who buys the table is a consumer."

Section 3 — Economic Systems

Prepare to Read

Key Questions
In this section you will
1. Examine different kinds of economies.
2. Investigate levels of economic development.
3. Study global trade patterns.

Taking Notes
Copy the table below. As you read this section, fill in the table with information about economic terms, kinds of economies, levels of development, and world trade. Add columns and rows as needed.

Economic Systems	
Kinds of Economies	• •
Levels of Development	• •

Target Reading Skill

Make Comparisons
Comparing economic systems enables you to see what they have in common. As you read this section, compare different kinds of economies and levels of economic development. Who makes decisions and how do people live?

Key Terms
- **economy** (ih KAHN uh mee) *n.* a system in which people make, exchange, and use things that have value
- **producers** (pruh DOOS urz) *n.* owners and workers
- **consumers** (kun SOOM urz) *n.* people who buy and use products
- **capitalism** (KAP ut ul iz um) *n.* an economic system in which individuals own most businesses
- **communism** (KAHM yoo niz um) *n.* an economic system in which the central government owns factories, farms, and offices
- **developed nations** (dih VEL upt NAY shunz) *n.* nations with many industries and advanced technology
- **developing nations** (dih VEL up ing NAY shunz) *n.* nations with few industries and simple technology

Consumers choose produce at a market in Honolulu, Hawaii.

74 Foundations of Geography

Different Kinds of Economies

An **economy** is a system in which people make, exchange, and use things that have value and that meet their wants or needs. Economies differ from one country to another. In any economy, owners and workers are **producers.** The things they sell are called products **Consumers** are people who buy and use products.

There are three basic economic questions: What will be produced? How will it be produced? And, for whom will it be produced? The answers to these questions depend on the economy.

Modern economies differ in who owns workplaces. The owners generally decide how products are produced. In some countries, most workplaces are privately owned. In others, the government owns most workplaces.

Target Reading Skill [L2]

Make Comparisons Point out the Target Reading Skill. Tell students that making comparisons will help them see what things have in common.

Model the skill by reading the last paragraph on p. 79 and comparing NAFTA and the European Union. (*Both groups are trade alliances and are made up of several countries in the same region.*)

Give students *Make Comparisons.* Have them complete the activity in groups.

All in One Foundations of Geography Teaching Resources, *Make Comparisons,* p. 179

Private Ownership Capitalism is an economic system in which private individuals own most businesses. Capitalism is also called a free-market economy because producers compete freely for consumers' business.

In capitalism, people may save money in banks. Banks lend money to people and businesses in return for interest, or a percentage fee for the use of money. Banks also pay interest to savers. Under capitalism, people may directly invest in, or commit money to, a business. Owners of a business are also investors in that business.

Government Ownership Communism is an economic system in which the central government owns farms, factories, and offices. It controls the prices of goods and services, how much is produced, and how much workers are paid. The government decides where to invest resources. Today, only a few of the world's nations practice communism.

Mixed Ownership Hardly any nation has a "pure" economic system. For example, the United States has a capitalist economy. However, governments run schools, build and maintain roads, and provide other services. In communist countries, you may find a few small private businesses.

In some countries, the government may own some industries, while others belong to private owners. This system of mixed ownership is sometimes called a mixed economy.

✓ Reading Check **What are the differences between capitalism and communism?**

New York Stock Exchange
Stocks are bought and sold on the busy trading floor of the New York Stock Exchange. **Draw Conclusions** *Would you expect to find a busy stock exchange in a communist economy? Explain why or why not.*

Instruct

Different Kinds of Economies L2

Guided Instruction

■ **Vocabulary Builder** Clarify the high-use words **exchange** and **value** before reading.

■ Read Different Kinds of Economies using the ReQuest Procedure (TE, p. T35).

■ Discuss with students the three different types of economies and the differences among them. *(In capitalism, private individuals own most businesses. In communism, the central government controls the economy. In a mixed economy, the government has partial control of the economy.)*

■ Ask **What kind of economy does the United States have?** *(capitalist economy, but the government runs schools, builds and maintains roads, and provides other services)*

Independent Practice

Have students create the Taking Notes graphic organizer on a blank piece of paper. Then have them begin to fill in the organizer with information they have just learned.

Monitor Progress

As students fill in the graphic organizer, circulate and make sure that individuals are choosing the correct details. Provide assistance as needed.

Vocabulary Builder

Use the information below to teach students this section's high-use words.

High-Use Word	Definition and Sample Sentence
exchange, p. 74	*v.* to give and receive Sarah had to **exchange** the large sweater for a smaller one.
value, p. 74	*n.* worth Because it was damaged, the car had little **value**.
alliance, p. 79	*n.* a union The two schools formed an **alliance** to help raise money for their music programs.

Answers

Draw Conclusions No; in a communist country there probably would be no need for a stock market, because the government controls the prices of goods, and goods and shares are not open to free buying and selling.

✓ Reading Check Capitalism is an economic system in which producers compete freely for consumers' business. Communism is an economic system in which the government controls the prices of goods and services.

Levels of Economic Development

L2

Guided Instruction

- Read about the differences between developed and developing countries in Levels of Economic Development.

- Have students describe the ways in which people in developed countries and in developing countries produce food. (*In developed countries, most of the food is grown by commercial farmers; in developing countries, most of the people are subsistence farmers.*)

- Ask **What challenges might commercial and subsistence farmers have in common?** (*Bad weather, pollution, and lack of water might be challenges that affect both types of farmers.*)

⟳ Target Reading Skill L2

Make Comparisons As a follow up, ask students to answer the Target Reading Skill question in the Student Edition. (*Both kinds of countries have farms.*)

Make Comparisons What do developed nations have in common with developing nations?

Levels of Economic Development

Three hundred years ago, most people made their own clothes. Then came a great change. People invented machines to make goods. They found new sources of power to run the machines. Power-driven machines were a new technology, or way of putting knowledge to practical use. This change in the way people made goods was called the Industrial Revolution.

The Industrial Revolution created a new economic pattern. Nations with more industries and more advanced technology are considered **developed nations.** Because they are still developing economically, nations with fewer industries and simpler technology are considered **developing nations.** People live differently in developed and developing nations.

Developed Nations Only about one fifth of the world's people live in developed nations. These nations include the United States, Canada, Japan, and most European nations. People in these nations use goods made in factories. Businesses use advanced technologies to produce goods and services.

In developed nations, most people live in towns and cities. They work in offices and factories. Machines do most of the work. Most people have enough food and water. Most citizens can get an education and healthcare.

In developed nations, most food is grown by commercial farmers. These are farmers who grow crops mainly for sale rather than for their own needs. Commercial farms use modern technologies, so they need fewer workers than traditional farms.

Developed nations can have some problems. Unemployment is a challenge. Not everyone can find a job. Industry and cars can cause air, land, and water pollution. Developed nations are working to solve these problems.

Most of Thailand's subsistence farmers grow rice.

Skills for Life — Skills Mini Lesson

Identifying Main Ideas

1. Tell students that to identify main ideas, they should identify the subject, identify details about the subject, and decide what their overall impression is of the details. Then they should draw a conclusion about what the details tell them.

2. Help students practice the skill by reading the first paragraph on this page with them. Have them note the details and use them to identify the main idea in that paragraph. (*Main idea: The Industrial Revolution changed the way people made goods.*)

3. Have students apply the skill by identifying the details and main idea in the third paragraph on page 77.

The World: Levels of Development

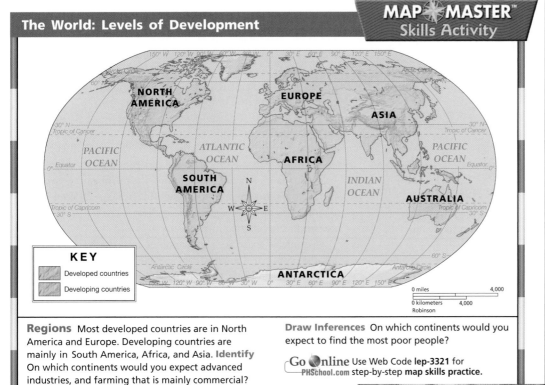

KEY

Developed countries

Developing countries

0 miles 4,000
0 kilometers 4,000
Robinson

Regions Most developed countries are in North America and Europe. Developing countries are mainly in South America, Africa, and Asia. **Identify** On which continents would you expect advanced industries, and farming that is mainly commercial?

Draw Inferences On which continents would you expect to find the most poor people?

Go Online Use Web Code lep-3321 for
PHSchool.com step-by-step **map skills practice**.

Developing Nations Not every economy is like that of the United States. Most of the people in the world live in developing nations, which are mainly in Africa, Asia, and Latin America.

Developing nations do not have great wealth. Many people are subsistence farmers, or farmers who raise food and animals mainly to feed their own families. Their farms have little or no machinery. People and animals do most of the work.

Many developing nations face great challenges. These include disease, food shortages, unsafe water, poor education and healthcare, and political unrest.

People in developing nations are confronting these challenges. Some nations, such as Saudi Arabia and South Africa, have grown richer by selling natural resources. Others, such as Thailand and China, have built successful industries. The more industrial developing nations are gradually becoming developed countries themselves.

Many people in developed nations work in offices.

✓ **Reading Check** How do developed nations differ from developing nations?

Chapter 3 Section 3 **77**

Independent Practice

Have students add a column entitled "Levels of Development" to their graphic organizers and fill it in with information from this section.

Monitor Progress

As students continue to fill in the graphic organizer, circulate and make sure they are filling in the correct details. Provide assistance as needed.

Answers

MAP★MASTER™ Skills Activity **Identify** North America, Europe, the northern half of Asia, Australia
Draw Inferences Africa, the southern half of Asia, the southern half of North America and South America

✓ **Reading Check** In developed nations food is grown by commercial farmers; in developing nations many people are subsistence farmers. Most people in developed countries live in towns and cities, and can get food, healthcare, good housing, and a good education; in developing countries many face a lack of food, clean water, education, healthcare, and land.

Go Online
PHSchool.com Students may practice their map skills using the interactive online version of this map.

Differentiated Instruction

For Less Proficient Readers [L1]

To help students better understand the differences and similarities among developed and developing countries have them create a Venn diagram. Have students label one circle "Developing Countries," and the other "Developed Countries." As they read, have students record information in the appropriate circles.

For Gifted and Talented [L3]

Divide students into groups and assign each group one world region: United States and Canada, Latin America, Asia and the Pacific, Africa, or Europe and Russia. Have each group do research to find out what economic systems the countries in their region have, and then create a table with this information.

Read the **Links Across Time** on this page. Ask students **Why was it important for traders to carry items of value instead of inexpensive items along the Silk Road?** *(To make the trip worthwhile, traders needed to have valuable items to trade along the route.)*

World Trade Patterns L2

Guided Instruction

- **Vocabulary Builder** Clarify the high-use word **alliance** before reading.

- Have students read World Trade Patterns and study the flow chart.

- Have students summarize the world trade diagram in their own words. *(Country A sells oil to Countries B and C so it can buy wheat and computers; Country B sells wheat to Countries A and C so it can buy computers and oil; Country C sells computers to countries A and B so it can buy wheat and oil.)*

- **What might be some benefits of belonging to a trade alliance? What might be some drawbacks?** *(Benefits: able to trade goods easily with other member countries. Drawbacks: cannot make decisions about trade alone; member countries might make better, cheaper goods than your country and take business away from your country's producers.)*

Independent Practice

Have students complete the graphic organizer by adding a row entitled "World Trade Patterns" and filling it in with information from this section.

Monitor Progress

- Show *Section Reading Support Transparency FG 51* and ask students to check their work.

  📖 **Foundations of Geography Transparencies,** *Section Reading Support Transparency FG 51*

- Tell students to fill in the last column of their *Reading Readiness Guides.*

  All in One Foundations of Geography Teaching Resources, *Reading Readiness Guide,* p. 170

Answer
Predict Country A

The Silk Road
Long-distance trade is nothing new. Hundreds of years ago, merchants brought silks and other luxuries from China to ancient Rome along the Silk Road across Asia. However, those merchants had to load goods on the backs of animals or carry the goods themselves. They could take only lightweight, valuable goods. Today, ships, trains, and trucks can carry heavy and inexpensive goods long distances.

World Trade Patterns

Different countries have different economic strengths. Developed nations have strong industries with advanced technology. Some developing nations have low-cost industries. Other developing nations may grow plantation cash crops, or they may produce oil or minerals.

Different Specialties Countries' economies differ not only because they are more or less developed. They also differ because each country has a different set of economic specialties. For example, Saudi Arabia has vast amounts of oil, and Switzerland has a long history of producing fine watches. Because each country has different specialties, each country has products that consumers in other countries want.

Countries trade with one another to take advantage of one another's special strengths. For example, the United States makes some of the world's best computers. But the United States needs oil. Saudi Arabia has plenty of oil, but it needs computers. So Saudi Arabia sells oil to the United States, and the United States sells computers to Saudi Arabia.

How Does World Trade Work?

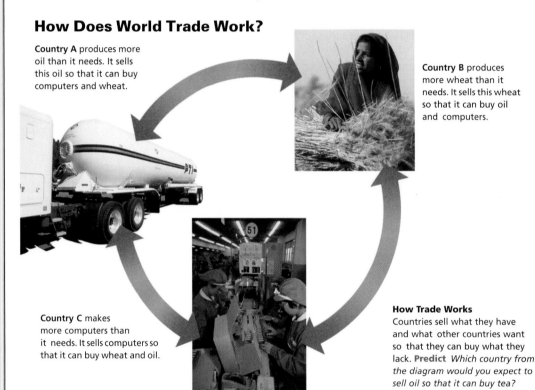

Country A produces more oil than it needs. It sells this oil so that it can buy computers and wheat.

Country B produces more wheat than it needs. It sells this wheat so that it can buy oil and computers.

Country C makes more computers than it needs. It sells computers so that it can buy wheat and oil.

How Trade Works
Countries sell what they have and what other countries want so that they can buy what they lack. **Predict** *Which country from the diagram would you expect to sell oil so that it can buy tea?*

78 Foundations of Geography

Background: Links Across Place

European Union The European Union, or EU, is an organization of European countries that work together on many issues. After the end of World War II, some European leaders believed that a union should be formed between European countries to rebuild Europe and try to prevent future wars. As a result, six countries formed the European Economic Community (EEC) in 1958. More countries eventually joined, and by 1993, the organization changed its name to the European Union. Today goods can be transported freely between countries within the European Union. Representatives from each member country decide on laws that all of the countries will follow. In 2002, 12 EU members replaced their currency with the Euro.

Interdependence As world trade has grown, countries have grown interdependent, or dependent on one another. The United States depends on other countries for oil and inexpensive industrial goods. Meanwhile, other countries depend on the United States for computers and other products.

Developed nations tend to sell products made using advanced technologies. Developing nations tend to sell foods, natural resources such as oil, and simple industrial products. In return, they buy high-technology goods from developed countries.

Some countries have formed trade alliances to reduce the costs of trade. For example, the United States, Canada, and Mexico belong to the North American Free Trade Area, or NAFTA. Most European countries belong to the European Union. Businesses may face increased competition from foreign competitors within these alliances, and workers may lose their jobs. However, businesses may benefit from increased sales in other countries. Consumers benefit from these alliances because they pay less for products from other countries.

✓ **Reading Check** Why do countries trade with one another?

Moving Goods
Much of the world's trade travels on container ships, like this one in Dubai, United Arab Emirates. These ships can carry huge loads across oceans. **Draw Conclusions** *How does technology make world trade easier?*

✦ Section 3 Assessment

Key Terms
Review the key terms at the beginning of this section. Use each term in a sentence that explains its meaning.

↻ Target Reading Skill
What are two ways developed and developing countries are similar?

Comprehension and Critical Thinking
1. (a) Identify Who owns farms, factories, and offices in a communist economy?
(b) Compare and Contrast How is ownership different in a capitalist economy?

2. (a) Identify What is a country's level of development?
(b) Describe What are the main differences in level of development between countries?
(c) Predict What can we predict about a country's economy if we know its level of development?
3. (a) List What are two major trade alliances?
(b) Explain What is the main purpose of these alliances?
(c) Analyze What are some reasons why a country might want to join a trade alliance?

Writing Activity
Suppose you run a company, and you want to expand to another nation. Would you choose a capitalist or communist nation? A developed or developing nation? Would you choose a nation that belongs to a trade alliance? Write a letter to investors explaining your choice.

For: An activity on economic systems
Visit: PHSchool.com
Web Code: led-3303

Chapter 3 Section 3 **79**

Section 3 Assessment

Key Terms
Students' sentences should reflect an understanding of each Key Term.

↻ Target Reading Skill
Both developed countries and developing countries have farms and trade with other nations.

Comprehension and Critical Thinking
1. (a) the government **(b)** Individuals own farms, factories, and offices.
2. (a) It is based on the numbers of industries and level of advanced technology it has.
(b) its level and type of food production; type of trade goods; the availability of healthcare, education, and housing; the kinds of work most people do **(c)** We can predict that the higher the level of development, the stronger the economy will be.

3. (a) NAFTA and the European Union
(b) to reduce costs of trade **(c)** to gain new places to sell its goods and to be able to get goods from its partners more cheaply.

Assess and Reteach

Assess Progress [L2]
Have students complete the Section Assessment. Then administer the *Section Quiz*.

All in One **Foundations of Geography Teaching Resources,** *Section Quiz,* p. 172

Reteach [L1]
If students need more instruction, have them read this section in the Reading and Vocabulary Study Guide.

📖 Chapter 3, Section 3, **Foundations of Geography Reading and Vocabulary Study Guide,** pp. 32–34

Extend [L3]
To extend the lesson, have students access the online activity *Trade in a Global Economy.*

Go **Online** PHSchool.com **For:** Environmental and Global Issues: *Trade in a Global Economy*
Visit: PHSchool.com
Web Code: led-3306

Answers

Draw Conclusions Technology allows more goods to be traded in a shorter amount of time and over long distances.

✓ **Reading Check** to take advantage of each other's special strengths

Writing Activity
Use the *Rubric for Assessing a Writing Assignment* to evaluate students' letters.

All in One **Foundations of Geography Teaching Resources,** *Rubric for Assessing a Writing Assignment,* p. 197

Go **Online** PHSchool.com Typing in the Web code when prompted will bring students directly to detailed instructions for this activity.

Section 4
Step-by-Step Instruction

Objectives

Social Studies
1. Examine different types of states.
2. Investigate types of government.
3. Learn about alliances and international organizations.

Reading/Language Arts
Recognize contrast signal words to understand how things are different.

Prepare to Read

Build Background Knowledge L2

Tell students that in this section they will learn about different kinds of rulers and types of governments. To introduce the topic, remind students that the United States is a representative democracy, headed by a President. Ask them to think of other titles they may know for leaders of a country (*prime minister, queen, king*). Conduct an Idea Wave (TE, p. T35) to elicit responses and make a list on the board.

Set a Purpose for Reading L2

■ Preview the Objectives.

■ Read each statement in *the Reading Readiness Guide* aloud. Ask students to mark the statements true or false.

  All in One Foundations of Geography Teaching Resources, *Reading Readiness Guide*, p. 174

■ Have students discuss the statements in pairs or groups of four, then mark their worksheets again. Use the Numbered Heads participation strategy (TE, p. T36) to call on students to share their group's perspectives.

Vocabulary Builder
Preview Key Terms L2

Pronounce each Key Term, and then ask students to say the word with you. Provide a simple explanation such as, "The constitution of the United States set the framework for our government."

Section
4 Political Systems

Prepare to Read

Objectives
In this section you will
1. Examine different types of states.
2. Investigate types of government.
3. Learn about alliances and international organizations.

Taking Notes
Copy the table below. As you read, fill the table with information about types of states, types of governments, and international organizations.

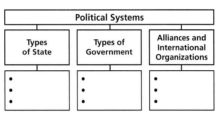

Target Reading Skill

Use Contrast Signal Words
Signal words point out relationships among ideas or events. Certain words, such as *like* or *unlike,* can signal a comparison or contrast. As you read this section, notice the comparisons and contrasts among different types of states and governments. What signal words indicate the comparisons and contrasts?

Key Terms
• **government** (GUV urn munt) *n.* a body that makes and enforces laws

• **state** (stayt) *n.* a region that shares a government
• **dependency** (dee PEN dun see) *n.* a region that belongs to another state
• **nation-state** (NAY shun stayt) *n.* a state that is independent of other states
• **city-state** (SIH tee stayt) *n.* a small city-centered state
• **empire** (EM pyr) *n.* a state containing several countries
• **constitution** (kahn stuh TOO shun) *n.* a set of laws that define and often limit a government's power

In 1994, Eritreans celebrated the first anniversary of their country's independence.

80 Foundations of Geography

Types of States

Long ago, most people lived in small, traditional communities. All adults took part in group decisions. Some small communities still make decisions this way, but they are now part of larger units called nations. Nations are too large for everyone to take part in every decision. Still, nations have to protect people and resolve conflicts between individuals and social groups. In modern nations, these needs are met by **governments**, or organizations that set up and enforce laws.

You may remember that a region is an area united by a common feature. A **state** is a region that shares a government. You probably live in a state that is part of the United States. But the political units that we call "states" in the United States are just one kind of state. The entire United States can also be called a state. It is a region that shares a common government—the federal government.

Target Reading Skill L2

Use Contrast Signal Words Point out the Target Reading Skill. Tell students that being able to recognize words that signal a contrast will let them know when a writer is showing how things are different.

Model recognizing contrast signal words using this passage on p. 80: "You probably live in a state that is part of the United States. But the political units that we call 'states' are

just one kind of state. The entire country can also be called a state." (*The word* but *signals a contrast. It alerts the reader that the word* "state" *can have two meanings.*)

Give students *Identify Contrasts*. Have them complete the activity in groups.

All in One Foundations of Geography Teaching Resources, *Identify Contrasts,* p. 178

Dependencies and Nation-States Some regions are **dependencies,** or regions that belong to another state. Others, like the United States, are **nation-states,** or states that are independent of other states. Each has a common body of laws. Nation-states are often simply called nations. Every place in the world where people live is part of a nation-state or dependency.

Most nation-states are large, but some are tiny. The smallest is Vatican City, which is surrounded by the city of Rome in Italy. Vatican City covers only about 109 acres (44 hectares)!

How States Developed The first real states formed in Southwest Asia more than 5,000 years ago when early cities set up governments. Small city-centered states are called **city-states.** Later, military leaders conquered large areas and ruled them as **empires,** or states containing several countries.

After about 1500, European rulers founded the first true nation-states. European nations established dependencies all over the world. When those dependencies became independent, they formed new nation-states.

✔ **Reading Check** What is the difference between a government and a state?

 **Use Contrast Signal Words**

The first sentence in the paragraph at the left begins with the word *some*. The second sentence begins with *others*. These words signal that a contrast will be made. What contrast is being made?

Vatican City
St. Peter's Basilica, shown below, is the seat of the pope. He leads the Roman Catholic Church and rules Vatican City. **Infer** *What must be true about Vatican City for it to be a nation-state?*

Vocabulary Builder

Use the information below to teach students this section's high-use words.

High-Use Word	Definition and Sample Sentence
surround, p. 81	*v.* to shut in on all sides The farmer decided to **surround** the field with a fence to keep his animals from wandering away.
dispute, p. 84	*n.* an argument or disagreement The neighbors settled the **dispute** by agreeing to build a fence between their properties.

Use Contrast Signal Words As a follow up, ask students to answer the Target Reading Skill question in the Student Edition. (*Two types of states—dependencies and nation-states—are being contrasted.*)

Instruct

Types of States L2

Guided Instruction

■ **Vocabulary Builder** Clarify the high-use word **surround** before reading.

■ Read Types of States using the Paragraph Shrinking technique (TE, p. T34).

■ Discuss with students the kinds of states that exist today or have in the past, and the characteristics of each type. (*A state is a region that shares the same government. Some regions like the United States are nation-states, which are states that are independent of other states. Some states have dependencies, or regions that belong to them. Empires are states that contain several countries, while many ancient states were small, contained city-states.*)

Independent Practice

Have students create the Taking Notes graphic organizer on a blank piece of paper. Then have them begin to fill in the chart with information they have just learned. Briefly model how to record details by using the *Tree Map/Flow Chart* transparency.

▱ **Foundations of Geography Transparencies,** *Transparency B3: Tree Map/Flow Chart*

Monitor Progress

As students fill in the graphic organizer, circulate and make sure that individuals are choosing the correct details. Provide assistance as needed.

Answers

Infer Vatican City must be independent of any other states.

✔ **Reading Check** Government is a system that sets up and enforces rules; a state is a region that shares a government.

Types of Government L2

Guided Instruction

- Have students read about the different kinds of governments in Types of Government.

- Have students name the different types of government and who makes the decisions in each. *(direct democracy, all adult residents; tribal rule, the chief or elders; absolute monarchy, the king or queen; dictatorship, the dictator; oligarchy, a small group of people; constitutional monarchy, representatives selected by the people; representative democracy, representatives selected by the people.)*

- Ask **What is the difference between a direct democracy and a representative democracy?** *(In a direct democracy, all adult residents take part in decisions; in a representative democracy, governments are run by representatives that the people choose.)*

Independent Practice

Have students continue to fill in the graphic organizer with details from this section.

Monitor Progress

Circulate to make sure that individuals are choosing relevant details and recording them in the appropriate box on their charts. Provide assistance as needed.

Answer

Analyze Images Kim Jong Il appears before the military, which may be a source of power for him.

Kim Jong Il
Kim Jong Il, the dictator of North Korea, making a rare public appearance.
Analyze Images *What group in North Korea might be a source of power for Kim Jong Il?*

Types of Government

Each state has a government. There are many different kinds of government. Some governments are controlled by a single person or a small group of people. Others are controlled by all of the people.

Direct Democracy The earliest governments were simple. People lived in small groups. They practiced direct democracy, a form of government in which all adults take part in decisions. Many towns in New England today practice direct democracy. Decisions are made at town meetings where all adult residents can speak and vote.

Tribal Rule In time, communities banded together into larger tribal groups. Members of the tribe had a say in group decisions. But chiefs or elders usually made the final decision about what to do. Decisions were based upon the culture's customs and beliefs.

Absolute Monarchy Until about 200 years ago, one of the most common forms of government was absolute monarchy. In that system, a king or queen who inherits the throne by birth has complete control. Few absolute monarchies still exist today. Saudi Arabia and Brunei are two surviving absolute monarchies.

Dictatorship There are other countries today, however, where just one person rules. A leader who is not a king or queen but who has almost total power over an entire country is called a dictator. Dictatorship is rule by such a leader. Nations ruled by dictators include Cuba, Libya, and North Korea. Dictatorships differ from absolute monarchies because most dictators don't inherit power. Instead, they seize power. Dictators usually remain in power by using violence against their opponents. Dictators deny their people the right to make their own decisions.

Oligarchy Oligarchies are governments controlled by a small group of people. The group may be the leadership of a ruling political party. For example, China is an oligarchy controlled by the leadership of the Communist Party. There are other types of oligarchy. Myanmar, also called Burma, is run by a group of military officers. A group of religious leaders controls Iran. As in a dictatorship, ordinary people have little say in decisions.

82 Foundations of Geography

Differentiated Instruction

For Advanced Readers L3

Tells students that sometimes the form of government may change within a country as a result of a revolution or change in leadership. Have students read *Your Government Has Returned to You!* to see an example of this event in the former European country of Czechoslovakia.

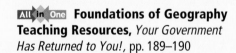 **Foundations of Geography Teaching Resources,** *Your Government Has Returned to You!*, pp. 189–190

Constitutional Monarchy Most monarchies today are constitutional monarchies, or governments in which the power of the king or queen is limited by law. The United Kingdom, the Netherlands, and Kuwait are examples. These nations have **constitutions,** or sets of laws that define and often limit the government's power. In a constitutional monarchy, the king or queen is often only a symbol of the country.

Representative Democracy Representative democracies are governments run by representatives that the people choose. Many constitutional monarchies are also representative democracies. In a representative democracy, the people indirectly hold power to govern and rule. They elect representatives who create laws. If the people do not like what a representative does, they can refuse to reelect that person. Citizens can also work to change laws they do not like. A constitution sets rules for elections, defines the rights of citizens, and limits the powers of the government. This system ensures that power is shared. The United States, Canada, and India are examples of representative democracies.

✓ **Reading Check** What do absolute monarchies, dictatorships, and oligarchies have in common?

Queen Beatrix of the Netherlands heads a constitutional monarchy.

Representative Democracy Members of the United States House of Representatives, shown below, are elected by the people of their districts. **Contrast** *How does a representative democracy differ from a direct democracy?*

Chapter 3 Section 4 **83**

International Organizations L2

Guided Instruction

- **Vocabulary Builder** Clarify the high-use word **dispute** before reading.

- Read about the different ways in which countries work together in International Organizations.

- Have students name three purposes of alliances or international organizations. *(Possible answers: to promote trade, to keep peace, for defense, to work for health and welfare of children.)*

- Ask **What is NATO, and what do its members agree to do?** *(the North Atlantic Treaty Organization; its members have agreed to defend any fellow member that is attacked)*

Independent Practice

As they read about alliances and international organizations, have students complete their charts by recording details in the third box.

Monitor Progress

- When students are finished with their flow charts, show *Section Reading Support Transparency FG 52* and ask students to check their work individually. Go over key concepts and clarify key vocabulary as needed.

  Foundations of Geography Transparencies, *Section Reading Support Transparency FG 52*

- Tell students to fill in the last column of their *Reading Readiness Guides.* Probe for what they learned that confirms or invalidates each statement.

  All in One Foundations of Geography Teaching Resources, *Reading Readiness Guide,* p. 174

Skills Mini Lesson

Decision Making

1. Tell students that when they make decisions, they should identify the problem, list the options, evaluate each option, and then choose the best one.

2. Help students practice the skill by reading the following scenario and then identifying how Tom made his decision: Tom had two choices for an activity on Saturday. He could baby-sit, which would be work, but he would get paid. He could play soccer with his friends which would be fun, but would depend on good weather. Tom decided to baby-sit because he wanted to get paid.

3. Have students apply the skill by writing a short description of a decision they made and how they arrived at that decision.

Answers

✓ **Reading Check** In all three types of government, one group or individual has all the power.

Contrast While all adults take part in decisions in a direct democracy, in a representative democracy, people choose representatives to make decisions on their behalf.

Assess and Reteach

Assess Progress L2
Have students complete the Section Assessment. Then administer the *Section Quiz*.

All in One **Foundations of Geography Teaching Resources,** *Section Quiz*, p. 176

Reteach L1
If students need more instruction, have them read this section in the Reading and Vocabulary Study Guide.

Chapter 3, Section 4, **Foundations of Geography Reading and Vocabulary Study Guide,** pp. 35–37

Extend L3
To extend the lesson, have students do research to learn more about any of the alliances or international organizations mentioned in this section. Students should work in groups to create a display with information about their organization. Then allow students to share their displays with the class.

Answer

✓ **Reading Check** Its purpose is to resolve disputes and promote peace among nations.

Section 4 Assessment

Key Terms
Students' sentences should reflect an understanding of each Key Term.

Target Reading Skill
Governments controlled by a single person are contrasted with governments controlled by all of the people. The words *some* and *others* signal the contrast.

Comprehension and Critical Thinking
1. (a) city-states **(b)** City-states were small and usually controlled only the lands around the city. Modern nation-states are larger.

International Organizations

Nations may make agreements to work together in an alliance. Members of an alliance are called allies. Alliances provide for nations to assist each other with defense. For example, members of the North Atlantic Treaty Organization (NATO) have agreed to defend any fellow member who is attacked.

Military bodies such as NATO are just one type of organization that is international, or involving more than one nation. Some international bodies are mainly economic in purpose. The European Union, for example, promotes economic unity among member nations in Europe.

The United Nations is an international organization meant to resolve disputes and promote peace. Almost all nations of the world belong to the United Nations. Every member has a vote in the General Assembly of the United Nations. But only the United Nations Security Council can make decisions over the use of force. The United States and four other permanent members have the power to prevent action in the Security Council.

The United Nations sponsors other international organizations with special purposes. For example, the Food and Agriculture Organization combats hunger worldwide. The United Nations Children's Fund (UNICEF) promotes the rights and well-being of children.

The United Nations headquarters in New York, New York

✓ **Reading Check** **What is the purpose of the United Nations?**

Section 4 Assessment

Key Terms
Review the key terms at the beginning of this section. Use each term in a sentence that explains its meaning.

Target Reading Skill
Reread the first paragraph on page 82. Which two main types of government are contrasted? Look for contrast signal words.

Comprehension and Critical Thinking
1. (a) Identify What were the earliest types of states?

(b) Compare and Contrast How did those early states differ from modern nation-states?

2. (a) List What are the main types of government?

(b) Categorize In which types of government do ordinary citizens take part in decisions?

3. (a) Define What is an alliance?

(b) Compare and Contrast What are the differences and similarities between alliances and other international organizations?

Writing Activity
Which type of government described in this section appeals most to you? Write a paragraph explaining your preference, and why it appeals to you.

> **Writing Tip** When you write a paragraph, state the main idea in a topic sentence. In this case, the topic sentence will tell the type of government that you prefer. Other sentences should support the main idea with arguments.

84 Foundations of Geography

---

2. (a) direct democracy, absolute monarchy, dictatorship, oligarchy, constitutional monarchy, representative democracy **(b)** direct democracy, constitutional monarchy, representative democracy

3. (a) a group of nations that has agreed to work together **(b)** An alliance is often created to assist members in the event of a military attack, while an international organization may mainly be economic in purpose.

Writing Activity
Use the *Rubric for Assessing a Writing Assignment* to evaluate students' paragraphs.

All in One **Foundations of Geography Teaching Resources,** *Rubric for Assessing a Writing Assignment*, p. 197

Review and Assessment

◆ Chapter Summary

Section 1: Population
- Where people live depends on factors such as climate, soil, and history.
- Population density measures the average number of people living in an area.
- Scientific progress has spurred population growth, which is straining Earth's resources.

Section 2: Migration
- People migrate to seek a better life, or, in some cases, because they have no other choice.
- Cities are growing rapidly in some regions.

Section 3: Economic Systems
- Economic systems may have private ownership of businesses, government ownership, or a mixture of both.
- Developed countries have more industry and technology than developing countries.
- Trade connects countries as buyers and sellers.

Section 4: Political Systems
- The world is divided into nation-states.
- States have governments that differ in the amount of power that citizens have.
- Nation-states may join together in alliances and international organizations.

Harvesting rice in China

◆ Key Terms

Each of the statements below contains a key term from the chapter. If the statement is true, write *true*. If it is false, rewrite the statement to make it true.

1. A country's population is the number of people who live there.
2. Population density measures the size of cities.
3. The movement of people from one region to another is migration.
4. Urbanization is the movement of people to cities.

5. An economy is a system of government.
6. Consumers are people who sell products.
7. Developing nations have few industries and simple technologies.
8. A government is a body that makes and enforces laws and resolves conflicts among its people.
9. A state is a system of government.

┌ Vocabulary Builder ─

Revisit this chapter's high-use words:

cluster	theory	rely
vary	unique	alliance
method	exchange	surround
aspect	value	dispute

Ask students to review the definitions they recorded on their *Word Knowledge* worksheets.

All in One Foundations of Geography Teaching Resources, *Word Knowledge,* p. 180

Consider allowing students to earn extra credit if they use the words in their answers to the questions in the Chapter Review and Assessment. The words must be used correctly and in a natural context to win the extra points.

Chapter 3
Review and Assessment
Review Chapter Content

- Review and revisit the major themes of this chapter by asking students to classify what Guiding Question each bulleted statement in the Chapter Summary answers. Have students write each statement down and work in pairs to determine which statement applies to which Guiding Question. Refer to page 1 in the Student Edition for text of Guiding Questions.

- Assign *Vocabulary Development* for students to review Key Terms.

  All in One Foundations of Geography Teaching Resources, *Vocabulary Development,* p. 196

Answers

Key Terms
1. True
2. False. Population density measures the average number of people living in an area.
3. True
4. True
5. False. An economy is a system in which people make, exchange, and use things that have value.
6. False. Consumers are people who buy products.
7. True
8. True
9. False. A state is a region that shares a government.

Review and Assessment

Comprehension and Critical Thinking

10. (a) the way a population is spread out over an area **(b)** climate, natural resources, availability of water, availability of soil for farming **(c)** Because of advancements in food production and transportation, not everyone needs to farm for a living and can therefore live away from rural areas, in cities.

11. (a) It has grown enormously. **(b)** Difficulties include: overcrowding, hunger, unemployment, lack of housing, fresh water, and schools, and inadequate public services

12. (a) when people move by their own choice **(b)** Some people are pulled to a new country by better opportunities, more jobs, or a better climate. Others are pushed to escape hunger, or war, or because they want political freedom.

13. (a) an economic system in which private individuals own most businesses **(b)** Capitalism is an economic system that is controlled by the producers and consumers while communism is an economic system controlled by the government.

14. (a) inadequate healthcare, housing, education, and public services, such as water and electricity **(b)** Developing countries do not have much wealth or industry and have shortages of land and water, which makes it difficult to overcome the challenges.

15. (a) direct democracy and representative democracy **(b)** In democracies a greater number of the citizens get to have a say in government actions than in other forms.

Skills Practice

Purple: more than 260 persons per sq. mile, more than 100 persons per sq. kilometer; pink: 52–259 persons per sq. mile, 21–100 per sq. kilometer; orange: 24–51 persons per sq. mile, 5–20 per sq. kilometer; yellow: less than 24 persons per sq. mile, less than 5 per sq. kilometer; most sparsely populated areas include parts of North and South America, Asia, Africa, and most of Australia; students' conclusions will vary, but may mention that areas that have small populations usually have difficult living conditions, such as climate or terrain, or are not easily accessible.

◆ Comprehension and Critical Thinking

10. (a) Define What is population distribution?
(b) Explain What factors affect population distribution in a region?
(c) Compare and Contrast How are those factors different today than they were when most people were farmers?

11. (a) Identify How has the size of world populations changed in recent years?
(b) Identify Cause and Effect What difficulties have resulted from the change in the size of world populations?

12. (a) Define What is voluntary migration?
(b) Make Generalizations Why do people choose to migrate?

13. (a) Define What is capitalism?
(b) Contrast How does capitalism differ from communism?

14. (a) List What are some challenges faced by developing countries?
(b) Infer Why do developing countries face these challenges?

15. (a) Identify What are two types of democracy?
(b) Contrast How do democracies differ from other forms of government?

◆ Skills Practice

Using Population Density Maps In the Skills for Life activity in this chapter, you learned how to read a population density map using the map key.

Review the steps you followed to learn this skill. Then review the map on pages 62 and 63, titled The World: Population Density. Using the map key, describe what each color on the map represents and then list the most sparsely populated areas shown. Finally, draw conclusions about why these areas have such small populations.

◆ Writing Activity: Math

Suppose you are a demographer projecting population growth for three countries. Use the following information to create a population bar graph for each country:

	Birthrate	Death Rate
Country A	14.2	8.7
Country B	9.8	9.7
Country C	9.4	13.9

Then, write a brief paragraph explaining your graph. For each country, is the population increasing, decreasing, or stable? Explain why.

MAP✶MASTER™ Skills Activity

Place Location For each place listed below, write the letter from the map that shows its location.

1. Asia
2. Antarctica
3. Africa
4. South America
5. North America
6. Europe
7. Australia

Go Online
PHSchool.com Use Web Code **lep-3215** for an **interactive map.**

Continents

Writing Activity: Math

Students' bar graphs should show that Country A has a growing population, Country B's population is staying about the same, and Country C's population is declining. Their paragraphs should explain these findings.

Use *Rubric for Assessing a Bar Graph* to evaluate students' graphs.

All in One Foundations of Geography Teaching Resources, *Rubric for Assessing a Bar Graph,* p. 198

Standardized Test Prep

Test-Taking Tips

Some questions on standardized tests ask you to analyze a reading selection for a main idea. Read the passage in the box below. Then follow the tips to answer the sample question.

This region has one of the highest population densities in the world. As many as 5,000 people per square mile live in parts of the region. There are good reasons for this heavy population density. The land is fertile. Though the desert is not far away, the river contains plenty of water for the people who live there.

TIP As you read each sentence, think about what main idea it supports.

Pick the letter that best answers the question.

Which sentence states this passage's main idea?

A ~~Demographers study human populations.~~

B Egypt's Nile River valley supports a large population.

C ~~People find ways to adapt to their environment.~~

D Many people live near the Mississippi River.

TIP Cross out answer choices that don't make sense. Then pick from the remaining choices the one that BEST answers the question.

Think It Through The passage does not mention demographers. So you can cross out answer A. You can also rule out C, because the passage does not discuss people adapting to their environment. Answers B and D both mention specific regions. Which region does the paragraph describe? The paragraph mentions a desert. There is no desert near the Mississippi River. So the answer is B.

Practice Questions

Use the tips above and other tips in this book to help you answer the following questions.

1. The number of people per square mile is a region's
   A population distribution.
   B population.
   C elevation.
   D population density.

2. People moving to a different region to seek better farming opportunities is an example of
   A trade.
   B voluntary migration.
   C involuntary migration.
   D urbanization.

3. In which of the following does the government own most workplaces?
   A capitalism
   B developing country
   C communism
   D developed country

Read the following passage, and answer the question that follows.

A constitutional monarch has little power. Under some constitutions, elected representatives have the law-making power instead of the monarch. In such cases, the government works much like other representative democracies.

4. What is the main idea of this passage?
   A An absolute monarch has great power.
   B Constitutions are always democratic.
   C A constitutional monarchy may also be a representative democracy.
   D A constitutional monarch cannot interfere with representative democracy.

Use Web Code **lea-3301** for a **Chapter 3 self-test.**

Standardized Test Prep

Answers

1. D
2. B
3. C
4. C

Go Online PHSchool.com Students may use the Chapter 3 self-test on PHSchool.com to prepare for the Chapter Test.

Assessment Resources

Use *Chapter Tests A and B* to assess students' mastery of chapter content.

All in One **Foundations of Geography Teaching Resources,** *Chapter Tests A and B,* pp. 199–204

Tests are also available on the *ExamView Test Bank CD-ROM*

⊙ *ExamView Test Bank CD-ROM*

Objectives

1. Identify the skills Sam needs to survive alone in the wilderness.

2. Discover how Sam came to understand the natural world.

3. Identify devices used by the author to create effects.

4. Analyze the effectiveness of elements of plot, such as setting and character.

Prepare to Read

Build Background Knowledge L2

Have students read the Background Information in the Student Edition. Then ask them to brainstorm a list of items they would want to have with them if they were going to live in the woods. Use the Think-Write-Pair-Share strategy (TE, p. T36) to elicit student responses. Then list them on the board.

Instruct

My Side of the Mountain L2

Guided Instruction

- Point out that some potentially unfamiliar words are defined in the margin. Clarify the meanings of the words before reading.

- Have students read the selection using the Silent Structured Reading strategy (TE p. T34).

- Tell students that the author of this story uses a literary technique called figurative language to convey Sam's ability to read the weather and animal behavior. One type of figurative language is personification, or describing an object, animal, or idea as if it had human characteristics. Ask students to look through the text to find examples of personification. *("the moods of storms;" "the air said snow," "trees cry out," and "wind gets caught in a ravine and screams until it dies.")*

- Similes, or phrases that compare things using the words *like* or *as*, are another form of figurative language. Ask students to look through the story and identify similes.

Literature

My Side of the Mountain
By Jean Craighead George

Prepare to Read

Background Information
Have you ever camped out overnight? Have you ever built a fire in order to keep warm? Suppose you had no electricity or your home had no heating system. How would you cope with the natural world without modern technology? Do you think that living closer to the natural world would change you in any significant way?

Sam Gribley is the fictional hero of the novel *My Side of the Mountain*. When he decided to live close to nature, he built a tree house in the Catskill Mountains of New York and then moved in with his only companion, Frightful, a falcon. This excerpt describes their first winter in the mountains.

Objectives
As you read this selection, you will
- Identify the skills Sam needed to survive alone in the wilderness.
- Discover how Sam came to understand the natural world.

I lived close to the weather. It is surprising how you watch it when you live in it. Not a cloud passed unnoticed, not a wind blew untested. I knew the moods of the storms, where they came from, their shapes and colors. When the sun shone, I took Frightful to the meadow and we slid down the mountain on my snapping-turtle-shell sled. She really didn't care much for this.

When the winds changed and the air smelled like snow, I would stay in my tree, because I had gotten lost in a blizzard one afternoon and had to hole up in a rock ledge until I could see where I was going. That day the winds were so strong I could not push against them, so I crawled under the ledge; for hours I wondered if I would be able to dig out when the storm blew on. Fortunately I only had to push through a foot of snow. However, that taught me to stay home when the air said "snow." Not that I

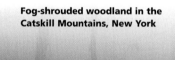

Fog-shrouded woodland in the Catskill Mountains, New York

Read Fluently

Form the class into partners. Choose a paragraph from the selection. Have students take turns reading the paragraph aloud. Ask them to underline words that give them trouble as they read. Then, have them decode the problem words with their partner. Provide assistance as needed. Have them reread the paragraph two more times to improve their reading speed. Remind them to stop at the commas and periods and to read with expression. Guide students to see that using figurative language allows the author to maker her points about Sam's life among nature more vividly.

was afraid of being caught far from home in a storm, for I could find food and shelter and make a fire anywhere, but I had become as attached to my hemlock house as a brooding bird to her nest. Caught out in the storms and weather, I had an urgent desire to return to my tree, even as The Baron Weasel returned to his den, and the deer to their copse. We all had our little "patch" in the wilderness. We all fought to return there.

I usually came home at night with the nuthatch that roosted in a nearby sapling. I knew I was late if I tapped the tree and he came out. Sometimes when the weather was icy and miserable, I would hear him high in the trees near the edge of the meadow, yanking and yanking and flicking his tail, and then I would see him wing to bed early. I considered him a pretty good barometer, and if he went to his tree early, I went to mine early too. When you don't have a newspaper or radio to give you weather bulletins, watch the birds and animals. They can tell when a storm is coming. I called the nuthatch "Barometer," and when he holed up, I holed up, lit my light, and sat by my fire whittling or learning new tunes on my reed whistle. I was now really into the teeth of winter, and quite fascinated by its activity. There is no such thing as a "still winter night." Not only are many animals running around in the breaking cold, but the trees cry out and limbs snap and fall, and the wind gets caught in a ravine and screams until it dies.

✓ Reading Check What did Sam name the nuthatch? Explain why.

hemlock (HEM lahk) *n.* an evergreen tree with drooping branches and short needles
copse (kahps) *n.* a thicket of small trees or shrubs
yank (yangk) *v.* to give the call made by a nuthatch
barometer (buh RAHM uh tur) *n.* an instrument for forecasting changes in the weather; anything that indicates a change
whittle (WHIT ul) *v.* to cut or pare thin shavings from wood with a knife
teeth of winter (teeth uv WIN tur) *n.* the coldest, harshest time of winter

About the Selection

My Side of the Mountain, by Jean Craighead George (New York: E. P. Dutton, 1959), includes sketches of Sam Gribley's adventures.

Review and Assessment

Comprehension and Critical Thinking

1. (a) Identify When the weather is bad, what is Sam's "urgent desire"?
(b) Compare To what does Sam compare this desire?
(c) Interpret What does Sam tell us about himself when he makes a comparison?
2. (a) Recall What are some of the clues Sam has about what the weather will be like?
(b) Describe What parts of the natural world does Sam seem to notice most?
(c) Evaluate Sometimes Sam talks about the wind and trees

as if they were alive. Think about your relationship with nature. How is it like Sam's? How is it different?

Writing Activity

Make a list of sounds you hear only in winter. What are the tastes and smells that make you think of winter? List them. What are the sights of winter? Add them to your list. Then write an essay describing the place you most like to be in winter and explain why.

About the Author

Jean Craighead George (b. 1919) often went camping, climbed trees, and studied living things as she grew up. Ms. George has been writing about nature and its lessons since she was eight years old, and has written more than 80 books for young readers.

Literature **89**

Review and Assessment

Comprehension and Critical Thinking

1. (a) to return to his tree **(b)** to the desire of animals to go to their shelters **(c)** that he relates to the animals because he thinks of himself as one of them

2. (a) the air smells like snow; the winds change; the nuthatch goes to bed early **(b)** the behavior of animals **(c)** Answers

will vary, but students should indicate how their relationship with nature is similar to or different than Sam's.

Writing Activity

Students should create lists of the sights, sounds, tastes, and smells of winter.

All in One **Foundations of Geography Teaching Resources,** *Rubric for Assessing a Writing Assignment,* p. 197

■ *Hint:* Have them look at how Sam describes the animals he lives near. *(Examples of similes are: on page 89, "I had become as attached to my hemlock house as a brooding bird to her nest." "...even as The Baron Weasel returned to his den."* Guide students to see that using figurative language allows the author to make her points about Sam's life among nature more vividly.

Independent Practice

Have students write a response to the following statement: "I would/would not want to live like Sam does because…" Make sure that students include at least three reasons why they would or would not like to live like Sam, and that they support each reason with details. Give students *Creating Paragraph Outlines* to help them prepare for writing.

All in One **Foundations of Geography Teaching Resources,** *Creating Paragraph Outlines,* p. 195

Monitor Progress

As students work on their paragraphs, circulate around the room and provide assistance as needed.

Assess and Reteach

Assess Progress L2
Have students answer the assessment questions.

Reteach L1
If students are having difficulty understanding the story, write the words *Plot, Character,* and *Setting* on the board. Help students identify these elements in the story and list them under the correct heading on the board.

Extend L3
To extend the lesson, have students read the selected excerpt from *Hatchet* and answer the questions that follow. Ask students to make a chart in which they compare and contrast the experiences of the boy in each selection.

All in One **Foundations of Geography Teaching Resources,** *Hatchet,* pp. 191–194

Answer

✓ Reading Check Barometer; because its actions told Sam when a storm might be coming.

Cultures of the World

Overview

 Section 1

Understanding Culture
1. Learn about culture.
2. Explore how culture has developed.

 Section 2

Culture and Society
1. Learn how people are organized into groups.
2. Investigate language.
3. Explore the role of religion.

 Section 3

Cultural Change
1. Explore how cultures change.
2. Learn how ideas spread from one culture to another.

Video

What is Culture?
Length: 5 minutes, 10 seconds
Use with Section 1
A broad overview of cultures around the world, this segment defines culture and discusses elements of culture. It focuses on the cultures of Sri Lanka as a case study.

Technology Resources

PHSchool.com

Students use embedded Web codes to access Internet activities, chapter self-tests, and additional map practice. They may also access Dorling Kindersley's Online Desk Reference to learn more about each country they study.

Use the Interactive Textbook to make content and concepts come alive through animations, videos, and activities that accompany the complete basal text—online and on CD-ROM.

PRENTICE HALL
TeacherEXPRESS™
Plan • Teach • Assess

Use this complete suite of powerful teaching tools to make planning lessons and administering tests quicker and easier.

Reading and Assessment

Reading and Vocabulary Instruction

🎯 Model the Target Reading Skill

Sequence Explain to students that recognizing the sequence, or order, of events in written material can help them organize ideas and analyze patterns. Becoming familiar with words that signal sequence is one way for students to strengthen and apply this skill. Have students practice identifying sequence and recognizing sequence signal words by putting the following statements in order:

1. *Then I remembered that there was a shopping list in my pocket.*
2. *Before I left my house, I wrote out a grocery list.*
3. *Later, when I start cooking, I will have all the ingredients I need.*
4. *When I first entered the store, I could not remember what items I needed.*
5. *Soon, my cart was filled up with groceries.*

Model the approach by thinking out loud: "I am going to look for signal words to put these sentences in order. I see the following signal words: *then, before, later, first, soon.* I think sentence two should be first in the sequence, because it happens *before* the person goes to the store. The first sentence that takes place in the store is four, when she *first entered*, so that comes next. I think sentence one comes after that because she needed the shopping list before she could fill her cart with groceries. She finishes her shopping in sentence five. Finally, she uses the future tense and the word *Later* in sentence three. The correct sequence should be: sentences 2, 4, 1, 5, 3."

Use the following worksheets from All-in-One Foundations of Geography Teaching Resources (pp. 221–222) to support this chapter's Target Reading Skill.

Vocabulary Builder
High-Use Academic Words

Use these steps to teach this chapter's high-use words:

1. Have students rate how well they know each word on their Word Knowledge worksheets (All-in-One Foundations of Geography Teaching Resources, p. 223).
2. Pronounce each word and ask students to repeat it.
3. Give students a brief definition or sample sentence (provided on TE pp. 93, 97, and 105).
4. Work with students as they fill in the "Definition or Example" column of their Word Knowledge worksheets.

Assessment

Formal Assessment

Test students' understanding of core knowledge and skills.

Chapter Tests A and B, All-in-One Foundations of Geography Teaching Resources, pp. 235–240

Customize the Chapter Tests to suit your needs.

ExamView Test Bank CD-ROM

Skills Assessment

Assess geographic literacy.

MapMaster Skills, Student Edition, pp. 99, 100, 110

Assess reading and comprehension.

Target Reading Skills, Student Edition, pp. 95, 97, 106, and in Section Assessments

Chapter 4 Assessment, Foundations of Geography Reading and Vocabulary Study Guide, p. 48

Performance Assessment

Assess students' performance on this chapter's Writing Activities using the following rubrics from All-in-One Foundations of Geography Teaching Resources.

Rubric for Assessing a Writing Assignment, p. 233

Rubric for Assessing a Journal Entry, p. 234

Assess students' work through performance tasks.

Small Group Activity: Creating a Report on World Music, All-in-One Foundations of Geography Teaching Resources, pp. 226–229

Online Assessment

Have students check their own understanding.

Chapter Self-Test

Section 1 **Understanding Culture**

 1.5 periods, .75 block

Social Studies Objectives

1. Learn about culture.
2. Explore how culture has developed.

Reading/Language Arts Objective

Identify the sequence of events to help you understand and remember them.

Prepare to Read	**Instructional Resources**	**Differentiated Instruction**
Build Background Knowledge Show students a video and discuss the elements that make up culture. **Set a Purpose for Reading** Have students begin to fill out the *Reading Readiness Guide*. **Preview Key Terms** Teach the section's Key Terms. **Target Reading Skill** Introduce the section's Target Reading Skill of **understanding sequence.**	**All in One Foundations of Geography Teaching Resources** L2 Reading Readiness Guide, p. 210 L2 Identify Sequence, p. 221 **World Studies Video Program** L2 What is Culture?	**Spanish Reading and Vocabulary Study Guide** L1 Chapter 4, Section 1, pp. 28–29 ELL

Instruct	**Instructional Resources**	**Differentiated Instruction**
What Is Culture? Discuss how elements of culture differ throughout the world. **The Development of Culture** Ask about the four major advances of early cultures. **Target Reading Skill** Review **understanding sequence.**	**All in One Foundations of Geography Teaching Resources** L2 Guided Reading and Review, p. 211 L2 Reading Readiness Guide, p. 210 **Foundations of Geography Transparencies** L2 Section Reading Support Transparency FG 53	**Spanish Support** L2 Guided Reading and Review (Spanish), p. 30 ELL

Assess and Reteach	**Instructional Resources**	**Differentiated Instruction**
Assess Progress Evaluate student comprehension with the section assessment and section quiz. **Reteach** Assign the Reading and Vocabulary Study Guide to help struggling students. **Extend** Extend the lesson by assigning a Book Project.	**All in One Foundations of Geography Teaching Resources** L2 Section Quiz, p. 212 L3 Book Project: Desktop Countries, pp. 33–35 Rubric for Assessing a Writing Assignment, p. 233 **Reading and Vocabulary Study Guide** L1 Chapter 4, Section 1, pp. 39–41	**Spanish Support** L2 Section Quiz (Spanish), p. 31 ELL

Key

L1 Basic to Average   L3 Average to Advanced

L2 For All Students

LPR Less Proficient Readers
AR Advanced Readers
SN Special Needs Students

GT Gifted and Talented
ELL English Language Learners

Section 2 Culture and Society

 3.5 periods, 1.75 blocks (includes Skills for Life)

Social Studies Objectives
1. Learn how people are organized into groups.
2. Investigate language.
3. Explore the role of religion.

Reading/Language Arts Objective
Learning to notice the sequence of important changes can help you understand, remember, and interpret these changes.

Prepare to Read	**Instructional Resources**	**Differentiated Instruction**
Build Background Knowledge Discuss three elements of culture: social structure, language, and religion. **Set a Purpose for Reading** Have students evaluate statements on the *Reading Readiness Guide*. **Preview Key Terms** Teach the section's Key Terms. **Target Reading Skill** Introduce the section's Target Reading Skill of **understanding sequence.**	**All in One Foundations of Geography Teaching Resources** L2 Reading Readiness Guide, p. 214 L2 Identify Sequence, p. 221	**Spanish Reading and Vocabulary Study Guide** L1 Chapter 4, Section 2, pp. 30–31 ELL

Instruct	**Instructional Resources**	**Differentiated Instruction**
How Society Is Organized Ask about extended and nuclear families. **Target Reading Skill** Review **understanding sequence.** **Language** Discuss language and how it can uphold or reflect particular customs. **Religion** Discuss features of different religions.	**All in One Foundations of Geography Teaching Resources** L2 Guided Reading and Review, p. 215 L2 Reading Readiness Guide, p. 214 **Foundations of Geography Transparencies** L2 Section Reading Support Transparency FG 54 L2 Transparency B15: Outline	**All in One Foundations of Geography Teaching Resources** L3 City Kids in China, pp. 230–231 AR, GT L2 Skills for Life, p. 225 AR, GT, LPR, SN **Teacher's Edition** L3 For Advanced Readers, TE p. 99 L3 For Gifted and Talented, TE p. 99 **Spanish Support** L2 Guided Reading and Review (Spanish), p. 32 ELL

Assess and Reteach	**Instructional Resources**	**Differentiated Instruction**
Assess Progress Evaluate student comprehension with the section assessment and section quiz. **Reteach** Assign the Reading and Vocabulary Study Guide to help struggling students. **Extend** Have students work in groups to learn about rituals of world religions.	**All in One Foundations of Geography Teaching Resources** L2 Section Quiz, p. 216 Rubric for Assessing a Journal Entry, p. 234 **Reading and Vocabulary Study Guide** L1 Chapter 4, Section 2, pp. 42–44	**All in One Foundations of Geography Teaching Resources** Rubric for Assessing a Writing Assignment, p. 233 **Teacher's Edition** L1 For Less Proficient Readers, TE p. 103 L1 For Special Needs Students, TE p. 103 **Social Studies Skills Tutor CD-ROM** L1 Making Valid Generalizations ELL, LPR, SN **Spanish Support** L2 Section Quiz (Spanish), p. 33 ELL

Key
L1 Basic to Average	L3 Average to Advanced	LPR Less Proficient Readers	GT Gifted and Talented
L2 For All Students		AR Advanced Readers	ELL English Language Learners
		SN Special Needs Students	

Section 3 Cultural Change

 3.5 periods, 1.75 blocks (includes Chapter Review and Assessment)

Social Studies Objectives
1. Explore how cultures change.
2. Learn how ideas spread from one culture to another.

Reading/Language Arts Objective
Identify signal words to help keep the order of events clear.

Prepare to Read

Build Background Knowledge
Ask students to identify elements of their cultures that have been borrowed from others.

Set a Purpose for Reading
Have students evaluate statements on the *Reading Readiness Guide*.

Preview Key Terms
Teach the section's Key Terms.

Target Reading Skill
Introduce the section's Target Reading Skill of **recognizing words that signal sequence.**

Instructional Resources

All in One Foundations of Geography Teaching Resources
- L2 Reading Readiness Guide, p. 218
- L2 Recognize Sequence Signal Words, p. 222

Differentiated Instruction

Spanish Reading and Vocabulary Study Guide
- L1 Chapter 4, Section 3, pp. 32–33 ELL

Instruct

How Cultures Change
Discuss cultural change and have students predict future changes in their own cultures.

How Ideas Spread
Discuss cultural diffusion.

Target Reading Skill
Review **recognizing words that signal sequence.**

Instructional Resources

All in One Foundations of Geography Teaching Resources
- L2 Guided Reading and Review, p. 219
- L2 Reading Readiness Guide, p. 218

Foundations of Geography Transparencies
- L2 Section Reading Support Transparency FG 55
- L2 Transparency B18: Concept Web

Differentiated Instruction

All in One Foundations of Geography Teaching Resources
- L3 Enrichment, p. 224 AR, GT

Teacher's Edition
- L3 For Advanced Readers, TE p. 106
- L1 For English Language Learners, TE p. 106

Spanish Support
- L2 Guided Reading and Review (Spanish), p. 34 ELL

Assess and Reteach

Assess Progress
Evaluate student comprehension with the section assessment and section quiz.

Reteach
Assign the Reading and Vocabulary Study Guide to help struggling students.

Extend
Extend the lesson by assigning a Small Group Activity.

Instructional Resources

All in One Foundations of Geography Teaching Resources
- L2 Section Quiz, p. 220
- L3 Small Group Activity: Creating a Report on World Music, pp. 226–229
  Rubric for Assessing a Writing Assignment, p. 233
- L2 Vocabulary Development, p. 232
- L2 Word Knowledge, p. 223
- L2 Chapter Tests A and B, pp. 235–240

Reading and Vocabulary Study Guide
- L1 Chapter 4, Section 3, pp. 45–47

Differentiated Instruction

Spanish Support
- L2 Section Quiz (Spanish), p. 35 ELL
- L2 Chapter Summary (Spanish), p. 36 ELL
- L2 Vocabulary Development (Spanish), p. 37 ELL

Key
- L1 Basic to Average
- L2 For All Students
- L3 Average to Advanced
- LPR Less Proficient Readers
- AR Advanced Readers
- SN Special Needs Students
- GT Gifted and Talented
- ELL English Language Learners

90e

Reading Background

Oral Cloze Reading

In Section 1 of this chapter, students may use the Oral Cloze Reading strategy to explore the section called Understanding Culture. Help students get the most out of this reading strategy by choosing meaningful words to leave out, such as nouns and verbs, rather than prepositions or conjunctions, and by choosing words that are not particularly long or difficult. For example, in the following paragraph from page 92 of the Student Edition, you might leave out the words indicated in bold.

What Is Culture?

*Culture is the way of life of a **people**, including their beliefs, customs, and practices. The **language** people speak and the way they **dress** are both parts of their **culture**. So are the work people do, what they do after **work** or school, and the **ideas** that influence them.*

Processing Information

Because students will be studying sequence in this chapter's Target Reading Skill, use this opportunity to talk to them about different plans or structures authors may use to organize, or craft, their ideas. Sequence, or chronological order, is one type of author's craft, and others may include comparison and contrast, or cause and effect. Ask students to read the two paragraphs on page 99 of the Student Edition and determine what kind of structure the author is using. Ask: *Is the information in sequence? Is there a clear cause and effect? Is the author highlighting similarities and differences?* Students should see that the author is comparing and contrasting the languages of different groups and countries.

World Studies Background

Folk Art

Folk art can tell us a great deal about a society. Folk artists do not follow the trends of popular art. They develop their own art that reflects the local culture. Folk art includes clothing, toys, and religious figurines that express the typical costumes, forms of entertainment, and beliefs of a society. Because the art is both decorative and functional, it reveals the aesthetic style and everyday routines of a people.

Languages Spread and Shrink

In the 1990s, scholars counted about 6,000 languages spoken across the world. However, scholars predict that within the next 100 years, as societies become more interconnected through improved com-munication, distinct languages will blend together and unique local languages will die out, leaving only 3000 languages in use. This equals a loss of one language every 12 days.

Computers Finding Cures

As technology advances, computer users can help scientists further their research toward curing diseases. In similar pro-grams launched in 2001 and 2003, volun-teers downloaded a screensaver that allowed their computers to perform com-plicated calculations related to disease research. The power of so many comput-ers working on a project is immensely more powerful than the largest supercom-puter and can yield faster results.

Get in-depth information on topics of global importance with **Prentice Hall NewsTracker,** powered by FT.com.

 Use Web Code **led-3400** for **Prentice Hall NewsTracker.**

Chapter 4

Guiding Questions

Remind students about the Guiding Questions introduced at the beginning of the book.

Section 1 relates to **Guiding Question** ③
What is a culture? *(A culture is the way of life of a people, including their beliefs, customs, and practices.)*

Section 2 relates to **Guiding Question** ③
What is a culture? *(Social organization, language, and religion are all parts of a culture.)*

Section 3 relates to **Guiding Question** ③
What is a culture? *(A culture changes through the spread of new technologies and new ideas.)*

⟳ Target Reading Skill

In this chapter, students will learn and apply the reading skill of sequence. Use the following worksheets to help students practice this skill:

> **All in One** **Foundations of Geography Teaching Resources,** *Identify Sequence,* p. 221, *Recognize Sequence Signal Words,* p. 222

Chapter 4 Cultures of the World

Chapter Preview

This chapter will introduce you to the concept of culture, the things that make up culture, and the ways in which cultures change.

Section 1
Understanding Culture

Section 2
Culture and Society

Section 3
Cultural Change

⟳ Target Reading Skill

Sequence In this chapter, you will focus on the text structure by identifying the order, or sequence, of events. Noting the sequence of events can help you understand and remember the events.

▶ Young women in traditional dress at a festival in Pushkar, India

---

Bibliography

For the Teacher

Kohl, MaryAnn F., and Jean Potter. *Global Art: Activities, Projects and Inventions from Around the World.* Gryphon House, 1998.

Knight, Margy Burns. *Talking Walls: The Stories Continue.* Tillbury House Publishers, 2003.

Perry, Phyllis Jean. *Keeping the Traditions: A Multicultural Resource.* Fulcrum Publishers, 2000.

For the Student

L1 Wroble, Lisa A. *Kids During the Industrial Revolution* (Kids Throughout History). Rosen Publishing Group, 2003.

L2 Macdonald, Fiona. *Clothing and Jewelry* (Discovering World Cultures). Bt Bound, 2001.

L3 Na, An. *A Step From Heaven.* Front Street Press, 2001.

Using the Visual $\boxed{\text{L2}}$

Reach Into Your Background Have students read the caption and study the photograph on pp. 90–91. Ask them if they have seen or participated in ceremonies where traditional dress is worn. Ask them why wearing traditional dress during special occasions might be important to Indian culture. Have students share their ideas.

Chapter 4 **91**

Chapter Resources

Teaching Resources
$\boxed{\text{L2}}$ Vocabulary Development, p. 232
$\boxed{\text{L2}}$ Skills for Life, p. 225
$\boxed{\text{L2}}$ Chapter Tests A and B, pp. 235–240

Spanish Support
$\boxed{\text{L2}}$ Spanish Chapter Summary, p. 36
$\boxed{\text{L2}}$ Spanish Vocabulary Development, p. 37

Media and Technology
$\boxed{\text{L1}}$ Student Edition on Audio CD
$\boxed{\text{L1}}$ Guided Reading Audiotapes, English and Spanish
$\boxed{\text{L2}}$ Social Studies Skills Tutor CD-ROM
ExamView Test Bank CD-ROM

DISCOVERY World Studies
CHANNEL Video Program
SCHOOL

Interactive Textbook

PRENTICE HALL
TeacherEXPRESS
Plan · Teach · Assess

Section 1
Step-by-Step Instruction

Objectives

Social Studies
1. Learn about culture.
2. Explore how culture has developed.

Reading/Language Arts
Identify the sequence of events to help you understand and remember them.

Prepare to Read

Build Background Knowledge   L2

Tell students that in this chapter they will be learning about the elements that make up culture. Show the video *What is Culture?* and as they watch, ask students to write down a definition of culture and some of its parts. Point out the definition in the text to help students sharpen their answers. Conduct an Idea Wave (TE, p. T35) to generate a list of definitions on the board.

📼 *What Is Culture?*, **World Studies Video Program**

Set a Purpose for Reading   L2

■ Preview the objectives.

■ Form students into pairs or groups of four. Distribute the *Reading Readiness Guide*. Ask the students to fill in the first two columns of the chart. Use the Numbered Heads participation strategy (TE, p. T36) to call on students to share one piece of information they already know and one piece of information they want to know.

All in One **Foundations of Geography Teaching Resources**, *Reading Readiness Guide*, p. 210

Vocabulary Builder
Preview Key Terms   L2

Pronounce each Key Term, then ask the students to say the word with you. Provide a simple explanation such as, "A civilization is a society advanced in art, science, and government."

Section 1
Understanding Culture

Prepare to Read

Objectives
In this section you will
1. Learn about culture.
2. Explore how culture has developed.

Taking Notes

Copy the concept web below. As you read this section, fill in the web with information about culture, its relation to the environment, and how it has developed. Add ovals as needed for concepts in the section.

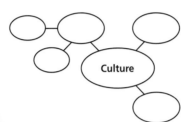

Culture

🎯 Target Reading Skill

Understand Sequence
A sequence is the order in which a series of events occurs. Noting the sequence of important events can help you understand and remember the events. You can show the order of events by making a sequence chart. Write the first event, or thing that sets the other events in motion, in the first box. Then write each additional event in a box. Use arrows to show how one event leads to the next.

Key Terms

• **culture** (KUL chur) *n.* the way of life of a people, including their beliefs and practices
• **cultural landscape** (KUL chur ul LAND skayp) *n.* the parts of a people's environment that they have shaped and the technology they have used to shape it
• **civilization** (sih vuh luh ZAY shun) *n.* an advanced culture with cities and a system of writing
• **institution** (in stuh TOO shun) *n.* a custom or organization with social, educational, or religious purposes

A grandfather in Japan teaching his grandson to use chopsticks

What Is Culture?

Culture is the way of life of a people, including their beliefs, customs, and practices. The language people speak and the way they dress are both parts of their culture. So are the work people do, what they do after work or school, and the ideas that influence them.

Elements of Culture Parents pass culture on to their children, generation after generation. Ideas and ways of doing things are called cultural traits. Over time, cultural traits may change.

Some elements of a culture are easy to see. They include material things, such as houses, television sets, food, and clothing. Sports and literature are visible elements of culture as well. Things you cannot see or touch are also part of culture. They include spiritual beliefs, government, and ideas about right and wrong. Finally, language is a very important part of culture.

92 Foundations of Geography

🎯 Target Reading Skill   L2

Understand Sequence Explain that one way to organize ideas is by sequence, or time order. Explain sequence by asking students to consider the order of events in their day. Tell students that events in history also can be organized in a logical sequence.

Model understanding sequence using the first two paragraphs under the head "Technology and Civilization" on p. 94 of the Student Edition. Make a sequence chart on the board using the events leading to the Agricultural Revolution.

Give students *Identify Sequence*. Have them complete the activity in groups.

All in One **Foundations of Geography Teaching Resources**, *Identify Sequence*, p. 221

People and Their Land Geographers study themes of culture, especially human activities related to the environment. The theme of human-environment interaction deals with these activities. Geographers want to know how the environment affects culture. For example, Japan is a nation of mountainous islands, with limited farmland. So the Japanese have turned to the sea. Fish and seaweed are popular foods in Japan.

However, environment does not dictate culture. Like Japan, Greece is a nation of mountainous islands and peninsulas surrounded by the sea. The Greeks eat some fish, but they have cleared mountainsides as well for use as pasture. Goats and sheep graze on the mountainsides and provide food for the Greeks.

Geographers are also interested in the effect people have on their environment. Often the effect is tied to a culture's technology, even if that technology is simple. For example, the Greeks have cleared their rugged land for pasture. The Japanese harvest seaweed.

A **cultural landscape** is the parts of a people's environment that they have shaped and the technology they have used to shape it. This varies from place to place. On hilly Bali (BAH lee), in Indonesia, farmers have carved terraces into hillsides. On the plains of northern India, farmers have laid out broad, flat fields.

✓ **Reading Check** How are culture and environment related?

Learn more about culture.

Balinese Terraces
A farmer on the island of Bali, in Indonesia, crosses terraced rice fields. **Analyze** How has Bali's environment affected its culture? How has Bali's culture affected its environment?

Chapter 4 Section 1 **93**

Vocabulary Builder

Use the information below to teach students this section's high-use words.

High-Use Word	Definition and Sample Sentence
trait, p. 92	*n.* distinguishing feature or characteristic One of Adam's **traits** is his unusual sense of humor.
dictate, p. 93	*v.* to control or command Culture often **dictates** the kinds of food people eat.
advance, p. 94	*n.* development Doctors made an important **advance** in fighting the disease.
complex, p. 95	*adj.* complicated, made up of several parts It took him almost an hour to solve the **complex** math problem.

Show students *What is Culture?* Ask students **What elements make up culture?** *(food, festivals, clothing, dance, architecture, spiritual beliefs, language, ideas)*

Instruct

What Is Culture? 📘2

Guided Instruction

■ **Vocabulary Builder** Clarify the high-use words **trait** and **dictate** before reading.

■ Read What Is Culture? using the Oral Cloze strategy (TE, p. T33).

■ Ask students **What are some elements of culture?** *(houses, television sets, food, clothing, sports, entertainment, literature, spiritual beliefs, government, ideas about right and wrong, and language)*

■ Point out to students that people in Japan and Greece share similar physical geography but have chosen to utilize their resources in different ways. Ask students **How do people in Greece interact with their environment differently than people in Japan?** *(The Greeks have cleared their rugged land for pasture; the Japanese fish and harvest seaweed.)*

Independent Practice

Ask students to create the Taking Notes graphic organizer on a blank piece of paper. Have students fill in some of the ovals with information from the passage. Model choosing appropriate details.

Monitor Progress

As students read the passage and expand the Taking Notes concept web, circulate through the classroom to answer questions and provide assistance as needed.

Answers

✓ **Reading Check** Physical environment may influence the types of food, housing, and work that are most common in a culture. The development of technology in a culture can influence environment by allowing people to change the landscape.

Analyze Bali's environment provides a climate suitable for raising rice. The technology of the Balinese culture allows farmers to modify the environment by terracing the land.

The Development of Culture

Guided Instruction

■ **Vocabulary Builder** Clarify the high-use words **advance** and **complex** before reading.

■ Ask students to read The Development of Culture. As students read, circulate to make sure individuals can answer the Reading Check question.

■ Ask **What are the four major advances of early cultures? Why do you think each is important?** (*Possible answers: Tools could be used for hunting and building shelters; fire allowed people to live in colder climates and cook food; farming provided a steady food supply; civilizations helped people live better through new technologies.*)

■ Ask students why they think the development of cities created a need for institutions such as armies and governments. (*People living together in large groups need more organization, such as laws to ensure safety, as well as means to protect themselves.*)

Independent Practice

Have students complete the Taking Notes graphic organizer by asking them to add more information from the section. Students may add ovals as needed.

Monitor Progress

■ Show *Section Reading Support Transparency FG 53* and ask students to check their graphic organizers individually. Go over key concepts and clarify key vocabulary as needed.

📖 **Foundations of Geography Transparencies,** *Section Reading Support Transparency FG 53*

■ Tell students to fill in the last column of the *Reading Readiness Guide.* Ask them to evaluate if what they learned was what they had expected to learn.

All in One Foundations of Geography Teaching Resources, *Reading Readiness Guide,* p. 210

Answer

Draw Conclusions Farmers were able to harvest more with more powerful tools.

The Development of Agricultural Technology

Sickle
The first farmers used hand-held sickles to harvest grain. The first sickles had stone blades. Later sickles, like the one shown here, had metal blades.

Horse-drawn reaper
By the late 1800s, farmers were using animal-powered machinery, such as this sail reaper, to harvest grain.

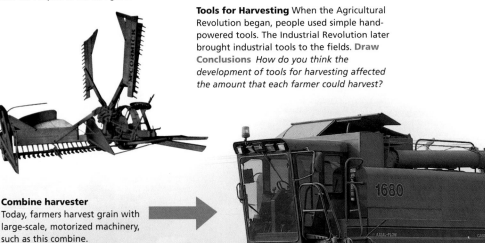

Combine harvester
Today, farmers harvest grain with large-scale, motorized machinery, such as this combine.

94 Foundations of Geography

The Development of Culture

Scientists think that early cultures had four major advances in technology. First was the invention of tools millions of years ago. Second and third were the control of fire and the beginnings of agriculture. Fourth was the development of **civilizations,** or advanced cultures with cities and the use of writing.

Technology and Civilization For most of human existence, people were hunters and gatherers. While traveling from place to place, they collected wild plants, hunted game, and fished.

Later, people discovered how to grow crops. They tamed wild animals to help them with work or to raise for food. Over time, more and more people relied on farming for most of their food. Historians call this great change the Agricultural Revolution.

Agriculture provided a steady food supply. Agriculture let farmers grow more food than they needed. In parts of Asia and Africa, some people worked full time on crafts such as metal-working. They traded their products for food. People began to develop laws and government. To store information, they developed writing. These advances in culture produced the first true civilizations about 5,000 years ago.

Early civilizations developed new technologies, such as irrigation, that let people grow more crops. Over time, farming and civilization spread throughout the world.

Tools for Harvesting When the Agricultural Revolution began, people used simple hand-powered tools. The Industrial Revolution later brought industrial tools to the fields. **Draw Conclusions** *How do you think the development of tools for harvesting affected the amount that each farmer could harvest?*

Skills Mini Lesson

Recognizing Bias

1. Define *bias* as a one-sided view. Explain that to detect bias students should look for false or missing information, words that express emotion, and how the writer's purpose affects the information.

2. Practice the skill using this statement from a school newspaper: *Our team will win the big game because we have better players.* Ask: What words express emotion rather than fact? (*better players*) Why might the paper show a bias? (*The writer wants his or her own team to win.*)

3. Discuss what could make the article less biased.

Then, about 200 years ago, people began to invent new technologies that used power-driven machinery. This change marked the beginning of the Industrial Revolution. It led to the growth of cities, science, and even more advanced technologies, such as computers and space flight.

Development of Institutions Before the Agricultural Revolution, people had simple **institutions,** customs and organizations with social, educational, or religious purposes. These included extended families and simple political institutions, such as councils of elders.

As people gathered in larger groups and formed cities, they needed more complex institutions. People developed organized religions, with priests, ceremonies, and temples. Armies and governments appeared with states. Teachers started schools.

In the modern world, we have many different kinds of institutions, including museums, sports clubs, corporations, political parties, and universities. These institutions are important parts of our culture.

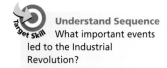

Understand Sequence What important events led to the Industrial Revolution?

✔ Reading Check What allowed civilizations to develop?

Oxford University, in Oxford, England, is more than 800 years old.

Section 1 Assessment

Key Terms
Review the key terms at the beginning of this section. Use each term in a sentence that explains its meaning.

Target Reading Skill
Place the following events in the order in which they occurred: the development of civilization; the invention of tools; the development of industry; and the beginnings of agriculture.

Comprehension and Critical Thinking
1. (a) **Define** What is a cultural landscape?
(b) **Explain** What are the most important cultural traits that shape a people's cultural landscape?
(c) **Identify Cause and Effect** If two cultures occupy similar environments, why might their cultural landscapes still differ?
2. (a) **Identify** What was the Agricultural Revolution?
(b) **Sequence** What cultural advances followed the Agricultural Revolution?

Writing Activity
Think of all the ways that the culture of your region has shaped its landscape. Write a short paragraph describing your cultural landscape and the cultural traits that shaped it.

Go Online
PHSchool.com

For: An activity on culture
Visit: PHSchool.com
Web Code: led-3401

Target Reading Skill ⬛ L2

Understand Sequence As a follow-up, ask students to answer the Target Reading Skill question in the Student Edition. *(the Agricultural Revolution; the invention of new technologies that used power-driven machinery)*

Assess and Reteach

Assess Progress ⬛ L2
Have students complete the Section Assessment. Administer the *Section Quiz.*

All in One **Foundations of Geography Teaching Resources,** *Section Quiz,* p. 212

Reteach ⬛ L1
If students need more instruction, have them read this section in the Reading and Vocabulary Study Guide.

📖 Chapter 4, Section 1, **Foundations of Geography Reading and Vocabulary Study Guide,** pp. 39–41

Extend ⬛ L3
Have students complete *Book Project: Desktop Countries.*

All in One **Foundations of Geography Teaching Resources,** *Book Project: Desktop Countries,* pp. 33–35

Answer

✔ Reading Check advances in culture such as agriculture and writing

Writing Activity
Use the *Rubric for Assessing a Writing Assignment* to evaluate students' paragraphs.

All in One **Foundations of Geography Teaching Resources,** *Rubric for Assessing a Writing Assignment,* p. 233

Section 1 Assessment

Key Terms
Students' sentences should reflect knowledge of each Key Term.

Target Reading Skill
the invention of tools; the beginnings of agriculture; the development of civilization; the development of industry

Comprehension and Critical Thinking
1. (a) the parts of a people's environment that they have shaped and the technology they have used to shape it (b) a group's customs, ideas, and ways of doing things (c) because of the way they have developed and applied technology, or because of their customs

2. (a) The Agricultural Revolution was a change in which people began growing crops and taming wild animals. They began to depend more on farming for food than hunting and gathering. (b) the rise of birthrates and population, the ability to grow excess crops, the development of crafts, the institution of laws and government, and the development of writing

Objectives

Social Studies

1. Learn how people are organized into groups.
2. Investigate language.
3. Explore the role of religion.

Reading/Language Arts

Learning to notice the sequence of important changes can help you understand and remember and interpret these changes.

Prepare to Read

Build Background Knowledge   L2

In this section, students will learn about three elements of culture: social structure, language, and religion. Have students look at the section's headings and photographs with this question in mind: **Why are these ideas important to a society's culture?** Conduct an Idea Wave (TE, p. T35) to generate a list.

Set a Purpose for Reading   L2

- Preview the Objectives.

- Read each statement in the *Reading Readiness Guide* aloud. Ask students to mark the statements true or false.

- Have students discuss the statements in pairs or groups of four, then mark their worksheets again. Use the Numbered Heads participation strategy (TE, p. T36) to call on students to share their group's perspectives.

  All in One Foundations of Geography Teaching Resources, *Reading Readiness Guide,* p. 214

Vocabulary Builder

Preview Key Terms   L2

Pronounce each Key Term, then ask the students to say the word with you. Provide a simple explanation such as, "An extended family can include grandparents, aunts, uncles, and cousins."

Prepare to Read

Objectives

In this section you will
1. Learn how people are organized into groups.
2. Investigate language.
3. Explore the role of religion.

Taking Notes

Copy the outline below. As you read this section, fill in the outline with information about how society is organized, about language, and about religion. Add letters and numbers as needed.

> I. How society is organized
>   A. Social classes
>   B.
>   1.
>   2.
> II. Language
>   A.

Target Reading Skill

Understand Sequence Noting the sequence of important changes can help you understand and remember the changes. You can show a sequence of changes by simply listing the changes in the order in which they occurred. As you read this section, list the sequence of the changes in people's ability to improve their status.

Key Terms

- **society** (suh SY uh tee) *n.* a group of people sharing a culture
- **social structure** (SOH shul STRUK chur) *n.* a pattern of organized relationships among groups of people within a society
- **social class** (SOH shul klas) *n.* a grouping of people based on rank or status
- **nuclear family** (NOO klee ur FAM uh lee) *n.* a mother, a father, and their children
- **extended family** (ek STEN did FAM uh lee) *n.* a family that includes several generations

A nuclear family in the United Kingdom

How Society Is Organized

Think about the people you see every day. Do you spend each day meeting random strangers? Or do you see the same family members, classmates, and teachers every day? Chances are, there is a pattern to your interactions.

A group of people sharing a culture is known as a **society.** Every society has a **social structure,** or a pattern of organized relationships among groups of people within the society. A society may be as small as a single community or as large as a nation or even a group of similar nations. Smaller groups within a society work together on particular tasks. Some groups work together to get food. Others protect the community. Still others educate children. Social structure helps people work together to meet one another's basic needs.

The family is the basic, most important social unit of any society. Families teach the customs and traditions of the culture to their children. Through their families, children learn how to dress, to be polite, to eat, and to play.

96 Foundations of Geography

Target Reading Skill   L2

Understand Sequence Explain to students that they can show a sequence of changes by listing the changes in the order in which they occurred.

Model understanding sequence using the text on p. 100 of the Student Edition. Ask **In what order did the religions of Christianity, Islam, and Judaism start?** Then write on the board, *1. Judaism; 2. Christianity; 3. Islam.* Point out the sentence in the passage in which the answer can be found, emphasizing the clue words "first," "then," and "finally."

Give students *Identify Sequence.* Have them complete the activity in groups.

All in One Foundations of Geography Teaching Resources, *Identify Sequence,* p. 221

Social Classes Cultures also have another kind of social organization—**social classes,** or groupings of people based on rank or status. A person's status or position may come from his or her wealth, land, ancestors, or education. In some cultures in the past, it was often hard—or impossible—for people to move from one social class to another. Today, people in many societies can improve their status. They can obtain a good education, make more money, or marry someone of a higher class.

Kinds of Families Not all cultures define family in the same way. In some cultures, the basic unit is a **nuclear family,** or a mother, a father, and their children. This pattern is common in developed nations such as the United States, Australia, and Germany. The nuclear family gets its name from the word *nucleus*, which means "center."

Other cultures have **extended families,** or families that include several generations. In addition to a central nuclear family of parents and their sons or daughters, there are the wives or husbands of those sons or daughters. The family also includes grandchildren, or the children of those sons or daughters. In extended families, older people often help care for the children. They are respected for their knowledge and experience. Older family members pass on traditions. Extended families are less common than they used to be. As rural people move to cities, nuclear families are becoming more common.

✓ **Reading Check** What is the basic social unit of societies?

 **Understand Sequence** How has people's ability to improve their status changed over time?

A Salvadoran-American Family This family includes grandparents and more than one set of parents. **Infer** *Is this a nuclear family or an extended family?*

Chapter 4 Section 2 **97**

Vocabulary Builder

Use information below to teach students this section's high-use words.

High-Use Word	Definition and Sample Sentence
status, p. 97	*n.* rank or position Going to college is one way to improve your **status** in life.
concept, p. 98	*n.* idea The **concept** behind the invention was very simple.
ritual, p. 101	*n.* ceremony or custom Many religions have a marriage **ritual.**

Instruct

How Society Is Organized L2

Guided Instruction

■ **Vocabulary Builder** Clarify the high-use word **status** before reading.

■ Read How Society Is Organized using the Structured Silent Reading technique (TE, p. T34). As students read, circulate to make sure individuals can answer the Reading Check question.

■ Have students explain the difference between a nuclear family and an extended family. *(nuclear family: mother, father, and their children; extended family: family that includes several generations)*

■ Ask students **Why might movement from rural to urban areas cause nuclear families to become more common?** *(Possible answer: In rural areas, extended families living together might share the work on farms, and there would probably be more room to provide housing for everyone. In urban areas, people generally work outside of the home, and homes are usually smaller and closer together.)*

Independent Practice

Ask students to create the Taking Notes graphic organizer on a blank piece of paper and begin filling in details about how society is organized.

Monitor Progress

As students fill in the graphic organizer, circulate and make sure that individuals are choosing the correct details. Provide assistance as needed.

◯ Target Reading Skill L2

Understand Sequence As a follow-up, ask students to answer the Target Reading Skill question in the Student Edition. *(In the past, it was difficult for people in some cultures to move from one social class to another. Today, people in many societies improve their social status through education, money, or marriage.)*

Answers

✓ **Reading Check** The family is the basic social unit of societies.

Infer This is an extended family.

Language

Guided Instruction

- **Vocabulary Builder** Clarify the high-use word **concept** before reading.

- Read Language and examine The World: Major Language Groups. Encourage students to ask questions about using the map.

- Ask students if they can think of examples of a word having different meanings in two different cultures. *(Possible answer: "Football" in the United States is not the same as "football" in England. There, "football" refers to soccer.)*

- Ask students to examine the photograph at the top of p. 98. Ask **What other forms of cultural communication might depend on senses other than hearing?** *(Answers will vary, but might include a green light that means "go," or a handshake that means "nice to meet you.")*

- Ask **Why might the customs of a French-speaking Canadian differ from those of an English-speaking Canadian?** *(because people who speak different languages may have different ideas and traditions)*

- Have students list the language groups found in Australia *(Indo-European, other)*. Ask **Why might Australia share a language group with Europe?** *(Most Australians are descended from British settlers.)*

A teacher using sign language with hearing-impaired students

Language

All cultures have language. In fact, language provides a basis for culture. People learn their cultures mainly through language. Most communication with others depends on language. Think how hard it would be if you had no way to say, "Meet me by the gate after school." How could you learn if you could not ask questions?

A culture's language reflects the things that are important in that culture. For example, English has words for Christian and Jewish concepts, such as *baptism* and *sabbath*. Some languages lack words for these concepts because their speakers are not Jewish or Christian. But those languages have words for concepts in their people's religions that have no English translation.

The World: Major Language Groups

This map shows the locations of the world's major language groups. Languages in each of these groups share a common ancestor, a language spoken long ago that gradually changed to become several related languages. For example, English and German are both Indo-European languages that share a common ancestor. Can you recognize the German words *Land, Mann,* and *Wagen?*

NORTH AMERICA

ATLANTIC OCEAN

PACIFIC OCEAN

SOUTH AMERICA

SOUTHERN OCEAN

ANTARCTICA

Arctic Circle

60° N

30° N

Tropic of Cancer

Equator

Tropic of Capricorn

30° S

60° S

Antarctic Circle

150° W   120° W   90° W   60° W   30°

0 miles 2,000
0 kilometers 2,000
Robinson

Young boy in China writing Chinese characters

Background: Daily Life

Religion Affects Daily Life Many religions require daily activities, such as prayers and rituals, to be performed by believers. In a Jewish group called Hasidim, or "pious ones," religion governs how believers dress, what they eat, and how they wear their hair. Men wear beards and have a long side lock of hair hanging on each side of their faces. Married women cover their hair with wigs or scarves in public. Like other Orthodox Jews, Hasidim observe special laws about food, called *kashrus*, which are outlined in the Jewish Torah. Shellfish and pork are forbidden. Meat and dairy foods may not be eaten at the same meal or cooked in the same pot.

In some countries, people speak more than one language. For example, Canada has two official languages, French and English. In the United States, you may usually hear English, but you can also hear Spanish, Chinese, Haitian Creole, and many other languages. India has 16 official languages, but people there speak more than 800 languages!

People who speak each language are culturally different in some ways from other people in their country who speak other languages. They may celebrate different festivals or have different customs for such things as dating or education. That is because each language preserves shared ideas and traditions.

✓ **Reading Check** **What is the relation between language and culture?**

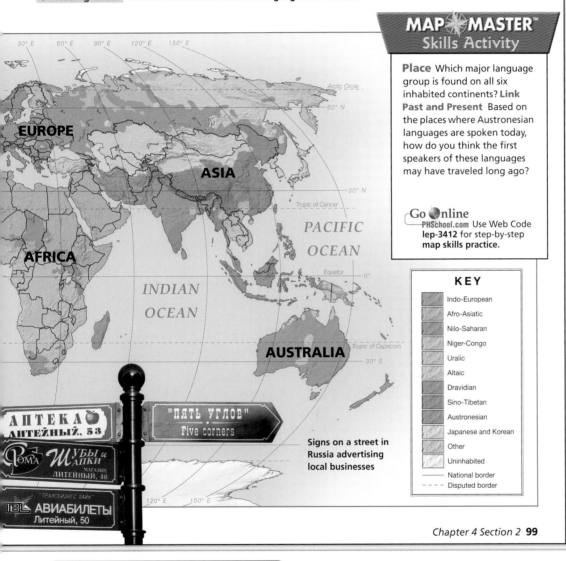

MAP MASTER™ Skills Activity

Place Which major language group is found on all six inhabited continents? **Link Past and Present** Based on the places where Austronesian languages are spoken today, how do you think the first speakers of these languages may have traveled long ago?

Go Online
PHSchool.com Use Web Code lep-3412 for step-by-step map skills practice.

KEY

- Indo-European
- Afro-Asiatic
- Nilo-Saharan
- Niger-Congo
- Uralic
- Altaic
- Dravidian
- Sino-Tibetan
- Austronesian
- Japanese and Korean
- Other
- Uninhabited
- — National border
- --- Disputed border

Signs on a street in Russia advertising local businesses

Chapter 4 Section 2 **99**

Differentiated Instruction

For Advanced Readers ▢3
Have students read the primary source *City Kids in China* and look for elements of social structure. Have them compare the Chinese students' experiences to their own and write a paragraph that describes an element of social structure in the United States.

All in One Foundations of Geography Teaching Resources, *City Kids in China,* pp. 230–231

For Gifted and Talented ▢3
Have students go on a "language hunt." By using the library or Internet and talking to their families, have each student learn ten words in another language. Each student should make a chart with the word, the English translation, and the name of the language. Have students share their new words with the class.

Independent Practice
Have students continue working with the Taking Notes graphic organizer by asking them to expand and complete the section of the outline on Language. If students need assistance, show the blank *Outline Transparency* as a model.

📖 **Foundations of Geography Transparencies,** *Transparency B15: Outline*

Monitor Progress
As students continue to fill in the graphic organizer, make sure individuals are adding appropriate details about language. Provide assistance as needed.

 АПТЕКА
ЛИТЕЙНЫЙ, 53

"ПЯТЬ УГЛОВ"
Five corners

РОМА ШУБЫ и ШАПКИ
МАГАЗИН
ЛИТЕЙНЫЙ, 46

ТВL АВИАБИЛЕТЫ
Литейный, 50

"ТРАНСБИЗНЕС ЛАЙН"

Religion

L2

Guided Instruction

- **Vocabulary Builder** Clarify the high-use word **ritual** before reading.

- Have students read Religion and examine The World: Major Religions map and its accompanying text. As students read, circulate to make sure individuals can answer the Reading Check question.

- Direct students' attention to the map and ask **What religions are practiced in South America?** *(Roman Catholic, Protestant, and traditional)*

- Ask students to look at the map key and consider what "Sunni" and "Shiite" might designate. *(Sunni and Shiite are branches of Islam, just as Roman Catholic, Protestant, and Eastern Churches are branches of Christianity.)*

- Ask students to list some of the common features among the world's religions. *(All have prayers and rituals, celebrate important places and times, and have standards of proper behavior.)*

Independent Practice

Have students complete the Taking Notes outline by adding a heading on Religion and filling in the appropriate details.

Monitor Progress

- Show *Section Reading Support Transparency FG 54* and ask students to check their graphic organizers individually.

    All in One Foundations of Geography Teaching Resources, *Section Reading Support Transparency FG 54*

- Tell students to fill in the last column of the *Reading Readiness Guide.*

    All in One Foundations of Geography Teaching Resources, *Reading Readiness Guide,* p. 214

Answers

MAP MASTER Skills Activity **Place** Asia **Draw Inferences** It is the largest continent.

Go Online PHSchool.com Students may practice their map skills using the interactive online version of this map.

100 *Foundations of Geography*

The World: Major Religions

The major religions of the world all began in Asia. India was the birthplace of Sikhism, Hinduism, and Buddhism, all of which later spread to other countries. The other great world religions had their start in Southwest Asia: first Judaism, then Christianity, and finally Islam. These religions also later spread to other parts of the world.

Young Buddhist monks in Thailand

MAP MASTER Skills Activity

Place Which of the continents has the greatest variety of religions?
Draw Inferences Why do you think this is so?

Go Online PHSchool.com Use Web Code **lep-3422** for step-by-step map skills practice.

Eastern Orthodox Christian priests in Greece

KEY	
Islam	**Other Major Groups**
Sunni	Hinduism
Shi'a	Buddhism
Christianity	Sikhism
Roman Catholic	Judaism
Protestant	Traditional
Eastern Churches	National border
	Disputed border

0 miles 3,000
0 kilometers 3,000
Robinson

100 Foundations of Geography

Skills for Life — Skills Mini Lesson

Synthesizing Information

1. Explain that to synthesize information, students should find the main idea of each fact, then find supporting details, and look for connections.

2. State the idea from the text on p. 101, "Most of the people of Saudi Arabia are Muslim." The map and text on p. 100 confirm the fact that Islam started in Southwest Asia. You can conclude: *Many people living near where Islam began are Muslims.*

3. Read the text on p. 101 that says that members of Islam, Judaism, and Christianity believe in one God. The map on p. 100 shows that people of these religions live in the same area. Ask: What conclusion can you draw from this information?

Religion

Religion is an important part of every culture. For example, most of the people of Saudi Arabia are Muslim. In some countries, such as the United States, people follow more than one religion. Beliefs and practices may differ among religions. However, religion remains important to many people.

Religion can help people make sense of the world. Religion can provide comfort and hope for people facing difficult times. And religion can help answer questions about the meaning and purpose of life. Religion also guides people in ethics, or standards of accepted behavior.

Religious beliefs vary. Members of some religions, such as Islam, Judaism, and Christianity, believe in one God. Members of other religions, such as Hinduism and traditional religions, believe in more than one god. But all religions have prayers and rituals. Every religion celebrates important places and times. And all religions expect people to treat one another well and to behave properly.

✓ **Reading Check** Why is religion important to people?

This temple, in Amritsar, India, is a holy place of Sikhism.

⭐ Section 2 Assessment

Key Terms
Review the key terms at the beginning of this section. Use each term in a sentence that explains its meaning.

🎯 Target Reading Skill
Place the following events in young people's lives in the correct sequence: learning their culture's language and learning their culture's beliefs.

Comprehension and Critical Thinking
1. (a) Identify What is the role of social structure in society?

(b) Explain What is the place of families in a social structure?
(c) Predict Would you expect the members of one family to fall within one social class or more than one?
2. (a) Recall How is language related to culture?
(b) Identify Cause and Effect Why do you think people who speak different languages tend to have different cultures?
3. (a) Identify What values do all religions share?
(b) Draw Conclusions How might those values help people of different religions overcome conflicts?

Writing Activity
In a journal entry, explore the ways in which family and language connect you to other people in your society.

> **Writing Tip** When you write a journal entry, write about experiences from your own life. You may also express your own opinions and perspectives. For this exercise, think about which of your activities and interests involve family or the use of language.

Assess Progress L2
Have students complete the Section Assessment. Administer the *Section Quiz*.

📋 **Foundations of Geography Teaching Resources,** *Section Quiz*, p. 216

Reteach L1
If students need more instruction, have them read this section in the Reading and Vocabulary Study Guide.

📄 Chapter 4, Section 2, **Foundations of Geography Reading and Vocabulary Study Guide,** pp. 42–44

Extend L3
Have students work in small groups to investigate the rituals of world religions. Assign each group a different religion, and ask the groups to use the library or Internet to find out about one major holiday celebrated as part of the religion, including the name of the holiday, what it celebrates, when it is celebrated, and how it is celebrated. Have students create posters using the information they have gathered, and present their posters to the class.

Answer

✓ **Reading Check** Religion is important to people because it helps them make sense of the world, answers questions about the meaning of life, and guides their behavior.

Writing Activity
Use the *Rubric for Assessing a Journal Entry* to evaluate students' journal entries.

📋 **Foundations of Geography Teaching Resources,** *Rubric for Assessing a Journal Entry*, p. 234

Section 2 Assessment

Key Terms
Students' sentences should reflect knowledge of each Key Term.

🎯 Target Reading Skill
Learning their culture's language; learning their culture's beliefs.

Comprehension and Critical Thinking
1. (a) Social structure organizes a society through a pattern of relationships, and helps people work together to meet the basic needs of individuals, families, and communities. **(b)** Families are the most basic and important unit in a social structure. **(c)** Members of one nuclear family would likely fall within one social class, but the members of an extended family might fall within more than one social class.

2. (a) People learn culture mainly through language. **(b)** Each language preserves shared ideas and traditions.

3. (a) All have prayers and rituals, celebrate important places and times, and have standards of behavior. **(b)** People may be able to focus on their similarities rather than their differences.

Skills for Life

Objective

Learn how to make valid generalizations.

Prepare to Read

Build Background Knowledge   L2

Ask students to think of words or terms they already know that may help them to determine the meaning of the word *generalization*. Suggest terms such as "generally," "general store," "in general," and "general idea" to get them started. Conduct an Idea Wave (TE, p. T35) to create a list, then point out that the word *general* usually means "for all" or "for the whole." Have students refer to a dictionary to sharpen their definitions.

Instruct

Making Valid Generalizations   L2

Guided Instruction

- Read the steps to make valid generalizations as a class and write them on the board.

- Practice the skill by following the steps on p. 103 as a class. Identify the topic of the text and three facts that support it *(corn in the Americas before the 1200s; corn was the principle crop of the Mayas of present-day Mexico and Central America, the Hohokam grew corn in Arizona and the Anasazi grew corn in the northeastern United States.)* Identify what the facts have in common *(all are about Native American groups who grew corn).* Work with students to create a generalization. *(Possible generalization: Corn was an important and versatile crop in the Americas before the 1200s.)* Ask students to test the generalization using the bulleted questions on p. 102.

Skills for Life — Making Valid Generalizations

A generalization is a broad conclusion. Some generalizations are valid—that is, they have value or worth—because they can be drawn reasonably from specific facts. Other generalizations are not valid, because they draw unreasonably broad conclusions and are not based on fact.

Many statements have clues that tell you they should be evaluated for validity. For example, statements with words such as *everybody* or *everyone* are very broad. They should always be evaluated. Is the statement "Everybody needs salt" a valid generalization? It is, because it is based on the scientifically proven fact that humans cannot survive without salt in our diet. However, generalizations such as "Everybody loves chocolate" are not valid. They draw unreasonably broad conclusions and cannot be proved.

You need to know how to evaluate a generalization to see if it is valid. You also have to know how to make a valid generalization yourself.

Testing for Validity

To find whether a generalization is valid, ask

- Are there enough facts—at least three in a short passage—to support the generalization?
- Do I know any other facts that support the generalization?
- Does the statement overgeneralize or stereotype a group of people? Words such as *all*, *always*, or *every* signal overgeneralization. Words such as *some*, *many*, *most*, and *often* help prevent a statement from being overgeneralized.

Learn the Skill

To make a valid generalization, follow these steps:

1. **Identify specific facts contained within a source of information.** Make sure you understand the topic that the facts support.

2. **State what the facts have in common, and look for patterns.** Do any of the facts fit together in a way that makes a point about a broad subject? Do data in a table or graph point toward a general statement?

3. **Make a generalization, or broad conclusion, about the facts.** Write your generalization as a complete sentence or a paragraph.

4. **Test the generalization and revise it if necessary.** You can test the validity of a generalization by using the guidelines in the box at the left.

102 Foundations of Geography

Practice the Skill

Read the passage at the right describing three cultures, and then make a generalization about these cultures.

1. What is the topic of the text? List at least three specific facts that relate to that topic.

2. What do the facts you listed have in common? Do they suggest a general idea about the topic?

3. Make a generalization about the topic. Write it in a complete sentence. List three facts that support it.

4. Test your generalization to see if it is valid. If it is not valid, try rewriting it so that it is more limited. Be careful of exaggerated wording.

Apply the Skill

Turn to page 97 and read the paragraph under the heading Kinds of Families. Make as many generalizations as you can, and test them for their validity. Explain why each generalization is or is not valid.

The Maya thrived in present-day Mexico and Central America from about A.D. 300 to 900. Corn was their principal crop. They developed a sophisticated civilization, but they had abandoned their great cities by about A.D. 900. At about that time, the Hohokam people were growing corn and beans in what is now Arizona. The Hohokam left their settlements during the 1400s, possibly because of drought. Meanwhile, between about A.D. 900 and 1300, the Anasazi people lived to the northeast. They also grew corn. The Anasazi built multistory dwellings up against high cliff walls. Many families lived in these homes. During a drought in the late 1200s, the Anasazi abandoned some of their villages.

An extended Islamic family, spanning three generations, from the rural east coast of Malaysia

Chapter 4 **103**

Independent Practice

Assign *Skills for Life* and have students complete it individually.

All in One Foundations of Geography Teaching Resources, *Skills for Life*, p. 225

Monitor Progress

As students are completing the *Skills for Life* worksheet, circulate and check to make sure they understand the skill steps.

Assess and Reteach

Assess Progress L2

Ask students to do the Apply the Skill activity.

Reteach L1

If students are having trouble applying the skill steps, have them review the skill using the interactive Social Studies Skills Tutor CD-ROM.

⊙ *Making Valid Generalizations,* **Social Studies Skills Tutor CD-ROM**

Extend L3

Ask students to read the last paragraph on p. 107 of the Student Edition. Point out that the first sentence, "Technology has brought many benefits," is a generalization. Ask them if the paragraph contains enough facts to support this generalization, and have them brainstorm other facts that support it. Students should then write a paragraph explaining whether or not the generalization is valid. Use *Rubric for Assessing a Writing Assignment* to evaluate students' paragraphs.

All in One Foundations of Geography Teaching Resources, *Rubric for Assessing a Writing Assignment*, p. 233

Differentiated Instruction

For Less Proficient Readers L1

Partner these students with more proficient readers to do Level 1 of the *Making Valid Generalizations* lesson on the interactive Social Studies Skills Tutor CD-ROM. When they have successfully completed Level 1, they can move on to Level 2 alone.

⊙ *Making Valid Generalizations,* **Social Studies Skills Tutor CD-ROM**

For Special Needs Students L1

Help students make valid generalizations about items or people in the classroom. Students should look for patterns, and then write sentences expressing their generalizations, such as, "Most of the chairs in this room are green." Help students discuss whether or not their generalizations are valid.

Answers
Apply the Skill

Answers will vary, but students should show that they made generalizations and tested them for their validity.

Chapter 4 **103**

Section 3
Step-by-Step Instruction

Objectives

Social Studies

1. Explore how cultures change.
2. Learn how ideas spread from one culture to another.

Reading/Language Arts

Identify signal words to help keep the order of events clear.

Prepare to Read

Build Background Knowledge `L2`

Tell students that in this section they will learn about how cultures change over time. Point out to students that some sports, foods, and words in American culture may have been borrowed or adapted from other cultures. Ask if they are familiar with the sport of karate or have ever eaten shish kebab. Point out that these both originated in different cultures. Have students engage in a Give One, Get One activity (TE, pp. T37) to identify other aspects of American culture that have been borrowed or adapted from different cultures.

Set a Purpose for Reading `L2`

■ Preview the Objectives.

■ Read each statement in the *Reading Readiness Guide* aloud. Ask students to mark the statements true or false.

■ Have students discuss the statements in pairs or groups of four, then mark their worksheets again. Use the Numbered Heads participation strategy (TE, p. T36) to call on students to share their group's perspectives.

All in One Foundations of Geography Teaching Resources, *Reading Readiness Guide,* p. 218

Vocabulary Builder
Preview Key Terms `L2`

Pronounce each Key Term, then ask the students to say the word with you. Provide a simple explanation such as "Playing the American sport of baseball in Japan is an example of cultural diffusion."

Section 3 Cultural Change

Prepare to Read

Objectives

In this section you will
1. Explore how cultures change.
2. Learn how ideas spread from one culture to another.

Taking Notes

Copy the concept web below. As you read this section, fill in the web with information about cultural change. Add ovals as needed for the concepts in the section.

Target Reading Skill

Recognize Words That Signal Sequence

Signal words point out relationships among ideas or events. To help keep the order of events clear, look for words such as *first, later,* or *at that time* that signal the order in which the events took place.

Key Terms

• **cultural diffusion** (KUL chur ul dih FYOO zhun) *n.* the movement of customs and ideas

• **acculturation** (uh kul chur AY shun) *n.* the process of accepting new ideas and fitting them into a culture

Blue jeans and denim shirts have changed with the times.

How Cultures Change

All cultures change over time. The history of blue jeans is an example of cultural change. Some people think that blue jeans are typical American clothes. But many cultures contributed to them. Blue jeans were invented in the United States in the 1800s. They were marketed by Levi Strauss. Strauss was a German-born merchant who moved to California. He made the jeans with a cloth called denim. This may be a shortened form of *serge de Nîmes,* the name of a similar cloth from France.

At first, only Americans wore blue jeans, but they later became popular in other countries. In the 1980s, the Japanese and the French developed stonewashing. It made brand-new denim jeans look worn. Since then, designers from Asia, Europe, and America have promoted new styles, such as ripped and "dirty" denim. Today, jeans are popular all over the world. And the word *jeans* comes from an old French name for Genoa, an Italian city where a cloth similar to denim was first made. What could be more American than jeans?

Target Reading Skill `L2`

Recognize Words That Signal Sequence Point out the Target Reading Skill. Explain that by identifying words that signal time order, readers can better understand the sequence of events being presented.

Model recognizing words that signal sequence by reading the second paragraph on p. 104 aloud. Then ask students to make a list of words and terms in the paragraph that signal sequence. On the board, list: "At first,"

"later," "In the 1980s," "Since then," and "Today." Have students brainstorm other sequence signal words and terms to add to the list *(before, after, then, soon, in the future.)*

Give students *Recognize Sequence Signal Words.* Have them complete the activity in groups.

All in One Foundations of Geography Teaching Resources, *Recognize Sequence Signal Words,* p. 222

Why Cultures Change Just as jeans have changed over time, so, too, has American culture. Cultures change all the time. Because culture is an entire way of life, a change in one part changes other parts. Changes in the natural environment, technology, and ideas all affect culture.

New Technologies New technologies also change a culture. During the 1800s and early 1900s, the growth of industry and the spread of factories drew large numbers of Americans from the countryside to the nation's cities. Factories offered jobs to thousands of men, women, and children. Limited transportation meant that people had to live close to the factories. Cities grew larger as a result.

This all changed after the invention of the car in the late 1800s. Within a few years, advances in technology made cars more affordable. By 1920, many Americans had cars. People could live farther from their jobs and drive to work. Soon after, the idea of owning a house with a yard became more popular. The result has been the growth of sprawling suburbs since the mid-1900s and a new culture based on car travel.

A teenager using a cell phone

A "bullet train" in Japan
Japanese engineers have developed new technologies that allow these trains to travel at speeds of more than 180 miles (300 kilometers) per hour. *Infer How might such high speeds affect how far away people can live from their work?*

Chapter 4 Section 3 **105**

Vocabulary Builder

Use the information below to teach students this section's high-use words.

High-Use Word	Definition and Sample Sentence
contribute, p. 104	*v.* to give Kim **contributed** cans of food to the food bank.
promote, p. 104	*v.* to help bring about Eating a healthy diet will **promote** a long life.
obtain, p. 106	*v.* to gain possession of You must **obtain** a passport before traveling out of the country.
focus, p. 106	*v.* to concentrate Jenny couldn't **focus** on her book in the noisy airport.

How Cultures Change 🄻🄴

Guided Instruction

- **Vocabulary Builder** Clarify the high-use words **contribute** and **promote** before reading.

- Read How Cultures Change using the Paragraph Shrinking strategy (TE, p. T34). As students read, circulate to make sure they can answer the Reading Check question.

- Ask students to identify three factors that can change a culture. *(changes in the natural environment, technology, and ideas)*

- Discuss the meaning of the sentence "What could be more American than jeans?" Ask students to discuss how, since the passage explains that jeans are a result of the contributions of many different cultures, they could also be called "American." *(America is often recognized as a place where culture is a combination of many different cultures, brought by immigrants from countries around the world. Jeans represent this blending of cultural ideas.)*

- Ask **Since cultures change over time, what kind of changes do you predict may happen to your culture in the future?** *(Answers will vary, but should indicate possible future changes in their culture.)*

Independent Practice

Ask students to create the Taking Notes graphic organizer on a blank piece of paper. Have them fill in some of the blank ovals connected to "Cultural Change." Model one example using the blank *Concept Web* transparency.

All in One Foundations of Geography Teaching Resources, *Transparency B18: Concept Web*

Monitor Progress

As students fill in the graphic organizer, circulate through the classroom to make sure individuals select the appropriate details.

Answer

Infer High-speed travel such as bullet trains allows people to commute much greater distances from homes to jobs.

How Ideas Spread

Guided Instruction

- **Vocabulary Builder** Clarify the high-use words **obtain** and **focus** before reading.

- Read How Ideas Spread and direct students' attention to the photographs, Links to Technology, and line graph on these pages.

- Ask students **What is cultural diffusion?** *(the movement of customs and ideas from one culture to another)*

- Ask **How does cultural diffusion occur?** *(As people move they bring customs and ideas with them, and also obtain new customs and ideas.)*

- Discuss with students how the use of computers and the Internet affects their daily lives. *(Libraries, schools, and many homes now have computers and access to the Internet. Students may suggest that this technology helps them with their homework, helps communicate with their friends or family, or provides entertainment.)*

➔ Target Reading Skill   L2

Recognize Words That Signal Sequence
As a follow-up, ask students to answer the Target Reading Skill question in the Student Edition. (*The words* before that *signal what comes first in sequence. The events after those words happened before the events in the preceding sentence.*)

Answer

✓ **Reading Check** The invention of cars allowed people to live farther away from their jobs, which led to the growth of suburbs.

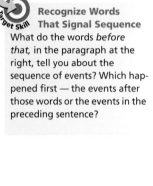

Recognize Words That Signal Sequence
What do the words *before that,* in the paragraph at the right, tell you about the sequence of events? Which happened first — the events after those words or the events in the preceding sentence?

A woman practicing yoga, a form of meditation that spread from Asia to Europe and North America

---

How One Change Can Lead to Others Think of other ways technology has changed the culture of the United States. Radio and television brought entertainment and news into homes. Today instant information is part of our culture. Computers change how and where people work. Computers even help people live longer since doctors use computers to diagnose and treat patients. Radio, television, and computers add new words to our language, such as *broadcast, channel surfing,* and *hacker.* What other new words can you think of?

Cultural Change Over Time Cultural change has been going on for a long time. Controlling fire helped early people survive in colder climates. When people started raising animals and growing crops, ways of life also changed. People began to work in the same fields year after year. Before that, they had roamed over a wider area looking for wild plant and animal foods.

✓ **Reading Check** How did the invention of cars change culture?

How Ideas Spread

Advances in transportation technology, such as the airplane, make it easier for people to move all over the world. When they move, people bring new kinds of clothing and tools with them. They also bring ideas about such things as ways to prepare food, teach children, practice their religion, or govern themselves.

Ideas can travel to new places in other ways. People may obtain goods from another culture by trade and then learn to make those goods themselves. People may also learn from other cultures through written material. The movement of customs and ideas is called **cultural diffusion.**

How Cultures Adopt New Ideas One example of cultural diffusion is the game of baseball. Baseball began as an American sport, but today it is played in countries all around the world. That is an example of cultural diffusion. The Japanese love baseball. However, they have changed the game to fit their culture. These changes are an example of **acculturation,** or the process of accepting new ideas and fitting them into a culture. Americans value competition. They focus on winning. A game of baseball does not end until one team wins. But in Japan, a game can end in a tie. The Japanese do not mind a tie game. In Japan, how well you play is more important than winning.

Differentiated Instruction

For Advanced Readers   L3
Have students complete the *Enrichment* activity, which centers on the spread of wheat-growing. After they have answered the questions, ask if they can think of other examples of ideas and customs that have spread around the world.

All in One Foundations of Geography Teaching Resources, *Enrichment,* p. 224

For English Language Learners   L1
As students read, ask them to list unfamiliar words and record any questions they may have about the section on a blank sheet of paper. Label a box "Questions" and tell students that they may place their papers in the box anonymously at a specific time. Go over all of the words and questions with the class.

Communication Technology and the Speed of Change

What's the fastest way to get from your house to Japan? Would you use a jet plane? A phone call? The Internet? A fax? All these answers can be correct. The answer depends on whether you want to transport your body, your voice, a picture, or just words on a sheet of paper.

For thousands of years, cultures changed slowly. People and goods moved by foot or wagon or sailing ship, so ideas and technology also moved slowly. Recently, communication technology has increased the speed of change. Faxes and computers transport information almost instantly. Magazines and television shows can bring ideas and information from all over the world to any home. This rapid exchange of ideas speeds up cultural change.

Technology has brought many benefits. Computers let scientists share information about how to cure diseases. Telephones let us instantly talk to relatives thousands of miles away. In the Australian Outback, students your age use closed-circuit television and two-way radios to take part in class from their own homes.

Links to
Technology

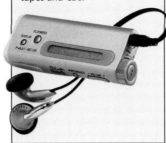

Digital Tunes Until recent years, music lovers had to lug around tapes or CDs. The invention of MP3s and MP3 players changed that. Fans can now download and store thousands of songs in MP3 format from the Internet. They no longer need bulky tapes and CDs.

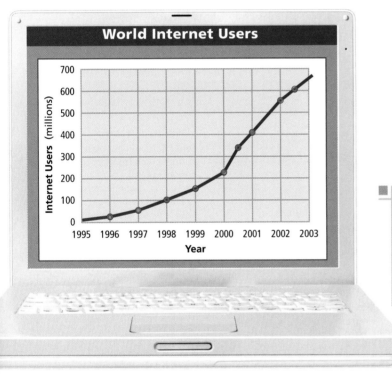

World Internet Users

Internet Users (millions) / Year

Graph Skills

Internet use grew rapidly after 1995. **Identify** What was the number of Internet users half-way through 2002?
Predict Based on the trend shown in the graph, how do you think the number of Internet users has changed since 2002?

Links

Read the **Links to Technology** on this page of the Student Edition. Ask **Why are MP3s more convenient than CDs or tapes?** *(Because MP3s are digital files, they are easier to transport and obtain than CDs or tapes.)*

Guided Instruction (continued)

- Direct students' attention to the graph at the bottom of the page. Ask **According to the graph, which year had the greatest increase of Internet users?** *(2000)*

- Ask students to name one benefit of technology and one challenge of technology. *(Students may say that technology helps people to communicate more quickly or assists people with research, but that the customs of traditional societies may be lost as technology spreads.)*

Independent Practice

Have students complete the Taking Notes graphic organizer by asking them to add more information from the section.

Monitor Progress

- Show *Section Reading Support Transparency FG 55* and ask students to check their graphic organizers individually. Go over key concepts and clarify key vocabulary as needed.
  All in One Foundations of Geography Teaching Resources, *Section Reading Support Transparency FG 55*

- Tell students to fill in the last column of the *Reading Readiness Guide*. Ask them to evaluate if what they learned was what they had expected to learn.
  All in One Foundations of Geography Teaching Resources, *Reading Readiness Guide*, p. 218

Skills Mini Lesson

Distinguishing Fact and Opinion

1. Explain that a fact can be proved to be true or false and an opinion is a personal belief. Tell students that facts answer the question *Who? What? When? Where?* or *Why?* Opinions often use words like *good, bad, think,* or *feel.*

2. Help students practice the skill by writing these statements on the board:

A. *"Dirty" denim jeans are the best jeans.*
B. *Blue jeans were invented in the 1800s.*
Then explain, "I can prove B is true or false using an encyclopedia. I can't prove A. A is an opinion, B is a fact."

3. Have students apply the skill to the following statements: A. *The first telephone was built in 1876.* B. *I think cell phones should be banned.*

Answers

Graph Skills Identify 600 million
Predict Because the graph shows a steady increase, it is likely that the number of Internet users has grown since 2002.

Assess and Reteach

Assess Progress `L2`

Have students complete the Section Assessment. Then administer the *Section Quiz*.

 Foundations of Geography Teaching Resources, *Section Quiz*, p. 220

Reteach `L1`

If students need more instruction, have them read this section in the Reading and Vocabulary Study Guide.

 Chapter 4, Section 3, **Foundations of Geography Reading and Vocabulary Study Guide,** pp. 45–47

Extend `L3`

To learn more about aspects of cultural diffusion, assign the small group activity *Creating a Report on World Music*. Students may work in pairs to complete the activity.

Foundations of Geography Teaching Resources, *Small Group Activity: Creating a Report on World Music*, pp. 226–229

Answers

Analyze Images The aborigines in the photo are wearing modern-day clothing.

✓ Reading Check New technology allows information to travel more quickly, speeding up cultural change.

Section 3 Assessment

Key Terms
Students' sentences should reflect knowledge of each Key Term.

Target Reading Skill
the words "For thousands of years" and "Recently"

Comprehension and Critical Thinking
1. (a) the ability of many people to live farther away from their jobs, and the rapid growth of suburbs **(b)** Cars allowed people to travel longer distances between their homes and workplaces, which meant they could live outside cities. **(c)** More Americans might choose to work from their homes, communicating electronically, rather than driving to work. Americans could live even farther away from their workplaces.

Defending Their Heritage
In 1988 Aborigines, descendants of Australia's original inhabitants, protested the 200th anniversary of the arrival of Europeans. **Analyze Images** *What evidence do you see that the Aborigines' culture has changed over the past 200 years?*

Defending Traditions Change can help, but it can also hurt. If things change too fast, people may feel that their culture is threatened. Valuable traditions can disappear. Once traditional knowledge has been lost, it can never be regained. In many parts of the world, people are working to preserve, or save, their own cultures before it is too late. They do not want to lose what is valuable in their culture. They want to save the artistic traditions, the religious beliefs, and the wisdom that enriched the lives of past generations for the sake of future generations.

✓ Reading Check **How has technology affected the speed of cultural change?**

 ### Section 3 Assessment

Key Terms
Review the key terms at the beginning of this section. Use each term in a sentence that explains its meaning.

Target Reading Skill
Review the second paragraph on page 107. Find the words that signal a sequence of events related to communication technologies.

Comprehension and Critical Thinking
1. (a) Describe What cultural changes in America followed the invention of cars?

(b) Explain How did cars change where people lived and worked?
(c) Predict Suppose that gasoline became more expensive and computers allowed more people to work at home. How might American culture change?
2. (a) List What are two main ways in which ideas travel from one culture to another?
(b) Describe Give an example of an idea that has passed from one culture to another.
(c) Compare and Contrast How has the spread of ideas changed with modern communication technologies?

Writing Activity
What parts of your own culture come from other countries? Make a list detailing the foods, fashions, music, or customs that are part of your life and that come from other countries.

For: An activity on cultural change
Visit: PHSchool.com
Web Code: led-3403

---

2. (a) trade and written materials **(b)** the people of the culture accepting the idea usually adapt it to fit in with their ideas, customs, and traditions through the process of acculturation. **(c)** The spread of ideas has become much faster due to modern communication technologies.

Writing Activity
Use *Rubric for Assessing a Writing Assignment* to evaluate students' lists.

Foundations of Geography Teaching Resources, *Rubric for Assessing a Writing Assignment*, p. 233

Go Online PHSchool.com Typing in the Web code when prompted will bring students directly to detailed instructions for this activity.

Review and Assessment

◆ Chapter Summary

Section 1: Understanding Culture

- Culture is an entire way of life that is shaped by people's environment and that also shapes people's environment.
- Culture developed over time from simple technologies and institutions to more advanced technologies and institutions.

Section 2: Culture and Society

- A society is a group of people sharing a culture and held together by a social structure.
- Language expresses the basic concepts of a culture and transmits those concepts to young people.
- Religions help people make sense of the world. They are an important source of values for cultures and teach people to treat one another fairly.

Section 3: Cultural Change

- Changes in the environment or in technology lead to changes in culture.
- Ideas move among cultures through the movement of people, through trade, and through communication technologies.

Traditional dress in India

◆ Key Terms

Each of the statements below contains a key term from the chapter. If the statement is true, write *true*. If it is false, rewrite the statement to make it true.

1. The culture of a people is their way of life, including their beliefs and customs.

2. A civilization is an organization with social, educational, or religious purposes.

3. An institution is an advanced culture with cities and the use of writing.

4. A society is a group of people sharing a culture.

5. A pattern of organized relationships among groups of people is a social structure.

6. An extended family consists of two parents and their children.

7. A nuclear family includes two grandparents, their children, and their grandchildren.

8. Cultural diffusion is the movement of customs or ideas from one culture to another.

9. Acculturation is an accumulation of several cultures in a single place.

Vocabulary Builder

Revisit this chapter's high-use words:

trait	status	promote
dictate	concept	obtain
advance	ritual	focus
complex	contribute	

Ask students to review the definitions they recorded on their *Word Knowledge* worksheets.

All in One Foundations of Geography Teaching Resources, *Word Knowledge,* p. 223

Consider allowing students to earn extra credit if they use the words in their answers to the questions in the Chapter Review and Assessment. The words must be used correctly and in a natural context to win the extra points.

Review and Assessment

Review Chapter Content

- Review and revisit the major themes of this chapter by asking students to classify what Guiding Questions each bulleted statement in the Chapter Summary answers. Have students work in groups to match the statements with the appropriate questions. Conduct an Idea Wave (TE, p. T35) with the class to share their answers. Refer to page 1 of the Student Edition for the text of the Guiding Questions.

- Assign *Vocabulary Development* for students to review Key Terms.

  All in One Foundations of Geography Teaching Resources, *Vocabulary Development,* p. 232

Answers

Key Terms

1. True

2. False. A civilization is an advanced culture with cities and the use of writing.

3. False. An institution is an organization with social, educational, or religious purposes.

4. True

5. True

6. False. An extended family includes several generations.

7. False. A nuclear family consists of two parents and their children.

8. True

9. Acculturation is the process of accepting new ideas and fitting them into a culture.

Review and Assessment

Comprehension and Critical Thinking

10. (a) material things, sports, entertainment, literature, spiritual beliefs, ideals, government, morals, language, and technology **(b)** Technology, because through even simple technology, people can change their land.

11. (a) the change from hunting and gathering food to raising crops and animals **(b)** Population increased. **(c)** because people could stay in one area year round, trade extra food for other goods, learn crafts, develop writing systems, and create technologies that gave rise to cities

12. (a) The social class to which a person belongs often comes from his or her wealth, education, or family connections, which affects his or her status in society. **(b)** People's ability to change their status has improved over time, as access to education, the ability to get a high-paying job, or the chance of marrying into a family of high status has increased.

13. (a) Sikhism, Hinduism, and Buddhism in India; and Judaism, Christianity, and Islam in Southwest Asia **(b)** The spread of these religions might be explained by cultural diffusion; as people of various religions traveled to new areas of the world, they brought their beliefs with them and taught them to others, and written materials of different religions could be read by people in other countries.

14. (a) The development of industry and factories led to the advancement of science, the development of even newer technologies, and the growth of cities and institutions, such as governments, schools, and armies. **(b)** Both caused the world to seem smaller by allowing people to work and communicate faster. One difference is that the Internet has changed the way that people find and handle information, while the Industrial Revolution changed the way physical goods were manufactured.

15. (a) forms of communication such as the Internet, scientific advancements in medicine, advances in transportation technology, and other areas **(b)** They have greatly increased the rate of cultural change.

Skills Practice

Students' answers will vary, but should include several facts from the paragraphs and a valid generalization about the information.

Review and Assessment (continued)

◆ Comprehension and Critical Thinking

10. (a) Describe What elements make up a culture? **(b) Apply Information** Which of these elements might influence a people's environment, and how?

11. (a) Describe What was the Agricultural Revolution? **(b) Explain** How did it affect population? **(c) Draw Conclusions** How did it allow the growth of cities?

12. (a) Describe How does social class affect a person's status in society? **(b) Link Past and Present** How has people's ability to improve their status changed?

13. (a) Recall Which major religions started in Asia? **(b) Infer** What might explain their spread?

14. (a) Describe How did the development of industry and factories change culture? **(b) Compare and Contrast** How do those changes compare with the ways technology has changed culture in your lifetime?

15. (a) List What technologies contribute to cultural change today? **(b) Draw Conclusions** How have new technologies affected the rate of cultural change?

◆ Skills Practice

Making Valid Generalizations In the Skills for Life activity in this chapter, you learned to make generalizations. You also learned how to make sure that generalizations are valid, or justified, based on facts. You learned not to overgeneralize, or make claims that go beyond the facts.

Review the steps that you followed to learn this skill. Then reread the paragraphs on pages 94 and 95 under the heading Development of Culture. List several facts about the changes described there. Finally, use these facts to make a valid generalization about those changes.

◆ Writing Activity: Math

Look at the graph titled World Internet Users on page 107. Find the number of Internet users at the end of 1995 and the number of Internet users almost seven years later in mid-2002. How many more users were there in mid-2002 than in 1995? Based on this information, predict how many Internet users there will be in 2009, seven years after the latest date shown on this graph. Write a short paragraph describing your results and your prediction.

MAP MASTER™ Skills Activity

World Religions

Place Location For each religion listed below, write the letter that marks its location on the map.
1. Buddhism
2. Eastern Christianity
3. Hinduism
4. Islam
5. Protestant Christianity
6. Roman Catholic Christianity
7. Traditional religions

Go Online
PHSchool.com Use Web Code **lep-3414** for an **interactive map.**

Writing Activity: Math

There were about 580 million more Internet users in 2002 than in 1995. Students' paragraphs should indicate that there is likely to be a similar dramatic increase in Internet users between 2002 and 2009. Students may express that as computer technology becomes more affordable and accessible, the number of Internet users should continue to rise.

Use *Rubric for Assessing a Writing Assignment* to evaluate students' paragraphs.

All in One Foundations of Geography Teaching Resources, *Rubric for Assessing a Writing Assignment,* p. 233

Standardized Test Prep

Test-Taking Tips

Some questions on standardized tests ask you to supply information using prior knowledge. Analyze the web diagram below. Then follow the tips to answer the sample question.

TIP The title in the center circle describes all of the languages. Think about the word *Indo-European* and how it describes languages.

Pick the letter that best answers the question.

Another language that belongs on this web is

A ~~Mandarin Chinese.~~

B Swahili.

C ~~Japanese.~~

D Greek.

TIP Use your prior knowledge—what you know about history, geography, or government—to help you rule out choices.

Think It Through The word *Indo-European* describes languages of India and Europe. Therefore, you can rule out answers A and C because these languages do not come from India or Europe. That leaves Swahili and Greek. You may not be sure about where Swahili is spoken, but you probably know from prior reading that Greece (where people speak Greek) is in Europe. The correct answer is D.

Practice Questions

Use the tips above and other tips in this book to help you answer the following questions:

1. The Agricultural Revolution led
   A to a rebellion by farmers against taxes.
   B to widespread hunger.
   C to an increase in population.
   D people to begin using tools.

2. How does family structure change when countries become more developed?
   A People lose interest in their families.
   B Nuclear families become more common.
   C People move in with their grandparents, aunts, and uncles.
   D Extended families become more common.

3. Which of the following does NOT contribute to cultural change?
   A technological change
   B migration
   C tradition
   D television

Read the following passage, and answer the question that follows.

This country is the birthplace of three major religions. It is located on Earth's largest continent. Its neighbors include Bangladesh and Sri Lanka. The country has more than a billion inhabitants. Its people speak hundreds of different languages. Many people from this country have migrated overseas.

4. What country does the passage describe?
   A Israel
   B Mexico
   C India
   D China

Use Web Code **lea-3401**
for a **Chapter 4 self-test.**

Chapter 4 **111**

Standardized Test Prep

Answers

1. C
2. B
3. C
4. C

Go Online PHSchool.com Students may use the Chapter 4 self-test on PHSchool.com to prepare for the Chapter Test.

Assessment Resources

Use *Chapter Tests A and B* to assess students' mastery of the chapter content.

All in One Foundations of Geography Teaching Resources, *Chapter Tests A and B,* pp. 235–240

Tests also available on the *ExamView Test Bank CD-ROM.*

⊙ *ExamView Test Bank CD-ROM*

Overview

Section 1 **Natural Resources**
1. Learn about natural resources.
2. Investigate energy.

Section 2 **Land Use**
1. Study the relation between land use and culture.
2. Investigate the relation between land use and economic activity.
3. Explore changes in land use.

Section 3 **People's Effect on the Environment**
1. Investigate how first-level activities affect the environment.
2. Explore how second- and third-level activities affect the environment.

The Natural Resources of an Island Nation

Length: 3 minutes, 57 seconds

Use with Section 1

This segment explores the relationship between natural resources and a nation's people and economy. We will see how sugarcane, tourism and the people of the island of Mauritius have been used to boost the economy.

Technology Resources

Students use embedded Web codes to access Internet activities, chapter self-tests, and additional map practice. They may also access Dorling Kindersley's Online Desk Reference to learn more about each country they study.

Use the Interactive Textbook to make content and concepts come alive through animations, videos, and activities that accompany the complete basal text—online and on CD-ROM.

Use this complete suite of powerful teaching tools to make planning lessons and administering tests quicker and easier.

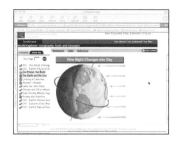

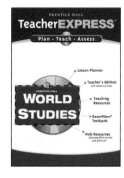

Reading and Assessment

Reading and Vocabulary Instruction

🔊 Model the Target Reading Skill

Main Idea The main idea is the most important point in a written passage. All of the details in a well-written paragraph or section should add up to the main idea. Write the paragraph below, from page 131, on the board. Explain that the main idea is usually stated in the first or last sentence. Model identifying the main idea by thinking aloud: "I will read the first and last sentences to see if either may be the main idea. I think the first sentence is the main idea because it is more general. Let me read the entire paragraph to see if I can find details that support the first sentence."

Point out the supporting details by underlining each one: *Other industrial and service activities have side effects on the environment. For example, shopping malls require large areas to be paved for parking. Industries use large amounts of resources and release industrial wastes into the environment. Service activities require the construction of roads, telephone lines, and power lines.*

Think aloud: "What do these details have in common? They are all examples of how service activities and industries negatively influence the environment. They support the main idea, that *other industrial and service activities have side effects on the environment.*"

Use the following worksheets from All-in-One Foundations of Geography Teaching Resources (pp. 256–258) to support this chapter's Target Reading Skill.

Vocabulary Builder
High-Use Academic Words

Use these steps to teach this chapter's high-use words:

1. Have students rate how well they know each word on their Word Knowledge worksheets (All-in-One Foundations of Geography Teaching Resources, p. 259).

2. Pronounce each word and ask students to repeat it.

3. Give students a brief definition or sample sentence (provided on TE pp. 115, 121, and 129).

4. Work with students as they fill in the "Definition or Example" column of their Word Knowledge worksheets.

Assessment

Formal Assessment

Test students' understanding of core knowledge and skills.

Chapter Tests A and B, Final Exams A and B, All-in-One Foundations of Geography Teaching Resources, pp. 278–283, 287–292

Customize the Chapter Tests to suit your needs.
ExamView Test Bank CD-ROM

Skills Assessment

Assess geographic literacy.

MapMaster Skills, Student Edition, pp. 115, 124, 134

Assess reading and comprehension.

Target Reading Skills, Student Edition, pp. 115, 122, 131 and in Section Assessments

Chapter 5 Assessment, Foundations of Geography Reading and Vocabulary Study Guide, p. 58

Performance Assessment

Assess students' performance on this chapter's Writing Activities using the following rubrics from All-in-One Foundations of Geography Teaching Resources.

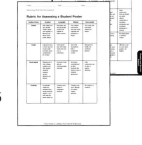

Rubric for Assessing a Student Poster, p. 274

Rubric for Assessing a Report, p. 275

Assess students' work through performance tasks.

Small Group Activity, All-in-One Foundations of Geography Teaching Resources, pp. 262–265

Online Assessment

Have students check their own understanding.

Chapter Self-Test

Test Preparation

Foundations of Geography Practice Tests A, B and C, Test Prep Workbook, pp. 49–60

Foundations of Geography Benchmark Test and Outcome Test, AYP Monitoring Assessments, pp. 80–85, 128–131

Section 1 **Natural Resources**

 1.5 periods, .75 block

Social Studies Objectives

1. Learn about natural resources.
2. Investigate energy.

Reading/Language Arts Objective

Learn how to identify the main idea of a paragraph.

Prepare to Read	**Instructional Resources**	**Differentiated Instruction**
Build Background Knowledge Discuss raw materials. **Set a Purpose for Reading** Have students evaluate statements on the *Reading Readiness Guide.* **Preview Key Terms** Teach the section's Key Terms. **Target Reading Skill** Introduce the section's Target Reading Skill of **identifying main ideas.**	**All in One Foundations of Geography Teaching Resources** **L2** Reading Readiness Guide, p. 245 **L2** Identify Main Ideas, p. 256 **World Studies Video Program** **L2** The Natural Resources of an Island Nation	**Spanish Reading and Vocabulary Study Guide** **L1** Chapter 5, Section 1, pp. 35–36 ELL

Instruct	**Instructional Resources**	**Differentiated Instruction**
What are Natural Resources? Ask for examples of natural resources and discuss some of them. **Target Reading Skill** Review **identifying main ideas.** **A Special Resource: Energy** Discuss different sources of energy and how they are consumed and protected.	**All in One Foundations of Geography Teaching Resources** **L2** Guided Reading and Review, p. 246 **L2** Reading Readiness Guide, p. 245 **Foundations of Geography Transparencies** **L2** Section Reading Support Transparency FG 56 **L2** Transparency B15: Outline	**All in One Foundations of Geography Teaching Resources** Rubric for Assessing a Student Poster, p. 274 GT, AR **L1** Reading a Natural Resources Map, p. 267 ELL, LPR, SN **L3** Reading an Economic Activity Map, p. 266 AR, GT **Teacher's Edition** **L3** For Gifted and Talented, TE p. 116 **L1** For Less Proficient Readers, TE p. 116 **L3** For English Language Learners, TE p. 117 **L3** For Advanced Readers, TE p. 117

Assess and Reteach	**Instructional Resources**	**Differentiated Instruction**
Assess Progress Evaluate student comprehension with the section assessment and section quiz. **Reteach** Assign the Reading and Vocabulary Study Guide to help struggling students. **Extend** Extend the lesson by assigning an online activity.	**All in One Foundations of Geography Teaching Resources** **L2** Section Quiz, p. 247 Rubric for Assessing a Journal Entry, p. 276 **Reading and Vocabulary Study Guide** **L1** Chapter 5, Section 1, pp. 49–51 **PHSchool.com** **L3** **For:** Environmental and Global Issues: Alternative Sources of Energy **Web Code:** led-3504	**Spanish Support** **L2** Section Quiz (Spanish), p. 39 ELL

Key

L1 Basic to Average   **L3** Average to Advanced   LPR Less Proficient Readers   GT Gifted and Talented

L2 For All Students   AR Advanced Readers   ELL English Language Learners

SN Special Needs Students

Section 2 Land Use

 3 periods, 1.5 blocks (includes Skills for Life)

Social Studies Objectives

1. Study the relation between land use and culture.
2. Investigate the relation between land use and economic activity.
3. Explore changes in land use.

Reading/Language Arts Objective

Learn how to identify sentences that include details that support the main idea of a paragraph.

Prepare to Read	Instructional Resources	Differentiated Instruction
Build Background Knowledge Discuss how land is used to extract raw materials. **Set a Purpose for Reading** Have students begin to fill out the *Reading Readiness Guide.* **Preview Key Terms** Teach the section's Key Terms. **Target Reading Skill** Introduce the section's Target Reading Skill of **identifying supporting details.**	**All in One Foundations of Geography Teaching Resources** **L2** Reading Readiness Guide, p. 249 **L2** Identify Supporting Details, p. 257	**Spanish Reading and Vocabulary Study Guide** **L1** Chapter 5, Section 2, pp. 37–38 ELL

Instruct	Instructional Resources	Differentiated Instruction
Land Use and Culture Discuss how different cultures use the materials in their environments. **Land Use and Economic Activity** Discuss first-, second-, and third-level activities related to land use. **Target Reading Skill** Review **identifying supporting details.** **Changes in Land Use** Discuss how human actions can affect land use.	**All in One Foundations of Geography Teaching Resources** **L2** Guided Reading and Review, p. 250 **L2** Reading Readiness Guide, p. 249 **Foundations of Geography Transparencies** **L2** Section Reading Support Transparency FG 57	**All in One Foundations of Geography Teaching Resources** **L2** Celia's Island Journal, pp. 270–271 AR, GT, LPR, SN **L3** The Road From Coorain, pp. 268–269 AR, GT **L2** Skills for Life, p. 261 AR, GT, LPR, SN **Teacher's Edition** **L3** For Advanced Readers, TE p. 123 **L1** For English Language Learners, TE p. 123 **Reading and Vocabulary Study Guide** **L1** Chapter 5, Section 2, pp. 52–54 ELL, LPR, SN

Assess and Reteach	Instructional Resources	Differentiated Instruction
Assess Progress Evaluate student comprehension with the section assessment and section quiz. **Reteach** Assign the Reading and Vocabulary Study Guide to help struggling students. **Extend** Extend the lesson by assigning a Book Project.	**All in One Foundations of Geography Teaching Resources** **L2** Section Quiz, p. 251 **L3** Book Project: World News Today, pp. 36–38 Rubric for Assessing a Report, p. 275 **Reading and Vocabulary Study Guide** **L1** Chapter 5, Section 2, pp. 52–54	**Spanish Support** **L2** Section Quiz (Spanish), p. 41 ELL **Teacher's Edition** **L1** For Special Needs Students, TE p. 127 **Social Studies Skills Tutor CD-ROM** **L1** Identifying Cause and Effect ELL, LPR, SN

Key

L1 Basic to Average	**L3** Average to Advanced	**LPR** Less Proficient Readers	**GT** Gifted and Talented
L2 For All Students		**AR** Advanced Readers	**ELL** English Language Learners
		SN Special Needs Students	

Section 3 People's Effect on the Environment

 3.5 periods, 1.75 blocks (includes Chapter Review and Assessment)

Social Studies Objectives
1. Investigate how first-level activities affect the environment.
2. Explore how second- and third-level activities affect the environment.

Reading/Language Arts Objective
Learn how to identify implied main ideas.

Prepare to Read	Instructional Resources	Differentiated Instruction
Build Background Knowledge Discuss the natural resources of soil, water and air. **Set a Purpose for Reading** Have students evaluate statements on the *Reading Readiness Guide.* **Preview Key Terms** Teach the section's Key Terms. **Target Reading Skill** Introduce the section's Target Reading Skill of **identifying implied main ideas.**	**All in One Foundations of Geography Teaching Resources** L2 Reading Readiness Guide, p. 253 L2 Identify Implied Main Ideas, p. 258	**Spanish Reading and Vocabulary Study Guide** L1 Chapter 5, Section 3, pp. 39–40 ELL

Instruct	Instructional Resources	Differentiated Instruction
First-Level Activities Discuss the negative effects of first-level activities on the environment. **Eyewitness Technology** Discuss the hybrid car. **Target Reading Skill** Review **identifying implied main ideas.** **Second- and Third-Level Activities** Discuss the effects of industrial and service activities on the environment.	**All in One Foundations of Geography Teaching Resources** L2 Guided Reading and Review, p. 254 L2 Reading Readiness Guide, p. 253 L2 Small Group Activity: Community Service Project: Protect the Environment, pp. 262–265 **Foundations of Geography Transparencies** L2 Section Reading Support Transparency FG 58	**Spanish Support** L2 Guided Reading and Review (Spanish), p. 42 ELL

Assess and Reteach	Instructional Resources	Differentiated Instruction
Assess Progress Evaluate student comprehension with the section assessment and section quiz. **Reteach** Assign the Reading and Vocabulary Study Guide to help struggling students. **Extend** Extend the lesson by assigning an Enrichment Activity.	**All in One Foundations of Geography Teaching Resources** L2 Section Quiz, p. 255 L3 Enrichment, p. 260 Rubric for Assessing a Journal Entry, p. 276 L2 Vocabulary Development, p. 273 Rubric for Assessing a Writing Assignment, p. 277 L2 Word Knowledge, p. 259 L2 Chapter Tests A and B, pp. 278–283 L2 Final Exams A and B, pp. 287–292 **Reading and Vocabulary Study Guide** L1 Chapter 5, Section 3, pp. 55–57	**Spanish Support** L2 Section Quiz (Spanish), p. 43 ELL L2 Chapter Summary (Spanish), p. 44 ELL L2 Vocabulary Development (Spanish), p. 45 ELL

Key

L1 Basic to Average   L3 Average to Advanced   LPR Less Proficient Readers   GT Gifted and Talented
L2 For All Students   AR Advanced Readers   ELL English Language Learners
     SN Special Needs Students

Section Lesson Planner

Reading Background

Summarizing

Research has shown that summarizing helps students understand and recall what they have read. Explain to students that good summarizers begin by taking notes while reading. They identify main ideas and list important supporting details. Describe the following steps for writing good summaries:

1. After reading the selection aloud, ask students to recall information from the text. List their responses on the board.
2. Have students reread the selection to verify the accuracy of the recalled information.
3. Have students eliminate any information that is not important enough to include in their summaries.
4. Write the summary together as a class.

   Use scaffolding to teach the skill by starting small; ask students to summarize a paragraph from their texts. Then have them extend their summarizing skills by gradually applying the skill to groups of paragraphs, entire sections, and complete chapters.

Using Paragraph Shrinking Effectively

The Paragraph Shrinking strategy can help students extract key ideas from each paragraph they read. To maximize success with this strategy, have students read the paragraph twice. The first time, students should scan the text to understand the general idea of the paragraph. The second time, students should read the paragraph more carefully to identify key ideas.

Demonstrate Paragraph Shrinking by modeling the following steps based on the last paragraph on page 115:

1. Identify the subject of the paragraph. *(types of energy that are renewable resources)*
2. Identify two to three important supporting details. *(The way the sun heats Earth causes wind, which can be used as energy. Solar power and geothermal energy, or the heat within Earth, are types of energy. These resources will never run out.)*
3. Help the student to "shrink" the paragraph by stating the main idea of the paragraph in a complete sentence. The sentence should use approximately ten words or less. *(Wind, solar, and geothermal energy are renewable resources used as energy.)*

World Studies Background

Solar Energy

Solar energy is free, but collecting and converting it to electricity is not. Solar cells can convert only about 10 percent of the sun's energy into electricity. Consequently, several cells must be connected to create power for large areas. This is costly and takes up a great deal of space. Smaller systems used to heat individual homes are more cost-effective.

Raw Materials in the United States

The demand for raw materials in the United States results in substantial internal trade. Forest products from the West are traded particularly to the Northeast and the Midwest. Oil from Texas is essential throughout the United States. Metals from the Midwest are a necessity in the Northeast and the West. These raw materials often travel through manufacturing centers in major cities before the final products are sent to their ultimate destinations.

The Amazon Rainforest and Medicine

Concerns about deforestation in the Amazon rainforest often focus on the threat posed to its unique gene pool. Many organisms found exclusively in the rainforest are essential to the development of pharmaceutical products. About twenty-five percent of the pharmaceuticals used in the Western world are created from rainforest ingredients.

Infoplease® provides a wealth of useful information for the classroom. You can use this resource to strengthen your background on the subjects covered in this chapter. Have students visit this advertising-free site as a starting point for projects requiring research.

Use Web Code **led-3500** for **Infoplease®**.

Chapter 5

Guiding Questions

Remind students about the Guiding Questions introduced at the beginning of the book.

Section 1 refers to **Guiding Question ③**
How do people use the world's natural resources? *(Everything that people use or consume is made with natural resources, which can be divided into renewable resources, living resources, and nonrenewable resources.)*

Section 2 refers to **Guiding Question ③**
How do people use the world's natural resources? *(People use land in a variety of ways, depending on culture, environment, history, and industrialization.)*

Section 3 refers to **Guiding Question ③**
How do people use the world's natural resources? *(People change Earth's landscape through farming and industrialization, and struggle to find a balance between industry and protecting the environment.)*

🎯 Target Reading Skill   L2

In this chapter, students will learn and apply the reading skill of identifying main ideas. Use the following worksheets to help students practice this skill.

All in One **Foundations of Geography Teaching Resources,** *Identify Main Ideas,* p. 256; *Identify Supporting Details,* p. 257; *Identify Implied Main Ideas,* p. 258

Differentiated Instruction

The following Teacher's Edition strategies are suitable for students of varying abilities.
Advanced Readers, pp. 117, 123
English Language Learners, pp. 117, 123
Gifted and Talented, p. 116
Less Proficient Readers, p. 116
Special Needs Students, p. 127

Chapter 5
Interacting With Our Environment

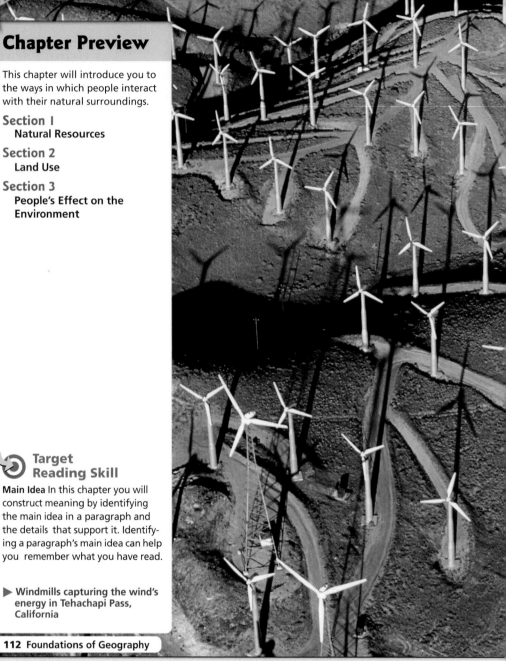

Chapter Preview

This chapter will introduce you to the ways in which people interact with their natural surroundings.

Section 1
Natural Resources

Section 2
Land Use

Section 3
People's Effect on the Environment

🎯 Target Reading Skill

Main Idea In this chapter you will construct meaning by identifying the main idea in a paragraph and the details that support it. Identifying a paragraph's main idea can help you remember what you have read.

► Windmills capturing the wind's energy in Tehachapi Pass, California

---

Bibliography

For the Teacher
Nadakavukaren, Anne. *Our Global Environment: A Health Perspective.* Waveland Press, 5th Edition, 2000.
Smith, Dan & Anne Braein. *The Penguin State of the World Atlas.* Penguin USA, 7th Edition, 2003.
The Worldwatch Institute. *State of the World 2003 (annual).* W.W. Norton & Company, 2003.

For the Student
L1 Ditchfield, Christian. *Oil (True Books: Natural Resources).* Children's Book Press, 2003.
L2 Allaby, Michael. *The Environment (How It Works).* Award Publications, 2002.
L3 Morgan, Sally. *Alternative Energy Sources (Science at the Edge).* Heinemann Library, 2002.

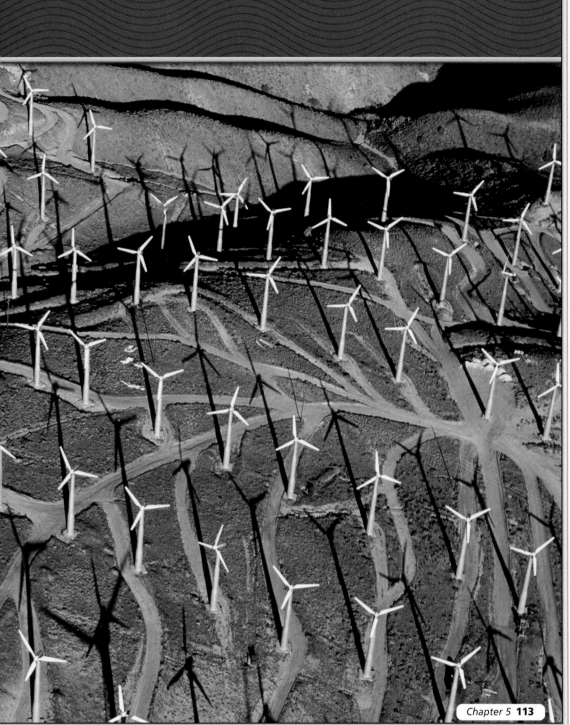

Reach Into Your Background Have students study the photo on pp. 112–113 and read the accompanying caption. Draw their attention to the title of the chapter. Ask students to think about how the photograph illustrates interaction between humans and their environment. *(People are using wind to create energy.)* Then ask them to think of some other examples of people interacting with their environment. *(Possible answers: damming rivers to create electricity and regulate water supply; farming; harnessing natural materials to make things used in everyday life, such as clothing)*

Chapter Resources

Teaching Resources
- L2 Vocabulary Development, p. 273
- L2 Skills for Life, p. 261
- L2 Chapter Tests A and B, pp. 278–283

Spanish Support
- L2 Spanish Chapter Summary, p. 44
- L2 Spanish Vocabulary Development, p. 45

Media and Technology
- L1 Student Edition on Audio CD
- L1 Guided Reading Audiotapes, English and Spanish
- L2 Social Studies Skills Tutor CD-ROM
- *ExamView Test Bank CD-ROM*

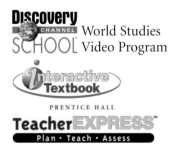

Discovery CHANNEL World Studies SCHOOL Video Program

Interactive Textbook PRENTICE HALL

Teacher**EXPRESS** Plan • Teach • Assess

Objectives
Social Studies
1. Learn about natural resources.
2. Investigate energy.

Reading/Language Arts
Learn how to identify the main idea of a paragraph.

Prepare to Read

Build Background Knowledge L2

Tell students that in this section they will learn about natural resources and how people use them. Ask students to identify things in the classroom that are in their natural forms, such as a glass of water or a plant. Then have the students name several objects in the room made of raw materials, such as a desk or an item of clothing. Ask them to identify what raw material each was made from and how the raw materials were changed for human use. Conduct an Idea Wave (TE, p. T35) to help students share their ideas.

Set a Purpose for Reading L2

- Preview the Objectives.

- Read each statement in the *Reading Readiness Guide* aloud. Ask students to mark the statements true or false.

  All in One Foundations of Geography Teaching Resources, *Reading Readiness Guide*, p. 245

- Have students discuss the statements in pairs or groups of four, then mark their worksheets again. Use the Numbered Heads participation strategy (TE, p. T36) to call on students to share their group's perspectives.

Vocabulary Builder
Preview Key Terms L2

Pronounce each Key Term, then ask the students to say the word with you. Provide a simple explanation such as, "Natural resources are things found in nature that people use."

Prepare to Read

Objectives
In this section you will
1. Learn about natural resources.
2. Investigate energy.

Taking Notes
Copy the outline below. Add letters, numbers, and headings as needed. As you read this section, fill in the outline with information about natural resources and energy.

```
I. Natural resources
   A. Renewable resources
   B.
      1.
      2.
II. Energy
   A.
```

Target Reading Skill
Identify Main Ideas
Good readers identify the main idea in every written paragraph. The main idea is the most important point—the one that includes all of the other points. Sometimes this idea is stated directly. For example, in the first paragraph below, the first sentence states the paragraph's main idea. As you read, note the main idea of each paragraph.

Key Terms
- **natural resources** (NACH ur ul REE sawr siz) *n.* useful materials found in the environment
- **raw materials** (raw muh TIHR ee ulz) *n.* natural resources that must be worked to be useful
- **renewable resources** (rih NOO uh bul REE sawr siz) *n.* natural resources that can be replaced
- **nonrenewable resources** (nahn rih NOO uh bul REE sawr siz) *n.* natural resources that cannot be replaced

Men constructing a wooden hut in Kenya

114 Foundations of Geography

What Are Natural Resources?

Everything that people use or consume is made with **natural resources,** or useful materials found in the environment. When people talk about natural resources, they usually mean such things as water, minerals, and vegetation.

All people need water, food, clothing, and shelter to survive. People drink water. People eat food that the soil produces. So do the animals that provide eggs, cheese, meat, and wool. Homes are made from wood, clay, and steel.

People can use some resources just as they are found in nature. Fresh water is one of these. But most resources must be changed before people can use them. Natural resources that must be worked to be useful are called **raw materials.** For example, people cannot just go out and cut down a tree if they want paper. Trees are the raw materials for paper and wood. To make paper, the wood must be soaked and broken up to create pulp. (Pulp is a kind of soup of wood fibers.) Machines collect the wet fibers on screens to form sheets of paper.

Target Reading Skill L2

Identify Main Ideas Direct students' attention to the Target Reading Skill. Tell them that identifying the main idea will help them to focus on the most important points of a paragraph.

Model identifying main ideas by having students read the third paragraph on this page. Students should make a list of the three ideas presented in the paragraph.

Then ask students **Which of these three points is the most important and includes all the other points?** (*Most resources must be changed before people use them.*)

Give students *Identify Main Ideas*. Have them complete the activity in groups.

All in One Foundations of Geography Teaching Resources, *Identify Main Ideas*, p. 256

Renewable Resources The environment is filled with natural resources, but not all resources are alike. Geographers divide them into two main groups.

The first group is **renewable resources,** or resources that can be replaced. Some resources are replaced naturally because of the way Earth works. In the water cycle, water evaporates into the air and falls as rain, snow, hail, or sleet. This happens over and over again. Therefore, Earth has an unchanging amount of water. Other materials that go through natural cycles include nitrogen and carbon.

Some types of energy are also renewable resources. Using wind to make electricity will not use the wind up. Wind results from differences in the way the sun heats Earth. As long as the sun shines, there will always be more wind. Solar energy, or energy from the sun, is a renewable resource. No matter how much people use, there will always be more. Geothermal energy uses differences in heat between Earth's surface and its interior. This heat difference will not disappear in the foreseeable future.

Explore the environment of an island nation.

 Identify Main Ideas Which sentence states the main idea of the paragraph at the left?

The World: Natural Resources

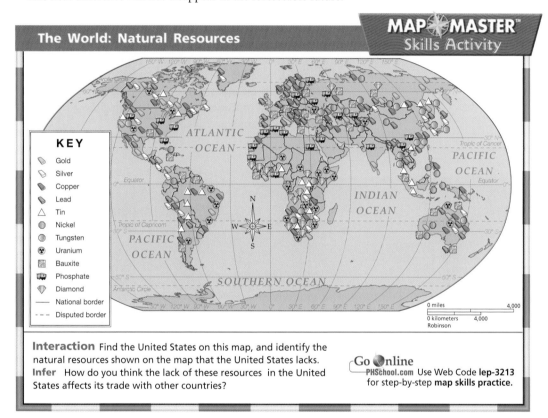

KEY
- 🔷 Gold
- 🔷 Silver
- 🔷 Copper
- 🔷 Lead
- △ Tin
- ◯ Nickel
- ◯ Tungsten
- ⊛ Uranium
- ▦ Bauxite
- ▨ Phosphate
- ⬡ Diamond
- —— National border
- - - - Disputed border

ATLANTIC OCEAN

PACIFIC OCEAN

Equator

Tropic of Cancer

Tropic of Capricorn

INDIAN OCEAN

PACIFIC OCEAN

SOUTHERN OCEAN

Antarctic Circle

0 miles 4,000
0 kilometers 4,000
Robinson

MAP MASTER Skills Activity

Interaction Find the United States on this map, and identify the natural resources shown on the map that the United States lacks.
Infer How do you think the lack of these resources in the United States affects its trade with other countries?

Go Online
PHSchool.com Use Web Code lep-3213 for step-by-step **map skills practice.**

Vocabulary Builder

Use the information below to teach students this section's high-use words.

High-Use Word	Definition and Sample Sentence
consume, p. 114	*v.* to use something Larger cars **consume** more gasoline than smaller ones.
evaporate, p. 115	*v.* to change from a liquid into a vapor Puddles **evaporate** quickly on a sunny day.
harness, p. 117	*v.* to bring under control and direct the force of something Windmills **harness** the energy of the wind.
hybrid, p. 119	*n.* something made up of two different elements A **hybrid** car runs on gasoline and electric power.

 Show students *The Natural Resources of an Island Nation.* Ask students to name two important parts of Mauritius' economy. *(sugarcane and tourism)* Ask students **How are these related to Mauritius' environment and natural resources?** *(Its climate is suitable for growing sugarcane, and its natural beauty attracts tourists.)*

Instruct

What Are Natural Resources? L2

Guided Instruction

- **Vocabulary Builder** Clarify the high-use words **consume** and **evaporate** before reading.

- Read What Are Natural Resources? using the ReQuest reading strategy (TE, p. T35). Ask students to study the map on p. 115.

- Ask students **What are natural resources?** *(useful materials found in the environment)*

- Ask students **What are renewable resources?** *(natural resources that can be replaced)* **What are some examples of renewable resources?** *(water, wind, solar energy, geothermal energy)*

- Have students examine the map and brainstorm what some of the natural resources shown might be used for. *(Possible answers: gold, silver, diamonds—jewelry; copper—coins, wire; tin—cans; lead—pipes)*

🎯 Target Reading Skill L2

Identify Main Ideas As a follow up, ask students to answer the Target Reading Skill question in the Student Edition. *(Some types of energy are also renewable resources.)*

Answers

 MAP MASTER Skills Activity Interaction nickel and diamonds **Infer** Since the United States does not have these resources, it probably has to purchase them from other countries.

Go Online PHSchool.com Students may practice their map skills using the interactive online version of this map.

Guided Instruction (continued)

- Ask students **What are living resources?** *(living things that provide natural resources, such as plants and animals)*

- Ask students to define nonrenewable resources and list examples. *(resources that cannot be replaced; metal ores, most minerals, natural gas, petroleum)*

- Ask students **How does recycling help conserve nonrenewable resources?** *(Recycling recovers and processes used materials so they can be used again.)*

- Ask students **What are examples of fossil fuels?** *(coal, natural gas, and petroleum)* Have students discuss how they are created and if they are renewable. *(They were created over millions of years from remains of prehistoric living things. They are renewable, but if used up they would take millions of years to form again. So for the purposes of people living today, fossil fuels are nonrenewable resources.)*

Independent Practice

Show students the *Outline Transparency.* Then ask students to create the Taking Notes graphic organizer on a blank piece of paper. Have them begin to fill in the outline by adding information about natural resources. Briefly model how to create and fill in the outline.

📖 **Foundations of Geography Transparencies,** *Transparency B15: Outline*

Monitor Progress

As students fill in the graphic organizer, circulate and make sure students are choosing appropriate headings and details. Provide assistance as needed.

Solar cells on the roof of a house in Felsberg, Germany

Living Resources Living things that provide natural resources, such as plants and animals, are also renewable resources. Like other resources, they must be properly managed so that people do not overuse them.

For example, a timber company may cut down all the trees in an area for use as wood. But the company may then plant new trees to replace the ones they cut. Even if they do not, seeds left in the ground will probably produce new trees. Every day, the people of the world eat many chickens and ears of corn. But farmers always make sure to grow more corn and chickens to replace what people eat. If people are careful, they can have a steady supply of these renewable living resources.

Nonrenewable Resources The second major group of resources is called **nonrenewable resources,** or resources that cannot be replaced. Most nonliving things, such as metal ores, most minerals, natural gas, and petroleum—or crude oil—are nonrenewable resources. If people keep mining minerals and burning fuels such as coal and oil, they will eventually run out. Therefore, people need to use these resources carefully. If they do run out, people will need to find substitutes for them.

Although they are nonrenewable, many metals, minerals, and materials such as plastics can be recycled. Recycling does not return these materials to their natural state. Still, they can be recovered and processed for reuse. Recycling these materials helps to conserve nonrenewable resources.

116 Foundations of Geography

Fossil Fuels Most scientists think that coal, natural gas, and petroleum are fossil fuels, or fuels created over millions of years from the remains of prehistoric living things. If people continue using coal at today's rate, known supplies may run out in several hundred years. At current rates of use, known supplies of oil and natural gas may run out in less than 100 years.

If oil and natural gas are fossil fuels, they are renewable, since living things today will become fossil fuels in millions of years. But if these fuels take so long to develop, they are nonrenewable for our purposes.

✓ **Reading Check** What is the difference between renewable and nonrenewable resources?

A Special Resource: Energy

Many natural resources are sources of energy. People use energy not only from fossil fuels, but also from the wind and the sun. Dams produce hydroelectric power by harnessing the power of falling water.

Energy is itself a resource that is needed to make use of other natural resources. Consider cotton. It takes energy to harvest cotton from a field, to spin the cotton into thread, and to weave it into fabric. Workers use energy to travel to a garment factory. It takes energy to sew a shirt with a sewing machine. It also takes energy to transport the shirt by ship and truck to a retail store. Finally, the consumer uses energy to bring the shirt home.

Located on the border between Oregon and Washington, the Bonneville Dam produces hydroelectric power.

Strip Mining Coal
The machine below extracts coal from this exposed deposit in Banwen Pyrddin, Wales, United Kingdom.
Apply Information *Do you think that coal is a recyclable, renewable, or nonrenewable resource?*

A Special Resource: Energy   L2

Guided Instruction

- **Vocabulary Builder** Clarify the high-use words **harness** and **hybrid** before reading.

- Read A Special Resource: Energy with students and have them examine the graph on p. 118. Circulate to make sure individuals can answer the Graph Skills questions.

- Ask students to name some different sources of energy. (*Possible answers: fossil fuels, wind, water, sun*) Ask students **How is energy needed to make use of other natural resources?** (*It takes energy to convert the natural resource into a usable form, to make it into a product, to transport the product, and to consume the product.*)

Answers

✓ **Reading Check** Renewable resources are natural resources that can be replaced, whereas nonrenewable resources are natural resources that cannot be replaced.

Apply Information Coal is a renewable resource; over millions of years more coal will be created from the remains of living things. Practically, coal is generally considered to be a nonrenewable resource because its supplies are limited.

- Have students name two countries that can sell oil and two countries that have to buy energy. *(Mexico and Saudi Arabia sell oil; Japan and the United States have to buy energy.)*

- Ask students to list energy alternatives to fossil fuels. *(wind energy, solar energy, tidal energy, geothermal energy, biomass, atomic energy)*

- Direct students' attention to the graph on this page to help them answer the following question: **What are the names of at least three countries that consume more petroleum than they produce?** *(Possible answers: Brazil, China, Germany, Japan, and the United States)*

- Have students list some ways of conserving energy discussed in the text. Then have them brainstorm other ways they could save energy at home or at school. *(In text: hybrid cars, new technologies that conserve energy used for heat and light; other possible answers: turning off lights when not in use at home or in school, turning down heat or air conditioning at night or when not at home)*

Independent Practice

Have students complete the graphic organizer by adding details about energy usage.

Monitor Progress

- Show *Section Reading Support Transparency FG 56* and ask students to check their graphic organizers individually. Go over key concepts and clarify key vocabulary as needed.

   📖 **Foundations of Geography Transparencies,** *Section Reading Support Transparency FG 56*

- Tell students to fill in the last column of their *Reading Readiness Guides.* Probe for what they learned that confirms or invalidates each statement.

   All in One Foundations of Geography Teaching Resources, *Reading Readiness Guide,* p. 245

Answers

Graph Skills Identify Germany and Japan **Compare and Contrast** the United States

Pipes running across an oil field in Meyal, Pakistan

Energy "Have's" and "Have Not's" People in every country need energy. But energy resources are not evenly spread around the world. Certain areas are rich in energy resources. Others have very few.

Countries with many rivers, such as Canada and Norway, can use water energy to create electricity. Countries like Saudi Arabia and Mexico have huge amounts of oil that they sell to other countries. Countries like Japan and the United States do not produce as much energy as they use. These countries have to buy energy from other countries.

Meeting Energy Needs in the Future Over time, energy use worldwide has grown rapidly. Yet our supplies of fossil fuels may be limited. It seems likely that the world's people will need to find other sources of energy. Many possibilities exist.

Already, some countries, such as Denmark and Germany, are developing renewable energy sources such as wind and solar energy. Other sources of energy that will not run out are tidal energy, from the rise and fall of Earth's oceans, and geothermal energy, or energy from the heat of Earth's interior. Biomass, or plant material, is a renewable source of energy. These energy sources can reduce a country's need for imported oil.

Atomic energy uses radioactive materials, which are nonrenewable but plentiful. Some people oppose atomic energy because radioactive materials can be dangerous. Others support it as a plentiful energy source that does not pollute the air.

Graph Skills

Some countries produce more oil than they use. These countries can sell their extra oil to other countries. Others consume more oil than they produce and have to buy it from other countries. **Identify** Which of the countries on this graph have to buy almost all of their oil? **Compare and Contrast** Which country buys the most oil?

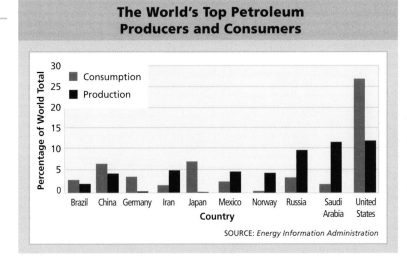

The World's Top Petroleum Producers and Consumers

SOURCE: *Energy Information Administration*

118 Foundations of Geography

Skills Mini Lesson

Problem-Solving

1. To solve a problem, students should identify the problem, evaluate its effect, identify possible solutions, choose a solution, and determine its effectiveness.

2. Have students read the second paragraph on this page to identify some problem-solving steps used to meet countries' energy needs.

3. Have students apply the skill by asking them to reread the text under Meeting Energy Needs in the Future on pp. 118–119. Have students suppose they live in a cloudy, windless place with a limited oil supply, no large bodies of water, and no biomass available. Ask them how problem-solving can be used to help them meet their energy needs. *(Possible solutions: geothermal or atomic energy)*

Geothermal power
In addition to producing energy, the geothermal power plant at Svartsengi, Iceland, heats the mineral-rich water of the Blue Lagoon. **Infer** *Are fossil fuels used to heat this pool?*

Fossil fuels will last longer if people use less energy. New technologies, such as hybrid cars, can reduce a country's need for imported oil by burning less gas per mile. Other technologies offer energy savings in heating and lighting buildings and in making new products. If people manage to use less energy, they will not need to buy as much from foreign countries. They will also have an easier time meeting their energy needs in the future.

 ✓ Reading Check Why do some countries have to import energy?

Section 1 Assessment

Key Terms
Review the key terms at the beginning of this section. Use each term in a sentence that explains its meaning.

Target Reading Skill
State the main idea of the paragraph on this page.

Comprehension and Critical Thinking
1. (a) **Identify** Why is wood considered a renewable resource?

(b) **Apply Information** What needs to happen after trees are cut in order for wood to remain a renewable resource?
2. (a) **List** Name some sources of energy other than fossil fuels.
(b) **Categorize** What do these energy sources have in common, and how do they differ from fossil fuels?
(c) **Draw Conclusions** Why might we need to use more of these energy sources in the future?

Writing Activity
Think about what you did this morning before you came to school. Write a journal entry describing the natural resources that you used and all of the ways that you used energy at home and on your way to school.

For: An activity on natural resources
Visit: PHSchool.com
Web Code: led-3501

Chapter 5 Section 1 **119**

Section 1 Assessment

Key Terms
Students' sentences should reflect knowledge of each Key Term.

Target Reading Skill
Fossil fuels will last longer if people use less energy.

Comprehension and Critical Thinking
1. (a) It can be replaced by the growth of new trees. (b) New trees need to be planted.
2. (a) wind energy, solar energy, geothermal energy, hydroelectric power, tidal energy, biomass, atomic energy (b) All of the types of energy listed above except atomic energy are renewable resources, and fossil fuels are not. (c) Reserves of important fossil fuels will eventually run out.

Assess and Reteach

Assess Progress   L2
Have students complete the Section Assessment. Administer the *Section Quiz.*

All in One Foundations of Geography Teaching Resources, *Section Quiz,* p. 247

Reteach   L1
If students need more instruction, have them read this section in the Reading and Vocabulary Study Guide.

Chapter 5, Section 1, **Foundations of Geography Reading and Vocabulary Study Guide,** pp. 49–51

Extend   L3
Have students explore alternative energy by completing *Alternative Sources of Energy.* Use the activity as a springboard for a discussion about the use of renewable sources of energy.

Go Online
PHSchool.com

For: Environmental and Global Issues: *Alternative Sources of Energy*
Visit: PHSchool.com
Web Code: led-3504

Answers

Infer Fossil fuels are not used; geothermal energy is used.

✓ Reading Check Some countries need to import energy because the energy they consume is greater than the energy they produce.

Go Online
PHSchool.com Typing in the Web code when prompted will bring students to detailed instructions for this activity.

Writing Activity
Use the *Rubric for Assessing a Journal Entry* to evaluate students' journals.

All in One Foundations of Geography Teaching Resources, *Rubric for Assessing a Journal Entry,* p. 276

Section 2
Step-by-Step Instruction

Objectives

Social Studies

1. Study the relation between land use and culture.

2. Investigate the relation between land use and economic activity.

3. Explore changes in land use.

Reading/Language Arts

Learn how to identify sentences that include details that support the main idea of a paragraph.

Prepare to Read

Build Background Knowledge L2

Tell students they will learn about how people use land resources in this section. Ask students to choose a familiar product *(such as a box of cereal)* that they use in their everyday lives. Then have them think about what raw materials were used to make the product. Finally, ask them to describe how the products are made and relate this process to land use *(For example, farm land is needed to grow the ingredients of cereal.)* Use the Think-Write-Pair-Share participation strategy (TE, p. T36) to structure the activity.

Set a Purpose for Reading L2

■ Preview the Objectives.

■ Form students into pairs or groups of four. Distribute the *Reading Readiness Guide.* Ask students to fill in the first two columns of the chart. Use the Numbered Heads participation strategy (TE, p. T36) to call on students to share one piece of information they already know and one piece of information they want to know.

All in One Foundations of Geography Teaching Resources, *Reading Readiness Guide,* p. 249

Vocabulary Builder
Preview Key Terms L2

Pronounce each Key Term, then ask the students to say the words with you. Provide a simple explanation such as, "Manufacturing refers to making many things by hand or using machines."

Section 2
Land Use

Prepare to Read

Objectives

In this section you will

1. Study the relation between land use and culture.

2. Investigate the relation between land use and economic activity.

3. Explore changes in land use.

Taking Notes

Copy the concept web below. As you read the section, fill in the ovals with information about land use. Add ovals as needed.

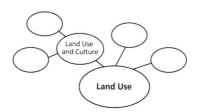

Target Reading Skill

Identify Supporting Details Sentences in a paragraph may provide details that support the main idea. These details may give examples or explanations. In the second paragraph on this page, this sentence states the main idea: "Even in similar environments, people may use land differently because they have different cultural traits." Note three details in the paragraph that explain this main idea.

Key Terms

• **environment** (en VY run munt) *n.* natural surroundings

• **manufacturing** (man yoo FAK chur ing) *n.* the large-scale production of goods by hand or by machine

• **colonization** (kahl uh nih ZAY shun) *n.* the movement of settlers and their culture to a new country

• **industrialization** (in dus tree ul ih ZAY shun) *n.* the growth of machine-powered production in an economy

A peanut farmer in Georgia inspecting his crop

120 Foundations of Geography

Land Use and Culture

How people use the land depends on their culture. People may use their land differently because their cultures have developed in different **environments**, or natural surroundings. For example, the Inuit live in a cold, arctic climate. It is too cold to grow crops, so the Inuit use their land mainly for hunting wild animals, and they rely heavily on fishing. The Japanese live in a warmer, moister climate. Although much of Japan is too steep to farm, the Japanese use much of the remaining land for crops. Their main crop is rice, which grows well in the warm, moist climate of Japan.

Even in similar environments, however, people may use land differently because they have different cultural traits. For example, Georgia has a warm, moist climate like that of southern Japan. But Georgia does not produce much rice. Instead, Georgians raise chickens and grow crops such as peanuts. While the Japanese eat rice at nearly every meal, Americans eat more meat and peanut butter.

Target Reading Skill L2

Identify Supporting Details Point out the Target Reading Skill. Tell students that sentences in a paragraph may provide additional details that support the main idea.

Model identifying supporting details by reading the first paragraph on p. 121 aloud. Ask students to identify the main idea. *(People's cultures help shape the landscapes where they live.)* Then ask them to identify one detail that supports the main idea. *(Possible supporting details: In some parts of the Philippines, a culture of rice farming and a shortage of level land has led people to carve terraces into hillsides; people cleared forests in Western Europe for farm land.)*

Give students *Identify Supporting Details.* Have them complete the activity in groups.

All in One Foundations of Geography Teaching Resources, *Identify Supporting Details,* p. 257

Cultures and Landscapes The examples of the Inuit and the Japanese show how people's environments help to shape their cultures. People's cultures, in turn, help shape the landscapes where they live. For example, in some parts of the Philippines, a culture of rice farming and a shortage of level land has led people to carve terraces into hillsides. Thousands of years ago, Western Europe was covered with forests. As farming cultures spread across that region, people cleared forests to use the land for farming. Today, most of Western Europe is open fields and pastures. Few forests remain.

Land Use and Cultural Differences As the examples of Japan and Georgia show, however, similar environments do not necessarily produce similar cultures. People may respond differently to those environments, depending on their culture. For example, much of the western United States has a dry climate. Many crops need irrigation, or an artificial water supply. The Middle East also has climates too dry for most crops to grow without irrigation. However, the two regions have different cultures and different responses to this challenge. In the western United States, farmers use modern irrigation systems. For example, drip irrigation provides water to each plant through little pipes or tubes. Some Middle Eastern farmers use qanats, or brick irrigation channels, to bring water to their crops. Both cultures face similar environments, but they interact with those environments differently.

✓ **Reading Check** How is land use related to culture?

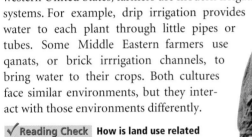
Drip irrigation of grape vines in eastern Washington State

Irrigation in Yemen
This man is walking along a qanat, or brick irrigation channel, in Jiblah, Yemen.
Analyze Images *What clues do you see in this landscape that suggest a need for irrigation?*

Chapter 5 Section 2 **121**

Land Use and Economic Activity

Guided Instruction

- **Vocabulary Builder** Clarify the high-use words **distribute** and **correspond** before reading.

- Have students read Land Use and Economic Activity. Review the photographs and captions on pp. 122 and 123 with students. Circulate to make sure individuals can answer the Reading Check question.

- Ask students **What are first-level activities?** (*economic activities in which people use land and resources directly to make products*)

- Ask students **How much of the world's land is used for first-level activities?** (*Most of the world's land is used for first-level activities.*) **How much land is used for these activities in developed countries like the United States?** (*In developed countries only a small percentage of the land is used for first-level activities.*)

Target Reading Skill

L2

Identify Supporting Details As a follow up, ask students to answer the Target Reading Skill question in the Student Edition. (*Possible answers: hunting, cutting wood, mining, fishing, herding animals, and raising crops*)

Land Use and Economic Activity

In some places, people use the land and its resources to make a living by farming, fishing, or mining. In other places, people work in factories, where they turn natural resources into finished products. In still other places, people sell or distribute products and make a living by providing services. These three ways of making a living correspond to three stages of economic activity. Geographers use stages of economic activity as a way to understand land use.

Identify Supporting Details
Which details in the paragraph at the right give examples of first-level activities?

First-Level Activities In the first stage, people use land and resources directly to make products. They may hunt, cut wood, mine, or fish. They also may herd animals or raise crops. This is the first stage of activities. At this stage, people interact directly with the land or the sea. Most of the world's land is used for first-level activities. However, in developed countries such as the United States, only a small percentage of the people make a living at first-level activities.

Stages of Economic Activity

A series of economic activities connect a flock of sheep in a pasture to a wool sweater in a store. Sheep-raising, a first-level activity, makes it possible to manufacture woolen goods such as sweaters, a second-level activity. Manufacturing makes it possible to deliver sweaters to stores. Stores can then sell the sweaters. Delivery and sales are both third-level activities.

A flock of sheep being driven to a pasture in New Zealand

▲ **Farming, a first-level activity**
This farmer is shearing a sheep, or trimming away its wool. Raising and shearing sheep are first-level activities, or direct uses of natural resources.

122 Foundations of Geography

Skills Mini Lesson

Analyzing Primary Sources
1. Help students define primary and secondary sources. To analyze these sources, students should identify who created the source, when, and why. They should then identify the main idea, separate facts from opinions, look for evidence of bias, and evaluate how reliable the source is.

2. In groups, have students use the steps above to analyze an encyclopedia article, a secondary source, about islands.

3. Have students analyze the primary source *Celia's Island Journal*.

All in One Foundations of Geography Teaching Resources, *Celia's Island Journal*, pp. 270–271

Second-Level Activities At the second stage, people process the products of first-level activities. Most second-level activity is **manufacturing**, or the large-scale production of goods by hand or by machine. Manufacturing may turn a farmer's corn crop into cornflakes for your breakfast. Manufacturing, especially in urban areas, is an important land use in developed countries.

Third-Level Activities At the third stage, a person delivers boxes of cornflakes to your local grocery store. Third-level activities are also known as services. These activities do not produce goods. They may help sell goods. They often involve working directly for customers or for businesses. Many businesses offering services—doctors' offices, banks, automobile repair shops, shopping malls, and fast-food restaurants—are part of everyday living. Services are also clustered in urban areas, especially in developed countries.

✓ Reading Check How is most of the world's land used?

▲ **Manufacturing, a second-level activity**
Second-level activities process natural resources to make goods, such as the wool this worker is processing at a New Zealand mill.

Retail sales, a third-level activity ▶
Selling manufactured goods, such as this sweater, in a store is a third-level activity. This woolen-goods store is in New Zealand.

GEOGRAPHY SKILLS PRACTICE

Human-Environment Interaction Each activity shown here occurs in a different part of New Zealand.
Apply Information Which activities occur in rural areas, and which activities are likely to occur in urban areas?

Chapter 5 Section 2 **123**

Changes in Land Use L2

Guided Instruction

- Have students examine the text and visuals on p. 124 and read Changes in Land Use on p. 125.

- Ask students **How has human-environment interaction shaped the city of Boston?** *(Colonists cleared forests and built structures along the waterfront; marshes were drained and filled in to create new land.)*

- Ask **How can colonization affect land use?** *(It may change a landscape to fit colonists' cultural practices.)*

- Ask students **How has industrialization changed land use in developed countries?** *(Since 1900, suburbs have increased around cities in developed countries.)*

Independent Practice

Have students complete the graphic organizer by filling in details about changes in land use.

Monitor Progress

- Show *Section Reading Support Transparency FG 57* and ask students to check their graphic organizers individually. Go over key concepts and clarify key vocabulary as needed.

   Foundations of Geography Transparencies, *Section Reading Support Transparency FG 57*

- Tell students to fill in the last column of their *Reading Readiness Guides.* Ask them if what they learned was what they had expected to learn.

   All in One Foundations of Geography Teaching Resources, *Reading Readiness Guide,* p. 249

Answers

MAP★MASTER Skills Activity **Identify** Only a small area to the west of South Boston remained forested after colonization. **Compare and Contrast** The city has grown because people created new land.

Go Online PHSchool.com Students may practice their map skills using the interactive online version of this map.

Boston: A Changing Landscape

English colonists founded Boston, Massachusetts, on a narrow peninsula surrounded by water, marshes, and forest. The colonists cleared most of the forest for farmland. The colonists also built dams, piers, and retaining walls along the waterfront. By the 1800s, Boston's growing industries and growing population of workers faced a land shortage. Boston's solution was to drain marshes and to create new land by filling in areas of water. At first, Boston's people filled in around existing piers. Then, they filled in tidal ponds behind dams. Finally, they filled in whole bodies of open water.

Human-Environment Interaction Colonization and industrialization transformed Boston's landscape. **Identify** How much of the forest around Boston remained after colonization? **Compare and Contrast** How did Boston's land area change between colonial times and today?

Go Online
PHSchool.com Use Web Code lep-3312 for step-by-step map skills practice.

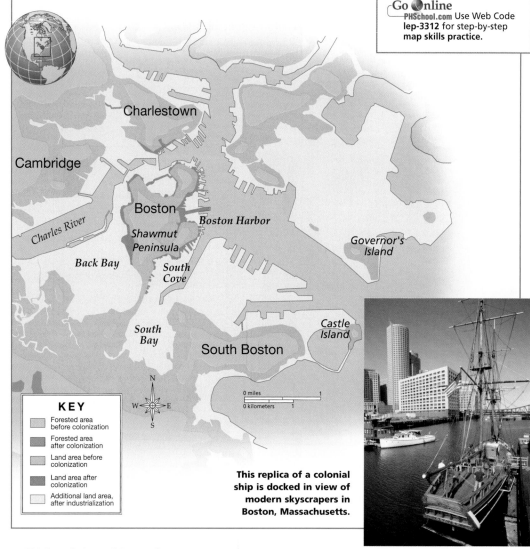

Charlestown

Cambridge

Boston

Charles River

Shawmut Peninsula

Boston Harbor

Governor's Island

Back Bay

South Cove

South Bay

South Boston

Castle Island

KEY

- Forested area before colonization
- Forested area after colonization
- Land area before colonization
- Land area after colonization
- Additional land area, after industrialization

This replica of a colonial ship is docked in view of modern skyscrapers in Boston, Massachusetts.

124 Foundations of Geography

Background: Links Across Place

The Netherlands Large portions of the Netherlands, a country in northwestern Europe, have been reclaimed from the sea much like the city of Boston. The country is mostly flat, low-lying land. Over one-quarter is located below sea level, and much of the land is naturally lakes or marshes and unusable for farming. However, ingenious civil engineering projects dating as far back as medieval times have managed to make the land more habitable. Lakes and marshes have been drained, and a series of dunes and dikes protect the land from the sea.

Changes in Land Use

When a region undergoes **colonization,** or a movement of new settlers and their culture to a country, the newcomers may change that region's landscape to fit their cultural practices. For example, if farmers move to a region without farms, they will create farms. Similarly, as people find new ways of making a living, they start using the land in new ways, too.

Colonization Before European colonists came to Australia, there was no farming and no livestock raising. In North and South America before colonization, European crops such as wheat and grapes were unknown. So were livestock such as cows and chickens. When Europeans settled these continents, they cleared large areas for use as farmland and livestock pasture.

Industrialization and Sprawl Since the 1800s, the growth of machine-powered production, or **industrialization,** has changed landscapes in many countries. Cities have grown around industrial facilities worldwide. Since 1900, suburbs have spread out from cities in the United States and other developed countries to cover more and more land. The spread of cities and suburbs is known as sprawl.

✓ **Reading Check** How did European colonization change landscapes in North and South America?

Vineyards in Australia
Grapes did not grow in Australia before European colonists arrived. Now grapes thrive in Australia's Hunter Valley. **Infer** *What would have been different about this landscape before European colonization?*

Section 2 Assessment

Key Terms
Review the key terms at the beginning of this section. Use each term in a sentence that explains its meaning.

Target Reading Skill
State three details that explain the main idea of the second paragraph on page 120.

Comprehension and Critical Thinking
1. (a) Describe How have rice farmers in the Philippines transformed the landscape?

(b) Infer Why is the Philippines' farm landscape different from Western Europe's?
2. (a) Recall What are second-level activities?
(b) Categorize Name some examples of second-level activities.
(c) Compare and Contrast How do second-level activities differ from third-level activities?
3. (a) Recall What is industrialization?
(b) Identify Causes How is industrialization related to sprawl?

Writing Activity
Write a short encyclopedia article on land use around your hometown. Describe how culture has affected land use. Mention the different levels of economic activity around your town. Finally, give an example of a change in land use in or near your hometown.

> **Writing Tip** Encyclopedia articles contain descriptions and statements of facts. Be careful not to express personal thoughts or opinions.

Chapter 5 Section 2 **125**

Section 2 Assessment

Key Terms
Students' sentences should reflect knowledge of each Key Term.

Target Reading Skill
Possible answers: Georgia and southern Japan both have moist, warm climates; rice is a major crop in Japan; people in Georgia raise chickens and grow crops such as peanuts.

Comprehension and Critical Thinking
1. (a) Due to a shortage of land, Philippine farmers have carved terraces into hillsides in order to grow rice. **(b)** There is a shortage of level land in the Philippines.

2. (a) Second-level activities are economic activities in which people process the products of first-level activities. **(b)** Possible answers include: processing food and making sweaters from wool. **(c)** Second-level activities are based upon the manufacture of goods, whereas third-level activities produce services rather than goods.

3. (a) the growth of machine-powered production in an economy **(b)** Cities tend to grow around industrial facilities. As cities grow, suburbs grow as well. As cities and suburbs spread out, sprawl is increased.

Objective
Learn how to make predictions.

Prepare to Read

Build Background Knowledge [L2]
Tell students that in this skill lesson they will learn how to make an educated prediction. Explain to students that they make predictions every day when they decide whether to take a certain action. For example, students who walk to school may have to choose among several routes they can take. They choose routes based on which they predict is the safest and will get them to school the fastest. Have students brainstorm other common examples of making predictions.

Instruct

Making Predictions [L2]

Guided Instruction
- Read the steps on p. 126 as a class and have student volunteers write them on the board.

- Practice the skill by following the steps on p. 127 as a class. First, identify the issue in the passage. *(Some countries control water supplies of downstream nations.)* Then have students explain how the issue in the passage is similar to oil issues they already learned about. *(Possible similarity: Both oil and water are important natural resources that are in short supply in some countries.)* Next, have students read aloud the possible effects shown in the graphic organizer. Finally, ask them to predict which effect seems most likely. *(Accept any of the three effects, but be sure students supply a valid reason for their choice.)*

Independent Practice
Assign *Skills for Life* and have students complete it individually.

All in One **Foundations of Geography Teaching Resources,** *Skills for Life,* p. 261

Making Predictions

The Oval Office, where leaders make predictions, is at the center of this photo of the White House.

When you watch an adventure movie, half the fun is in predicting what happens next. Decision makers, such as American presidents, make predictions, too, and their predictions guide their decisions. Good decision makers take actions that they predict will have good results. When you predict, you make an educated guess about the effects of a certain cause. The key word here is *educated*. Without knowledge, you can't predict—you just guess.

Learn the Skill
Follow these steps to make a good prediction.

1 **Identify a situation that has not been resolved.** As you read information, ask yourself questions, such as, "What will happen next? What effects will this situation produce?"

2 **Make a list of probable outcomes, or effects.** If possible, analyze examples of similar causes that have known effects.

3 **Make an educated guess about which outcome is most likely.** In order to make an *educated* guess, use information that you know or that you research.

4 **State your prediction.** In your prediction, explain why you think the cause will produce a particular effect, or outcome.

126 Foundations of Geography

Monitor Progress
As students are completing the *Skills for Life* worksheet, circulate to make sure students are applying the skill steps effectively. Provide assistance as needed.

Practice the Skill

Read the text in the box at the right. Then predict the consequences of global struggles for water.

1 From what you have read about water supplies in Southwest Asia, identify a major issue that has not been resolved. State the problem as a question.

2 This chapter discusses problems in global oil supply. How are oil and water issues similar? What effects have resulted from world oil shortages? Study the graphic organizer below. It shows results that might occur when one country controls other countries' water.

3 Of the possible outcomes in the graphic organizer, which seems the most likely? Make an educated guess, using what you know about the oil issue.

4 Here's how your prediction might begin: "As the world's need for water grows, water-rich countries will probably _____."

During the 1900s, oil-rich nations became wealthy and powerful by controlling world oil supplies. In the present century, water supplies may determine who is rich or poor. Much of the world's usable fresh water comes from rivers that flow through many countries. Nearly half the people in the world live in international river basins. Yet many of the countries that share rivers have no water treaties. Countries along these rivers build dams to store water for themselves. Nations downstream worry that they might run out of water. In Southwest Asia, Turkey controls sources of water flowing south into Syria and Iraq. A proposed system of 22 dams could allow Turkey to withhold water from its neighbors. Syria and Iraq have plentiful oil but not enough water.

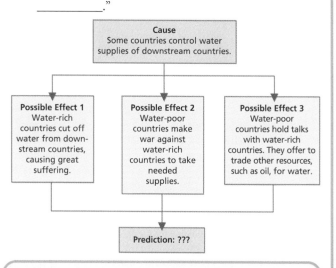

Cause
Some countries control water supplies of downstream countries.

Possible Effect 1
Water-rich countries cut off water from downstream countries, causing great suffering.

Possible Effect 2
Water-poor countries make war against water-rich countries to take needed supplies.

Possible Effect 3
Water-poor countries hold talks with water-rich countries. They offer to trade other resources, such as oil, for water.

Prediction: ???

Apply the Skill

Study the graph on page 118. Note how much oil the United States consumes and produces. What do you learn from these facts? Make a prediction about what America might do when world oil supplies run low. Create a graphic organizer like the one on this page to help you make a prediction.

Differentiated Instruction

For Special Needs Students 🔲 L1
Partner special needs students with more proficient students to complete Level 1 of the *Identifying Cause and Effect* lesson on the Social Studies Skills Tutor CD-ROM together. When students feel more confident, have them complete Level 2 individually.

⦿ *Identifying Cause and Effect,* **Social Studies Skills Tutor CD-ROM**

Assess and Reteach

Assess Progress 🔲 L2
Ask students to do the Apply the Skill activity.

Reteach 🔲 L1
Identifying cause and effect is a vital part of making predictions. If students are having trouble with this skill, have them review it using the Social Studies Skills Tutor CD-ROM.

⦿ *Identifying Cause and Effect,* **Social Studies Skills Tutor CD-ROM**

Extend 🔲 L3

■ Have students reread p. 124. Ask them to identify the effect of Boston's growing population and industrialization. (*Boston's people filled in some bodies of water to create more land.*) Explain that this effect can also be a cause.

■ Tell students to make a graphic organizer like the one on p. 127. Have them identify two to three possible effects of Boston's people filling in bodies of water to create more land. (*Possible effects: Industries that rely on bodies of water and their resources, such as fishing, may no longer exist; goods may no longer be able to be shipped to and from Boston via waterways.*) Then tell them to predict which effect is most likely. (*Accept any of the effects, but be sure students supply a valid reason for their choice.*)

Answers
Apply the Skill

Students should note from the graph that the United States consumes more oil than any other country in the world.

Students' graphic organizers should look like the graphic organizer on p. 127. Cause: The United States is highly dependent on oil, but world oil supplies are running low. Possible effects: The United States looks for other sources of energy. The United States taps into any oil resources it has not yet used. The United States conserves energy and uses less oil.

Students should choose one of the effects they listed as their prediction and supply a valid reason for their choice.

Objectives

Social Studies

1. Investigate how first-level activities affect the environment.

2. Explore how second- and third-level activities affect the environment.

Reading/Language Arts

Learn how to identify implied main ideas.

Prepare to Read

Build Background Knowledge · L2

In this section, students will learn about people's effect on the environment. Write the following words on the board: *soil, water, air.* Ask students to list some ways that these natural resources are important. *(Possible answers: soil for growing food, water to irrigate crops and drink, air to breathe)* Then have students describe human activities that could threaten these natural resources. Use the Give One, Get One participation strategy (TE, p. T37) to generate student responses. *(Driving cars can lead to air pollution; cutting down trees can lead to soil erosion and deforestation; dumping trash can cause water pollution.)*

Set a Purpose for Reading · L2

■ Preview the Objectives.

■ Read each statement in the *Reading Readiness Guide* aloud. Ask students to mark the statements true or false.

   All in One Foundations of Geography Teaching Resources, *Reading Readiness Guide,* p. 253

■ Have students discuss the statements in pairs or groups of four, then mark their worksheets again. Use the Numbered Heads participation strategy (TE, p. T36) to call on students to share their group's perspectives.

Vocabulary Builder

Preview Key Terms · L2

Pronounce each Key Term, then ask the students to say the word with you. Provide a simple explanation such as, "Pollution is waste, such as the exhaust that comes out of cars when we drive, that makes our air, water, or soil less clean."

 **Section 3**

People's Effect on the Environment

Prepare to Read

Objectives

In this section you will

1. Investigate how first-level activities affect the environment.

2. Explore how second- and third-level activities affect the environment.

Taking Notes

Copy the table below. As you read this section, fill in the table with information about people's effect on the environment. Add rows to the table as needed.

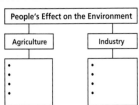

Target Reading Skill

Identify Implied Main Ideas Identifying main ideas can help you remember what you read. The details in a paragraph can add up to the main idea, even if it is not stated directly. For example, the details in the first paragraph below add up to this main idea: "While first-level activities are necessary for human survival, they also reshape the environment."

Key Terms

- **deforestation** (dee fawr uh STAY shun) *n.* a loss of forest cover in a region
- **biodiversity** (by oh duh VUR suh tee) *n.* a richness of different kinds of living things in a region
- **civil engineering** (SIV ul en juh NIHR ing) *n.* technology for building structures that alter the landscape, such as dams, roads, and bridges
- **pollution** (puh LOO shun) *n.* waste, usually man-made, that makes the air, water, or soil less clean

First-Level Activities

First-level activities, or direct interaction with raw materials, provide the food and resources that people need to live. They also transform the physical environment. For example, agriculture replaces wild plants and animals with the domesticated plants and animals that people need for food and other products.

Creating Farmland As countries have grown, they have met the challenge of feeding their people in different ways. The Great Plains of North America once supported wild grasses and buffalo. Today, farmers in that region grow corn and wheat and raise cattle. In the Netherlands, the people have drained lakes, bays, and marshes to create dry farmland. While creating new farmland destroyed wild grasslands and wetlands, the new land has fed millions.

A rancher driving cattle in Manitoba, Canada

Target Reading Skill · L2

Identify Implied Main Ideas Point out the Target Reading Skill. Tell students that identifying implied main ideas can help them to remember what they read.

Model identifying implied main ideas by reading the first paragraph on p. 132. Think aloud as you read to show how you arrived at the main idea. *(There are many different sources of pollution.)*

Give students *Identify Implied Main Ideas.* Have them complete the activity in groups.

   All in One Foundations of Geography Teaching Resources, *Identify Implied Main Ideas,* p. 258

Environmental Challenges Agriculture, forestry, and fishing provide food and resources that people need to live. At the same time, they sometimes have harmful effects on the environment. For example, wood is needed to build houses. But cutting down too many trees can result in **deforestation,** or the loss of forest cover in a region. Cutting forests may result in the loss of more than trees and other plants. Animals that depend on the forest for survival may also suffer. Deforestation can lead to a loss of **biodiversity,** which is a richness of different kinds of living things. So timber companies face the challenge of harvesting needed wood while limiting damage to the environment.

Farmers often use fertilizers and other chemicals to grow more crops. This makes it possible to feed more people. But when rain washes these chemicals into streams, they sometimes harm fish and other water-dwelling creatures. Fish are a tasty and healthy food source. But if fishers catch too many, they may threaten the fishes' survival. Farmers and fishers face the challenge of feeding the world's people without harming important resources.

Finding a Balance The key is to find a balance. Around the world, governments, scientists, and business people are working to find ways of meeting our need for food and resources without harming the environment. One solution is planting tree farms for timber. When the trees are mature, they can be cut and new trees can be replanted without harming ancient forests. Farmers can grow crops using natural methods or use chemicals that will not damage waterways. Fishers can limit their catch of endangered fish and harvest fish that are more plentiful.

√ **Reading Check** How do people benefit when new farmland is created?

Deforestation
Timber companies and farmers have cut down rain forests in Indonesia.
Apply Information *What are some of the advantages and disadvantages of cutting down forests?*

Links to Math

Acres and Timber Yields
Tree farms, like the one below, in Newbury, England, are one way to fight deforestation. If these oak trees grow to yield 80,000 board feet of timber per acre (466 cubic meters per hectare), and the farm covers 300 acres (121 hectares), how much timber will the farm produce?

Vocabulary Builder

Use the information below to teach students this section's high-use words.

High-Use Words	Definition and Sample Sentence
interaction, p. 128	*n.* the process of acting together Jake's new job calls for **interaction** with customers.
transform, p. 128	*v.* to change the form or look of Dusting **transformed** the room's appearance.
domesticated, p. 128	*adj.* tamed to be used by humans Our cat is **domesticated.**
prosperity, p. 131	*n.* the condition of being successful or wealthy Good times brought **prosperity** to the town.

Instruct

First-Level Activities   L2

Guided Instruction

- **Vocabulary Builder** Clarify the high-use words **interaction, transform,** and **domesticated** before reading.

- Read First-Level Activities using the Paragraph Shrinking technique (TE, p. T34).

- Ask students **What can people do to limit the negative effects of first-level activities?** *(Tree farms can be planted to help preserve ancient forests. Crops can be grown without fertilizers or with chemicals that do not harm the environment. Fishers can avoid catching endangered fish.)*

- Ask students **Why do you think it is important to limit the negative impact of first-level activities on the environment?** *(Possible answer: so that resources such as fish and trees are available to future generations)*

Independent Practice

Ask students to create the Taking Notes graphic organizer on a blank piece of paper. As students read, have them fill in the table with information about people's effect on the environment. Briefly model how to identify which information to record.

Monitor Progress

Circulate throughout the classroom to ensure that individuals are filling in their tables correctly. Provide assistance as needed.

Links

Read the **Links to Math** on this page and have them answer the question. *(Help students calculate that the farm will produce 24 million feet, or 56,386 cubic meters of timber.)*

Answers

Apply Information Advantages: wood can be used to make products; clears land for farming. Disadvantages: threatens the survival of animals and plants; a loss of biodiversity.

√ **Reading Check** New farmland allows more people to be fed.

The Hybrid Car

Guided Instruction
Ask students to study the Eyewitness Technology feature on this page. Have them silently read the introduction. Then read each caption together with students. Pause after each caption is read aloud to solicit comments and questions from students. Then answer the Analyzing Images question as a class.

Independent Practice
Distribute *Small Group Activity: Community Service Project: Protect the Environment*. Have students work in small groups to propose community education and project proposals that focus on transportation and improving the environment. Possible projects include: an educational campaign about the benefits of using hybrid-car technology; a proposal to establish bike paths for commuters; an education program that encourages carpooling for commuters.

All in One Foundations of Geography Teaching Resources, *Small Group Activity: Community Service Project: Protect the Environment,* pp. 262–265

Answer
ANALYZING IMAGES by drawing energy from the battery; being lighter in weight reduces the amount of fuel used; higher tire pressure helps reduce energy loss and conserve fuel

---

The Hybrid Car

Cars with gasoline engines are fast and can go long distances, but they pollute. Electric cars don't emit dangerous chemicals, but they can be driven only for a short distance before their batteries need to be recharged. The hybrid car combines the best features of gasoline and electric cars. It is fast and can go long distances, but it uses less gasoline and pollutes less. The hybrid car gets about 46 miles per gallon, while the conventional car of the same size gets about 33.

Traffic Jam
Today, traffic jams are common as drivers commute daily in and out of cities. Waiting in traffic jams wastes a lot of fuel and adds to air pollution.

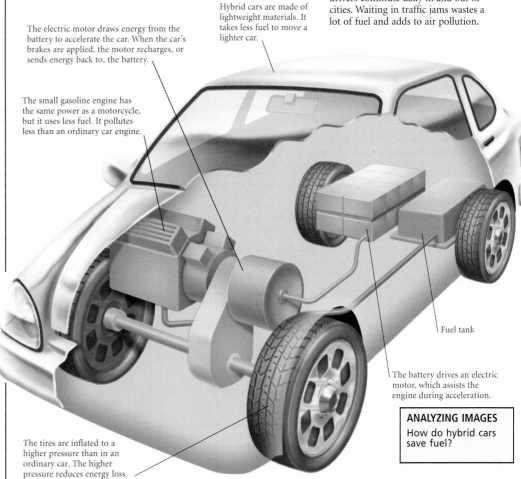

The electric motor draws energy from the battery to accelerate the car. When the car's brakes are applied, the motor recharges, or sends energy back to, the battery.

Hybrid cars are made of lightweight materials. It takes less fuel to move a lighter car.

The small gasoline engine has the same power as a motorcycle, but it uses less fuel. It pollutes less than an ordinary car engine.

Fuel tank

The battery drives an electric motor, which assists the engine during acceleration.

The tires are inflated to a higher pressure than in an ordinary car. The higher pressure reduces energy loss.

ANALYZING IMAGES
How do hybrid cars save fuel?

Background: Global Perspectives

The Kyoto Protocol In 1997, representatives from 160 nations met in Kyoto, Japan, to discuss concerns about increasing global gas emissions. Many scientists believe that these gases cause global warming, a gradual increase in the average temperature on Earth that could lead to melting of polar ice caps and flooding of coastal areas.

At Kyoto, the nations reached an agreement, called the Kyoto Protocol, to reduce the amount of certain gases released into the atmosphere. The agreement called for global emissions to be reduced by approximately 5 percent by 2012. The United States has not ratified the agreement.

Second- and Third-Level Activities

Over the years, industry, or second-level activities, and services, or third-level activities, have transformed deserts, prairies, woodlands, and marshes. They have created our familiar urban landscapes of housing developments, offices, factories, railroads, and highways.

Providing Jobs, Reshaping the Environment Industrial and service activities provide most of the jobs in developed countries such as the United States. Those activities are the basis for the developed countries' prosperity. They are also the main land use in urban areas.

The main purpose of some of these activities is to change the environment. **Civil engineering** is technology for building structures that alter the landscape, such as dams, canals, roads, and bridges. Dams create reservoirs that cover large areas with water. They also provide water for farms and cities and protect areas downstream from flooding.

Other industrial and service activities have side effects on the environment. For example, shopping malls require large areas to be paved for parking. Industries use large amounts of resources and release industrial wastes into the environment. Service activities require the construction of roads, telephone lines, and power lines.

Identify Implied Main Ideas
In one sentence, state what all the details in the paragraph at the left are about.

A Landscape Shaped by Industry
The waterfront in Rotterdam, Netherlands, has been shaped to meet the needs of industry. **Analyze Images** *How might this landscape have been different before it was shaped by industry?*

Chapter 5 Section 3 **131**

 Skills Mini Lesson

Supporting a Position

1. To support a position, tell students they should state their position clearly in a sentence; identify at least three reasons to support their position; support each reason with accurate evidence; put their reasons and supporting evidence in an effective order; and add a conclusion.

2. Have students practice the skill using information from the section to support this position: All communities should have a recycling program.

3. Have students apply the skill by asking them to follow the steps to state and support their position on reducing car emissions.

Target Reading Skill

Identify Implied Main Ideas As a follow up, ask students to answer the Target Reading Skill question in the Student Edition. *(Second- and third-level activities have reshaped the environment we live in.)*

Second- and Third-Level Activities

Guided Instruction

■ **Vocabulary Builder** Clarify the high-use word **prosperity** before reading.

■ Ask students to read Second- and Third-Level Activities. As students read, circulate and make sure individuals can answer the Reading Check question.

■ Ask **How is most land used in urban areas?** *(for industrial and service activities)* **Why are these activities important to developed countries?** *(They provide most of the jobs and are the basis of developed countries' prosperity.)*

■ Ask students **How are people trying to reduce pollution?** *(by using fuel-efficient vehicles, developing renewable energy resources, and recycling)*

Independent Practice

Have students complete the table by filling in details about people's effect on the environment.

Monitor Progress

■ Show *Section Reading Support Transparency FG 58* and ask students to check their graphic organizers individually.

   Foundations of Geography Transparencies, *Section Reading Support Transparency FG 58*

■ Tell students to fill in the last column of their *Reading Readiness Guides*. Probe for what they learned that confirms or invalidates each statement.

   All in One Foundations of Geography Teaching Resources, *Reading Readiness Guide,* p. 253

Answer

Analyze Images Possible answer: The land along the water may have been covered by vegetation.

Assess and Reteach

Assess Progress

Have students complete the Section Assessment. Administer the *Section Quiz*.

 Foundations of Geography Teaching Resources, *Section Quiz,* p. 255

Reteach L1

If students need more instruction, have them read this section in the Reading and Vocabulary Study Guide.

Chapter 5, Section 3, **Foundations of Geography Reading and Vocabulary Study Guide,** pp. 55–57

Extend L3

Have students complete the *Enrichment* activity so that they may study an instance in which environmental concerns and providing jobs had to be balanced.

Foundations of Geography Teaching Resources, *Enrichment,* p. 260

Answers

Apply Information Recycling reduces the amount of waste that local governments must burn or dump and saves natural resources.

✓ **Reading Check** Some industrial activities, such as building dams and bridges, change the environment. Others use large amounts of resources and can harm the environment with the release of industrial wastes.

Section 3 Assessment

Key Terms
Students' sentences should reflect knowledge of each Key Term.

Target Reading Skill
(1) There are many sources of pollution that affect our air, water, and soil. (2) People are working together to find ways to reduce pollution. (3) Recycling is being used in the United States to reduce waste and save natural resources. (4) By working together, we can find solutions to environmental problems.

Comprehension and Critical Thinking
1. (a) cutting trees to clear land for farms and to use for timber **(b)** Deforestation threatens the survival of animals and plants and can lead to a loss of biodiversity.

2. (a) Industrial and service activities have transformed deserts, prairies, woodlands, and marshes into urban landscapes that include housing developments, offices,

Recycling
These seventh-grade students in Syracuse, New York, are sorting materials for recycling. **Apply Information** *What environmental problems does recycling help to solve?*

Environmental Challenges Industry is not the only source of **pollution**, waste that makes the air, soil, or water less clean. The trash that we throw away may pollute the soil, water, or air. Exhaust from cars and trucks is another source of air pollution. Many scientists believe that air pollution may cause higher temperatures or other changes in our climate.

Finding Solutions Working together, scientists, governments, businesses, and ordinary people can find solutions to these problems. One solution is to use more fuel-efficient vehicles, such as hybrid cars. Vehicles that burn less fuel create less air pollution. Renewable energy sources, such as solar power and wind power, can also reduce the need to burn fuels that pollute the air. In addition, reducing pollution may reduce the risk of harmful climate changes.

Many cities and counties in the United States have introduced waste recycling. Recycling reduces the amount of waste that local governments must burn or dump. It also saves natural resources. For example, when paper is recycled, fewer trees must be cut down to make new paper.

Finding solutions to environmental problems is one of the greatest challenges of our time. If we all work together, we can meet this challenge.

✓ **Reading Check** **How do industrial activities affect the environment?**

Section 3 Assessment

Key Terms
Review the key terms at the beginning of this section. Use each term in a sentence that explains its meaning.

Target Reading Skill
State the main idea of each paragraph on this page.

Comprehension and Critical Thinking
1. (a) Recall What are the causes of deforestation?

(b) Identify Cause and Effect How does deforestation threaten the environment?
2. (a) List List ways in which industrial and service activities transform landscapes.
(b) Categorize Which of these ways are common to both industrial and service activities?
(c) Analyze How are industrial activities different from service activities in their impact on the environment?

Writing Activity
Write a journal entry in which you discuss how your own activities today may have affected the environment.

For: An activity on the environment
Visit: PHSchool.com
Web Code: led-3503

132 Foundations of Geography

---

factories, roads, railroads, highways, dams, canals, bridges, reservoirs, shopping malls, and telephone and power lines. **(b)** Service and industrial activities both often require railroads, roads, and telephone and power lines. **(c)** Possible answer: Industrial activities seem to harm the environment more than service activities.

Writing Activity
Use the *Rubric for Assessing a Journal Entry* to evaluate students' entries.

 Foundations of Geography Teaching Resources, *Rubric for Assessing a Journal Entry,* p. 276

Go Online
PHSchool.com Typing in the Web code when prompted will bring students to detailed instructions for this activity.

Review and Assessment

◆ Chapter Summary

Section 1: Natural Resources
- Almost everything that people use or consume is made with natural resources, which are either renewable or nonrenewable.
- Energy is a special resource needed for most economic activities, but some sources of energy are in limited supply, and some nations need to buy energy resources from others.

Section 2: Land Use
- How people use the land depends on their culture.
- Three levels of economic activity account for most land use.
- Land use changes when newcomers settle a region and as cultures change over time.

Section 3: People's Effect on the Environment
- First-level activities provide needed food and resources, but they reduce the land available for wild plants and animals.
- Second- and third-level activities provide jobs, but they can also pollute the environment.

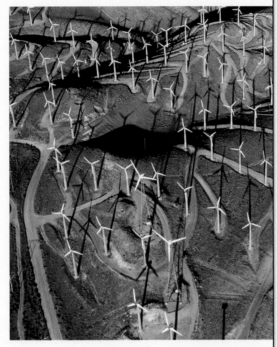

Windmills in California

◆ Key Terms

Each of the statements below contains a key term from the chapter. If the statement is true, write *true*. If it is false, rewrite the statement to make it true.

1. Raw materials are natural resources that can be used without reworking.
2. Renewable resources are natural resources that can be replaced.
3. Natural resources that cannot be replaced are called nonrenewable resources.
4. Our environment is our natural surroundings.

5. Manufacturing does not produce goods but involves working directly for customers.
6. Industrialization is the growth of manufacturing in an economy.
7. Deforestation is the planting of trees to replace forests cut down for timber.
8. Biodiversity is the loss of plant and animal life due to deforestation.
9. Pollution is waste, usually made by people, that makes air, soil, or water less clean.

┌ **Vocabulary Builder** ─────

Revisit this chapter's high-use words:

consume	respond	interaction
evaporate	channel	transform
harness	distribute	domesticated
hybrid	correspond	prosperity

Ask students to review the definitions they recorded on their *Word Knowledge* worksheets.

All in One Foundations of Geography Teaching Resources, *Word Knowledge,* p. 259

Consider allowing students to earn extra credit if they use the words in their answers to the questions in the Chapter Review and Assessment. The words must be used correctly and in a natural context to win the extra points.

Review and Assessment

Review Chapter Content

- Review and revisit the major themes of the chapter by asking students to classify what Guiding Question each bulleted statement in the Chapter Summary answers. Form students into groups and ask them to complete the activity together. Use the Numbered Heads participation strategy (TE, p. T36) to have the groups share their answers in the group discussion. Refer to page 1 of the Student Edition for the text of the Guided Questions.

- Assign *Vocabulary Development* for students to review Key Terms.

  All in One Foundations of Geography Teaching Resources, *Vocabulary Development,* p. 273

Answers

Key Terms
1. False. Raw materials are natural resources that must be reworked to be useful.
2. True
3. True
4. True
5. False. Manufacturing is the large-scale production of goods by hand or by machine.
6. False. Industrialization is the growth of machine-powered production in an economy.
7. False. Deforestation is a loss of forest cover in a region.
8. False. Biodiversity is a richness of different kinds of living things in a region.
9. True

Comprehension and Critical Thinking

10. (a) Possible answers: water; wind, geo-thermal energy, solar energy; living things **(b)** because they can be replaced **(c)** Renewable resources can be replaced, while non-renewable resources cannot be replaced.

11. (a) no **(b)** solar and wind energy and biomass

12. (a) yes **(b)** Possible answer: The land might be used differently, based on how the colonial culture traditionally uses the type of land available in the region.

13. (a) Possible answers: fishing, hunting, cutting wood, mining, herding, raising crops **(b)** Workers engaging in first-level activities use the land and its resources directly to make products. Second-level activities process the products of first-level activities. Third-level activities do not involve the process of creating goods at all; they may involve working directly for customers or for businesses.

14. (a) Tree farms can be planted and used to produce wood. **(b)** Biodiversity would be preserved.

15. (a) industrial and service activities, trash disposal, and car exhaust **(b)** Possible answers: by using more fuel-efficient vehicles such as hybrids, using renewable energy sources such as solar and wind power, and waste recycling

Skills Practice

Students' answers will vary, but should show an understanding of the skill steps.

Possible facts Worldwide energy usage has grown rapidly; fossil fuel supplies may be limited; some countries are using alternative energy resources; alternative energy resources include wind, solar, tidal, atomic, and geo-thermal energy, as well as biomass; atomic energy uses radioactive materials, which are plentiful; some people oppose atomic energy because radioactive materials can be danger-ous; new technologies that help people to use less energy, such as hybrid cars and those that offer energy savings in heating and lighting, can be used to help fossil fuels last longer.

Possible prediction Advancements in energy technology will help us meet the energy needs of the future.

◆ Comprehension and Critical Thinking

10. (a) List List at least three renewable resources.
(b) Explain Why is each of these resources renewable?
(c) Compare and Contrast How do renewable resources differ from nonrenewable resources?

11. (a) Recall Do all countries have adequate energy supplies?
(b) Analyze What energy sources are available to all countries?

12. (a) Recall Does culture affect land use?
(b) Predict What might happen to land use in a region if people with a different culture colonized it?

13. (a) List List three first-level activities.
(b) Compare and Contrast How do those activities differ from second- and third-level activities?

14. (a) Describe How can people obtain wood without cutting down wild forests?
(b) Predict How would leaving forests in place affect biodiversity?

15. (a) Describe What causes pollution?
(b) Infer How might companies and individuals reduce pollution?

◆ Skills Practice

Making Predictions In the Skills for Life activity on pages 126 and 127, you learned to make predictions. You also learned how to make sure that a prediction is an educated guess. That is, predictions should be based on information about the situation or about similar situations.

Review the steps that you followed to learn this skill. Then reread the paragraphs on pages 118 and 119 under the heading Meeting Energy Needs in the Future. List several facts about the issues described there. Finally, use these facts to make a prediction about how those issues might be resolved in the future.

◆ Writing Activity: Language Arts

Identify an environmental problem that interests you. Write a story about people solving the environmental problem. For your story, create characters with different roles in creating or solving the environmental problem. You should also create a plot for your story that describes how people come up with a solution to the problem and carry out that solution.

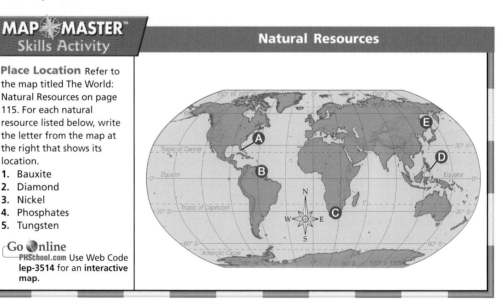

MAP MASTER™
Skills Activity

Place Location Refer to the map titled The World: Natural Resources on page 115. For each natural resource listed below, write the letter from the map at the right that shows its location.
1. Bauxite
2. Diamond
3. Nickel
4. Phosphates
5. Tungsten

Go Online
PHSchool.com Use Web Code
lep-3514 for an **interactive map.**

Natural Resources

Writing Activity: Language Arts

Students' stories will vary, but should include a problem, a solution, characters with various roles, and a plot.
Use *Rubric for Assessing a Writing Assignment* to evaluate students' stories.

All in One Foundations of Geography Teaching Resources, *Rubric for Assessing a Writing Assignment,* p. 277

Standardized Test Prep

Test-Taking Tips

Some questions on standardized tests ask you to find a main idea by analyzing a reading selection. Read the passage below. Then follow the tips to answer the sample question.

Saudi Arabia, Mexico, Iraq, Venezuela, and Russia have large oil reserves. The United States and China are rich in coal and natural gas. Many Northern European countries have rivers with water energy to create electricity. By contrast, Japan has few energy sources.

TIP As you read the paragraph, try to identify its main idea, or most important point. Every sentence in a paragraph supports this main idea.

Pick the letter that best answers the question.

This paragraph describes which kind of resources?

A capital resources

B human resources

C natural resources

D entrepreneurial resources

TIP Look for key words in the question and in the answer choices that connect to the paragraph. In this case, the key word is *resources*.

Think It Through Start with the main idea of the paragraph: Different countries have different energy sources. What kind of resources are these energy sources: oil, coal, gas, and water? Energy is not a human resource. You may not know the words *entrepreneurial* or *capital*. But you probably recognize *natural resources* as useful materials found in the environment—such as oil, coal, gas, and water. The correct answer is C.

Practice Questions

Use the tips above and other tips in this book to help you answer the following questions:

1. Wind energy is a
   A fossil fuel.
   B raw material.
   C renewable resource.
   D nonrenewable resource.

2. When colonists settle in a new environment,
   A they will use land just as they did in their old environment.
   B the environment will not change.
   C they will adjust their previous land uses to the new environment.
   D they will give up all familiar land uses.

3. Which of the following environmental problems does paper recycling help solve?
   A deforestation
   B pollution
   C deforestation and pollution
   D neither deforestation nor pollution

Read the following passage and answer the question that follows.

Sierra Leone's economy produces raw materials and cash crops. The country's people mine diamonds, iron ore, and aluminum ore. People on the coast catch fish. Its farmers produce coffee, cocoa, rice, and palm oil. They also raise poultry and other livestock.

4. The passage's main idea refers to which type of activities?
   A first-level activities
   B second-level activities
   C third-level activities
   D financial activities

Use Web Code **lea-3501**
for a **Chapter 5 self-test.**

Chapter 5 **135**

MAP★MASTER
Skills Activity
1. B   2. C
3. D   4. A
5. E

Go Online
PHSchool.com Students may practice their map skills using the interactive online version of this map.

Standardized Test Prep

Answers

1. C
2. C
3. C
4. A

Go Online
PHSchool.com Students may use the Chapter 5 self-test on PHSchool.com to prepare for the Chapter Test.

Assessment Resources

Teaching Resources
Chapter Tests A and B, pp. 190–195
Final Exams A and B, pp. 196–201

Test Prep Workbook
Foundations of Geography Study Sheet, pp. 113–115
Foundations of Geography Practice Tests A, B, and C, pp. 49–60

AYP Monitoring Assessments
Foundations of Geography Benchmark Test 2 and Report Sheet, pp. 85–88
Foundations of Geography Outcome Test, pp. 170–175

Technology
ExamView Test Bank CD-ROM

Projects

- Students can further explore the Guiding Questions by completing hands-on projects.

- Three pages of structured guidance in All-in-One Foundations of Geography Teaching Resources support each of the projects described on this page.

  All in One Foundations of Geography Teaching Resources, *Book Project: Focus on Part of the Whole,* pp. 27–29; *Book Project: Desktop Countries,* pp. 33–35

- There are also two additional projects introduced, explained, and supported in the All-in-One Foundations of Geography Teaching Resources.

  All in One Foundations of Geography Teaching Resources, *Book Project: The Geography Game,* pp. 30–32; *Book Project: World News Today,* pp. 36–38

- Go over the four project suggestions with students.

- Ask each student to select one of the projects, or design his or her own. Work with students to create a project description and a schedule.

- Post project schedules and monitor student progress by asking for progress reports.

- Assess student projects using rubrics from the All-in-One Foundations of Geography Teaching Resources.

  All in One Foundations of Geography Teaching Resources, *Rubric for Assessing a Student Performance on a Project,* p. 39; *Rubric for Assessing Performance of an Entire Group,* p. 40; *Rubric for Assessing Individual Performance in a Group,* p. 41

 Portfolio Activity Tell students they can add their completed Book Project as the final item in their portfolios. Assess student portfolios with *Rubric for Assessing a Student Portfolio.*

  All in One Foundations of Geography Teaching Resources, *Rubric for Assessing a Student Portfolio,* p. 42

Projects

Create your own projects to learn more about geography. At the beginning of this book, you were introduced to the **Guiding Questions** for studying the chapters and the special features. But you can also find answers to these questions by doing projects on your own or with a group. Use the questions to find topics you want to explore further. Then try the projects described on this page or create your own.

1. **Geography** What are Earth's major physical features?
2. **History** How have people's ways of life changed over time?
3. **Culture** What is a culture?
4. **Government** What types of government exist in the world today?
5. **Economics** How do people use the world's natural resources?

Project

CREATE A PHYSICAL MAP

Focus on Part of the Whole

The world and its population are extremely varied. Choose a particular region or country. If you are working with a group, have each person choose a different country on a continent. Learn everything you can about the country's physical geography, the population, and the lifestyles of the people there. Use encyclopedias, almanacs, or other books.

Set up a display based on your research. Prepare a large map that includes important physical features of the land. Add captions that explain how the land's physical geography affects people's lives.

Project

RESEARCH A COUNTRY'S CULTURE

Desktop Countries

What countries did your ancestors come from? Select one country and do some research on it. Interview someone, perhaps a relative from that country, or read about it. Find a recipe you can prepare to share with the class. Then make a desktop display about the country you have chosen. Write the name of the country on a card and put it on your desk. Add a drawing of the country's flag or map, or display a souvenir. On place cards, write several sentences about each object. Take turns visiting everyone's "desktop countries."

Contents

The World: Political

ARCTIC OCEAN

RUSSIA   Arctic Circle   ALASKA
                                           (U.S.)

GREENLAND
(Denmark)

Reykjavik

C A N A D A

**NORTH
AMERICA**   Ottawa

40° N   UNITED STATES

A T L A N T I C
O C E A N

AZORES
(Portugal)

Washington, D.C.

MEXICO

Tropic of Cancer

HAWAII (U.S)

20° N   Mexico City

**CENTRAL AMERICA
AND THE CARIBBEAN**
For detail, see map
North and South
America: Political.

CAPE
VERDE

Praia

MARSHALL
ISLANDS
Majuro

Caracas

VENEZUELA Georgetown
Bogotá   Paramaribo
           GUYANA   FRENCH GUIANA
COLOMBIA SURINAME (France)

K I R I B A T I

PALMYRA ATOLL (U.S.)

GALÁPAGOS ISLANDS
(Ecuador)

Quito

NAURU

Equator   ECUADOR

0°   Bairiki

W   N   E

**SOUTH
AMERICA**

TUVALU
Fongafale

PERU

B R A Z I L

SOLOMON
ISLANDS
Honiara

COOK
ISLANDS
(New Zealand)

P A C I F I C
O C E A N

S

Lima

Brasília

VANUATU
Port-Vila   FIJI   Apia AMERICAN
           Suva   SAMOA
                        (U.S.)

SAMOA

FRENCH POLYNESIA
(France)

La Paz
BOLIVIA

Sucre

NIUE (New Zealand)

20° S   Nuku'alofa TONGA

PITCAIRN
ISLANDS
(U.K.)

PARAGUAY
Asunción

NEW
CALEDONIA
(France)

Tropic of Capricorn

CHILE

URUGUAY
Montevideo

ARGENTINA

Santiago

Buenos Aires

NEW
ZEALAND

40° S

Wellington

FALKLAND ISLANDS
(U.K.)

SOUTH GEORGIA &
SOUTH SANDWICH ISLANDS
(U.K.)

60° S

S O U T H E R N   O C E A N

Antarctic Circle

80° S   **ANTARCTICA**

0 miles   2,000

0 kilometers   2,000
Robinson

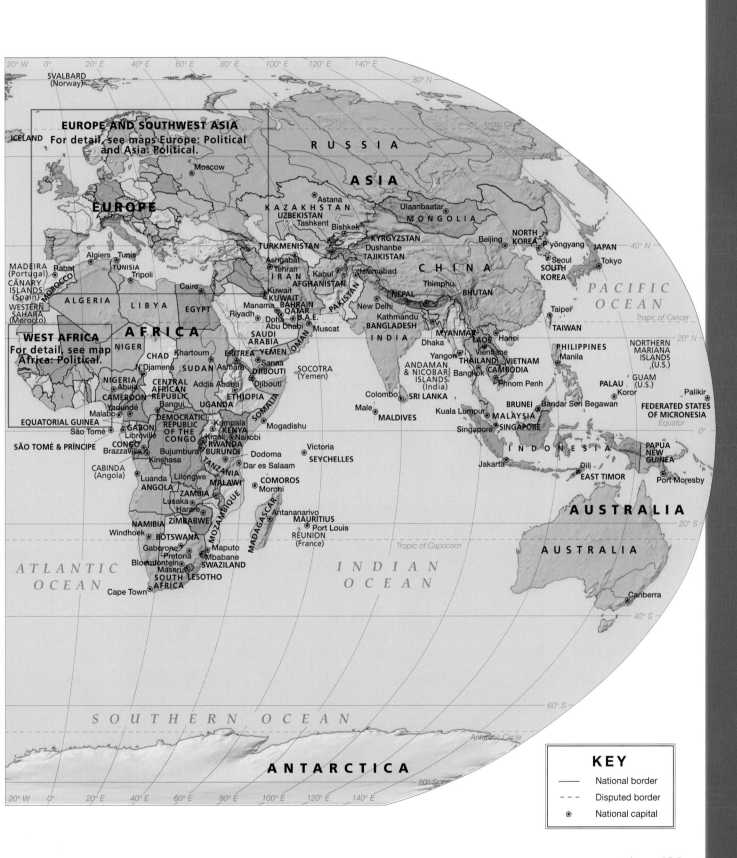

20° W | 0° | 20° E | 40° E | 60° E | 80° E | 100° E | 120° E | 140° E

SVALBARD
(Norway)

80° N
Arctic Circle

ICELAND

EUROPE AND SOUTHWEST ASIA
For detail, see maps Europe: Political
and Asia: Political.

RUSSIA

ASIA

⊛ Moscow

EUROPE

KAZAKHSTAN

⊛ Astana

Ulaanbaatar ⊛

MONGOLIA

60° N

UZBEKISTAN

⊛ Tashkent

Bishkek ⊛

KYRGYZSTAN

Beijing ⊛

NORTH
KOREA

P'yŏngyang ⊛

JAPAN

40° N

Algiers Tunis

TURKMENISTAN

Dushanbe
TAJIKISTAN

⊛ Seoul
SOUTH
KOREA

⊛ Tokyo

MADEIRA
(Portugal)

Rabat ⊛

TUNISIA

Ashgabat ⊛
Tehran ⊛

IRAN

Kabul ⊛

Islamabad ⊛

CHINA

Thimphu ⊛

PACIFIC
OCEAN

CANARY
ISLANDS
(Spain)

MOROCCO

Tripoli

AFGHANISTAN

PAKISTAN

NEPAL

BHUTAN

Taipei ⊛

Tropic of Cancer

WESTERN
SAHARA
(Morocco)

ALGERIA

LIBYA

EGYPT

Cairo ⊛

Kuwait ⊛
KUWAIT
Manama ⊛ BAHRAIN
QATAR
Riyadh ⊛ ⊛ Doha
Abu Dhabi ⊛ U.A.E.
⊛ Muscat

New Delhi ⊛

Kathmandu ⊛
BANGLADESH

⊛ Dhaka

MYANMAR

TAIWAN

20° N

WEST AFRICA
For detail, see map
Africa: Political.

AFRICA

NIGER

CHAD

Khartoum ⊛

SAUDI
ARABIA

ERITREA YEMEN

OMAN

INDIA

LAOS

Yangon ⊛

Hanoi ⊛

PHILIPPINES

NORTHERN
MARIANA
ISLANDS
(U.S.)

N'Djamena ⊛

SUDAN

Asmara ⊛
⊛ Sanaa
DJIBOUTI

SOCOTRA
(Yemen)

Vientiane ⊛
THAILAND VIETNAM

Manila ⊛

NIGERIA

CENTRAL
AFRICAN
REPUBLIC

Addis Ababa ⊛

Djibouti ⊛

Bangkok ⊛ CAMBODIA

GUAM
(U.S.)

⊛ Abuja

ETHIOPIA

Colombo ⊛

SRI LANKA

Phnom Penh ⊛

PALAU

⊛ Koror

CAMEROON

Bangui ⊛

UGANDA

SOMALIA

BRUNEI

Bandar Seri Begawan ⊛

FEDERATED STATES
OF MICRONESIA

Yaoundé ⊛

Malabo ⊛

Male ⊛

MALDIVES

Kuala Lumpur ⊛

⊛ Palikir

EQUATORIAL GUINEA

DEMOCRATIC
REPUBLIC
OF THE
CONGO

Kampala ⊛

KENYA

Mogadishu ⊛

MALAYSIA

SÃO TOMÉ

GABON

Libreville ⊛

Kigali ⊛
RWANDA
BURUNDI

⊛ Nairobi

Singapore ⊛ SINGAPORE

Equator

SÃO TOMÉ & PRÍNCIPE

CONGO

Brazzaville ⊛

Bujumbura ⊛

Dodoma ⊛

Victoria ⊛

INDONESIA

PAPUA
NEW
GUINEA

0°

CABINDA
(Angola)

Kinshasa ⊛

TANZANIA

Dar es Salaam ⊛

SEYCHELLES

Jakarta ⊛

Dili ⊛

Port Moresby ⊛

Luanda ⊛ Lilongwe ⊛

MALAWI

COMOROS

EAST TIMOR

ANGOLA

ZAMBIA

Moroni ⊛

AUSTRALIA

Lusaka ⊛

MOZAMBIQUE

Harare ⊛

MADAGASCAR

Antananarivo ⊛
MAURITIUS
⊛ Port Louis

20° S

NAMIBIA

ZIMBABWE

Windhoek ⊛

BOTSWANA

RÉUNION
(France)

Tropic of Capricorn

AUSTRALIA

Gaborone ⊛ ⊛ Maputo

ATLANTIC
OCEAN

Bloemfontein ⊛ Pretoria ⊛
⊛ Mbabane
SWAZILAND

INDIAN
OCEAN

SOUTH Maseru ⊛
Cape Town ⊛ AFRICA LESOTHO

Canberra ⊛

40° S

60° S

SOUTHERN OCEAN

Antarctic Circle

ANTARCTICA

80° S

20° W | 0° | 20° E | 40° E | 60° E | 80° E | 100° E | 120° E | 140° E

KEY

——— National border

- - - Disputed border

⊛ National capital

The World: Physical

ARCTIC OCEAN

Beaufort Sea

Greenland

Baffin Island

Yukon R.

Mackenzie R.

Hudson Bay

Labrador Sea

Bering Sea

NORTH AMERICA

ROCKY MOUNTAINS

CANADIAN SHIELD

Aleutian Islands

GREAT PLAINS

Missouri R.

Great Lakes

St. Lawrence R.

ATLANTIC OCEAN

40° N

Colorado R.

Mississippi R.

APPALACHIAN MTS.

Rio Grande

Gulf of Mexico

Tropic of Cancer

Hawaiian Islands

West Indies

20° N

Caribbean Sea

MICRONESIA

N

Galápagos Islands

Orinoco R.

GUIANA HIGHLANDS

Equator

0°

W   E

S

AMAZON BASIN

Amazon R.

SOUTH AMERICA

P O L Y N E S I A

PACIFIC OCEAN

ANDES

BRAZILIAN HIGHLANDS

M E L A N E S I A

20° S

Tropic of Capricorn

Tasman Sea

North Island

ANDES

PAMPAS

Río de la Plata

40° S

South Island

PATAGONIA

Cape Horn

60° S

S O U T H E R N   O C E A N

Drake Passage

Antarctic Circle

ANTARCTIC PENINSULA

Ross Sea

Weddell Sea

80° S

ANTARCTICA

180°   160° W   140° W   120° W   100° W   80° W   60° W   40° W   20° W

0 miles   2,000
0 kilometers   2,000
Robinson

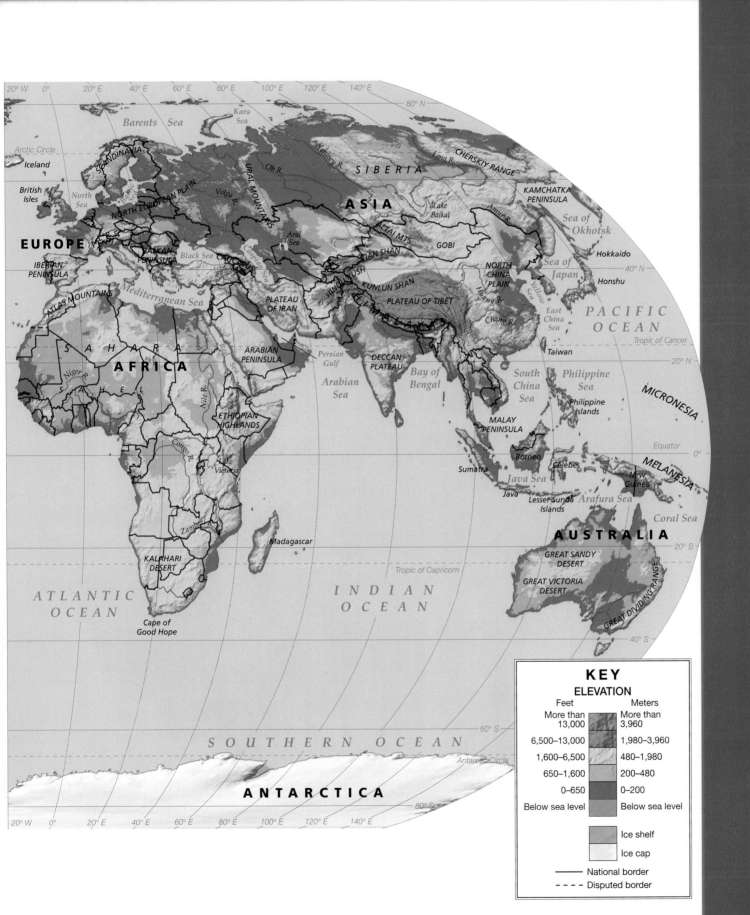

KEY

ELEVATION

Feet		Meters
More than 13,000		More than 3,960
6,500–13,000		1,980–3,960
1,600–6,500		480–1,980
650–1,600		200–480
0–650		0–200
Below sea level		Below sea level

Ice shelf

Ice cap

——— National border

- - - Disputed border

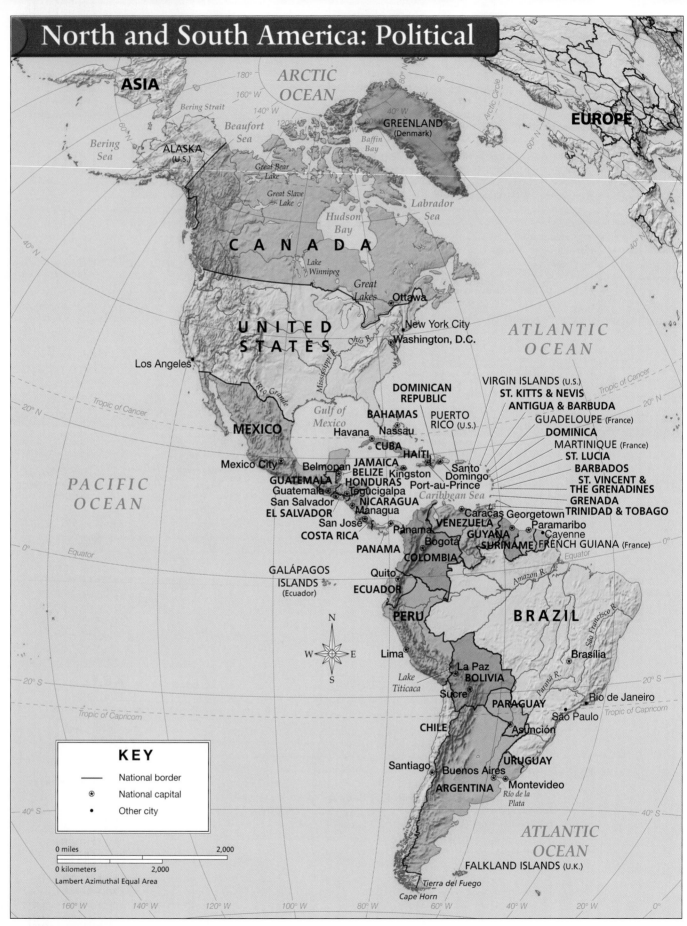

North and South America: Political

ASIA

ARCTIC OCEAN

EUROPE

Bering Strait

Beaufort Sea

Bering Sea

ALASKA (U.S.)

GREENLAND (Denmark)

Baffin Bay

Great Bear Lake

Great Slave Lake

Hudson Bay

Labrador Sea

C A N A D A

Lake Winnipeg

Great Lakes

Ottawa

New York City
Washington, D.C.

U N I T E D S T A T E S

Ohio R.

Mississippi R.

ATLANTIC OCEAN

Los Angeles

Rio Grande

Tropic of Cancer

VIRGIN ISLANDS (U.S.)
ST. KITTS & NEVIS
ANTIGUA & BARBUDA
GUADELOUPE (France)
DOMINICA
MARTINIQUE (France)
ST. LUCIA
BARBADOS
ST. VINCENT &
THE GRENADINES
GRENADA
TRINIDAD & TOBAGO

DOMINICAN REPUBLIC

BAHAMAS

PUERTO RICO (U.S.)

Gulf of Mexico

MEXICO

Havana   Nassau

CUBA

HAITI

Mexico City

Belmopan

JAMAICA

GUATEMALA   BELIZE   Kingston

Santo Domingo

Port-au-Prince

Guatemala

HONDURAS

Tegucigalpa

San Salvador

NICARAGUA

Caribbean Sea

EL SALVADOR   Managua

San José

Panama

Caracas   Georgetown

Paramaribo

VENEZUELA   GUYANA

Cayenne

PACIFIC OCEAN

COSTA RICA

Bogotá

SURINAME   FRENCH GUIANA (France)

PANAMA

COLOMBIA

Equator

GALÁPAGOS ISLANDS (Ecuador)

Quito

ECUADOR

Amazon R.

PERU

B R A Z I L

São Francisco R.

Lima

Brasília

La Paz
BOLIVIA

Lake Titicaca

Sucre

Paraná R.

Rio de Janeiro

PARAGUAY

São Paulo

Tropic of Capricorn

CHILE

Asunción

Tropic of Capricorn

URUGUAY

Santiago   Buenos Aires

Montevideo

ARGENTINA

Río de la Plata

KEY

—— National border

⊛ National capital

• Other city

0 miles _____ 2,000
0 kilometers _____ 2,000
Lambert Azimuthal Equal Area

ATLANTIC OCEAN

FALKLAND ISLANDS (U.K.)

Tierra del Fuego

Cape Horn

180°   160° W   140° W   120° W   100° W   80° W   60° W   40° W   20° W   0°

North and South America: Physical

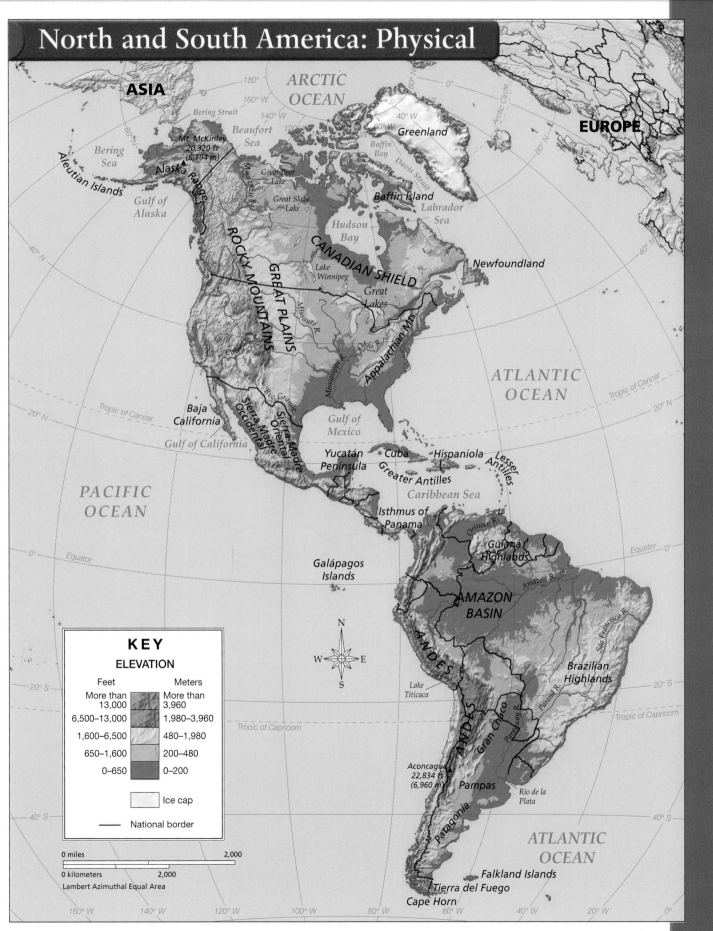

ASIA

ARCTIC OCEAN

EUROPE

Bering Strait

Beaufort Sea

Bering Sea

Mt. McKinley 20,320 ft (6,194 m)

Alaska Range

Aleutian Islands

Gulf of Alaska

Greenland

Baffin Bay

Davis Strait

Great Bear Lake

Mackenzie R.

Great Slave Lake

Baffin Island

Labrador Sea

CANADIAN SHIELD

Hudson Bay

Newfoundland

ROCKY MOUNTAINS

GREAT PLAINS

Lake Winnipeg

Great Lakes

Missouri R.

Colorado R.

Mississippi R.

Ohio R.

Appalachian Mts.

ATLANTIC OCEAN

Tropic of Cancer

Baja California

Sierra Madre Occidental

Rio Grande

Sierra Madre Oriental

Tropic of Cancer

Gulf of Mexico

Gulf of California

PACIFIC OCEAN

Yucatán Peninsula

Cuba

Hispaniola

Lesser Antilles

Greater Antilles

Caribbean Sea

Isthmus of Panama

Galápagos Islands

Orinoco R.

Guiana Highlands

Equator

Equator

Amazon R.

AMAZON BASIN

ANDES

Brazilian Highlands

São Francisco R.

Lake Titicaca

Tropic of Capricorn

Gran Chaco

Paraguay R.

Paraná R.

Tropic of Capricorn

Aconcagua 22,834 ft (6,960 m)

ANDES

Pampas

Río de la Plata

Patagonia

ATLANTIC OCEAN

Falkland Islands

Tierra del Fuego

Cape Horn

KEY
ELEVATION

Feet	Meters
More than 13,000	More than 3,960
6,500–13,000	1,980–3,960
1,600–6,500	480–1,980
650–1,600	200–480
0–650	0–200

Ice cap

National border

0 miles 2,000

0 kilometers 2,000

Lambert Azimuthal Equal Area

N W E S

United States: Political

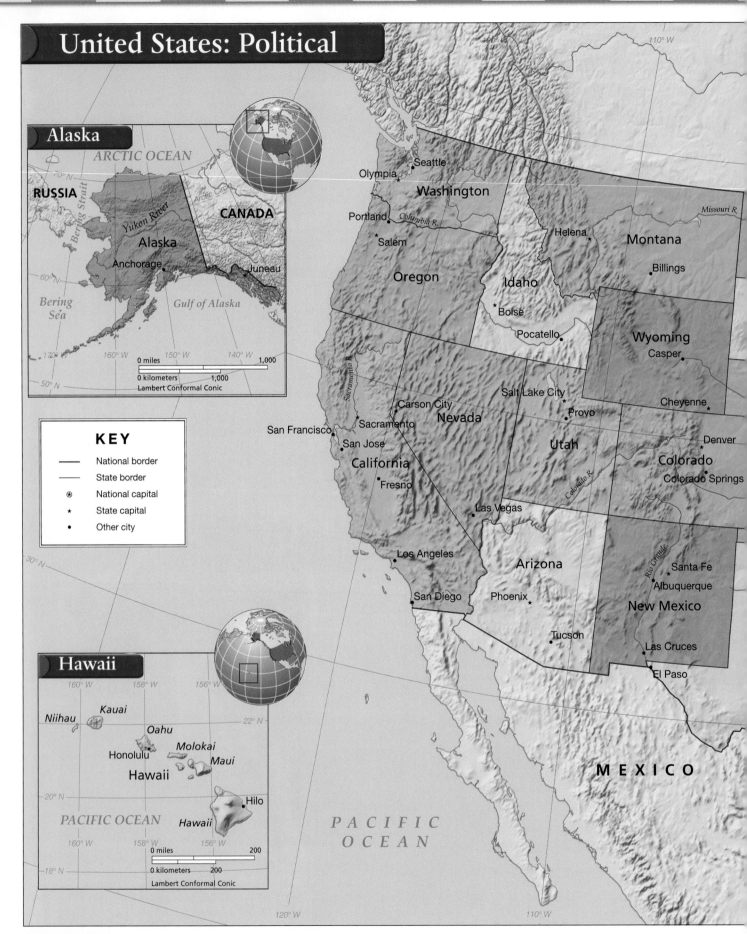

Alaska

ARCTIC OCEAN

RUSSIA

CANADA

Bering Strait

Yukon River

Arctic Circle

Alaska

Anchorage

Juneau

Bering Sea

Gulf of Alaska

0 miles 1,000
0 kilometers 1,000
Lambert Conformal Conic

70° N
60° N
170° W   160° W   150° W   140° W
50° N

KEY

—	National border
—	State border
⊛	National capital
★	State capital
•	Other city

Hawaii

160° W   158° W   156° W

Niihau   Kauai

Oahu

Honolulu   Molokai

Hawaii   Maui

22° N
20° N
18° N

PACIFIC OCEAN   Hawaii

Hilo

160° W   158° W   156° W

0 miles 200
0 kilometers 200
Lambert Conformal Conic

30° N

Seattle
Olympia
Washington
Portland   Columbia R.
Salem
Oregon
Helena
Montana
Billings
Idaho
Boise
Pocatello
Wyoming
Casper
Sacramento R.
Carson City
Salt Lake City
Cheyenne
San Francisco
Sacramento   Nevada
Provo
San Jose
Utah
Denver
California
Colorado
Fresno
Colorado Springs
Colorado R.
Las Vegas
Los Angeles
Arizona
Rio Grande
Santa Fe
San Diego
Phoenix
Albuquerque
New Mexico
Tucson
Las Cruces
El Paso

Missouri R.

MEXICO

PACIFIC OCEAN

110° W
120° W   110° W

CANADA

North Dakota
•Bismarck
  Fargo•

Minnesota
St. Paul••
Minneapolis•

South Dakota
•Pierre
•Sioux Falls

Lake Superior

Wisconsin
•Milwaukee
Madison★

Michigan
•Grand Rapids
Lansing★ •Detroit

Lake Huron

Lake Michigan

Lake Ontario

Maine
•Augusta
Portland•
Vermont
Montpelier★ New Hampshire
            ★Concord

Albany★   Boston
New York   Providence Massachusetts
       Hartford★ Rhode Island
                Connecticut

Buffalo•

Lake Erie

40° N

50° N

Iowa
•Des Moines

Nebraska
Omaha•
•Lincoln

Chicago•
Cedar Rapids•

Fort Wayne•

Ohio
Columbus★

Cleveland•
Pittsburgh•

Pennsylvania
Harrisburg★

New York City

New Jersey
•Trenton
Philadelphia•

Baltimore•
Washington, D.C.★ Delaware
              •Dover
              ★Annapolis
              Maryland

Illinois
Springfield★

Indiana
Indianapolis★

Missouri R.

Mississippi R.

Kansas
Topeka★
Kansas City•
Jefferson City★
St. Louis•

Wichita•

Arkansas R.

Springfield

Cincinnati•

Ohio R.

Louisville•

Frankfort★

Kentucky

Charleston★
West Virginia

Richmond★
District of Columbia
Norfolk•

Virginia

Raleigh•

Oklahoma
★Oklahoma City

Tulsa•

Arkansas
Fort Smith•
Little Rock★

Memphis•

Mississippi R.

Tennessee R.

Nashville• Knoxville•
Tennessee

North Carolina
•Charlotte

South Carolina
•Columbia★
Charleston•

ATLANTIC
OCEAN

Red R.

Texas

Fort Worth• •Dallas

Austin•

San Antonio•

Houston•

Mississippi

Jackson★

Shreveport•
Louisiana

Baton Rouge• Gulfport•
New Orleans

Alabama
•Birmingham
Montgomery★

Mobile•

Georgia
Atlanta★
Columbus•

Savannah•

Jacksonville•

Tallahassee★

Florida
•Orlando

Tampa•

Gulf of Mexico

Miami•

N
W   E
S

0 miles   250
0 kilometers   250
Lambert Azimuthal Equal Area

30° N

100° W

90° W

80° W

70° W

Europe: Political

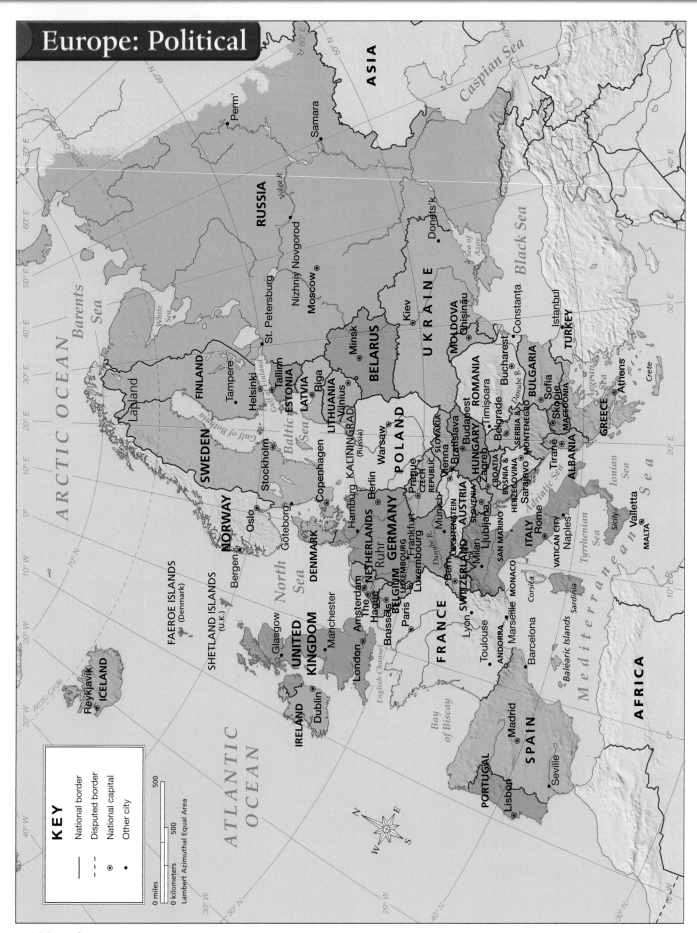

ASIA

Caspian Sea

Perm'

Samara

RUSSIA

Volga R.

Donets'k

Nizhniy Novgorod

Moscow ⊛

St. Petersburg

Sea of Azov

Black Sea

UKRAINE

Kiev

MOLDOVA
Chişinău

Constanţa

Istanbul

TURKEY

ARCTIC OCEAN

Barents Sea

White Sea

Minsk ⊛

BELARUS

ROMANIA

Bucharest

Danube R.

BULGARIA

Sofia ⊛

Aegean Sea

Athens ⊛

Crete

FINLAND

Tampere

Helsinki

Tallinn

ESTONIA

LATVIA

Riga

LITHUANIA

Vilnius

Gulf of Finland

Lapland

SWEDEN

Gulf of Bothnia

Baltic Sea

KALININGRAD
(Russia)

Warsaw

POLAND

SLOVAKIA

Bratislava

Budapest

HUNGARY

Timişoara

Belgrade

SERBIA &
MONTENEGRO

Skopje

MACEDONIA

Tiranë

ALBANIA

GREECE

Ionian Sea

Stockholm

Copenhagen

Hamburg

Berlin

Prague

CZECH
REPUBLIC

Vienna

Munich

AUSTRIA

SLOVENIA

Ljubljana

Zagreb

CROATIA

BOSNIA &
HERZEGOVINA

Sarajevo

Adriatic Sea

NORWAY

Oslo

Göteborg

DENMARK

North Sea

NETHERLANDS

Amsterdam

The Hague

BELGIUM

Brussels

GERMANY

Ruhr

Frankfurt

LUXEMBOURG

Luxembourg

LIECHTENSTEIN

Bern

SWITZERLAND

Milan

SAN MARINO

MONACO

ITALY

Rome

VATICAN CITY

Naples

Tyrrhenian Sea

Sicily

MALTA

Valletta

Mediterranean Sea

Bergen

FAEROE ISLANDS
(Denmark)

SHETLAND ISLANDS
(U.K.)

Glasgow

UNITED
KINGDOM

Manchester

London

English Channel

Paris

FRANCE

Lyon

Toulouse

Marseille

Corsica

Sardinia

ANDORRA

Barcelona

Balearic Islands

Reykjavik

ICELAND

Arctic Circle

IRELAND

Dublin

Bay
of Biscay

ATLANTIC
OCEAN

Madrid

SPAIN

Seville

PORTUGAL

Lisbon

AFRICA

KEY

—— National border

- - - Disputed border

⊛ National capital

• Other city

0 miles   500

0 kilometers   500

Lambert Azimuthal Equal Area

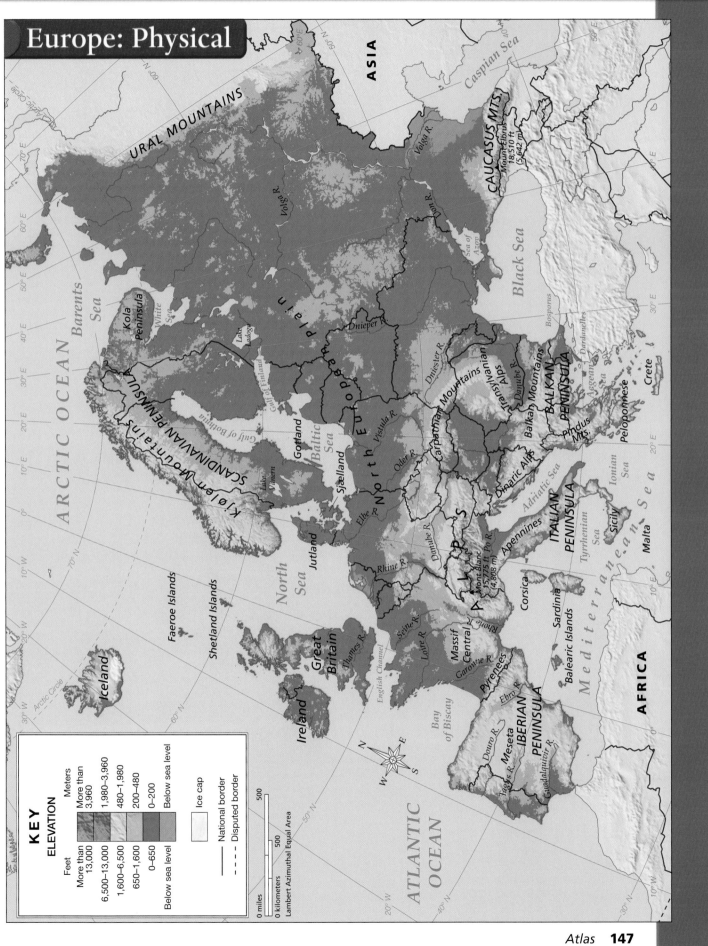

Europe: Physical

ASIA

URAL MOUNTAINS

Caspian Sea

CAUCASUS MTS.
Mount Elbrus
18,510 ft
(5,642 m)

Volga R.

Don R.

Black Sea

Sea of Azov

Barents Sea

Kola Peninsula

White Sea

Lake Ladoga

Dnieper R.

U r a l

E u r o p e a n

P l a i n

Bosporus

ARCTIC OCEAN

SCANDINAVIAN PENINSULA

Kjølen Mountains

Gulf of Bothnia

Gulf of Finland

Gotland

Baltic Sea

Sjælland

Lake Vänern

Vistula R.

North European Plain

Oder R.

Dniester R.

Carpathian Mountains

Transylvanian Alps

Danube R.

Balkan Mountains

BALKAN PENINSULA

Dinaric Alps

Pindus Mts.

Peloponnese

Dardanelles

Aegean Sea

Crete

30° E

North Sea

Jutland

Elbe R.

Rhine R.

A   L   P   S

Danube R.

Mont Blanc
15,775 ft
(4,808 m)

Po R.

Adriatic Sea

Apennines

ITALIAN PENINSULA

Tyrrhenian Sea

Sicily

Malta

Ionian Sea

Mediterranean Sea

Faeroe Islands

Shetland Islands

Great Britain

Thames R.

English Channel

Seine R.

Loire R.

Massif Central

Rhône R.

Garonne R.

Corsica

Sardinia

Balearic Islands

Ireland

Bay of Biscay

Pyrenees

Ebro R.

IBERIAN PENINSULA

Douro R.

Meseta

Tagus R.

Guadalquivir R.

Iceland

Arctic Circle

ATLANTIC OCEAN

AFRICA

KEY

ELEVATION

Feet	Meters
More than 13,000	More than 3,960
6,500–13,000	1,980–3,960
1,600–6,500	480–1,980
650–1,600	200–480
0–650	0–200
Below sea level	Below sea level

Ice cap

— National border
- - - Disputed border

0 miles 500
0 kilometers 500
Lambert Azimuthal Equal Area

Africa: Political

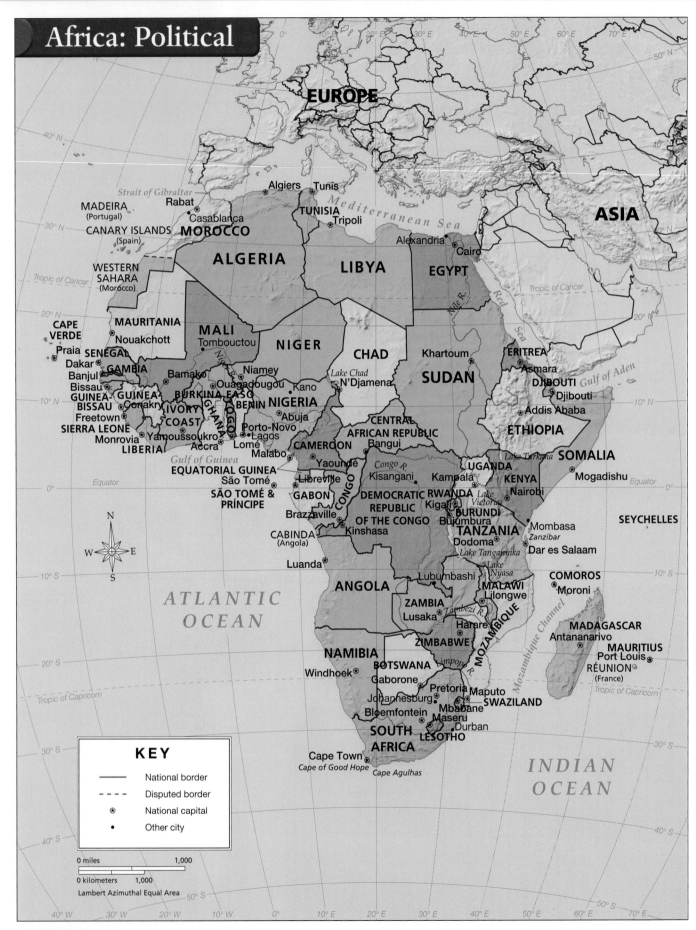

EUROPE

ASIA

Strait of Gibraltar

Mediterranean Sea

MADEIRA (Portugal)

Algiers ⊗ • Tunis

Rabat ⊗

• Casablanca

TUNISIA

• Tripoli ⊗

Alexandria •

CANARY ISLANDS (Spain)

MOROCCO

Cairo ⊗

Tropic of Cancer

WESTERN SAHARA (Morocco)

ALGERIA

LIBYA

EGYPT

Nile R.

Red Sea

Tropic of Cancer

MAURITANIA

CAPE VERDE

⊗ Nouakchott

MALI

Tombouctou •

NIGER

CHAD

Khartoum ⊗

ERITREA

Asmara ⊗

Praia ⊗

SENEGAL

Dakar ⊗

GAMBIA

Banjul ⊗

Bamako ⊗

Niamey ⊗

Lake Chad

N'Djamena ⊗

SUDAN

DJIBOUTI *Gulf of Aden*

• Djibouti ⊗

Bissau ⊗

Ouagadougou ⊗

Kano •

GUINEA BISSAU

GUINEA

BURKINA FASO

• Addis Ababa ⊗

Conakry ⊗

IVORY COAST

GHANA

BENIN

NIGERIA

• Abuja ⊗

CENTRAL AFRICAN REPUBLIC

Bangui ⊗

ETHIOPIA

Freetown ⊗

SIERRA LEONE

Yamoussoukro ⊗

Porto-Novo ⊗

Lake Turkana

SOMALIA

Monrovia ⊗

Accra ⊗

Lomé ⊗

• Lagos

LIBERIA

Malabo ⊗

CAMEROON

Gulf of Guinea

Yaoundé ⊗

Congo R.

UGANDA

Kisangani •

Kampala ⊗

KENYA

Mogadishu ⊗

Equator

EQUATORIAL GUINEA

São Tomé ⊗

Libreville ⊗

Nairobi ⊗

Equator

SÃO TOMÉ & PRÍNCIPE

GABON

CONGO

DEMOCRATIC REPUBLIC OF THE CONGO

RWANDA

Kigali ⊗

Lake Victoria

Brazzaville ⊗

BURUNDI

Bujumbura ⊗

SEYCHELLES

Kinshasa ⊗

TANZANIA

Mombasa •

CABINDA (Angola)

Dodoma ⊗

Zanzibar

Dar es Salaam •

Luanda ⊗

Lake Tanganyika

Lake Nyasa

COMOROS

Moroni ⊗

ANGOLA

Lubumbashi •

MALAWI

Lilongwe ⊗

ATLANTIC OCEAN

ZAMBIA

Lusaka ⊗

Zambezi R.

MOZAMBIQUE

MADAGASCAR

Antananarivo ⊗

ZIMBABWE

Harare ⊗

Mozambique Channel

MAURITIUS

Port Louis ⊗

NAMIBIA

BOTSWANA

Limpopo R.

RÉUNION (France)

Windhoek ⊗

Gaborone ⊗

Pretoria ⊗

Maputo ⊗

Tropic of Capricorn

Johannesburg •

Bloemfontein •

Mbabane ⊗

Maseru ⊗

SWAZILAND

Durban •

SOUTH AFRICA

LESOTHO

INDIAN OCEAN

Cape Town ⊗

Cape of Good Hope

Cape Agulhas

N

W — E

S

KEY

——	National border
- - -	Disputed border
&#8855;	National capital
&#8226;	Other city

0 miles 1,000

0 kilometers 1,000

Lambert Azimuthal Equal Area

Africa: Physical

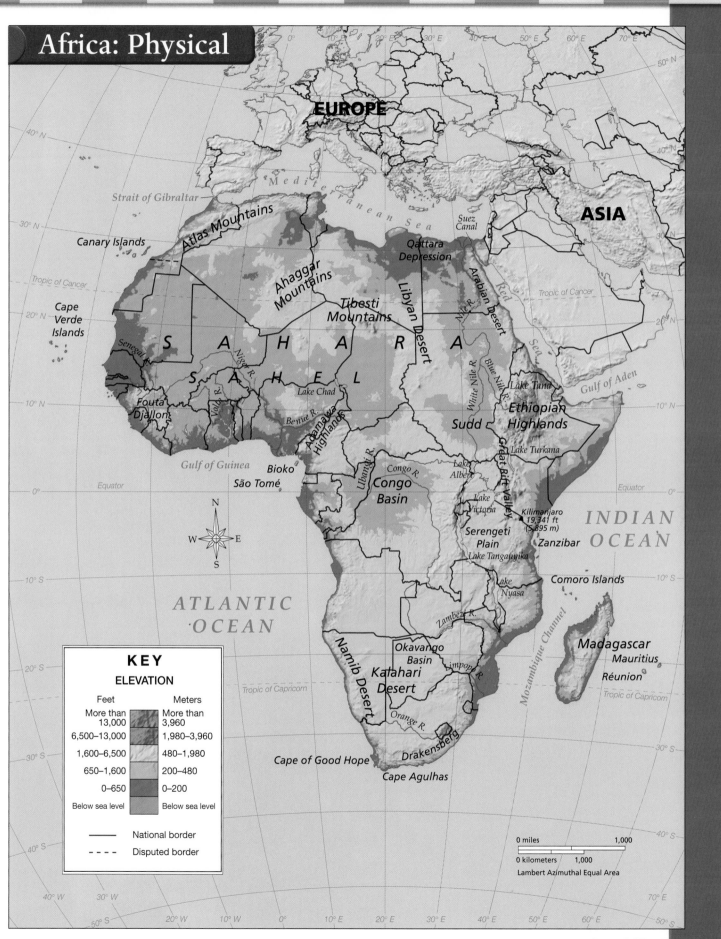

EUROPE

ASIA

Mediterranean Sea

Strait of Gibraltar

Canary Islands

Atlas Mountains

Qattara Depression

Suez Canal

Cape Verde Islands

Ahaggar Mountains

Tibesti Mountains

Libyan Desert

Arabian Desert

Red Sea

Nile R.

S   A   H   A   R   A

Senegal R.

Niger R.

S   A   H   E   L

White Nile R.

Blue Nile R.

Lake Tana

Gulf of Aden

Fouta Djallon

Volta R.

Lake Chad

Benue R.

Adamawa Highlands

Sudd

Ethiopian Highlands

Lake Turkana

Gulf of Guinea

Bioko

São Tomé

Ubangi R.

Congo R.

Congo Basin

Lake Albert

Great Rift Valley

Equator

Lake Victoria

Kilimanjaro 19,341 ft (5,895 m)

INDIAN OCEAN

Serengeti Plain

Zanzibar

Lake Tanganyika

N
W   E
S

ATLANTIC OCEAN

Lake Nyasa

Comoro Islands

Zambezi R.

Mozambique Channel

Madagascar

Mauritius

Réunion

Namib Desert

Okavango Basin

Kalahari Desert

Limpopo R.

Tropic of Capricorn

Orange R.

Drakensberg

Cape of Good Hope

Cape Agulhas

KEY
ELEVATION

Feet		Meters
More than 13,000		More than 3,960
6,500–13,000		1,980–3,960
1,600–6,500		480–1,980
650–1,600		200–480
0–650		0–200
Below sea level		Below sea level

——— National border

- - - - Disputed border

0 miles 1,000

0 kilometers 1,000

Lambert Azimuthal Equal Area

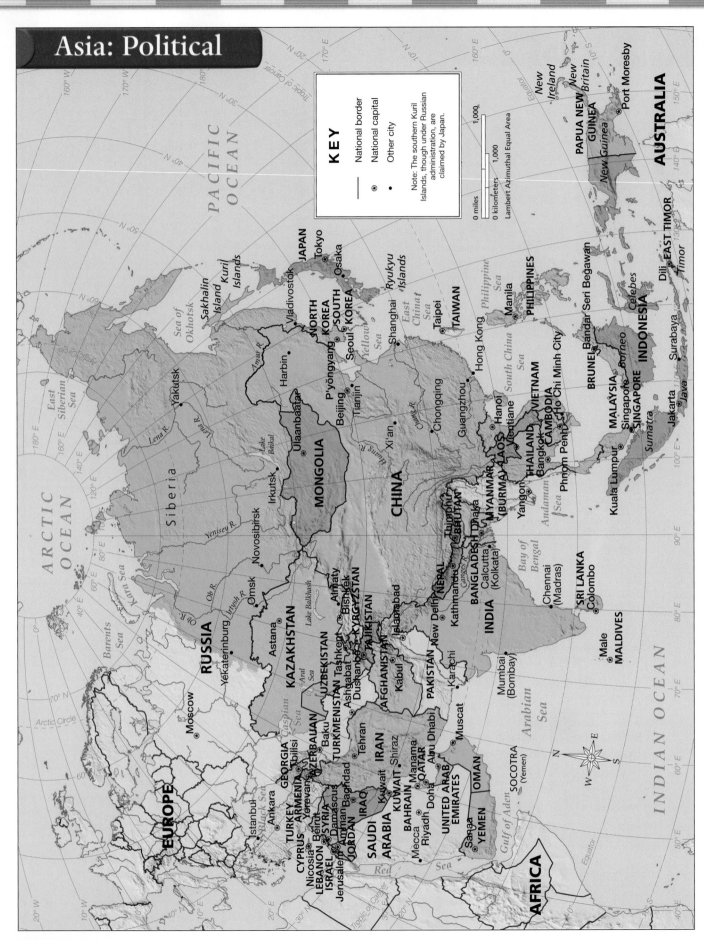

Asia: Political

KEY

— National border

⊛ National capital

• Other city

Note: The southern Kuril Islands, though under Russian administration, are claimed by Japan.

0 miles   1,000

0 kilometers   1,000

Lambert Azimuthal Equal Area

PACIFIC OCEAN

ARCTIC OCEAN

East Siberian Sea

Barents Sea

Arctic Circle

EUROPE

RUSSIA

Siberia

Moscow

Yekaterinburg

Omsk

Novosibirsk

Irkutsk

Yakutsk

Lena R.

Yenisey R.

Ob R.

Irtysh R.

Lake Baikal

Sea of Okhotsk

Sakhalin Island

Kuril Islands

Vladivostok

Amur R.

Harbin

MONGOLIA

Ulaanbaatar

JAPAN

Tokyo

Osaka

Ryukyu Islands

NORTH KOREA

P'yŏngyang

SOUTH KOREA

Seoul

Beijing

Tianjin

Shanghai

Yellow Sea

East China Sea

CHINA

Xi'an

Chang R.

Chongqing

Guangzhou

Hong Kong

Taipei

TAIWAN

Philippine Sea

PHILIPPINES

Manila

South China Sea

Huang R.

KAZAKHSTAN

Astana

Aral Sea

Lake Balkhash

Almaty

Bishkek

KYRGYZSTAN

Tashkent

UZBEKISTAN

TAJIKISTAN

Dushanbe

TURKMENISTAN

Ashgabat

Caspian Sea

Kura R.

GEORGIA

Tbilisi

ARMENIA

Yerevan

AZERBAIJAN

Baku

TURKEY

Ankara

Istanbul

Black Sea

CYPRUS

Nicosia

LEBANON

Beirut

SYRIA

Damascus

ISRAEL

Jerusalem

JORDAN

Amman

Baghdad

IRAQ

Kuwait

KUWAIT

BAHRAIN

Manama

QATAR

Doha

Riyadh

Mecca

SAUDI ARABIA

Sanaa

YEMEN

SOCOTRA (Yemen)

Gulf of Aden

Red Sea

AFRICA

IRAN

Tehran

Shiraz

UNITED ARAB EMIRATES

Abu Dhabi

OMAN

Muscat

Arabian Sea

AFGHANISTAN

Kabul

PAKISTAN

Islamabad

Karachi

INDIA

New Delhi

Mumbai (Bombay)

Calcutta (Kolkata)

Chennai (Madras)

Ganges R.

NEPAL

Kathmandu

BHUTAN

Thimphu

BANGLADESH

Dhaka

Bay of Bengal

SRI LANKA

Colombo

Male

MALDIVES

INDIAN OCEAN

MYANMAR (BURMA)

Yangon

Andaman Sea

THAILAND

Bangkok

LAOS

Vientiane

VIETNAM

Hanoi

CAMBODIA

Phnom Penh

Ho Chi Minh City

MALAYSIA

Kuala Lumpur

SINGAPORE

Singapore

BRUNEI

Bandar Seri Begawan

Borneo

INDONESIA

Celebes

Sumatra

Jakarta

Surabaya

Java

EAST TIMOR

Dili

Timor

PAPUA NEW GUINEA

New Guinea

New Ireland

New Britain

Port Moresby

AUSTRALIA

Equator

Tropic of Cancer

Tropic of Cancer

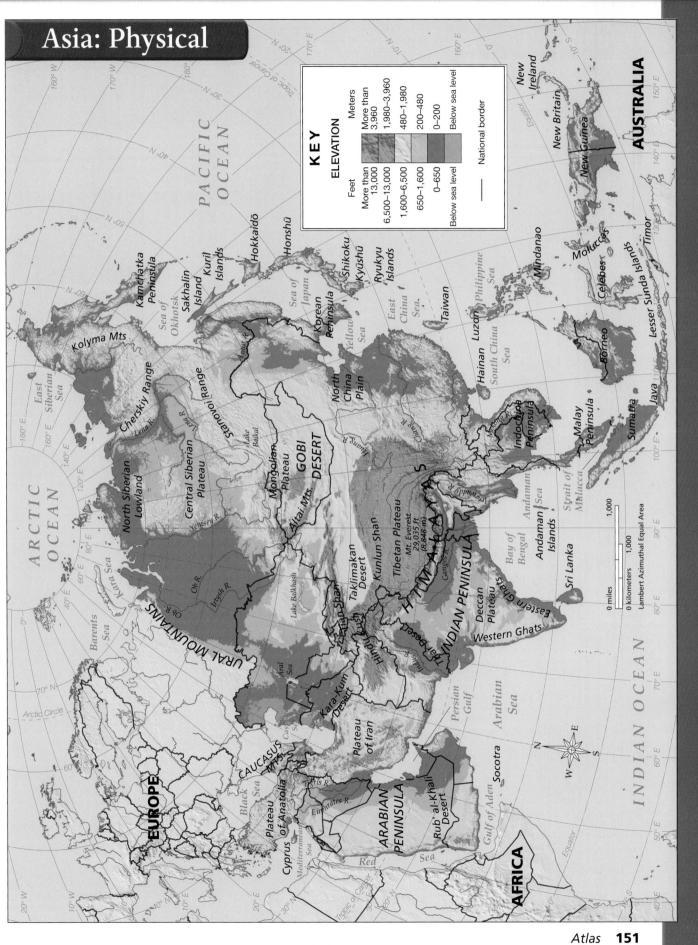

Asia: Physical

KEY

ELEVATION

Feet	Meters
More than 13,000	More than 3,960
6,500–13,000	1,980–3,960
1,600–6,500	480–1,980
650–1,600	200–480
0–650	0–200
Below sea level	Below sea level

—— National border

ARCTIC OCEAN

PACIFIC OCEAN

INDIAN OCEAN

EUROPE

AFRICA

AUSTRALIA

East Siberian Sea

Kolyma Mts

Kamchatka Peninsula

Sea of Okhotsk

Sakhalin Island

Kuril Islands

Hokkaidō

Honshū

Sea of Japan

Cherskiy Range

Stanovoi Range

Lena R.

Amur R.

Lake Baikal

Korean Peninsula

Shikoku

Kyūshū

Ryukyu Islands

East China Sea

Taiwan

Yellow Sea

North China Plain

Mongolian Plateau

GOBI DESERT

Central Siberian Plateau

North Siberian Lowland

Yenisey R.

Ob R.

Irtysh R.

Altai Mts.

Tian Shan

Taklimakan Desert

Kunlun Shan

Tibetan Plateau

Mt. Everest 29,035 ft (8,848 m)

HIMALAYAS

Huang R.

Chang R.

Mekong R.

Hainan

South China Sea

Luzon

Mindanao

Philippine Sea

Moluccas

Celebes

Borneo

Sumatra

Java

Lesser Sunda Islands

Timor

New Guinea

New Britain

New Ireland

Equator

Indochina Peninsula

Malay Peninsula

Strait of Malacca

Irrawaddy R.

Andaman Sea

Andaman Islands

Bay of Bengal

INDIAN PENINSULA

Deccan Plateau

Eastern Ghats

Western Ghats

Sri Lanka

Ganges R.

Brahmaputra R.

Indus R.

Hindu Kush

Kara Kum Desert

Aral Sea

Lake Balkhash

URAL MOUNTAINS

Ob R.

Kara Sea

Barents Sea

Arctic Circle

Plateau of Iran

Caspian Sea

CAUCASUS MTS.

Black Sea

Plateau of Anatolia

Cyprus

Mediterranean Sea

Tigris R.

Euphrates R.

ARABIAN PENINSULA

Rub' al-Khali Desert

Persian Gulf

Arabian Sea

Socotra

Gulf of Aden

Red Sea

Gulf of Aden

Tropic of Cancer

Tropic of Cancer

Lambert Azimuthal Equal Area

0 miles 1,000

0 kilometers 1,000

N
S
E
W

Oceania

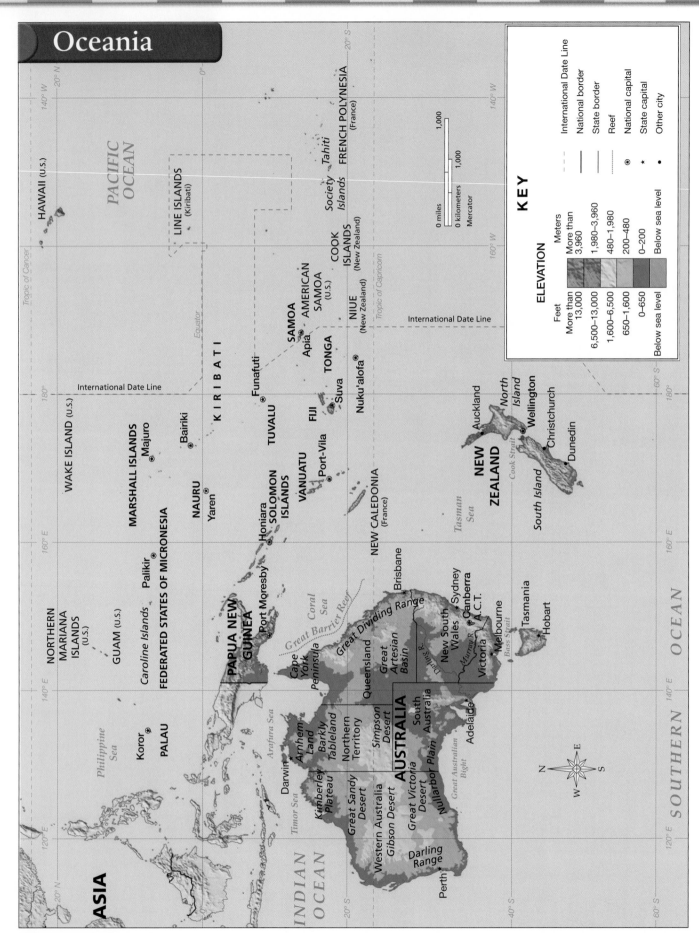

KEY

⊛	National capital
★	State capital
•	Other city

--- International Date Line
— National border
— State border
⋯⋯ Reef

ELEVATION

Feet	Meters
More than 13,000	More than 3,960
6,500–13,000	1,980–3,960
1,600–6,500	480–1,980
650–1,600	200–480
0–650	0–200
Below sea level	Below sea level

0 miles 1,000
0 kilometers 1,000
Mercator

HAWAII (U.S.)

PACIFIC OCEAN

Tropic of Cancer

LINE ISLANDS (Kiribati)

FRENCH POLYNESIA (France)

Society Islands *Tahiti*

COOK ISLANDS (New Zealand)

NIUE (New Zealand)

AMERICAN SAMOA (U.S.)

SAMOA
Apia ⊛

TONGA
Nuku'alofa ⊛

Tropic of Capricorn

International Date Line

Equator

K I R I B A T I

Funafuti ⊛

TUVALU

FIJI
Suva •

MARSHALL ISLANDS
Majuro ⊛

WAKE ISLAND (U.S.)

Bairiki ⊛

NAURU
Yaren ⊛

VANUATU
Port-Vila ⊛

SOLOMON ISLANDS
Honiara ⊛

NEW CALEDONIA (France)

NORTHERN MARIANA ISLANDS (U.S.)

GUAM (U.S.)

Caroline Islands Palikir ⊛
FEDERATED STATES OF MICRONESIA

International Date Line

NEW ZEALAND
Auckland •
North Island
Wellington ⊛
Christchurch •
Dunedin •
South Island
Cook Strait

Tasman Sea

Philippine Sea

Koror ⊛
PALAU

PAPUA NEW GUINEA
Port Moresby ⊛

Coral Sea

Great Barrier Reef

Brisbane •
Great Dividing Range
Sydney •
New South Wales
Canberra ⊛
A.C.T.
Murray R.
Melbourne ⊛
Victoria
Bass Strait
Tasmania
Hobart ★

Darling R.
Queensland
Great Artesian Basin

Arafura Sea

Darwin ★
Arnhem Land
Barkly Tableland
Northern Territory
Simpson Desert
South Australia
AUSTRALIA
Adelaide ⊛

Timor Sea

Kimberley Plateau
Great Sandy Desert
Western Australia
Gibson Desert
Great Victoria Desert
Nullarbor Plain
Great Australian Bight
Darling Range
Perth ★

Cape York Peninsula

ASIA

INDIAN OCEAN

SOUTHERN OCEAN

N
W E
S

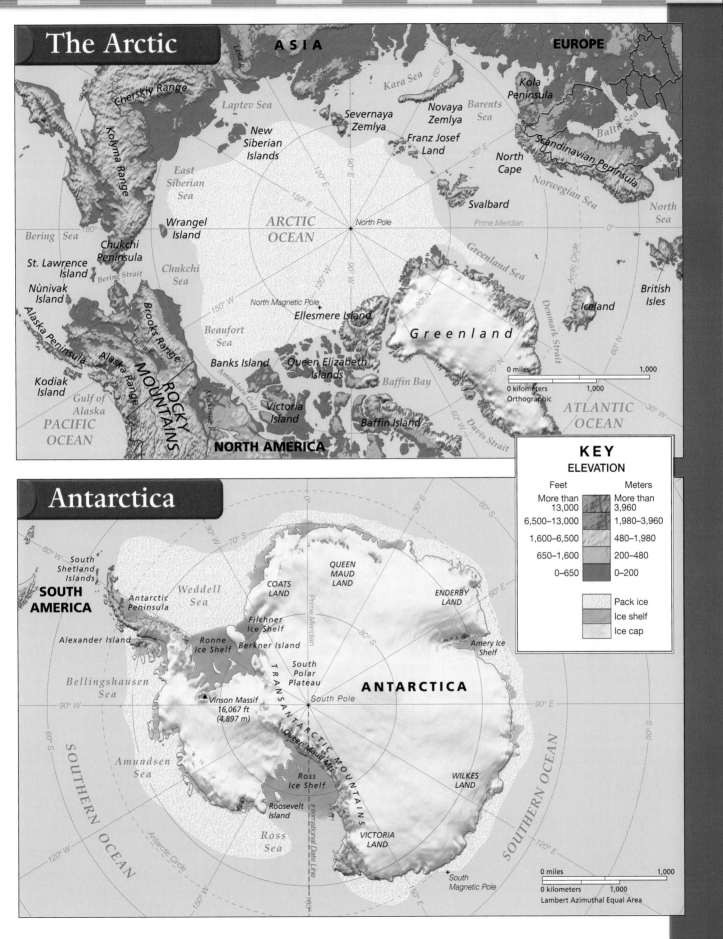

The Arctic

ASIA   EUROPE

Cherskiy Range
Laptev Sea
Kolyma Range
Severnaya Zemlya
New Siberian Islands
East Siberian Sea
Kara Sea
Novaya Zemlya
Barents Sea
Franz Josef Land
Kola Peninsula
North Cape
Baltic Sea
Scandinavian Peninsula
Svalbard
60° E
90° E
120° E
150° E
Prime Meridian
0°
Norwegian Sea
Bering Sea
Wrangel Island
ARCTIC OCEAN
North Pole
180°
Chukchi Peninsula
St. Lawrence Island
Chukchi Sea
Bering Strait
120° W
90° W
Greenland Sea
North Sea
Nunivak Island
Arctic Circle
Iceland
British Isles
80° N
North Magnetic Pole
Ellesmere Island
150° W
Beaufort Sea
Greenland
Denmark Strait
Alaska Peninsula
Brooks Range
Yukon R.
Alaska Range
ROCKY MOUNTAINS
Banks Island
Queen Elizabeth Islands
70° N
60° N
Kodiak Island
Amundsen Gulf
Mackenzie R.
Victoria Island
Baffin Bay
Baffin Island
Davis Strait
0 miles 1,000
0 kilometers 1,000
Orthographic
ATLANTIC OCEAN
30° W
Gulf of Alaska
PACIFIC OCEAN
NORTH AMERICA
60° W

Antarctica

South Shetland Islands
SOUTH AMERICA
Antarctic Peninsula
Weddell Sea
COATS LAND
QUEEN MAUD LAND
ENDERBY LAND
30° W
70° S
Prime Meridian
30° E
60° E
Filchner Ice Shelf
Alexander Island
Ronne Ice Shelf
Berkner Island
South Polar Plateau
80° S
Amery Ice Shelf
Bellingshausen Sea
Vinson Massif 16,067 ft (4,897 m)
TRANSANTARCTIC MOUNTAINS
ANTARCTICA
90° W
South Pole
Queen Maud Mts.
90° E
60° W
Amundsen Sea
Ross Ice Shelf
WILKES LAND
50° S
Roosevelt Island
International Date Line
VICTORIA LAND
SOUTHERN OCEAN
120° W
Ross Sea
South Magnetic Pole
120° E
Antarctic Circle
150° W
0 miles 1,000
0 kilometers 1,000
Lambert Azimuthal Equal Area
SOUTHERN OCEAN
90° S

KEY
ELEVATION

Feet		Meters
More than 13,000		More than 3,960
6,500–13,000		1,980–3,960
1,600–6,500		480–1,980
650–1,600		200–480
0–650		0–200

Pack ice
Ice shelf
Ice cap

Country Databank

Africa

Algeria
Capital: Algiers
Population: 32.3 million
Official Languages: Arabic and Tamazight
Land Area: 2,381,740 sq km; 919,590 sq mi
Leading Exports: petroleum, natural gas, petroleum products
Continent: Africa

Angola
Capital: Luanda
Population: 10.6 million
Official Language: Portuguese
Land Area: 1,246,700 sq km; 481,551 sq mi
Leading Exports: crude oil, diamonds, refined petroleum products, gas, coffee, sisal, fish and fish products, timber, cotton
Continent: Africa

Benin
Capital: Porto-Novo
Population: 6.9 million
Official Language: French
Land Area: 110,620 sq km; 42,710 sq mi
Leading Exports: cotton, crude oil, palm products, cocoa
Continent: Africa

Botswana
Capital: Gaborone
Population: 1.6 million
Official Language: English
Land Area: 585,370 sq km; 226,011 sq mi
Leading Exports: diamonds, copper, nickel, soda ash, meat, textiles
Continent: Africa

Burkina Faso
Capital: Ouagadougou
Population: 12.6 million
Official Language: French
Land Area: 273,800 sq km; 105,714 sq mi
Leading Exports: cotton, animal products, gold
Continent: Africa

Burundi
Capital: Bujumbura
Population: 6.4 million
Official Languages: Kirundi and French
Land Area: 25,650 sq km; 9,903 sq mi
Leading Exports: coffee, tea, sugar, cotton, hides
Continent: Africa

Cameroon
Capital: Yaoundé
Population: 16.1 million
Official Languages: English and French
Land Area: 469,440 sq km; 181,251 sqmi
Leading Exports: crude oil and petroleum products, lumber, cocoa, aluminum, coffee, cotton
Continent: Africa

Cape Verde
Capital: Praia
Population: 408,760
Official Language: Portuguese
Land Area: 4,033 sq km; 1,557 sq mi
Leading Exports: fuel, shoes, garments, fish, hides
Location: Atlantic Ocean

Central African Republic
Capital: Bangui
Population: 3.6 million
Official Language: French
Land Area: 622,984 sq km; 240,534 sq mi
Leading Exports: diamonds, timber, cotton, coffee, tobacco
Continent: Africa

Chad
Capital: N'Djamena
Population: 9 million
Official Languages: Arabic and French
Land Area: 1,259,200 sq km; 486,177 sq mi
Leading Exports: cotton, cattle, gum arabic
Continent: Africa

Comoros
Capital: Moroni
Population: 614,382
Official Languages: Arabic, Comoran, and French
Land Area: 2,170 sq km; 838 sq mi
Leading Exports: vanilla, ylang-ylang, cloves, perfume oil, copra
Location: Indian Ocean

Congo, Democratic Republic of the
Capital: Kinshasa
Population: 55.2 million
Official Language: French
Land Area: 2,267,600 sq km; 875,520 sq mi
Leading Exports: diamonds, copper, coffee, cobalt, crude oil
Continent: Africa

Congo, Republic of the
Capital: Brazzaville
Population: 3.3 million
Official Language: French
Land Area: 341,500 sq km; 131,853 sq mi
Leading Exports: petroleum, lumber, sugar, cocoa, coffee, diamonds
Continent: Africa

Djibouti
Capital: Djibouti
Population: 472,810
Official Languages: Arabic and French
Land Area: 22,980 sq km; 8,873 sq mi
Leading Exports: reexports, hides and skins, coffee (in transit)
Continent: Africa

Egypt
Capital: Cairo
Population: 70.7 million
Official Language: Arabic
Land Area: 995,450 sq km; 384,343 sq mi
Leading Exports: crude oil and petroleum products, cotton, textiles, metal products, chemicals
Continent: Africa

Equatorial Guinea
Capital: Malabo
Population: 498,144
Official Languages: Spanish and French
Land Area: 28,050 sq km; 10,830 sq mi
Leading Exports: petroleum, timber, cocoa
Continent: Africa

Eritrea
Capital: Asmara
Population: 4.5 million
Official Language: Tigrinya
Land Area: 121,320 sq km; 46,842 sq mi
Leading Exports: livestock, sorghum, textiles, food, small manufactured goods
Continent: Africa

Ethiopia
Capital: Addis Ababa
Population: 67.7 million
Official Language: Amharic
Land Area: 1,119,683 sq km; 432,310 sq mi
Leading Exports: coffee, qat, gold, leather products, oilseeds
Continent: Africa

Gabon
Capital: Libreville
Population: 1.2 million
Official Language: French
Land Area: 257,667 sq km; 99,489 sq mi
Leading Exports: crude oil, timber, manganese, uranium
Continent: Africa

Gambia
Capital: Banjul
Population: 1.5 million
Official Language: English
Land Area: 10,000 sq km; 3,861 sq mi
Leading Exports: peanuts and peanut products, fish, cotton lint, palm kernels
Continent: Africa

Ghana
Capital: Accra
Population: 20.2 million
Official Language: English
Land Area: 230,940 sq km; 89,166 sq mi
Leading Exports: gold, cocoa, timber, tuna, bauxite, aluminum, manganese ore, diamonds
Continent: Africa

Guinea
Capital: Conakry
Population: 7.8 million
Official Language: French
Land Area: 245,857 sq km; 94,925 sq mi
Leading Exports: bauxite, alumina, gold, diamonds, coffee, fish, agricultural products
Continent: Africa

Guinea-Bissau
Capital: Bissau
Population: 1.4 million
Official Language: Portuguese
Land Area: 28,000 sq km; 10,811 sq mi
Leading Exports: cashew nuts, shrimp, peanuts, palm kernels, lumber
Continent: Africa

Ivory Coast
Capital: Yamoussoukro
Population: 16.8 million
Official Language: French
Land Area: 318,000 sq km; 122,780 sq mi
Leading Exports: cocoa, coffee, timber, petroleum, cotton, bananas, pineapples, palm oil, cotton, fish
Continent: Africa

Kenya
Capital: Nairobi
Population: 31.3 million
Official Languages: Swahili and English
Land Area: 569,250 sq km; 219,787 sq mi
Leading Exports: tea, horticultural products, coffee, petroleum products, fish, cement
Continent: Africa

Lesotho
Capital: Maseru
Population: 2.2 million
Official Languages: Sesotho and English
Land Area: 30,355 sq km; 11,720 sq mi
Leading Exports: manufactured goods (clothing, footwear, road vehicles), wool and mohair, food and live animals
Continent: Africa

Liberia
Capital: Monrovia
Population: 3.3 million
Official Language: English
Land Area: 96,320 sq km; 37,189 sq mi
Leading Exports: rubber, timber, iron, diamonds, cocoa, coffee
Continent: Africa

Libya
Capital: Tripoli
Population: 5.4 million
Official Language: Arabic
Land Area: 1,759,540 sq km; 679,358 sq mi
Leading Exports: crude oil, refined petroleum products
Continent: Africa

Madagascar
Capital: Antananarivo
Population: 16.5 million
Official Languages: French and Malagasy
Land Area: 581,540 sq km; 224,533 sq mi
Leading Exports: coffee, vanilla, shellfish, sugar, cotton cloth, chromite, petroleum products
Location: Indian Ocean

Malawi
Capital: Lilongwe
Population: 10.7 million
Official Languages: English and Chichewa
Land Area: 94,080 sq km; 36,324 sq mi
Leading Exports: tobacco, tea, sugar, cotton, coffee, peanuts, wood products, apparel
Continent: Africa

Mali
Capital: Bamako
Population: 11.3 million
Official Language: French
Land Area: 1,220,000 sq km; 471,042 sq mi
Leading Exports: cotton, gold, livestock
Continent: Africa

Mauritania
Capital: Nouakchott
Population: 2.8 million
Official Language: Arabic
Land Area: 1,030,400 sq km; 397,837 sq mi
Leading Exports: iron ore, fish and fish products, gold
Continent: Africa

Mauritius
Capital: Port Louis
Population: 1.2 million
Official Language: English
Land Area: 2,030 sq km; 784 sq mi
Leading Exports: clothing and textiles, sugar, cut flowers, molasses
Location: Indian Ocean

Morocco
Capital: Rabat
Population: 31.2 million
Official Language: Arabic
Land Area: 446,300 sq km; 172,316 sq mi
Leading Exports: phosphates and fertilizers, food and beverages, minerals
Continent: Africa

Mozambique
Capital: Maputo
Population: 19.6 million
Official Language: Portuguese
Land Area: 784,090 sq km; 302,737 sq mi
Leading Exports: prawns, cashews, cotton, sugar, citrus, timber, bulk electricity
Continent: Africa

Namibia
Capital: Windhoek
Population: 1.8 million
Official Language: English
Land Area: 825,418 sq km; 318,694 sq mi
Leading Exports: diamonds, copper, gold, zinc, lead, uranium, cattle, processed fish, karakul skins
Continent: Africa

Niger
Capital: Niamey
Population: 11.3 million
Official Language: French
Land Area: 1,226,700 sq km; 489,073 sq mi
Leading Exports: uranium ore, livestock products, cowpeas, onions
Continent: Africa

Nigeria
Capital: Abuja
Population: 129.9 million
Official Language: English
Land Area: 910,768 sq km; 351,648 sq mi
Leading Exports: petroleum and petroleum products, cocoa, rubber
Continent: Africa

Rwanda
Capital: Kigali
Population: 7.4 million
Official Languages: Kinyarwanda, French, and English
Land Area: 24,948 sq km; 9,632 sq mi
Leading Exports: coffee, tea, hides, tin ore
Continent: Africa

São Tomé and Príncipe
Capital: São Tomé
Population: 170,372
Official Language: Portuguese
Land Area: 1,001 sq km; 386 sq mi
Leading Exports: cocoa, copra, coffee, palm oil
Location: Atlantic Ocean

Senegal
Capital: Dakar
Population: 10.6 million
Official Language: French
Land Area: 192,000 sq km; 74,131 sq mi
Leading Exports: fish, groundnuts (peanuts), petroleum products, phosphates, cotton
Continent: Africa

Seychelles
Capital: Victoria
Population: 80,098
Official Languages: English and French
Land Area: 455 sq km; 176 sq mi
Leading Exports: canned tuna, cinnamon bark, copra, petroleum products (reexports)
Location: Indian Ocean

Sierra Leone
Capital: Freetown
Population: 5.6 million
Official Language: English
Land Area: 71,620 sq km; 27,652 sq mi
Leading Exports: diamonds, rutile, cocoa, coffee, fish
Continent: Africa

Somalia
Capital: Mogadishu
Population: 7.8 million
Official Languages: Somali and Arabic
Land Area: 627,337 sq km; 242,215 sq mi
Leading Exports: livestock, bananas, hides, fish, charcoal, scrap metal
Continent: Africa

South Africa
Capital: Cape Town, Pretoria, and Bloemfontein
Population: 43.6 million
Official Languages: Eleven official languages: Afrikaans, English, Ndebele, Pedi, Sotho, Swazi, Tsonga, Tswana, Venda, Xhosa, and Zulu
Land Area: 1,219,912 sq km; 471,008 sq mi
Leading Exports: gold, diamonds, platinum, other metals and minerals, machinery and equipment
Continent: Africa

Sudan
Capital: Khartoum
Population: 37.1 million
Official Language: Arabic
Land Area: 2,376,000 sq km; 917,374 sq mi
Leading Exports: oil and petroleum products, cotton, sesame, livestock, groundnuts, gum arabic, sugar
Continent: Africa

Swaziland
Capital: Mbabane
Population: 1.1 million
Official Languages: English and siSwati
Land Area: 17,20 sq km; 6,642 sq mi
Leading Exports: soft drink concentrates, sugar, wood pulp, cotton yarn, refrigerators, citrus and canned fruit
Continent: Africa

Tanzania
Capital: Dar es Salaam and Dodoma
Population: 37.2 million
Official Languages: Swahili and English
Land Area: 886,037 sq km; 342,099 sq mi
Leading Exports: gold, coffee, cashew nuts, manufactured goods, cotton
Continent: Africa

Togo
Capital: Lomé
Population: 5.2 million
Official Language: French
Land Area: 54,385 sq km; 20,998 sq mi
Leading Exports: cotton, phosphates, coffee, cocoa
Continent: Africa

Tunisia
Capital: Tunis
Population: 9.8 million
Official Language: Arabic
Land Area: 155,360 sq km; 59,984 sq mi
Leading Exports: textiles, mechanical goods, phosphates and chemicals, agricultural products, hydrocarbons
Continent: Africa

Uganda
Capital: Kampala
Population: 24.7 million
Official Language: English
Land Area: 199,710 sq km; 77,108 sq mi
Leading Exports: coffee, fish and fish products, tea, gold, cotton, flowers, horticultural products
Continent: Africa

Zambia
Capital: Lusaka
Population: 10.1 million
Official Language: English
Land Area: 740,724 sq km; 285,994 sq mi
Leading Exports: copper, cobalt, electricity, tobacco, flowers, cotton
Continent: Africa

Zimbabwe
Capital: Harare
Population: 11.3 million
Official Language: English
Land Area: 386,670 sq km; 149,293 sq mi
Leading Exports: tobacco, gold, iron alloys, textiles and clothing
Continent: Africa

Asia and the Pacific

Afghanistan
Capital: Kabul
Population: 27.8 million
Official Languages: Pashtu and Dari
Land Area: 647,500 sq km;
250,000 sq mi
Leading Exports: agricultural products, hand-woven carpets, wool, cotton, hides and pelts, precious and semiprecious gems
Continent: Asia

Armenia
Capital: Yerevan
Population: 3.3 million
Official Language: Armenian
Land Area: 29,400 sq km; 10,965 sq mi
Leading Exports: diamonds, scrap metal, machinery and equipment, brandy, copper ore
Continent: Asia

Australia

Capital: Canberra
Population: 19.6 million
Official Language: English
Land Area: 7,617,930 sq km;
2,941,283 sq mi
Leading Exports: coal, gold, meat, wool, alumina, iron ore, wheat, machinery and transport equipment
Continent: Australia

Azerbaijan
Capital: Baku
Population: 7.8 million
Official Language: Azerbaijani
Land Area: 86,100 sq km; 33,243 sq mi
Leading Exports: oil and gas, machinery, cotton, foodstuffs
Continent: Asia

Bahrain
Capital: Manama
Population: 656,397
Official Language: Arabic
Land Area: 665 sq km; 257 sq mi
Leading Exports: petroleum and petroleum products, aluminum, textiles
Continent: Asia

Bangladesh
Capital: Dhaka
Population: 133.4 million
Official Language: Bengali
Land Area: 133,910 sq km; 51,705 sq mi
Leading Exports: garments, jute and jute goods, leather, frozen fish and seafood
Continent: Asia

Bhutan
Capital: Thimphu
Population: 2.1 million
Official Language: Dzongkha
Land Area: 47,000 sq km; 18,147 sq mi
Leading Exports: electricity, cardamom, gypsum, timber, handicrafts, cement, fruit, precious stones, spices
Continent: Asia

Brunei
Capital: Bandar Seri Begawan
Population: 350,898
Official Language: Malay
Land Area: 5,270 sq km; 2,035 sq mi
Leading Exports: crude oil, natural gas, refined products
Continent: Asia

Cambodia
Capital: Phnom Penh
Population: 12.8 million
Official Language: Khmer
Land Area: 176,520 sq km; 68,154 sq mi
Leading Exports: timber, garments, rubber, rice, fish
Continent: Asia

China
Capital: Beijing
Population: 1.29 billion
Official Languages: Mandarin and Chinese
Land Area: 9,326,410 sq km;
3,600,927 sq mi
Leading Exports: machinery and equipment, textiles and clothing, footwear, toys and sports goods, mineral fuels
Continent: Asia

Cyprus
Capital: Nicosia
Population: 767,314
Official Languages: Greek and Turkish
Land Area: 9,240 sq km; 3,568 sq mi
Leading Exports: citrus, potatoes, grapes, wine, cement, clothing and shoes
Location: Mediterranean Sea

East Timor
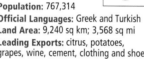
Capital: Dili
Population: 952,618
Official Languages: Tetum and Portuguese
Land Area: 15,007 sq km; 5,794 sq mi
Leading Exports: coffee, sandalwood, marble
Continent: Asia

Fiji
Capital: Suva
Population: 856,346
Official Language: English
Land Area: 18,270 sq km; 7,054 sq mi
Leading Exports: sugar, garments, gold, timber, fish, molasses, cocnut oil
Location: Pacific Ocean

Georgia
Capital: Tbilisi
Population: 5 million
Official Languages: Georgian and Abkhazian
Land Area: 69,700 sq km; 26,911 sq mi
Leading Exports: scrap metal, machinery, chemicals, fuel reexports, citrus fruits, tea, wine, other agricultural products
Continent: Asia

India
Capital: New Delhi
Population: 1.05 billion
Official Languages: Hindi and English
Land Area: 2,973,190 sq km;
1,147,949 sq mi
Leading Exports: textile goods, gems and jewelry, engineering goods, chemicals, leather manufactured goods
Continent: Asia

Indonesia
Capital: Jakarta
Population: 231.3 million
Official Language: Bahasa Indonesia
Land Area: 1,826,440 sq km;
705,188 sq mi
Leading Exports: oil and gas, electrical appliances, plywood, textiles, rubber
Continent: Asia

Iran

Capital: Tehran
Population: 66.6 million
Official Language: Farsi
Land Area: 1,636,000 sq km;
631,660 sq mi
Leading Exports: petroleum, carpets, fruits and nuts, iron and steel, chemicals
Continent: Asia

Iraq
Capital: Baghdad
Population: 24.7 million
Official Language: Arabic
Land Area: 432,162 sq km;
166,858 sq mi
Leading Exports: crude oil
Continent: Asia

Israel
Capital: Jerusalem
Population: 6.0 million
Official Language: Hebrew, Arabic
Land Area: 20,330 sq km; 7,849 sq mi
Leading Exports: machinery and equipment, software, cut diamonds, agricultural products, chemicals, textiles and apparel
Continent: Asia

Japan
Capital: Tokyo
Population: 127 million
Official Language: Japanese
Land Area: 374,744 sq km;
144,689 sq mi
Leading Exports: motor vehicles, semiconductors, office machinery, chemicals
Continent: Asia

Jordan
Capital: Amman
Population: 5.3 million
Official Language: Arabic
Land Area: 91,971 sq km; 35,510 sq mi
Leading Exports: phosphates, fertilizers, potash, agricultural products, manufactured goods, pharmaceuticals
Continent: Asia

Kazakhstan
Capital: Astana
Population: 16.7 million
Official Language: Kazakh
Land Area: 2,669,800 sq km;
1,030,810 sq mi
Leading Exports: oil and oil products, ferrous metals, machinery, chemicals, grain, wool, meat, coal
Continent: Asia

Kiribati

Capital: Bairiki (Tarawa Atoll)
Population: 96,335
Official Language: English
Land Area: 811 sq km; 313 sq mi
Leading Exports: copra, coconuts, seaweed, fish
Location: Pacific Ocean

Korea, North
Capital: Pyongyang
Population: 22.3 million
Official Language: Korean
Land Area: 120,410 sq km; 46,490 sq mi
Leading Exports: minerals, metallurgical products, manufactured goods (including armaments), agricultural and fishery products
Continent: Asia

Korea, South
Capital: Seoul
Population: 48.3 million
Official Language: Korean
Land Area: 98,190 sq km; 37,911 sq mi
Leading Exports: electronic products, machinery and equipment, motor vehicles, steel, ships, textiles, clothing, footwear, fish
Continent: Asia

Kuwait

Capital: Kuwait City
Population: 2.1 million
Official Language: Arabic
Land Area: 17,820 sq km; 6,880 sq mi
Leading Exports: oil and refined products, fertilizers
Continent: Asia

Kyrgyzstan

Capital: Bishkek
Population: 4.8 million
Official Languages: Kyrgyz and Russian
Land Area: 191,300 sq km; 73,861sq mi
Leading Exports: cotton, wool, meat, tobacco, gold, mercury, uranium, hydropower, machinery, shoes
Continent: Asia

Laos

Capital: Vientiane
Population: 5.8 million
Official Language: Lao
Land Area: 230,800 sq km;
89,112 sq mi
Leading Exports: wood products, garments, electricity, coffee, tin
Continent: Asia

Lebanon
Capital: Beirut
Population: 3.7 million
Official Language: Arabic
Land Area: 10,230 sq km; 3,950 sq mi
Leading Exports: foodstuffs and tobacco, textile, chemicals, precious stones, metal and metal products, electrical equipment and products, jewelry, paper and paper products
Continent: Asia

Malaysia
Capital: Kuala Lumpur and Putrajaya
Population: 22.7 million
Official Language: Bahasa Malaysia
Land Area: 328,550 sq km; 126,853 sq mi
Leading Exports: electronic equipment, petroleum and liquefied natural gas, wood and wood products, palm oil, rubber, textiles, chemicals
Continent: Asia

Maldives
Capital: Malé
Population: 320,165
Official Language: Dhivehi (Maldivian)
Land Area: 300 sq km; 116 sq mi
Leading Exports: fish, clothing
Location: Indian Ocean

Marshall Islands
Capital: Majuro
Population: 73,360
Official Languages: Marshallese and English
Land Area: 181.3 sq km; 70 sq mi
Leading Exports: copra cake, coconut oil, handicrafts
Location: Pacific Ocean

Micronesia, Federated States of
Capital: Palikir (Pohnpei Island)
Population: 135,869
Official Language: English
Land Area: 702 sq km; 271 sq mi
Leading Exports: fish, garments, bananas, black pepper
Location: Pacific Ocean

Mongolia
Capital: Ulaanbaatar
Population: 2.6 million
Official Language: Khalkha Mongolian
Land Area: 1,555,400 sq km; 600,540 sq mi
Leading Exports: copper, livestock, animal products, cashmere, wool, hides, fluorspar, other nonferrous metals
Continent: Asia

Myanmar (Burma)
Capital: Rangoon (Yangon)
Population: 42.2 million
Official Language: Burmese (Myanmar)
Land Area: 657,740 sq km; 253,953 sq mi
Leading Exports: apparel, foodstuffs, wood products, precious stones
Continent: Asia

Nauru
Capital: Yaren District
Population: 12,329
Official Language: Nauruan
Land Area: 21 sq km; 8 sq mi
Leading Exports: phosphates
Location: Pacific Ocean

Nepal
Capital: Kathmandu
Population: 25.9 million
Official Language: Nepali
Land Area: 136,800 sq km; 52,818 sq mi
Leading Exports: carpets, clothing, leather goods, jute goods, grain
Continent: Asia

New Zealand
Capital: Wellington
Population: 3.8 million
Official Languages: English and Maori
Land Area: 268,680 sq km; 103,737 sq mi
Leading Exports: dairy products, meat, wood and wood products, fish, machinery
Location: Pacific Ocean

Oman
Capital: Muscat
Population: 2.7 million
Official Language: Arabic
Land Area: 212,460 sq km; 82,030 sq mi
Leading Exports: petroleum, reexports, fish, metals, textiles
Continent: Asia

Pakistan
Capital: Islamabad
Population: 147.7 million
Official Languages: Urdu and English
Land Area: 778,720 sq km; 300,664 sq mi
Leading Exports: textiles (garments, cotton cloth, and yarn), rice, other agricultural products
Continent: Asia

Palau
Capital: Koror
Population: 19,409
Official Languages: English and Palauan
Land Area: 458 sq km; 177 sq mi
Leading Exports: shellfish, tuna, copra, garments
Location: Pacific Ocean

Papua New Guinea
Capital: Port Moresby
Population: 5.2 million
Official Language: English
Land Area: 452,860 sq km; 174,849 sq mi
Leading Exports: oil, gold, copper ore, logs, palm oil, coffee, cocoa, crayfish, prawns
Location: Pacific Ocean

Philippines
Capital: Manila
Population: 84.5 million
Official Languages: Filipino and English
Land Area: 298,170 sq km; 115,123 sq mi
Leading Exports: electronic equipment, machinery and transport equipment, garments, coconut products
Continent: Asia

Qatar
Capital: Doha
Population: 793,341
Official Language: Arabic
Land Area: 11,437 sq km; 4,416 sq mi
Leading Exports: petroleum products, fertilizers, steel
Continent: Asia

Samoa
Capital: Apia
Population: 178,631
Official Languages: Samoan and English
Land Area: 2,934 sq km; 1,133 sq mi
Leading Exports: fish, coconut oil cream, copra, taro, garments, beer
Location: Pacific Ocean

Saudi Arabia
Capital: Riyadh and Jiddah
Population: 23.5 million
Official Language: Arabic
Land Area: 1,960,582 sq km; 756,981 sq mi
Leading Exports: petroleum and petroleum products
Continent: Asia

Singapore
Capital: Singapore
Population: 4.5 million
Official Languages: Malay, English, Mandarin, Chinese, and Tamil
Land Area: 683 sq km; 264 sq mi
Leading Exports: machinery and equipment (including electronics), consumer goods, chemicals, mineral fuels
Continent: Asia

Solomon Islands
Capital: Honiara
Population: 494,786
Official Language: English
Land Area: 27,540 sq km; 10,633 sq mi
Leading Exports: timber, fish, copra, palm oil, cocoa
Location: Pacific Ocean

Sri Lanka
Capital: Colombo
Population: 19.6 million
Official Language: Sinhala, Tamil, and English
Land Area: 64,740 sq km; 24,996 sq mi
Leading Exports: textiles and apparel, tea, diamonds, coconut products, petroleum products
Continent: Asia

Syria
Capital: Damascus
Population: 17.2 million
Official Language: Arabic
Land Area: 184,050 sq km; 71,062 sq mi
Leading Exports: crude oil, textiles, fruits and vegetables, raw cotton
Continent: Asia

Taiwan
Capital: Taipei
Population: 22.5 million
Official Language: Mandarin Chinese
Land Area: 32,260 sq km; 12,456 sq mi
Leading Exports: machinery and electrical equipment, metals, textiles, plastics, chemicals
Continent: Asia

Tajikistan
Capital: Dushanbe
Population: 6.7 million
Official Language: Tajik
Land Area: 142,700 sq km; 55,096 sq mi
Leading Exports: aluminum, electricity, cotton, fruits, vegetables, oil, textiles
Continent: Asia

Thailand
Capital: Bangkok
Population: 62.5 million
Official Language: Thai
Land Area: 511,770 sq km; 197,564 sq mi
Leading Exports: computers, transistors, seafood, clothing, rice
Continent: Asia

Tonga
Capital: Nuku'alofa
Population: 106,137
Official Languages: Tongan and English
Land Area: 718 sq km; 277 sq mi
Leading Exports: squash, fish, vanilla beans, root crops
Location: Pacific Ocean

Turkey
Capital: Ankara
Population: 67.3 million
Official Language: Turkish
Land Area: 770,760 sq km; 297,590 sq mi
Leading Exports: apparel, foodstuffs, textiles, metal manufactured goods, transport equipment
Continent: Asia

Turkmenistan
Capital: Ashgabat
Population: 4.7 million
Official Language: Turkmen
Land Area: 488,100 sq km; 188,455 sq mi
Leading Exports: gas, oil, cotton fiber, textiles
Continent: Asia

Asia and the Pacific (continued)

Tuvalu

Capital: Fongafale
Population: 10,800
Official Language: English
Land Area: 26 sq km; 10 sq mi
Leading Exports: copra, fish
Location: Pacific Ocean

United Arab Emirates
Capital: Abu Dhabi
Population: 2.4 million
Official Language: Arabic
Land Area: 82,880 sq km; 32,000 sq mi
Leading Exports: crude oil, natural gas, reexports, dried fish, dates
Continent: Asia

Uzbekistan
Capital: Tashkent
Population: 25.5 million
Official Language: Uzbek
Land Area: 425,400 sq km; 164,247 sq mi
Leading Exports: cotton, gold, energy products, mineral fertilizers, ferrous metals, textiles, food products, automobiles
Continent: Asia

Vanuatu
Capital: Port-Vila
Population: 196,178
Official Languages: English, French, and Bislama
Land Area: 12,200 sq km; 4,710 sq mi
Leading Exports: copra, kava, beef, cocoa, timber, coffee
Location: Pacific Ocean

Vietnam
Capital: Hanoi
Population: 81.1 million
Official Language: Vietnamese
Land Area: 325,320 sq km; 125,621 sq mi
Leading Exports: crude oil, marine products, rice, coffee, rubber, tea, garments, shoes
Continent: Asia

Yemen
Capital: Sanaa
Population: 18.7 million
Official Language: Arabic
Land Area: 527,970 sq km; 203,849 sq mi
Leading Exports: crude oil, coffee, dried and salted fish
Continent: Asia

Europe and Russia

Albania
Capital: Tiranë
Population: 3.5 million
Official Language: Albanian
Land Area: 27,398 sq km; 10,578 sq mi
Leading Exports: textiles and footwear, asphalt, metals and metallic ores, crude oil, vegetables, fruits, tobacco
Continent: Europe

Andorra
Capital: Andorra la Vella
Population: 68,403
Official Language: Catalan
Land Area: 468 sq km; 181 sq mi
Leading Exports: tobacco products, furniture
Continent: Europe

Austria
Capital: Vienna
Population: 8.2 million
Official Language: German
Land Area: 82,738 sq km; 31,945 sq mi
Leading Exports: machinery and equipment, motor vehicles and parts, paper and paperboard, metal goods, chemicals, iron and steel, textiles, foodstuffs
Continent: Europe

Belarus
Capital: Minsk
Population: 10.3 million
Official Languages: Belarussian and Russian
Land Area: 207,600 sq km; 80,154 sq mi
Leading Exports: machinery and equipment, mineral products, chemicals, textiles, food stuffs, metals
Continent: Europe

Belgium
Capital: Brussels
Population: 10.3 million
Official Languages: Dutch and French
Land Area: 30,230 sq km; 11,172 sq mi
Leading Exports: machinery and equipment, chemicals, metals and metal products
Continent: Europe

Bosnia and Herzegovina
Capital: Sarajevo
Population: 4.0 million
Official Language: Serbo-Croat
Land Area: 51,129 sq km; 19,741 sq mi
Leading Exports: miscellaneous manufactured goods, crude materials
Continent: Europe

Bulgaria
Capital: Sofía
Population: 7.6 million
Official Language: Bulgarian
Land Area: 110,550 sq km; 42,683 sq mi
Leading Exports: clothing, footwear, iron and steel, machinery and equipment, fuels
Continent: Europe

Croatia
Capital: Zagreb
Population: 4.4 million
Official Language: Croatian
Land Area: 56,414 km; 21,781 sq mi
Leading Exports: transport equipment, textiles, chemicals, foodstuffs, fuels
Continent: Europe

Czech Republic

Capital: Prague
Population: 10.3 million
Official Language: Czech
Land Area: 78,276 sq km; 29,836 sq mi
Leading Exports: machinery and transport equipment, intermediate manufactured goods, chemicals, raw materials and fuel
Continent: Europe

Denmark

Capital: Copenhagen
Population: 5.4 million
Official Language: Danish
Land Area: 42,394 sq km; 16,368 sq mi
Leading Exports: machinery and instruments, meat and meat products, dairy products, fish, chemicals, furniture, ships, windmills
Continent: Europe

Estonia

Capital: Tallinn
Population: 1.4 million
Official Language: Estonian
Land Area: 43,211 sq km; 16,684 sq mi
Leading Exports: machinery and equipment, wood products, textiles, food products, metals, chemical products
Continent: Europe

Finland
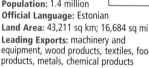
Capital: Helsinki
Population: 5.2 million
Official Languages: Finnish and Swedish
Land Area: 305,470 sq km; 117,942 sq mi
Leading Exports: machinery and equipment, chemicals, metals, timber, paper, pulp
Continent: Europe

France
Capital: Paris
Population: 59.8 million
Official Language: French
Land Area: 545,630 sq km; 310,668 sq mi
Leading Exports: machinery and transportation equipment, aircraft, plastics, chemicals, pharmaceutical products, iron and steel, beverages
Continent: Europe

Germany

Capital: Berlin
Population: 83 million
Official Language: German
Land Area: 349,223 sq km; 134,835 sq mi
Leading Exports: machinery, vehicles, chemicals, metals and manufactured goods, foodstuffs, textiles
Continent: Europe

Greece

Capital: Athens
Population: 10.6 million
Official Language: Greek
Land Area: 130,800 sq km; 50,502 sq mi
Leading Exports: food and beverages, manufactured goods, petroleum products, chemicals, textiles
Continent: Europe

Hungary

Capital: Budapest
Population: 10.1 million
Official Language: Hungarian
Land Area: 92,340 sq km; 35,652 sq mi
Leading Exports: machinery and equipment, other manufactured goods, food products, raw materials, fuels and electricity
Continent: Europe

Iceland
Capital: Reykjavík
Population: 279,384
Official Language: Icelandic
Land Area: 100,250 sq km;
38,707 sq mi
Leading Exports: fish and fish products, animal products, aluminum, diatomite, ferrosilicon
Location: Atlantic Ocean

Ireland
Capital: Dublin
Population: 3.9 million
Official Languages: Irish Gaelic and English
Land Area: 68,890 sq km; 26,598 sq mi
Leading Exports: machinery and equipment, computers, chemicals, pharmaceuticals, live animals, animal products
Continent: Europe

Italy
Capital: Rome
Population: 57.7 million
Official Language: Italian
Land Area: 294,020 sq km;
113,521 sq mi
Leading Exports: fruits, vegetables, grapes, potatoes, sugar beets, soybeans, grain, olives, beef, diary products, fish
Continent: Europe

Latvia
Capital: Riga
Population: 2.4 million
Official Language: Latvian
Land Area: 63,589 sq km; 24,552 sq mi
Leading Exports: wood and wood products, machinery and equipment, metals, textiles, foodstuffs
Continent: Europe

Liechtenstein
Capital: Vaduz
Population: 32,842
Official Language: German
Land Area: 160 sq km; 62 sq mi
Leading Exports: small specialty machinery, dental products, stamps, hardware, pottery
Continent: Europe

Lithuania
Capital: Vilnius
Population: 3.6 million
Official Language: Lithuanian
Land Area: 65,200 sq km; 25,174 sq mi
Leading Exports: mineral products, textiles and clothing, machinery and equipment, chemicals, wood and wood products, foodstuffs
Continent: Europe

Luxembourg
Capital: Luxembourg
Population: 448,569
Official Languages: Luxembourgish, French, and German
Land Area: 2,586 sq km; 998 sq mi
Leading Exports: machinery and equipment, steel products, chemicals, rubber products, glass
Continent: Europe

Macedonia, The Former Yugoslav Republic of
Capital: Skopje
Population: 2.1 million
Official Languages: Macedonian and Albanian
Land Area: 24,856 sq km; 9,597 sq mi
Leading Exports: food, beverages, tobacco, miscellaneous manufactured goods, iron and steel
Continent: Europe

Malta
Capital: Valletta
Population: 397,499
Official Languages: Maltese and English
Land Area: 316 sq km; 122 sq mi
Leading Exports: machinery and transport equipment, manufactured goods
Location: Mediterranean Sea

Moldova
Capital: Chişinău
Population: 4.4 million
Official Language: Moldovan
Land Area: 33,371 sq km; 12,885 sq mi
Leading Exports: foodstuffs, textiles and footwear, machinery
Continent: Europe

Monaco
Capital: Monaco
Population: 31,987
Official Language: French
Land Area: 1.95 sq km; 0.75 sq mi
Leading Exports: no information available
Continent: Europe

Netherlands
Capital: Amsterdam and The Hague
Population: 16.1 million
Official Language: Dutch
Land Area: 33,883 sq km; 13,082 sq mi
Leading Exports: machinery and equipment, chemicals, fuels, foodstuffs
Continent: Europe

Norway
Capital: Oslo
Population: 4.5 million
Official Language: Norwegian
Land Area: 307,860 sq km;
118,865 sq mi
Leading Exports: petroleum and petroleum products, machinery and equipment, metals, chemicals, ships, fish
Continent: Europe

Poland
Capital: Warsaw
Population: 38.6 million
Official Language: Polish
Land Area: 304,465 sq km;
117,554 sq mi
Leading Exports: machinery and transport equipment, intermediate manufactured goods, miscellaneous manufactured goods, food and live animals
Continent: Europe

Portugal
Capital: Lisbon
Population: 10.1 million
Official Language: Portuguese
Land Area: 91,951 sq km; 35,502 sq mi
Leading Exports: clothing and footwear, machinery, chemicals, cork and paper products, hides
Continent: Europe

Romania
Capital: Bucharest
Population: 22.3 million
Official Language: Romanian
Land Area: 230,340 sq km;
88,934 sq mi
Leading Exports: textiles and footwear, metals and metal products, machinery and equipment, minerals and fuels
Continent: Europe

Russia
Capital: Moscow
Population: 145 million
Official Language: Russian
Land Area: 16,995,800 sq km;
6,592,100 sq mi
Leading Exports: petroleum and petroleum products, natural gas, wood and wood products, metals, chemicals, and a wide variety of civilian and military manufactured goods
Continents: Europe and Asia

San Marino
Capital: San Marino
Population: 27,730
Official Language: Italian
Land Area: 61 sq km; 24 sq mi
Leading Exports: building stone, lime, wood, chestnuts, wheat, wine, baked goods, hides, ceramics
Continent: Europe

Serbia and Montenegro
Capital: Belgrade
Population: 10.7 million
Official Language: Serbo-Croat
Land Area: 102,136 sq km;
39,435 sq mi
Leading Exports: manufactured goods, food and live animals, raw materials
Continent: Europe

Slovakia
Capital: Bratislava
Population: 5.4 million
Official Language: Slovak
Land Area: 48,800 sq km; 18,842 sq mi
Leading Exports: machinery and transport equipment, intermediate manufactured goods, miscellaneous manufactured goods, chemicals
Continent: Europe

Slovenia
Capital: Ljubljana
Population: 1.9 million
Official Language: Slovene
Land Area: 20,151 sq km; 7,780 sq mi
Leading Exports: manufactured goods, machinery and transport equipment, chemicals, food
Continent: Europe

Spain
Capital: Madrid
Population: 40.1 million
Official Languages: Spanish, Galician, Basque, and Catalan
Land Area: 499,542 sq km;
192,873 sq mi
Leading Exports: machinery, motor vehicles, foodstuffs, other consumer goods
Continent: Europe

Sweden
Capital: Stockholm
Population: 8.9 million
Official Language: Swedish
Land Area: 410,934 sq km;
158,662 sq mi
Leading Exports: machinery, motor vehicles, paper products, pulp and wood, iron and steel products, chemicals
Continent: Europe

Europe and Russia (continued)

Switzerland
Capital: Bern
Population: 7.3 million
Official Languages: German, French, and Italian
Land Area: 39,770 sq km; 15,355 sq mi
Leading Exports: machinery, chemicals, metals, watches, agricultural products
Continent: Europe

Ukraine
Capital: Kiev
Population: 48.4 million
Official Language: Ukrainian
Land Area: 603,700 sq km; 233,090 sq mi
Leading Exports: ferrous and nonferrous metals, fuel and petroleum products, machinery and transport equipment, food products
Continent: Europe

United Kingdom
Capital: London
Population: 59.8 million
Official Languages: English and Welsh
Land Area: 241,590 sq km; 93,278 sq mi
Leading Exports: manufactured goods, fuels, chemicals, food, beverages, tobacco
Continent: Europe

Vatican City
(Holy See)
Capital: Vatican City
Population: 900
Official Languages: Latin and Italian
Land Area: 0.44 sq km; 0.17 sq mi
Leading Exports: no information available
Continent: Europe

Latin America

Antigua and Barbuda
Capital: Saint John's
Population: 67,448
Official Language: English
Land Area: 442 sq km; 171 sq mi
Leading Exports: petroleum products, manufactured goods, machinery and transport equipment, food and live animals
Location: Caribbean Sea

Argentina
Capital: Buenos Aires
Population: 37.8 million
Official Language: Spanish
Land Area: 2,736,690 sq km; 1,056,636 sq mi
Leading Exports: edible oils, fuels and energy, cereals, feed, motor vehicles
Continent: South America

Bahamas
Capital: Nassau
Population: 300,529
Official Language: English
Land Area: 10,070 sq km; 3,888 sq mi
Leading Exports: fish and crawfish, rum, salt, chemicals, fruit and vegetables
Location: Caribbean Sea

Barbados
Capital: Bridgetown
Population: 276,607
Official Language: English
Land Area: 431 sq km; 166 sq mi
Leading Exports: sugar and molasses, rum, other foods and beverages, chemicals, electrical components, clothing
Location: Caribbean Sea

Belize
Capital: Belmopan
Population: 262,999
Official Language: English
Land Area: 22,806 sq km; 8,805 sq mi
Leading Exports: sugar, bananas, citrus, clothing, fish products, molasses, wood
Continent: North America

Bolivia
Capital: La Paz and Sucre
Population: 8.5 million
Official Language: Spanish, Quechua, and Aymara
Land Area: 1,084,390 sq km; 418,683 sq mi
Leading Exports: soybeans, natural gas, zinc, gold, wood
Continent: South America

Brazil
Capital: Brasília
Population: 176 million
Official Language: Portuguese
Land Area: 8,456,510 sq km; 3,265,059 sq mi
Leading Exports: manufactured goods, iron ore, soybeans, footwear, coffee, autos
Continent: South America

Chile
Capital: Santiago
Population: 15.5 million
Official Language: Spanish
Land Area: 748,800 sq km; 289,112 sq mi
Leading Exports: copper, fish, fruits, paper and pulp, chemicals
Continent: South America

Colombia
Capital: Bogotá
Population: 41 million
Official Language: Spanish
Land Area: 1,038,700 sq km; 401,042 sq mi
Leading Exports: petroleum, coffee, coal, apparel, bananas, cut flowers
Continent: South America

Costa Rica
Capital: San José
Population: 3.8 million
Official Language: Spanish
Land Area: 51,660 sq km; 19,560 sq mi
Leading Exports: coffee, bananas, sugar, pineapples, textiles, electronic components, medical equipment
Continent: North America

Cuba
Capital: Havana
Population: 11.2 million
Official Language: Spanish
Land Area: 110,860 sq km; 42,803 sq mi
Leading Exports: sugar, nickel, tobacco, fish, medical products, citrus, coffee
Location: Caribbean Sea

Dominica
Capital: Roseau
Population: 73,000
Official Language: English
Land Area: 754 sq km; 291 sq mi
Leading Exports: bananas, soap, bay oil, vegetables, grapefruit, oranges
Location: Caribbean Sea

Dominican Republic
Capital: Santo Domingo
Population: 8.7 million
Official Language: Spanish
Land Area: 48,380 sq km; 18,679 sq mi
Leading Exports: ferronickel, sugar, gold, silver, coffee, cocoa, tobacco, meats, consumer goods
Location: Caribbean Sea

Ecuador
Capital: Quito
Population: 13.5 million
Official Language: Spanish
Land Area: 276,840 sq km; 106,888 sq mi
Leading Exports: petroleum, bananas, shrimp, coffee, cocoa, cut flowers, fish
Continent: South America

El Salvador
Capital: San Salvador
Population: 6.4 million
Official Language: Spanish
Land Area: 20,720 sq km; 8,000 sq mi
Leading Exports: offshore assembly exports, coffee, sugar, shrimp, textiles, chemicals, electricity
Continent: North America

Grenada
Capital: Saint George's
Population: 89,211
Official Language: English
Land Area: 344 sq km; 133 sq mi
Leading Exports: bananas, cocoa, nutmeg, fruit and vegetables, clothing, mace
Location: Caribbean Sea

Guatemala
Capital: Guatemala City
Population: 13.3 million
Official Language: Spanish
Land Area: 108,430 sq km; 41,865 sq mi
Leading Exports: coffee, sugar, bananas, fruits and vegetables, cardamom, meat, apparel, petroleum, electricity
Continent: North America

Guyana
Capital: Georgetown
Population: 698,209
Official Language: English
Land Area: 196,850 sq km; 76,004 sq mi
Leading Exports: sugar, gold, bauxite/alumina, rice, shrimp, molasses, rum, timber
Continent: South America

Haiti
Capital: Port-au-Prince
Population: 7.1 million
Official Language: French and French Creole
Land Area: 27,560 sq km; 10,641 sq mi
Leading Exports: manufactured goods, coffee, oils, cocoa
Location: Caribbean Sea

Honduras
Capital: Tegucigalpa
Population: 6.6 million
Official Language: Spanish
Land Area: 111,890 sq km; 43,201 sq mi
Leading Exports: coffee, bananas, shrimp, lobster, meat, zinc, lumber
Continent: North America

Jamaica
Capital: Kingston
Population: 2.7 million
Official Language: English
Land Area: 10,831 sq km; 4,182 sq mi
Leading Exports: alumina, bauxite, sugar, bananas, rum
Location: Caribbean Sea

Mexico
Capital: Mexico City
Population: 103.4 million
Official Language: Spanish
Land Area: 1,923,040 sq km; 742,486 sq mi
Leading Exports: manufactured goods, oil and oil products, silver, fruits, vegetables, coffee, cotton
Continent: North America

Nicaragua
Capital: Managua
Population: 5 million
Official Language: Spanish
Land Area: 120,254 sq km; 46,430 sq mi
Leading Exports: coffee, shrimp and lobster, cotton, tobacco, beef, sugar, bananas, gold
Continent: North America

Panama
Capital: Panama City
Population: 2.9 million
Official Language: Spanish
Land Area: 75,990 sq km; 29,340 sq mi
Leading Exports: bananas, shrimp, sugar, coffee, clothing
Continent: North America

Paraguay
Capital: Asunción
Population: 5.9 million
Official Language: Spanish
Land Area: 397,300 sq km; 153,398 sq mi
Leading Exports: electricity, soybeans, feed, cotton, meat, edible oils
Continent: South America

Peru
Capital: Lima
Population: 28 million
Official Languages: Spanish and Quechua
Land Area: 1,280,000 sq km; 494,208 sq mi
Leading Exports: fish and fish products, gold, copper, zinc, crude petroleum and byproducts, lead, coffee, sugar, cotton
Continent: South America

Saint Kitts and Nevis
Capital: Basseterre
Population: 38,736
Official Language: English
Land Area: 261 sq km; 101 sq mi
Leading Exports: machinery, food, electronics, beverages, tobacco
Location: Caribbean Sea

Saint Lucia
Capital: Castries
Population: 160,145
Official Language: English
Land Area: 606 sq km; 234 sq mi
Leading Exports: bananas, clothing, cocoa, vegetables, fruits, coconut oil
Location: Caribbean Sea

Saint Vincent and the Grenadines
Capital: Kingstown
Population: 116,394
Official Language: English
Land Area: 389 sq km; 150 sq mi
Leading Exports: bananas, eddoes and dasheen, arrowroot starch, tennis racquets
Location: Caribbean Sea

Suriname
Capital: Paramaribo
Population: 436,494
Official Language: Dutch
Land Area: 161,470 sq km; 62,344 sq mi
Leading Exports: alumina, crude oil, lumber, shrimp and fish, rice, bananas
Continent: South America

Trinidad and Tobago
Capital: Port-of-Spain
Population: 1.2 million
Official Language: English
Land Area: 5,128 sq km; 1,980 sq mi
Leading Exports: petroleum and petroleum products, chemicals, steel products, fertilizer, sugar, cocoa, coffee, citrus, flowers
Location: Caribbean Sea

Uruguay
Capital: Montevideo
Population: 3.4 million
Official Language: Spanish
Land Area: 173,620 sq km; 67,100 sq mi
Leading Exports: meat, rice, leather products, wool, vehicles, dairy products
Continent: South America

Venezuela
Capital: Caracas
Population: 24.3 million
Official Language: Spanish
Land Area: 882,050 sq km; 340,560 sq mi
Leading Exports: petroleum, bauxite and aluminum, steel, chemicals, agricultural products, basic manufactured goods
Continent: South America

United States and Canada

Canada
Capital: Ottawa
Population: 31.9 million
Official Languages: English and French
Land Area: 9,220,970 sq km; 3,560,217 sq mi
Leading Exports: motor vehicles and parts, industrial machinery, aircraft, telecommunications equipment, chemicals, plastics, fertilizers, wood pulp, timber, crude petroleum, natural gas, electricity, aluminum
Continent: North America

United States
Capital: Washington, D.C.
Population: 281.4 million
Official Language: English
Land Area: 9,158,960 sq km; 3,536,274 sq mi
Leading Exports: capital goods, automobiles, industrial supplies and raw materials, consumer goods, agricultural products
Continent: North America

SOURCE: CIA World Factbook Online, 2002

Glossary of Geographic Terms

basin
an area that is lower than surrounding land areas; some basins are filled with water

bay
a body of water that is partly surrounded by land and that is connected to a larger body of water

butte
a small, high, flat-topped landform with cliff-like sides

▲ **butte**

canyon
a deep, narrow valley with steep sides; often with a stream flowing through it

cataract
a large waterfall or steep rapids

◀ **cataract**

delta
a plain at the mouth of a river, often triangular in shape, formed where sediment is deposited by flowing water

flood plain
a broad plain on either side of a river, formed where sediment settles during floods

glacier
a huge, slow-moving mass of snow and ice

hill
an area that rises above surrounding land and has a rounded top; lower and usually less steep than a mountain

island
an area of land completely surrounded by water

isthmus
a narrow strip of land that connects two larger areas of land

mesa
a high, flat-topped landform with cliff-like sides; larger than a butte

mountain
a landform that rises steeply at least 2,000 feet (610 meters) above surrounding land; usually wide at the bottom and rising to a narrow peak or ridge

▶ **glacier**

◀ delta

mountain pass
a gap between mountains

peninsula
an area of land almost completely surrounded by water but connected to the mainland

plain
a large area of flat or gently rolling land

plateau
a large, flat area that rises above the surrounding land; at least one side has a steep slope

river mouth
the point where a river enters a lake or sea

strait
a narrow stretch of water that connects two larger bodies of water

tributary
a river or stream that flows into a larger river

valley
a low stretch of land between mountains or hills; land that is drained by a river

volcano
an opening in Earth's surface through which molten rock, ashes, and gases escape from the interior

▶ volcano

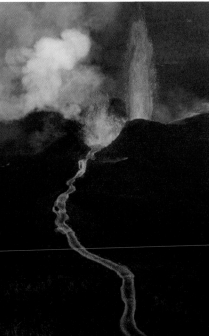

Glossary of Geographic Terms **163**

Gazetteer

A

Africa (10° N, 22° E) the world's second-largest continent, surrounded by the Mediterranean Sea, the Atlantic Ocean, the Indian Ocean, and the Red Sea (p. 15)

Antarctic Circle (66°30′ S) line of latitude around Earth near the South Pole (p. 32)

Antarctica (87° S, 60° E) the continent that contains the South Pole; almost completely covered by an ice sheet (p. 35)

Antofagasta (23°39′ S, 70°24′ W) a coastal city in Chile (p. 43)

Appalachian Mountains (41° N, 77° W) a mountain system in eastern North America (p. 39)

Arctic Circle (66°30′ N) line of latitude around Earth near the North Pole (p. 30)

Arctic region located around the North Pole (p. 31)

Asia (50° N, 100° E) the world's largest continent, the main part of the Eurasian landmass, surrounded by the Arctic Ocean, the Pacific Ocean, the Indian Ocean, the Red Sea, the Mediterranean Sea, and Europe (p. 54)

Australia (25° S, 135° E) a continent in the Southern Hemisphere, the world's smallest continent; also a country including the continent and Tasmania (p. 68)

B

Bangladesh (24° N, 90° E) a country in South Asia (p. 66)

Brazil (10° S, 55° W) a large country in South America (p. 71)

Brunei (5° N, 115° E) a country in Southeast Asia, on the island of Borneo (p. 82)

C

Canada (60° N, 95° W) a large country in North America (p. 31)

Central America the part of Latin America between Mexico and South America; an area including the seven republics of Guatemala, Honduras, El Salvador, Nicaragua, Costa Rica, Panama, and Belize (p. 103)

China (35° N, 105° E) a large country in East Asia, officially the People's Republic of China (p. 20)

Cuba (22° N, 80° W) the largest island country in the Caribbean Sea (p. 15)

D

Denmark (56° N, 10° E) a country in northern Europe (p. 118)

E

Egypt (27° N, 30° E) a country in North Africa (p. 60)

Equator (0°) a line of latitude that circles Earth at the center of the tropics, midway between the North and South poles, along which days and nights are always equal in length (p. 11)

Europe (50° N, 28° E) the world's second-smallest continent; a peninsula of the Eurasian landmass bounded by the Arctic Ocean, the Atlantic Ocean, the Mediterranean Sea, and Asia (p. 43)

F

Florida (28° N, 82° W) a state in the United States that is largely a peninsula (p. 12)

G

Genoa (44°25′ N, 8°57′ E) a seaport city of Italy (p. 104)

Georgia (33° N, 83° W) a state in the southeastern United States; also a nation of southwestern Asia (p. 12)

Germany (51° N, 10° E) a country in central Europe (p. 97)

Great Plains (42° N, 100° W) a semiarid plain located in North America, stretching from the Rio Grande at the U.S.-Mexico border in the south to the Mackenzie River Delta in the north, and from the Canadian Shield in the east to the Rocky Mountains in the west (p. 128)

Greece (39° N, 22° E) a country in southeastern Europe (p. 93)

Greenland (70° N, 40° W) a self-governing island in the northern Atlantic Ocean, Earth's largest island; a possession of Denmark (p. 18)

Greenwich (51°28′ N, 0°) a borough of London, England, and location of the Royal Greenwich Observatory, whose location serves as the basis for longitude and for setting standard time (p. 12)

Gulf Stream a warm ocean current in the North Atlantic, flowing northeastward off the North American coast (p. 43)

I

India (20° N, 77° E) a large country occupying most of the Indian subcontinent in South Asia (p. 13)

Indonesia (5° S, 120° E) a country in Southeast Asia consisting of many islands (p. 93)

Iran (32° N, 53° W) a country in Southwest Asia (p. 118)

Italy (43° N, 13° E) a boot-shaped country in southern Europe (p. 104)

J

Jakarta (6°10′ S, 106°48′ E) the capital and largest city of Indonesia (p. 71)

Japan (36° N, 138° E) an island country in the Pacific Ocean off the east coast of Asia, consisting of four main islands (p. 63)

L

Libya (27° N, 17° E) a country in North Africa (p. 82)

London (51°30′ N, 0°10′ W) the capital and largest city of the United Kingdom (p. 22)

M

Mexico (23° N, 102° W) a country in North America (p. 67)

Miami (25°46′ N, 80°11′ W) a coastal city in Florida (p. 12)

Milky Way a galaxy consisting of several billion stars, including the sun (p. 28)

Mount Everest (27°59′ N, 86°56′ E) highest point on Earth, located in the Himalayas on the border between Nepal and China (p. 54)

Myanmar (22° N, 98° E) a country in Southeast Asia, also known as Burma (p. 82)

N

Nepal (28° N, 83° E) a country in South Asia (p. 54)

New York (43° N, 75° W) a state in the northeastern United States (p. 132)

New York City (40°43′ N, 74°1′ W) a coastal city in New York State; the largest city in the United States (p. 84)

New Zealand (41° S, 174° E) an island country in the Pacific Ocean (p. 122)

Nile Valley the fertile land located on both sides of the Nile River in northeastern Africa; site of one of the earliest civilizations (p. 63)

North America (45° N, 100° W) the world's third-largest continent, consisting of Canada, the United States, Mexico, Central America, and many islands (p. 17)

North Atlantic Current a warm ocean current in the North Atlantic, flowing eastward toward western and northern Europe (p. 43)

North Korea (40° N, 127° E) a country in East Asia, officially the Democratic People's Republic of Korea (p. 82)

North Pole (90° N) the northernmost end of Earth's axis, located in the Arctic Ocean (p. 11)

Norway (62° N, 10° E) a country in northern Europe (p. 118)

P

Pangaea according to scientific theory, a single landmass that broke apart to form today's separate continents; thought to have existed about 200 million years ago (p. 38)

Peru Current a cold-water current of the southeast Pacific Ocean; flowing northward between 40° S and 4° S (p. 43)

Philippines (13° N, 122° E) an island country in Southeast Asia (p. 67)

R

Ring of Fire a circle of volcanic mountains that surrounds the Pacific Ocean, including those on the islands of Japan and Indonesia, the Cascades of North America, and the Andes of South America (p. 33)

Rocky Mountains the major mountain range in western North America, extending south from western Canada, through the western United States, to Mexico (p. 12)

Rotterdam (51°55′ N, 4°28′ E) a seaport city in the Netherlands (p. 131)

Russia (60° N, 80° E) a country stretching across eastern Europe and northern Asia; the largest country in the world (p. 3)

S

Sahara the largest desert in the world, covering almost all of North Africa (p. 53)

St. Louis (38°37′ N, 90°11′ W) a city in Missouri (p. 45)

San Francisco (37°46′ N, 122°25′ W) a coastal city in California (p. 45)

São Paulo (23°32′ S, 46°37′ W) the largest city in Brazil (p. 48)

Saudi Arabia (25° N, 45° E) a country in Southwest Asia (p. 101)

South Africa (30° S, 26° E) a country in southern Africa (p. 70)

South America (15° S, 60° W) the world's fourth-largest continent, bounded by the Caribbean Sea, the Atlantic Ocean, and the Pacific Ocean, and linked to North America by the Isthmus of Panama (p. 17)

A cloud forest in the mountains of Ecuador, a country in South America

South Korea (37° N, 128° E) a country in East Asia (p. 67)

South Pole (90° S) the southernmost end of Earth's axis, located in Antarctica (p. 12)

Switzerland (47° N, 8° E) a country in central Europe (p. 78)

T

Texas (32° N, 99° W) a state in the south central United States (p. 15)

Tokyo (35°42′ N, 139°46′ E) the capital and largest city of Japan; the largest city in the world (p. 63)

Tropic of Cancer (23°30′ N) the northern boundary of the tropics; the band of Earth, on either side of the Equator, that receives the most direct light and heat energy from the sun (p. 30)

Tropic of Capricorn (23°30′ S) the southern boundary of the tropics (p. 31). *See* **Tropic of Cancer.**

U

United States (38° N, 97° W) a large country in North America (p. 12)

V

Vatican City (41°54′ N, 12°27′ E) a nation-state of southern Europe; the smallest nation-state in the world, completely surrounded by the city of Rome, Italy (p. 81)

Venezuela (8° N, 66° W) a country in northern South America (p. 135)

Vietnam (16° N, 108° E) a country located in Southeast Asia (p. 67)

Glossary

A

absolute location (AB suh loot loh KAY shun) *n.* the exact position of a place on Earth (p. 12)

absolute monarchy (AB suh loot MAHN ur kee) *n.* a system of complete control by a king or queen who inherits the throne by birth (p. 82)

acculturation (uh kul chur AY shun) *n.* the process of accepting new ideas from one culture and fitting them into another culture (p. 106)

aerial photograph (EHR ee ul FOHT uh graf) *n.* a photographic image of Earth's surface taken from the air (p. 17)

agriculture (AG rih kul chur) *n.* farming; including growing crops and raising livestock (p. 94)

arid (A rid) *adj.* dry (p. 44)

atmosphere (AT muh sfeer) *n.* a layer of gases surrounding a planet (p. 35)

axis (AK sis) *n.* an imaginary line around which a planet turns. Earth's axis runs through the center of the planet from the North to the South Pole. (p. 29)

B

barometer (buh RAHM uh tur) *n.* an instrument for forecasting changes in the weather; anything that indicates a change (p. 89)

biodiversity (by oh duh VUR suh tee) *n.* a large variety of living things in a region (p. 129)

birthrate (BURTH rayt) *n.* the number of live births each year per 1,000 people (p. 64)

blizzard (BLIZ urd) *n.* a heavy snowstorm with strong winds (p. 47)

A blizzard in Bavaria, Germany

C

canopy (KAN uh pea) *n.* the layer formed by the uppermost branches of the rain forest (p. 52)

capitalism (KAP ut ul iz um) *n.* an economic system in which private individuals or groups of people own most businesses (p. 75)

cardinal directions (KAHR duh nul duh REK shunz) *n.* north, east, south, and west (p. 11)

city-state (SIH tee stayt) *n.* a small city-centered state (p. 81)

civil engineering (SIV ul en juh NIHR ing) *n.* technology for building structures that alter the landscape, such as dams, roads, and bridges (p. 131)

civilization (sih vuh luh ZAY shun) *n.* an advanced culture with cities and the use of writing (p. 94)

climate (KLY mut) *n.* the average weather of a place over many years (p. 40)

colonization (kahl uh nih ZAY shun) *n.* movement of settlers and their culture to a new country (p. 125)

commercial farmers (kuh MUR shul FAHR murz) *n.* farmers who grow most of their food for sale rather than for their own needs (p. 76)

communism (KAHM yoo niz um) *n.* an economic system in which the central government owns farms, factories, and offices (p. 75)

compass rose (KUM pus rohz) *n.* a diagram of a compass showing direction on a map (p. 21)

conformal map (kun FAWR mul map) *n.* a flat map of the entire planet Earth, which shows correct shapes but not true distances or sizes; also known as a Mercator projection after geographer Gerardus Mercator (p. 18)

coniferous trees (koh NIF ur us treez) *n.* trees that produce cones to carry seeds (p. 52)

constitution (kahn stuh TOO shun) *n.* a set of laws that defines and limits a government's power (p. 83)

constitutional monarchy (kahn stuh TOO shun ul MAHN ur kee) *n.* a government in which the power of the king or queen is limited by law (p. 83)

consumer (kun SOO mur) *n.* a person who buys and uses goods and services (p. 74)

copse (kahps) *n.* a thicket of small trees or shrubs (p. 89)

core (kawr) *n.* the ball of very hot metal at the center of Earth (p. 34)

crust (krust) *n.* the thin layer of rocks and minerals that surrounds Earth's mantle (p. 34)

cultural diffusion (KUL chur ul dih FYOO zhun) *n.* the movement of customs and ideas from one culture to another (p. 106)

cultural landscape (KUL chur ul LAND skayp) *n.* the parts of a people's environment that they have shaped and that reflect their culture (p. 93)

cultural trait (KUL chur ul trayt) *n.* a skill, custom, idea, or way of doing things that forms part of a culture (p. 92)

culture (KUL chur) *n.* the way of life of a people, including their language, beliefs, customs, and practices (p. 92)

D

death rate (deth rayt) *n.* the number of deaths each year per 1,000 people (p. 64)

deciduous trees (dih SIJ oo us treez) *n.* trees that lose their leaves in the fall (p. 52)

deforestation (dee fawr uh STAY shun) *n.* a loss of forest cover in a region (p. 129)

degrees (dih GREEZ) *n.* units that measure angles (p. 11)

demography (dih MAH gruh fee) *n.* the scientific study of population change and population distribution (p. 60)

dependency (dee PEN dun see) *n.* a region that belongs to another state (p. 81)

desert (DEZ urt) *n.* a hot, dry region with little vegetation (p. 52)

desert scrub (DEZ urt skrub) *n.* desert vegetation that needs little water (p. 52)

developed nations (dih VEL upt NAY shunz) *n.* nations with many industries and advanced technology (p. 76)

developing nations (dih VEL up ing NAY shunz) *n.* nations with few industries and simple technology (p. 76)

dictator (DIK tay tur) *n.* a leader who has almost total power over an entire country (p. 82)

direct democracy (duh REKT dih MAHK ruh see) *n.* a form of government in which all adults take part in decisions (p. 82)

distortion (dih STAWR shun) *n.* loss of accuracy. Every map projection causes some distortion of shape. (p. 17)

E

economy (ih KAHN uh mee) *n.* a system in which people make, exchange, and use things that have value (p. 74)

empire (EM pyr) *n.* a state containing several countries (p. 81)

energy (EN ur jee) *n.* usable heat or power; capacity for doing work (p. 115)

environment (en VY run munt) *n.* natural surroundings (p. 120)

equal-area map (EEK wul EHR ee uh map) *n.* a map showing the correct size of landmasses but with altered shapes (p. 19)

Equator (ee KWAYT ur) *n.* the line of latitude around the middle of the globe (p. 11)

equinox (EE kwih nahks) *n.* one of two days in the year when the sun is directly over the Equator and the days are almost exactly as long as the nights; known as spring and fall equinoxes (p. 30)

erosion (ee ROH zhun) *n.* a process in which water, ice, or wind remove small pieces of rock (p. 39)

ethics (ETH iks) *n.* the standards or code of moral behavior distinguishing between right and wrong (p. 101)

extended family (ek STEN did FAM uh lee) *n.* a family that includes several generations (p. 97)

F

faults (fawlts) *n.* cracks in Earth's crust (p. 37)

fossil fuels (FAHS ul FYOO ulz) *n.* fuels created over millions of years from the remains of prehistoric living things (p. 117)

G

geographic information systems (jee uh GRAF ik in fur MAY shun SIS tumz) *n.* computer-based systems that store and use information linked to geographic locations (p. 17)

geography (jee AHG ruh fee) *n.* the study of Earth (p. 10)

globe (glohb) *n.* a model of Earth with the same round shape as Earth itself (p. 16)

goods (gudz) *n.* physical products (p. 75)

government (GUV urn munt) *n.* a system that creates and enforces laws and institutions in a region (p. 80)

Green Revolution (green rev uh LOO shun) *n.* the increased use of chemicals, machinery, and new crop varieties in agriculture since the 1950s that has greatly increased the world's food supply. It has also created environmental challenges. (p. 65)

A hill in northern England

H

hemisphere (HEM ih sfeer) *n.* one half of Earth (p. 11)

hemlock (HEM lahk) *n.* an evergreen tree with drooping branches and short needles (p. 89)

high latitudes (hy LAT uh toodz) *n.* the areas north of the Arctic Circle and south of the Antarctic Circle (p. 32)

hill (hil) *n.* a landform with a rounded top that rises above the surrounding land but is lower and less steep than a mountain (p. 35)

human-environment interaction (HYOO mun en VY run munt in tur AK shun) *n.* how people affect the environment and the physical characteristics of their surroundings and how the environment affects them (p. 13)

humid continental climate (HYOO mid kahn tuh NENT ul KLY mut) *n.* climate with moderate to hot summers but very cold winters; supporting grasslands and forests (p. 51)

hurricane (HUR ih kayn) *n.* a tropical cyclone, or violent storm, that forms over the Atlantic Ocean (p. 47)

I

immigrant (IM uh grunt) *n.* a person who moves into one country from another (p. 67)

industrialization (in dus tree ul ih ZAY shun) *n.* the growth of manufacturing in an economy (p. 125)

institution (in stuh TOO shun) *n.* a custom or organization with social, educational, or religious purposes (p. 95)

interdependent (in tur dee PEN dunt) *adj.* dependent on one another (p. 79)

international (in tur NASH un ul) *adj.* involving more than one nation (p. 84)

irrigation (ih ruh GAY shun) *n.* supplying dry land with water for farming (p. 94)

K

key (kee) *n.* the section of a map that explains the symbols and shading on the map (p. 21)

L

landform (LAND fawrm) *n.* a shape or type of land (p. 35)

landmass (LAND mas) *n.* a large area of land (p. 19)

latitude (LAT uh tood) *n.* the distance north or south of the Equator, measured in units called degrees (p. 11)

lichen (LY kun) *n.* a plant that is a combination of a fungus and an alga and that grows and spreads over rocks and tree trunks (p. 39)

life expectancy (lyf ek SPEK tun see) *n.* the average number of years that people live (p. 65)

longitude (LAHN juh tood) *n.* the distance east or west of the Prime Meridian, measured in degrees (p. 11)

low latitudes (loh LAT uh toodz) *n.* the area between the Tropic of Cancer and the Tropic of Capricorn (p. 32)

M

magma (MAG muh) *n.* soft, nearly molten rock (p. 36)

mantle (MAN tul) *n.* the thick, rocky layer around Earth's core (p. 34)

manufacturing (man yoo FAK chur ing) *n.* processing a raw material to make a finished product, (p. 123)

marine west coast climate (muh REEN west kohst KLY mut) *n.* moderate climate occurring in areas cooled by ocean currents; supporting forests more often than grasses (p. 51)

Mediterranean climate (med uh tuh RAY nee un KLY mut) *n.* moderate climate that receives most of its rain in winter and has hot and dry summers; supporting plants with leathery leaves that hold water (p. 51)

meridian (muh RID ee un) *n.* a line of longitude (p. 12)

middle latitudes (MID ul LAT uh toodz) *n.* the areas between the high and low latitudes (p. 32)

migration (my GRAY shun) *n.* movement from one place or region to another (p. 67)

mineral (MIN ur ul) *n.* a natural resource that is obtained by mining, such as gold, iron, or copper (p. 114)

mountain (MOWN tun) *n.* a steep landform that rises usually more than 2,000 feet (610 m) above sea level or the surrounding flatlands (p. 35)

A mountain in British Columbia, Canada

N

nation-state (NAY shun stayt) *n.* a state that is independent of other states (p. 81)

natural resource (NACH ur ul REE sawrs) *n.* a useful material found in the environment (p. 114)

nonrenewable resource (nahn rih NOO uh bul REE sawrs) *n.* a resource that cannot be replaced (p. 116)

nuclear family (NOO klee ur FAM uh lee) *n.* a mother, a father, and their children (p. 97)

O

ocean current (OH shun KUR unt) *n.* a fast-moving stream of water in the ocean created by uneven heating of Earth's surface (p. 42)

oligarchy (AHL ih gahr kee) *n.* a government controlled by a small group of people (p. 82)

orbit (AWR bit) *n.* the path one body makes as it circles around another (p. 28)

P

parallel (PA ruh lel) *n.* in geography, a line of latitude (p. 12)

petroleum (puh TROH lee um) *n.* an oily substance found under Earth's crust; the source of gasoline and other fuels; an energy resource (p. 116)

plain (playn) *n.* a large area of flat or gently rolling land (p. 35)

plate (playt) *n.* in geography, a huge section of Earth's crust (p. 36)

plateau (pla TOH) *n.* a large, mostly flat area that rises above the surrounding land (p. 35)

polar climate (POH lur KLY mut) *n.* a climate of the high latitudes that is cold all year and has short summers (p. 50)

pollution (puh LOO shun) *n.* waste, usually made by people, that makes a place's air, water, or soil less clean (p. 132)

population (pahp yuh LAY shun) *n.* total number of people in an area (p. 60)

population density (pahp yuh LAY shun DEN suh tee) *n.* the average number of people per square mile or square kilometer (p. 62)

population distribution (pahp yuh LAY shun dis truh BYOO shun) *n.* the way the population is spread out over an area (p. 60)

precipitation (pree sip uh TAY shun) *n.* water that falls to the ground as rain, sleet, hail, or snow (p. 40)

Prime Meridian (prym muh RID ee un) *n.* the meridian that runs through Greenwich, England (p. 11)

producer (pruh DOO sur) *n.* a person who makes products that are used by other people (p. 74)

projection (proh JEK shun) *n.* method of mapping Earth on a flat surface (p. 18)

push-pull theory (push pul THEE uh ree) *n.* a theory of migration claiming that difficulties "push" people to leave their old homes, while a hope for better living conditions "pulls" them to a new country (p. 68)

The Prime Meridian runs through the middle of the Royal Observatory in Greenwich, England.

R

raw materials (raw muh TIHR ee ulz) *n.* natural resources that must be processed to be useful (p. 114)

region (REE jun) *n.* an area with a unifying characteristic such as climate, land, population, or history (p. 12)

relative location (REL uh tiv loh KAY shun) *n.* the location of a place described in relation to places near it (p. 12)

renewable resource (rih NOO uh bul REE sawrs) *n.* a natural resource that can be replaced (p. 115)

representative democracy (rep ruh ZEN tuh tiv dih MAHK ruh see) *n.* a government run by representatives that the people choose (p. 83)

revolution (rev uh LOO shun) *n.* a circular journey (p. 28)

rotation (roh TAY shun) *n.* a complete turn (p. 29)

rural (ROOR ul) *adj.* located in the countryside (p. 71)

S

sanitation (san uh TAY shun) *n.* disposal of sewage and waste (p. 65)

satellite image (SAT uh lyt IM ij) *n.* an image of Earth's surface taken from a satellite in orbit (p. 17)

savanna (suh VAN uh) *n.* a parklike landscape of grasslands with scattered trees that can survive dry spells (p. 52)

scale (skayl) *n.* relative size (p. 16)

semiarid climate (sem ee A rid KLY mut) *n.* hot, dry climate with little rain, supporting only shrubs and grasses (p. 44)

services (SUR vih siz) *n.* kinds of work that producers perform for other people (p. 123)

social class (SOH shul klas) *n.* a grouping of people based on rank or status (p. 97)

social structure (SOH shul STRUK chur) *n.* a pattern of organized relationships among groups of people within a society (p. 96)

society (suh SY uh tee) *n.* a group of people sharing a culture and social structure (p. 96)

solstice (SAHL stis) *n.* one of two days in the year when the sun is directly overhead at its farthest point from the Equator. Summer solstice, in the hemisphere where the sun is overhead, is the longest day and shortest night of the year. Winter solstice, in the opposite hemisphere, is the shortest day and longest night of the year. (p. 30)

state (stayt) *n.* a region that shares a government (p. 80)

subarctic climate (sub AHRK tik KLY mut) *n.* a continental dry climate with cool summers and cold winters (p. 51)

subsistence farmers (sub SIS tuns FAHR murz) *n.* farmers who raise food and animals mainly to feed their own families (p. 77)

T

technology (tek NAHL uh jee) *n.* a way of putting knowledge to practical use (p. 76)

temperature (TEM pur uh chur) *n.* the hotness or coldness of the air or some other substance (p. 40)

tornadoes (tawr NAY dohz) *n.* swirling funnels of wind moving as fast as 200 miles (320 kilometers) per hour (p. 47)

treaty (TREE tee) *n.* a formal written agreement between states (p. 84)

tropical cyclone (TRAHP ih kul SY klohn) *n.* an intense wind and rain storm that forms over oceans in the tropics or low latitudes (p. 47)

tundra (TUN druh) *n.* an area of cold climate and low-lying vegetation (p. 51)

U

urban (UR bun) *adj.* located in cities and nearby towns (p. 71)

urbanization (ur ban ih ZAY shun) *n.* the movement of people to cities (p. 70)

V

vegetation (vej uh TAY shun) *n.* plants that grow in a region, (p. 50)

vertical climate (VUR tih kul KLY mut) *n.* the overall weather patterns of a region as influenced by elevation; the higher the elevation, the colder the climate (p. 54)

W

weather (WETH ur) *n.* the condition of the air and sky from day to day (p. 40)

weathering (WETH ur ing) *n.* a process that breaks rocks down into tiny pieces (p. 39)

Index

C

California, *53p, 133p*
Cambodia, 156
Cameroon, 154
Canada, 161, 164
  economy 76
  energy resources 118
  government 83
  languages 99
  population density *62p*, 63
  trade 79
canopy, rain forest, 50, 52, 169
Cape Verde, 154
Cape Town, South Africa, *70p*
capitalism, 74, 75, 169
carbon cycle, 115
carbon dioxide, 35
cardinal directions, 10, 11, 169
Caribbean, migration, 67
cars,
  air pollution 132
  and cultural change 105
  energy consumption 119
  hybrid cars 119, 130, *130p*, 132
  and suburbanization 70
  traffic jams *130p*
cells, air circulation, *42p*
Central African Republic, 154
Central America, 164
  migration 67, 68
  Maya 103
Chad, 154
Cherrapunji, India, *41p*
children, families, 96, 97
Chile, 43, 160
China, 135, 156, 164
  economy 77
  government 82
  language *98p*, 99
  migration 67, 68
  rice harvest *58–59p, 85p*
  Silk Road 78
Christianity, 98, 100, 101
Churchill, Manitoba, 51
cities,
  development of culture 94
  growth of 61
  and industrialization 125

suburbs 70, 105, 125
  urbanization 67, 70–71, *70c*
citizenship, 83
city-states, 80, 81, 169
civil engineering, 128, 131, 169
civilization, 92, 94, 169
class, social, 96, 97, 175
climate, 40–55
  air pollution and 132
  arid and semiarid *44p*, 51
  climate change 132
  defined 40, 169
  differences from weather 40
  dry *42p*, 50, 51
  effect on vegetation 50–54, *53m*
  graphs 48–49, *48c*, 56
  and land use 121
  latitude and 32, 41
  polar *42p*, 50, 51
  regions *44–45m*, 50
  temperate continental 50, 51
  temperate marine 50, 51
  tropical 50
  vertical 54, 175
  See also weather
clothes, cultural change, 104
clouds, water cycle, 41
coal, 117, *117p*
cold climates, 41
Colombia, 160
colonization, 120, 125, 169
Colorado River, 44
colors, maps, 21
commercial farmers, 76, 169
communications,
  and cultural change 107
  language 98
communism, 74, 75, 82, 169
communities,
  political systems 80, 82–83
  social structure 96
Comoros, 154
comparisons, reading and
    writing skills,
  comparing and contrasting 54, 60
  making comparisons 74
compass rose, 16, *20m*, 21, 169
computers,
  cultural change 106, 107

finding cures for disease 90f
geographic information systems (GIS)
    16, 17
  trade 78, 79
conclusions, generalizations, 102–103
conformal maps, 18, 169
Congo, Democratic Republic of
    the, 154
Congo, Republic of the, 154
coniferous forests, 51, 52, *53p*, 54
coniferous trees, 50, 52, 169
constitutional monarchy, 83, 169
constitutions, 80, 83, 169
consumers, 74, 79, 169
container ships, 79
context clues, reading skill, 28, 30, 32,
    33, 35, 39, 40, 50, 52
continental climates, 51
continents,
  location of 86
  origins of 38
  movement of 36, *36p*, 38
contrasts, reading and writing skills,
  comparing and contrasting 54, 60
  identifying contrasts 67
  signal words 80
copses, 89, 169
core, Earth's, 33, 34, *34p*, 169
Costa Rica, 160
Côte D'Ivoire, 154
cotton, 177
Croatia, 158
crust, Earth's, 33, 34, *34p*, 36–37,
    36–37p, 169
Cuba, 160, 164
  dictatorship 82
  migration 68, *68p*
culture, 90–111, 136
  cultural change 104–108
  cultural diffusion 104, 106, 169
  cultural landscape 92, 93, *93p*, 169
  cultural traits 92, 169
  defined 92–93, 169
  development of 94–95
  and environment 93
  land use and 120–121
  language and 92, 98–99, *98–99m*
  project possibilities 136

S

W

Wales, coal mining, *117p*
warfare, and migration, 68
waste recycling, 132, *132p*
water, 35
 hydroelectric power 117, *117p*
 irrigation 94, 121, *121p*, 172
 natural resources 114, 115
 oasis *53p*
 pollution 129
 reservoirs 131
 water cycle *41p*, 115
 water supply 35, 65, 66, 127
 weathering and erosion 39
 See also lakes; oceans; rain; rivers; seas
weather, 88–89
 defined 40, 175
 differences from climate 40
 forecasting 26g, 46, *46p*
 storms 47
 See also climate
weathering, 33, 39, *39p*, 175
west, 11
Western hemisphere, *11p*
White House, Washington, DC, *126p*
wind,
 and ocean currents 43
 patterns *42p*
 tornadoes 47
 tropical cyclones 47
 wind energy *112–113p*, 115, 117, 132, *133p*
winter, 32, 51
winter solstice, 31, *31p*
wood, and deforestation, 129
wool, 122, *122p*
workplaces, ownership, 74
writing, and development of culture, 94
Writing Activities,
 five themes of geography 24
 language arts 134
 math 86, 110
 science 56
writing skills,
 comparing and contrasting 54
 paragraphs 47
 See also reading skills
Wyoming, *51 p*

Y

year, Earth's orbit, 28
Yemen, *121p*, 158

Z

Zambia, 155
Zimbabwe, 155

Acknowledgments

Cover Design

Pronk&Associates

Staff Credits

The people who made up the World Studies © 05 team—representing design services, editorial, editorial services, educational technology, marketing, market research, photo research and art development, production services, project office, publishing processes, and rights & permissions—are listed below. Bold type indicates core team members.

Greg Abrom, Ernie Albanese, Rob Aleman, Susan Andariese, **Rachel Avenia-Prol,** Leann Davis Alspaugh, Penny Baker, Barbara Bertell, **Peter Brooks,** Rui Camarinha, John Carle, **Lisa DelGatto,** Paul Delsignore, Kathy Dempsey, Anne Drowns, Deborah Dukeshire, Marlies Dwyer, **Frederick Fellows,** Paula C. Foye, Lara Fox, Julia Gecha, **Mary Hanisco,** Salena Hastings, Lance Hatch, Kerri Hoar, **Beth Hyslip,** Katharine Ingram, Nancy Jones, John Kingston, Deborah Levheim, Constance J. McCarty, **Kathleen Mercandetti,** Art Mkrtchyan, Ken Myett, **Mark O'Malley,** Jen Paley, Ray Parenteau, **Gabriela Pérez Fiato,** Linda Punskovsky, Kirsten Richert, **Lynn Robbins,** Nancy Rogier, Bruce Rolff, Robin Samper, Mildred Schulte, **Malti Sharma,** Lisa Smith-Ruvalcaba, Roberta Warshaw, Sarah Yezzi

Additional Credits

Jonathan Amber, Tom Benfatti, Lisa D. Ferrari, Paul Foster, Florrie Gadson, Phil Gagler, Ella Hanna, Jeffrey LaFountain, Karen Mancinelli, Michael McLaughlin, Lesley Pierson, Debi Taffet

 The DK Designs team who contributed to World Studies © 05 were as follows: Hilary Bird, Samantha Borland, Marian Broderick, Richard Czapnik, Nigel Duffield, Heather Dunleavy, Cynthia Frazer, James A. Hall, Lucy Heaver, Rose Horridge, Paul Jackson, Heather Jones, Ian Midson, Marie Ortu, Marie Osborn, Leyla Ostovar, Ralph Pitchford, Ilana Sallick, Pamela Shiels, Andrew Szudek, Amber Tokeley.

Maps

Maps and globes were created by **DK Cartography.** The team consisted of Tony Chambers, Damien Demaj, Julia Lunn, Ed Merritt, David Roberts, Ann Stephenson, Gail Townsley, Iorwerth Watkins.

Illustrations

31, 34, 36, 41, 43, DK images; 140, Kevin Jones Associates

Photos

Cover Photos

tl, Alec Pytlowany/Masterfile; tm, David Muir/Masterfile; tr, Gordon Wiltsie; b, Royalty Free/CORBIS/MAGMA/Artbase, Inc.

Title Page

Royalty Free/CORBIS/MAGMA/Artbase, Inc.

Table of Contents

T4–T5, Philip Blenkinsop/DK Images; T6–T7, Brenda Tharp/Corbis; T8, sun, DK Images; globes, Planetary Visions

Professional Development

T35, Royalty Free/CORBIS; T36, PhotoDisc/Getty Images, Inc.; T37, Comstock

Reading and Writing Handbook

RW, Michael Newman/PhotoEdit; RW1, Walter Hodges/Getty Images, Inc.; RW2, Digital Vision/Getty Images, Inc.; RW3, Will Hart/PhotoEdit; RW5, Jose Luis Pelaez, Inc./Corbis

Guiding Questions

1, Christine Osborne/World Religions Photo Library

World Overview

2 l, 2 t, DK Images; 3 l, Daniel Laine/Corbis; 3 tr, DK Images; 3 br, Sipa/Rex Features; 4 bl, Layne Kennedy/Corbis; 4 tr, DK Images; 5 t, Royalty Free Images/Corbis; 6 t, Roger Ressmeyer/Corbis; 7 br, Amet Jean Pierre/Sygma/Corbis; 7 tr, DK Images

Chapter One

8e l, Royalty-Free/Corbis; 8e r, PhotoDisc/Getty Images, Inc.; 8f l, GeoStock/Getty Images, Inc.; 8f ml, Comstock; 8f mr, PhotoDisc/Getty Images, Inc.; 8f r, SW Productions/Getty Images, Inc.; 8–9, Johnson Space Center/NASA; 10, Steve Gorton/DK Images; 13, M. Balan/DK Images; 14, Will & Deni McIntyre/Corbis; 15 b, Richard Powers/Corbis; 15 t, DK Images; 16, Peter Wilson/DK Images; 17, MSFC/NASA; 23, Johnson Space Center/NASA

Chapter Two

26g l, Royalty-Free/Corbis; 26g r, PhotoDisc/Getty Images, Inc.; 26h l, GeoStock/Getty Images, Inc.; 26h ml, Comstock; 26h mr, PhotoDisc/Getty Images, Inc.; 26h r, SW Productions/Getty Images, Inc.; 26–27, George H. Huey/Corbis; 28, Daniel Pyne/DK Images; 30 bl, Alan Briere/DK Images; 30–31, sun, DK Images; globes, Planetary Visions; 31 tr, Barnabas Kindersley/DK Images; 33, Brenda Tharp/Corbis; 35, C.M. Leask/Eye Ubiquitous; 36 bl, James Balog/Getty Images; 37 tr, James A. Sugar/Corbis; 39, Alan Hills/DK Images; 40, Galen Rowell/Corbis; 41 tr, Hutchison Library; 43 tr, Royalty Free Images/Corbis; 44 b, Demetrio Carrasco/DK Images; 45 bl, Chris Stowers/DK Images; 46 m, DK Images; 46 bl, NASA; 46 tr, N.H.P.A.; 46 mr, Lelan Statom, meteorologist; Mark Martin, photojournalist/network operations manager, WTVF-Newschannel 5 Network, Nashville, Tenn.; 47, Claude Charlier/Corbis; 48 t, Michael S. Yamashita/Corbis; 50, Liu Liqun/Corbis; 51 br, Terry W. Eggers/Corbis; 51 tr, Denver Museum of Nature and Science; 52, Alan Watson/DK Images; 53 t, Photowood Inc./Corbis; 53 bl, Neil Lukas; 53 br, Stephen Hayward/DK Images; 54, Galen Rowell/Corbis; 55, George H. Huey/Corbis

Chapter Three

58g l, Royalty-Free/Corbis; 58g r, PhotoDisc/Getty Images, Inc.; 58h l, GeoStock/Getty Images, Inc.; 58h ml, Comstock; 58h mr, PhotoDisc/Getty Images, Inc.; 58h r, SW Productions/Getty Images, Inc.; 58–59, Keren Su/Corbis; 60, James Strachan/Getty Images; 61 t, Royalty Free Images/Corbis; 62 bl, Wolfgang Kaehler/Corbis; 63 br, Peter Wilson/DK Images; 64 t, Howard Davies/Corbis; 65 b, Patricia Aithie/Ffotograff; 66, Dirk R. Frans/Hutchison Library; 67, Bettmann Corbis; 68, Dave King/DK Images; 69 bl, Bettmann/Corbis; 70 bl, Hulton-Deutsch Collection/Corbis; 70 br, Paul Almasy/Corbis; 71, Stephanie Maze/Corbis; 72, Bill Ross/Corbis; 74, Rob Reichenfeld/DK Images; 75 t, Corbis; 76, Philip Blenkinsop/DK Images; 77 b, Tom Wagner/Corbis; 78 l, Mark E. Gibson/Corbis; 78 b, Annebicque Bernard/Sygma/Corbis; 78 r, Mary Ann McDonald/Corbis; 79, Peter Blakely/SABA/Corbis; 80, Patrick Durand/Sygma/Corbis; 81, Franz-Marc Frei/Corbis; 82, Tom Haskell/Sygma/Corbis; 83 t, Pa Photos; 83 b, Ron Sachs/Rex Features; 84, Joseph Sohm/Chromosohm Inc./Corbis; 85, Keren Su/Corbis; 88, Peter Finger/Corbis

Chapter Four

90f l, Royalty-Free/Corbis; 90f r, PhotoDisc/Getty Images, Inc.; 90–91, Bryan Colton/Assignments Photographers/Corbis; 92, Royalty Free Images/Corbis; 93 b, Dennis Degnan/Corbis; 94 tl, Geoff Brightling/DK Images; 94 b, Richard Leeney/DK Images; 94 ml, Museum of English Rural Life; 95, Kim Sayer/DK Images; 96, DK Images; 97, Rob Lewine/Corbis; 98 t, Richard T. Nowitz/Corbis; 98 b, Barnabas Kindersley/DK Images; 99 b, Demetrio Carrasco/DK Images; 100 t, Barnabas Kindersley/DK Images; 100 b, Peter Wilson/DK Images; 101, B.P.S. Walia/DK Images; 102, Foodpix/Getty Images; 103 l, Christine Osborne/World Religions Photo Library; 104, DK Images; 105 b, Dallas and John Heaton/Corbis; 105 t, Royalty Free Images/Corbis; 106, DK Images;